ANTHROPOLOGICAL STUDIES

Number 6

PAUL J. BOHANNAN, Editor

Dominance and Defiance

*a study of marital instability
in an Islamic African society*

RONALD COHEN

Published by the

AMERICAN ANTHROPOLOGICAL ASSOCIATION
1703 New Hampshire Avenue, N.W.
Washington, D.C. 20009

This book is dedicated to
Suleman Audu

CONTENTS

Introduction

It is unfashionable today for anthropologists to speak of "my people." The expression seems to conjure up connotations of paternalism, ownership, unelected representation, or even worse—unwanted—spokesman for a group of people to whom the anthropologist has attached himself. He can do this, so goes the criticism, because he was or is a member of a colonial, ex-colonial, or wealthy and powerful nation that can afford, or wants, or needs (depending upon the ideology of the critic) to know about people and events all over the world.

A contrary view that does not really refute the criticism is the case put forward for "objective" social science. Comparative data on the human condition is necessary if we wish to understand man, his history, variety, and development on this planet. Thus the anthropologist is engaged in a purely scientific venture that is required by all mankind if self-knowledge of the species and its fate is to be fully appreciated and understood. However, a side product of this quest is an identification by the social scientist with his informants, their culture, and its development in the modern world. Thus he becomes a spokesman for them and their interests in the outside world just as many a European official or missionary did during the colonial period.

These views have some truth in them (and some untruth!) but somehow do not express all of my own feelings on the relationship of an anthropologist to the people he has studied. I have carried out extensive field work among the Kanuri, the people depicted in this book, covering a period of a decade which has straddled colonial status, independence, and a Nigerian civil war. I have spent years studying their history and analyzing field data collected from living members of the society. I have also carried out field work in the Canadian arctic, and hope ultimately to work elsewhere in Africa and other parts of the world. However, certain truths about my own experience must be faced. Never will I invest so much in understanding another culture as I have that of the Kanuri. Language learning, history, participant observation in several villages, and getting students and other social scientists interested in the area, have all contributed to this investment.

Such an investment has produced several results. First, I am interested in and concerned with the fate of Bornu and its people. In this sense they are "my people" because I have chosen to identify with them and to sympathize with their needs, desires, and point of view in the modern world. This has even led me of late to write critically of them and their participation in the nation-building efforts of Nigeria as a whole. As a sympathetic observer, I feel I have the right to criticize the failings as well as extol the virtues of my friends and their society.

It is not only my right to do so but my responsibility. This was pointed out to me recently by a very high official of the Nigerian government who said that if we, the foreign social scientists, had been more carefully and clearly critical of Nigeria during its early phases, then possibly we would have been unpopular, but we would have helped them to see themselves as they really were. Instead, we avoided criticism and the Western press gave out an image of Nigeria as a model democracy whose economy was developing in the Western way. We, the experts with more detailed knowledge of the country, kept silent or muffled our insights into the deep rifts in the nation so that when these rifts led to civil war the world was shocked and the Nigerians themselves were surprised at the intensity of the conflict that occurred.

In this same vein, and more to the point, the depth and scope of my own field experience with the Kanuri is a responsibility that cannot easily be shed. One thing my professors did not tell me was how enslaved I would be to my data once it was collected. Having spent so much time on the

Kanuri, I feel, as do all anthropologists, an enormous weight of obligation to myself, to my colleagues, and to the people whose way of life I have studied. Publication of my research results is one of the ways among several that I can discharge this debt. But this means many more hours of work trying to put one's understanding into language that communicates to others what has been learned. This is a more profound and personal way in which the society becomes "my people." They are my people because I not only have spent many months living with them, but years trying to sort out my impressions of those months and a systematic analysis of information collected during that time. They are "my people" then because like my wife I am "married" to them; I can't escape the relationship nor the obligations that seem to accompany it any more than I can any other long term and intensely personal human interaction. Nor do I want to. For I am now part of them and can only hope that my attempt to describe and understand their society is not so dictated by my inadequacies that I will have done an injustice to its intricacy and complexity.

Does all this mean that I disagree with the ideological interpretation of the anthropologist as a colonial creation, or the "objective" science view of his role as a collector of important comparative data? Certainly not. Both of these social and political analyses of anthropology are true. But I only wish to suggest that they ride roughshod over the personal experience that anthropology provides and creates, an experience that I believe to be one of the most profound, shocking, and ultimately enriching ones available in any culture. It is this non-political part of anthropology that also makes anthropologists speak of "my people." Although contemporary ideology may be casting a pall over such usage, there are I believe some of us who though avoiding the term in public discussion (for good and even relevant reasons) will still use it in our hearts.

But why divorce? Among all the things I could have chosen to concentrate on, why choose marital instability? Some of the theoretical reasons for the choice are given in Chapter 1. Some of my other reasons were personal, others ethnocentric. Kanuri marital instability is a common, well-established feature of their society. They are not concerned or aware of it as a problem in much the same way that we in the West were not concerned until recently about the air we breathe. Yet to an outsider from the West the instability is a striking feature of their society. So I am led to admit that it is my (or "our") problems that led me to focus on Kanuri marital instability. This is legitimate and can indeed shed light on a universal problem, that of marriage and the family. However, in the future I hope to balance this and concentrate more of my writing and research on problems seen to be such by the people themselves, thus shifting the origin of problems from one determined by Western scientific interests to ones more clearly identified with the needs of the people themselves.

No anthropologist has ever carried out a study by himself. Besides his training he needs the cooperation of many people and without a minimum of acceptance he cannot succeed in his work. The present work, like all of my other writings on Bornu, is primarily dependent upon the patience, interest, and cooperation of hundreds of Kanuri men and women who took the time to speak to us about their lives and to answer our innumerable questions. Added to this was the kindness and effort put forward on our behalf by the Bornu Emirate Native Authority and the government officials of Bornu Province and Nigeria who gave permission for the study to be carried out and who helped immeasurably with the sampling problems connected with survey research in the field. My assistants on the project, especially Suleman Audu, Abba Gambo, and Mallama Gona, all of Bornu, were invaluable in helping to prepare the materials and administer the questionnaires. They were aided in this by David and Catherine Spain and Norma Perchonock.

In the analysis of the data, Inez Oberteuffer and Vivian Smoker helped with coding and computer analyses of the data, and my wife, Diana, did yeoman service in turning much of our field scrawls into something more systematic and then helped to prepare the first drafts of our code book for the analysis of the sociological data. I am also grateful to Freda Segel of Evanston, Illinois, who spent innumerable evenings (with my wife posing in Kanuri clothes) poring over photographs in order to sketch the TAT pictures used in the field. David Spain and Remi Clignet have read a draft of the manuscript and provided many useful comments and criticisms.

All of this assistance, including a number of trips back and forth to Bornu plus time off to write up the data, required financial help for which I am very grateful. The pilot study for this project was carried out under a grant from the National Institute of Mental Health and funds for the major study came from the National Science Foundation. In addition, the Program of African Studies and the Council for Intersocietal Studies at Northwestern University provided backup support for secretarial help, and time off to write up the material. To all of these agencies I must say thank you, and sincerely hope that the product of all this support has justified the expense.

Nares Inlet
August, 1970

PART I
THEORY AND METHOD

Chapter 1
Introduction: Marriage and Divorce as a Theoretical Problem

The Problem and its Place in Social Theory

The problem of continuity and discontinuity has hovered in the background and the foreground of social science for decades. The first anthropologists to live for extended periods in non-Western societies seemed almost transfixed by their desire to understand why people continue day after day, month after month, to repeat the same exotic behaviors. Words, concepts, and theories have tumbled after one another to cope with these regularities. Early on, they were "patterns" or repeated actions, later there was "structure" and now "structural anthropology." Others speak of invariant principles, behavioral regularities, normative systems, and so on.

At the center of such thinking is functionalism. In essence, functional anthropology, especially in its early phases in the work of the social anthropologists, concerned itself primarily with explanations of social continuity. The Trobriand Islanders practiced their customs because it contributed to the maintenance of their social life; so did the Andaman Islanders, the Nuer, the Lozi, the Tallensi, and many others. As Homans (1950) pointed out, these services operate for some theorists at the societal level, while for others the beneficiaries are individuals. Thus a certain level of unemployment may be good for the economy as a whole, but it is less beneficial for those who are thereby thrown out of work. Winch (1950) calls this the Janus-faced quality of functionalism in that it sometimes refers to individuals and at other times to society as a whole.

No matter what level of analysis we go to, however, the problem presents us with scientific cul-de-sacs. As critics have pointed out (Jarvie 1964; Cohen 1970), functionalism is at best a practical guide to social planning or at worst a set of self-delusions based on circular reasoning. For social planning we can posit a set of requisites that any new social organization, e.g., a factory or a suburb, must have, and then try to construct the best system of components to achieve these goals. The efficiency and utility of the plan are dependent upon our foreknowledge of the goals and the relationship among the components which are supposed to interact to achieve the pre-set ends. This has proved easier to do for factories than suburbs, or new African townships, because of the larger number of unknown parameters in the latter case (Boguslaw 1965).

In other instances, functionalism is simple tautology trotted out with trappings of scientific jargon and cloaked with the respectability of pseudo-explanations. Thus, Fortes (1962) explains the fact that people who are close to one another in sociological characteristics tend to marry:

> Structural propinquity between the parties is conducive to marriage because it facilitates continuity and consistency between the network of status relations in which they and their kin were placed before their marriage and the status arrangements that are the result of marriage.

In other words, people marry others who are more like themselves (structural propinquity) because such marriages maintain their similarity through time (facilitates continuity), i.e., the regularity persists through time because it is continuous! Obviously this is coming quite close to nonsense, although the reduction of such functional "explanations" to their logical postulates does one useful thing. It points the way to more adequate statements and therefore toward more adequate research designs. Thus the Fortes statement given above could easily be improved if it referred comparatively to the differences among marriages between those from similar social backgrounds as opposed to those from quite different ones. Even then, the explanatory problems can become quite complex because of the correlative nature of research results. If, for example,

1

divorce rates are significantly lower among those from similar social backgrounds and this holds across societies, then we still cannot—as Fortes does—say why this should be so. People who marry outside their own social group may be more prone to break rules and relationships in general, and so the very proclivity to marry someone different (in religion, race, ethnicity, etc.) may also be the reason such unions are more brittle. Conversely, or in addition, the differences in background may produce more conflicts in a marriage. The final answer is not easily available, even when we have improved the simple functional statement and made it into a testable proposition.

In general, the analysis of social institutions in terms of the contribution they make to the persistence of the social system of which they are a part, is unproductive. This results from the fact that such statements are often untestable unless revised so that the *absence* of the so-called function or benefit can be observed as well. In other words, the continuity of social and cultural systems cannot be understood by simply inventing words like "pattern," or "structure." Instead, we must examine carefully the nature of discontinuity within the same framework of analysis. If a pattern or structure *does* certain things, then what happens when the pattern is not present? In other words, if the pattern contributes to the continuity of the system, then what happens when the continuity stops?

To some extent, this kind of approach has been forced upon observers confronted by social change. They have had to admit that the system is in fact not persisting and therefore behavior may be serving different functions at an earlier and then a later date. Thus Marcel Block (1968) shows that two urban sections of the same ethnic group in the Malagasy Republic—one with community autonomy, the other with burial obligations in a "home" community—have adapted differently to modernization. Those with the home town burial obligations have active social contacts between rural and urban areas and are more upwardly mobile as a group in the society as a whole. Thus a traditional funeral behavior is now functioning to create greater access by some rural people to the modernized sector of the Malagasy Republic.

Those working with social change have been able to see either changing continuity or, as in the example above, innovation of new goals. However, this has not occurred so easily among those working with "traditional" and assumedly stable ethnographic materials. At this level, that of the "ethnographic present," a stable equilibrated system is posited and much of the functional explanation of the parts refers to the contributions each of them makes to this assumed stability.

Within the space allotted to one or even several field trips, it is quite difficult to find some quality of society that can be studied in such a way as to meet the criticisms directed at previous functional studies. The requirements are that the phenomenon be continuous and also *discontinuous* so that we can examine it with and without or before and after its continuity. In the political organization, war and peace are such conditions as are pre- and post-revolutionary periods if the revolution changes not only the regime but rules of the game as well. In such situations we can see what conditions promote continuity and discontinuity rather than making the simplistic functional error of attributing as a working hypothesis positive continuity functions to all aspects of the system.[1] But data on war and peace, or revolution, is not so easily come by using ordinary field work techniques of data collection to provide intensive and detailed material on behavior.

On the other hand, marital stability is almost ideal for this purpose. Marriage is an ubiquitous social organization that is constantly being terminated in all societies through death, desertion, annulment, or divorce. Thus the continuity and discontinuity or persistence of the organization is a variable quality in all societies since no marriage lasts forever and all marriages tend to vary in their capacity to persist. By focusing attention on the strength of marital bonds, we are automatically saved from making the mistakes of oversimplified functional analysis. Some qualities can be envisaged as contributing to the persistence and continuity of the organization, but if we wish to understand dissolutions and varying durations we must also theorize about the lack of persistence in the organization under analysis and develop ideas about what produces such a dissolution and what consequences occur once the discontinuity or destruction of the organization has occurred.

Obviously, such an approach cannot solve all problems. Marriage and divorce are behavioral qualities when they are studied through field work investigations. Thus we can theorize about continuity and discontinuity at the level of individual behavior, whereas it becomes difficult to extend such analysis to the structural level without some ability to vary the structural features themselves, such as the rules governing marriage and divorce. This problem—stemming out of Winch's recognition of the Janus-like quality of functionalism in which effects upon individuals and upon society can be quite different—leads to methodological difficulties in research design and interpretation that will be taken up in greater detail in the next chapter. It is sufficient to state at this point that the choice of marriage and divorce as a form of study does tend to solve the problem of not having both continuity and discontinuity available for observation and analysis. However, it does not per se solve the problem of which level of functionalist theory—that of society or the individual—we shall or should try to understand within any one investigation. Marriage and its stability are among the most universal experiences of mankind and therefore provide a universal basis for the comparative study of persistence and durability of interpersonal relations within an organizational setting. Furthermore, marriage is an area of research that is documented, at least in a descriptive sense, for a great many societies; thus comparative study is not so difficult as it might be for other possible foci such as war and peace, or revolution. This wealth of material points to another quality of the family as an organization which is attractive to the researcher. Although we have data on a large variety of cultures and societies, the known variance among types of family systems is quite limited. If we construct a typology from marriage rules which define who may marry whom, and residence rules which define where the family will live, then using four types of marriage rules—monogamy, polygyny, polyandry, and extended (i.e., some progeny must bring their spouses into the family)—and five types of residence patterns— neolocal, patrilocal, matrilocal, bilocal, and matri-patrilocal—we get twenty possible types of families. Even if we add more residence rules, such as uxorilocal and virilocal, this would still increase the potential number of our types to twenty-eight, which is miniscule considering the number of societies extant in the world which consider themselves distinct from their neighbors (possibly 2500?). Furthermore, this limitation upon variance means that explanations for under- standing and predicting behavior should be more easily arrived at than for other areas of human experience where variations are much greater and the number of possible factors to be accounted for much more complex than that of the human family.

In summary, the family is a universal organization amenable to comparative study. When we add to this its quality of being constantly created and dissolved as an organization, then family research can satisfy the classic criticism of functional analysis—namely that we cannot say what the functions of an organization are unless we study its absence, loss, or destruction, as well as its presence and/or its emergency and development. By posing the problem of continuity, not in terms of explaining observed behavior as if it were a persistent entity requiring support, but rather in terms of comparison to lack of continuity *as observed*, i.e., the destruction of the marriage relationship, we can now phrase classical functionalist questions in an empirical way. Thus, we do not have to ask how customs x, y, and z, or their specific practice by individuals, contribute to the continuity of marriage. Instead, we can more directly ask, what produces, or is associated with, more or less continuity or break-up of marriage? In terms of the society as a whole, we can ask what kinds of provisions are made for people affected by such lack of continuity of marriage, i.e., what sorts of "back-up" institutions are there to provide services discontinued by the destruction of the marriage relationship and possibly of the family as it was previously constituted? What is the relationship between marital stability and the rest of the social system?

These questions are not new; I have merely tried to place them into a functionalist perspective to show that they are crucial to the development of social theory. Answers to these questions have been sought in anthropology and sociology. Let us go over these briefly to assess what the status of our knowledge is at present.

Sociological Theories of Marital Stability

The amount of research and data available in sociology concerning marital stability is staggering to the outsider. Journals, books, readers, even special bibliographies, are available. Yet the theoretical understanding of this mass of empirical data seems piecemeal and lacking in integra- tion. Instead of attempting to bring together research findings under one set of logically related ideas, workers in the field generally list variables that have been related to the continuity or dissolution of marriage.[2] Levinger (1968), on the other hand, has tried an initial synthesis of such findings by using the Festinger concept of group cohesiveness defined as "the total field of forces which act on members to remain in the group" (Levinger 1968:580). This allows Levinger to look at marriage as a system of social relations in which there are first of all inducements to remain inside the relationship coming from (a) the relationship itself and (b) barriers to its dissolution which stem from the social and cultural setting of the marriage. Secondly, there are inducements to leave the group which stem from the attraction of other relationships and the restraints imposed on an actor to maintain and even strengthen these at the cost of his or her marriage. Levinger (1968:580) states, "Thus the strength of the marital relationship would be a direct function of the attractions within and barriers around the marriage, and an inverse function of such attractions and barriers from other groups."

Levinger (1968) then arranges research findings in sociology under three columns: (1) sources of attraction inside marriage (sub-divided into affectional and socio-economic rewards, as well as similarity of social status), (2) sources of barrier strength (sub-divided into feelings of obligation, moral prescriptions, and external social and legal pressures, and finally (3) sources of alternative attraction (sub-divided into affectional and economic rewards outside of marriage). Under this three-part division, he is then able to organize a large body of research findings correlating specific behavioral measures to high or low divorce. However, if the research findings are not available, his "theory" can neither predict nor explain what the results should be. Thus he notes that more refined research techniques have indicated that childless couples in the U.S. divorce more often than those with children, but this difference is much less than was previously believed. Indeed, children may be a negative attraction in some cases of divorce, but the author's theory gives no way of locating or predicting when this is so and when it is not. The theory then is simply a technique for categorizing specific correlations associated with high or low divorce. It states that some things act from within to hold a marriage together or break it up and other things act from without. The author notes (Levinger 1968:592) that his schema is not a general theory but a means of understanding the research results already available on any human society.

Although Levinger's work can be thought of as helping to organize predictions about the continuity and discontinuity of marital relations, it tells us little if anything about why these correlations should exist at all. A review of various types of explanatory theories of divorce has been ably brought together by Jessie Bernard (1964). Rather than worrying over predictions based on specified sets of variables, Bernard asks why some people decide to remain together while others decide to break up the relationship. To Bernard, the marriage must involve some form of adjustment. Both partners come from another family and they must work out some means of adjusting to one another; in general ". . .it is the women who are most likely to do the adjusting" (Bernard 1964:681). The implication here is that human marriage always involves some conflict in which ends desired by one or both partners can in fact only be achieved realistically by one or both sacrificing other desired ends. Marriage is then a system of scarce means to valued ends, and adjustments by one or both partners are necessary. Such adjustments involve changes in behavior after marriage, and if such changes are consistently avoided or denied then the relationship will not persist, and dissolution will occur or become more probable.

Three "models" of such adjustments are then discussed. The first one referred to by Bernard (1964) is the assimilation model. In this explanation, one spouse tries to win the other over to his/her way of thinking. As long as each is willing to listen and be persuaded, or if a pattern of persuasion for given compromises can be developed, then the organization can persist. When compromise becomes less possible, then the probability of dissolution increases.

The second model is somewhat similar, although it is more overtly political in character than the first. In this "strategic" model marital partners are seen as more clearly aware of the conflicts inherent in marriage and tend to develop a bargaining process in which scarce and alternative means are in fact understood to be a limitation to the achievement of alternative ends. Neither husbands nor wives have all the power, and each uses whatever he has to manipulate the other in order to gain control of the decision-making process. This may result in constant bargaining, or the unperceived manipulation of one spouse by the other; or in some cases it can result in a "stand-off" or balance of power situation in which genuine compromises are made on both sides in order to maintain the relationship. Unlike previously mentioned theories, strategic models can also be conceived of as operating in time. Thus there are concepts taken from game theory such as "first move," "fait accompli," or "strategic threat" in which future interactions and decisions are pre-set by statements and actions made at a previous interaction.

Within this same framework, divorce is seen as one choice among a set of alternatives. The values in the society, and those held by the spouses then tend to be criteria for choosing among such alternatives, only one of which is divorce. The value of alternatives can, however, change over time. Thus a spouse views divorce as having a different value before and after a new love appears on the scene. Bernard (1964) also points out that on a comparative basis, the easier divorce is to obtain, the higher its probability as an alternative among the possible outcomes of conflict (1964:723).

The third theory comes from international relations theory and is aptly dubbed the "escalation" model (1964:723). In this context, marriage is a lack of "escalation" while divorce is the normal outcome of a process of additive hostility. In such an organization or interaction, conflicts grow rather than decline and differences "snowball" until the only possible outcome is the destruction of the relationship. The understanding of divorce then becomes an attempt to isolate and analyze those factors that create the escalation of conflict such that divorce becomes the only possible alternative. Two descriptive equations are given in the original model (for an arms race) which explains the relations between the components in an escalation situation.

$$dk/dt = ay\text{-}mk\text{+}g$$
$$dy/dt = bk\text{-}ny\text{+}h$$

Where dk/dt refers to the rate of change; y and k indicate the amount of hostility present in the two partners; m and n are the costs or effort required to maintain or increase the hostility; while g and h are the permanent grievances. In the original usage of the model by Rapoport (1960), there are four different situations: (1) stability, (2) cessation of hostility, (3) declining hostility, and (4) runaway escalation. In the latter case, which can be applied to divorce, escalation occurs when mn (the effort or cost involved in pursuing hostility—called the "braking force") is less than ab (the mutual dependence of the actors), and g and h (underlying grievances) both have positive values—that is to say, there are real grievances that continue to affect the relationship. Bernard (1964:724) points out that although the model is very useful in making us look at the processes at work in causing divorce, it does not predict the exact point at which a divorce will take place. Instead, it explains why the conflict increases, and predicts an increase or decrease in the hostility. However, very few of the other "theories," including Levinger's (1968) predictive attempts, point toward the exact time at which a divorce will take place. On the other hand, the escalation model does seem to have formalized into potentially quantifiable relationships the causes for continuity and discontinuity in interaction systems of which marriage is only one example among many.

Anthropological Theories of Marital Stability

When we move from sociology to anthropology, theory becomes much more concrete and specific, and with one major exception (Ardener 1962) the tradition of research and theory has been much more unified. Even when different methods and techniques are used, the same problems are given primary importance by researchers.

Attention to divorce as an aspect of marriage has always been present in anthropology, although it began to receive specific attention as a subject for study in the late 1940's and early 1950's. In 1949, Barnes published his technique for gathering divorce statistics in the field and thereby gave anthropologists the means of collecting data comparable to that available in the record-keeping societies. Although the data required for the Barnes computations are quite simple, larger samples than those usually questioned by anthropologists are required for proper computations. This did not fit in with the field work of many anthropologists and so the Barnes analyses and computations, although now over two decades old, have not become standard procedures for field workers. This means that much of the data on marital dissolution in anthropology is still qualitative. Words like "frequent," "easy," "rare," "infrequent," or "common" are still used to describe the rate of divorce making comparisons difficult, although a few attempts at scaling and comparing these qualitative judgments have been carried out (Murdock 1950; Ackerman 1963).

Some awareness of the large variety of divorce customs and rates was made apparent by Murdock's work (1950). In this study, qualitative words were scaled and turned into comparative rates relative to Western society. It was shown (a) that divorce rates vary greatly from society to society in the non-Western world and (b) that it is quite common for divorce rates to be much higher in these societies than in the West. Thus, concern over the so-called high divorce of the U.S. is somewhat misplaced since it tends to rank on the low side when compared to a large sample of societies rather than to other Western areas, or its own past history.

A most important development was the publication of Gluckman's (1951) hypotheses about variations in divorce rate among different types of societies. A large portion of the societies dealt with by anthropologists use kinship as their most important and pervasive basis of organization. Divorce is an aspect of kinship systems, as is marriage. Gluckman argued that the descent system is the most important independent variable for predicting the frequency of divorce and the nature of bridewealth payments. In his view, societies possessing corporate patrilineages obtain new members by marriage with women from outside the patrilineage. Given the rules of exogamy, the patrilineage can survive only by securing rights over the reproductive powers of women from other lineages. Marriage then involves the permanent incorporation of these women into their husband's patrilineages, and divorce is infrequent because the husband and his group have in fact made her a new and essential member of their own group. In such cases there is, says Gluckman, most probably a high bridewealth payment compared to societies where such transfers of women are not so total and a girl's group does not give up so much. Gluckman later commented that bridewealth is not a simple function of descent because it is also affected by many other factors.[3] However, he still maintained that "it is unusual for there to be a high marriage payment in a system with unstable marriage" (Leach 1961).

In societies having corporate matrilineages, Gluckman theorized that the woman is in the position of producing children for her own descent group, not that of her husband. Her descent group does not give up her reproductive powers and "the duration of the marriage does not affect the welfare of the child nor the rights of its matrilineal kinsmen over it" (Mitchell 1961). Marital stability is thus determined simply by personality attributes of the couple and divorce is frequent. Since the husband and his group are not obtaining the childbearing properties, and often not even the work of the bride, compensation in the form of bridewealth is low.

In cognatic or bilateral descent systems, marriage is rarely ever a matter of membership in a corporate descent group and therefore descent neither strengthens nor weakens the marital union. Again, as in the case of matrilineages, it is more a matter of personal choice, and is therefore usually quite high in divorce rate and low in bridewealth.

Leach, in commenting on this theory, obtained Gluckman's acceptance of a scale running from patriliny through cognatic descent to matriliny. If such a scale could be constructed, then as we move from patriliny to cognatic to matrilineal descent we move from low to high divorce and conversely from high to low bridewealth payments.

In order to more fully explain why this theory should work, Mitchell introduces Bohannan's concept of *uxorial* rights, i.e., those domestic and sexual rights stemming out of the wife role, as opposed to *genetricial* rights, i.e., those rights stemming out of the woman's role as a mother— particularly the ownership of children (Bohannan 1949). Mitchell goes on to point out that in corporate patrilineages the entire patrilineage acquires genetricial rights in the woman while one member of the group obtains uxorial rights over her. In such a situation, the group does not easily give up its rights, no matter what the interpersonal relations between husband and wife may be, and divorce is therefore difficult and infrequent. Similarly, the bride's group has given up all rights in the girl and requires compensation so that they can import her replacement who will contribute to the survival of the group as she could not because of exogamous rules.

Contrarily, in matrilineage societies, the husband acquires only uxorial rights, while genetricial rights are retained by the wife's group. Uxorial rights can then be changed from husband to husband without in any way affecting the women's procreative powers which are kept by her own lineage. Thus, divorce does not affect the system and is frequent and easy. The same transfer of uxorial rights can occur in cognatic or bilateral societies because there is in fact no corporate descent group that can obtain genetricial rights; here again, divorce is frequent and easy. Furthermore, where divorce is easy, bridewealth is low because the husband and/or his group cannot obtain a permanent interest in the woman and her procreative powers.

A little later, both Fallers (1957) and Leach (1957) published materials which called for a reformulation of the Gluckman theses. Both of these writers showed how societies which should fall into Gluckman's low divorce category could be characterized as having high divorce because of the connections of the wife to her own lineage. Rather than throwing out the hypothesis, Fallers reformulated it to take into account the degree to which a wife retains rights and obligations in her own patrilineage after marriage. When such is the case, this is hypothesized to be a source of conflict and leads to divorce as an aspect of such descent rules. Descent is still the predictor of divorce for Fallers, but it can go either way depending upon the degree to which the wife is absorbed into her husband's lineage. Two years later, Stenning (1959) published his material on the Fulani of Bornu and claimed that for this group, and contrary to the descent group theory, a wife is completely taken over by her husband's local patrilineage. Moreover, the levirate (widow inheritance) was practiced if the woman was still of childbearing age. Yet, divorce is frequent and easy. Stenning (1959:182) explains Fulani high divorce by referring instead to men's desire for children and the high sterility of the population, as well as the desire of women for milk to sell so that men with small herds find it difficult to keep wives. In pursuing this line of reasoning, Stenning was backing up Schneider's (1953) approach in which divorce was viewed not simply as a result of structural rules but as a consequence of an actor's actions, wishes, desires, and frustrations. This same line of reasoning was taken up in my own earlier article on Kanuri divorce (Cohen 1961) in which I tried to show that Kanuri divorce stemmed primarily from the dissatisfactions of women who subvert culturally sanctioned male dominance because the men are dependent upon them for labor. This produces a conflict in marriage that often leads toward divorce. In situations as described by Stenning (1959) and myself (Cohen 1970), descent and bridewealth become less important and interpersonal conflict and personal desires increase in importance as explanatory factors.

Soon afterwards Ackerman (1963) attempted a cross-cultural test of some of these theoretical ideas. A sample of sixty societies having some definite judgments about divorce frequency as being "high" or "low" was obtained from the Human Relations Area Files. The sample included thirty-two bilateral, twenty-one patrilineal, six matrilineal, and three bilineal societies. Ackerman (1963:19-20) found that bilateral societies cannot be characterized as having high or low divorce. But if marriages within a community or a kin group are combined and compared to marriages outside such a group, then divorce is positively associated with exogamy and negatively related to endogamy. Similarly, patrilineality is not associated with low divorce, and isolating the genetricial or procreative powers of the woman does not help to create a relationship. However, when the levirate is used as a measure of a woman's absorption into her husband's lineage (the Fallers reformulation [1957]) then high divorce is very strongly related to a lack of the levirate in lineal societies.

Ackerman (1963:17) interprets these findings to mean that "as the network of conjunctive affiliations 'tightens' around the spouses, marital stability increases." In other words, the more similar are the social worlds and interaction networks from which spouses come, and in which they interact after marriage, then the greater is the stability of the union. The extremely strong association of low divorce with the levirate (p. = .0002) is interpreted by Ackerman (1963) to mean that the wife has been more fully severed from her own kin group and more fully incorporated into that of her husband. This in turn means, again, that the relationships of spouses to others is more conjunctive than disjunctive. These data tie the anthropological material into that of the sociologists who have for years been arguing that homogeneity of interests and status in background and in networks of affective affiliations after marriage is crucial to the success of the marriage (Burgess and Cotrell 1939).

The more recent discussions of divorce theory in anthropology (Lewis 1962) have tended to refine the original theory of Gluckman by showing that the transfer of genetricial rights need not be permanent. Another study (Goody and Goody 1967) has shown that the pattern of divorce using age-specific rates may differentiate two societies very significantly into one that has an initially high rate that steadily falls off while the other has a consistently high rate throughout the life span of individuals. In this latter case, the authors develop a complex theory which relates a large set of variables to each of these different divorce rate patterns. In one type, there is said to be patrilineal descent groups, high (returnable) bridewealth, low fostering, "social" paternity, increasingly stable marriage, high ratio of conjugal residence (amount of time spent with husbands over amount of time spent elsewhere), and widow inheritance. In the other type, there are no unilineal descent groups (or weak non-exogamous ones), low (non-returnable) bridewealth, biological paternity, high fostering, consistently high divorce, high ratio of sibling residence (time spent with siblings as opposed to others), and no widow inheritance (levirate). Obviously, this theory (Goody and Goody 1967) supports previous findings that kin type is related to divorce, and Ackerman's correlation of the levirate with lower divorce. However, by introducing a large cluster of variables, the theory provides greater leeway for testing both across and within societies having any one of these characteristics.

Two anthropologists have not followed the general tradition of investigation laid down by Gluckman and those who have followed in his path. One of these is Gibbs (1963) who has a theory of "tightly" structured society (epainogamous) in which little variation from the ideal is allowed. This type, he claims, has a low divorce rate. On the other hand, "loosely" structured societies (non-epainogamous) have high divorce because much deviation is allowed as a general characteristic of the socio-cultural environment in which marriage takes place. The other researcher is Ardener (1962), who has taken a strictly demographic view of divorce among the Bakweri of west Cameroon. He interviewed 1062 women who had contracted 2199 unions. These data were then analyzed into variables related to fertility and divorce. They reveal correlations between lower divorce and the following: recency of union, literacy, children, husband occupying a political position, senior as compared to junior wife in a polygynous union or monogamy as opposed to polygyny, and membership in the same Christian sect. He found as well that higher divorce rates and break-ups in non-conjugal unions were related to junior wife status in a polygynous household, paganism and unskilled worker status for husbands (both are indicators of low status), illiteracy of husband, and childlessness.

Although Ardener's study has weaknesses (no men interviewed, no behavioral insights into family life) it is still one of the most extensive social surveys ever conducted on marriage in Africa. His findings make firm something already well known—that social change is disruptive to family life. His important contribution therefore is a methodological one. For after his efforts, and the earlier work of Barnes, it seems arbitrary to claim that careful quantitative research is not possible in the African setting.

Summary and Discussion

Divorce or, more broadly, marital instability is an intriguing subject. It is, as I suggested at the beginning, a crucial test of functional theory because it represents a regular occasion when a social organization breaks down. In research terms, this gives us an opportunity to isolate those factors which contribute to both continuity and discontinuity not logically but empirically because it does in fact occur. Elsewhere in the literature there are grandiose debates about continuity and discontinuity which people try to solve logically. Thus incest has been said to be universal because those societies not practicing it died out long ago. Perhaps, but at present it is impossible to prove or disprove such an idea. On the other hand it is relatively easy to record information on the persistence, or even the degree of persistence, among a set of marriages and to ask and isolate what may have caused more and less stability and instability.

Two research traditions, one in anthropology, the other in sociology, have dealt with marital stability. Anthropologists have for the most part collected non-quantitative data, even though techniques for such data collection have been available for over twenty years. Thus there is a paucity of good comparative materials on marital stability from non-Western societies, although a few such studies do exist (Barnes 1951; Mitchell 1956). Theoretical development in anthropology has been almost totally concerned with comparing societies, using such comparisons to isolate structural features that might explain high or low divorce. Much of this work has concentrated on the descent system as a basic causal variable whose ramifying effects tend to produce more or less divorce. Unlike their sociological cousins, anthropologists have not taken any interest in low divorce as "success" and high divorce as "failure" in marital experience. These were alien people and alien cultures, and it would be a simple breach of cross-cultural sophistication to make value judgment about divorce rates. As far as change is concerned, except for some work by Barnes and some speculations by others, very little is known as yet about trends in divorce over time for the non-Western societies in which anthropologists usually carry on research. Anthropology therefore lacks good quantitative data on marital stability in non-Western society and it has only one theoretical tradition that has produced any empirical research. Basically this theory states that divorce is an aspect of kinship; therefore the type of kinship rules and practices in the society are the primary reasons why the divorce rate is at its observed level. Attempts to show that similar kinship systems are correlated with different divorce rates has in general produced refined typological statements about kinship, so that the general theory has in effect been salvaged and retained. One anthropologist, Ackerman (1963), has attempted to gear anthropological theory into that of sociology, but though this attempt has been widely accepted in sociology, scant attention has been given to it by anthropologists.

Finally, it is important to notice that there have been few attempts in anthropology to look into more general theories of interpersonal conflict for explanatory models of divorce. Anthropologists are not marriage counselors; consequently, it is not easy to get information on the full range of husband-wife interactions in the ordinary course of field work. So anthropologists have instead tended to emphasize those things they can see and possibly even measure such as kinship, family obligations after marriage, and culturally defined attitudes to husband and wife roles rather than actual interpersonal problems within marriage. In sociology there has been an ever increasing body of excellent empirical data on marriage and divorce providing time depth, as well as taking in large samples of the population (cf. Jacobsen 1959). Such detailed knowledge has led recently to several theoretical approaches, a number of which we have summarized. Many of these theoretical approaches, however, have one very important element in common. Basically they try to discover and assess the causes of "successful" (no-divorce) as opposed to "unsuccessful" (divorce) marriages. One major goal of sociological theory then is to understand how people can achieve happier lives by knowing beforehand whether a marriage has more or less chance of "success." Data having some time depth have also given sociologists the capacity to theorize about the long or short term effects of such things as war, the changing status of women, urbanization, industrialization, etc., on marital stability.

Unspoken yet present in the sociological material is a view of human nature, or at the very least, of the Western individual and his social psychological needs and dispositions. He and she are happier, more rewarded, less punished, less fearful, etc., if interpersonal relations in marriage can be maintained without serious disruption, breakage, and hostility. These latter qualities exist especially in marriage but are to be avoided if possible. This presumption is so strong that one of the theoretical models used to explain marital relations equates husband-wife conflict to the escalation of hostilities preceding the outbreak of open warfare between nations. Leaving aside the conceptual adequacy of such ideas, it is hard to imagine a condition more universally disliked and one that must be so strongly avoided as war. Are we then being asked to look at divorce in this same way? If so, why? Why look at marital instability as "escalation" or "war"? Conversely, what would happen if everyone divorced, not once but several times, and therefore marital instability and break-up ("escalation" and "warfare") were the most common result of marriage? Is such a society in a continual state of anarchy and chaos? How can ordered family life survive if it is always breaking up? How can healthy personalities develop when their crucible (the family) is constantly being shattered? The material in this book on Kanuri marriage presents such a high divorce society. Indications are that it has been like this for quite a long time, and it has prospered.

The discussion above shows that by asking questions of theory and about a high divorce society we are ultimately asking questions about ourselves and the nature of our own marriage system. If a Kanuri were writing these words about this study of the Americans, he would, I believe, stress the opposite point of view and ask questions about how these American men and women who fight, dislike each other, and are both attracted to other mates, remain married while we (the Kanuri) simply break things off. In both cases, a Westerner asking about higher divorce (than ours) elsewhere, and my fictional Kanuri colleague would be asking the same question—how does this unfamiliar human experience compare with my own? How can I explain these differences, and finally what does all of this tell about my own group and about me? Ultimately then, the present study holds up a mirror for each of us to see not the Kanuri or "them" but ourselves, and this, not the depiction of an exotic family system, is what this book is all about.

Chapter 2
Methodology: The Logic and Techniques of Enquiry

Method, Technique, and Approach

Generally in anthropological monographs there is a foreword or introduction in which the means by which information was collected are summarized. In several cases, anthropologists have written separate books discussing such matters, and recently several books devoted to methodology have been published (Epstein 1967; Jongmens and Gutkind 1967; Naroll and Cohen 1970). However, careful separation and discussion of each aspect of the methodology connected with a particular study is still a rare occurrence. This chapter is designed to fill such a gap for this particular study, and hopefully to provide a model for others so that standards of methodological rigor can be appraised and compared.

Elsewhere I have defined and separated three aspects of method that are important and qualitatively distinct (Cohen 1970). Methodology is a set of logical steps that unites theory to data collection whether research is primarily inductive or deductive. It involves, therefore, the entire research process from interpretation to the design of a specific test or exploratory probe. The answers to the question, "How should we research that problem?" are the comprehensive set of statements that in fact describes the method. Technique, on the other hand, is only one small aspect of method since a technique is a standardized means of collecting information. Finally, an approach is a set of assumptions which delimits out of all possible variables, that set which the investigator decides is most important to his particular problem. Thus a psychological approach focuses on psychological variables, an historical approach—on historical ones, and so on.

In devising the present study, I asked questions about all of these levels of research, although not necessarily as systematically as I shall write about them.

The Approach

The present level of theory as described in chapter one gives some, but not very precise, guidelines about the approach we should take to the topic. Sociological variables have been stressed and seem to have explained many of the variations both within, and certainly between, societies. On the other hand, divorce—as Schneider (1953) pointed out in anthropology, as well as Bernard (1964) in sociology—is also the result of personal decisions by actors. Thus psychological factors cannot be ruled out, and may indeed provide basic insight into why some people divorce while others do not. Finally, historical materials, although rarely used in anthropology for divorce studies, have been of enormous value in sociology, providing as they do the basic insights into what changes are taking place in the divorce rate over time and thereby posing a set of questions which must be answered.

The above discussion indicates that the ideal approach would be one in which we could gather sociological and psychological materials and stability measures over a considerable time period. We could then compare results across societies and relate these rates to a whole series of independent variables derived from previous research. Then, from such an analysis we would construct a theory to explain marital stability and instability. At this point, however, the real world begins to demand compromises. Unfortunately, there are very little, if any, psychological and sociological data on divorce or any other indicator of stability and its possible correlates which provide us with a respectable time depth outside the Western world. We are thus limited to data which, if available at all, have been collected at only one time period. Furthermore, as already noted in chapter one, almost all of these data are qualitative such that Ackerman (1963), for example, found he had to scale it into a dichotomy of "high" and "low" divorce. More specifically, Ackerman warned that his cross-cultural materials on divorce were so poor in quality that his research results were of necessity only tentative. Besides this, information on other theoretically related variables may or may not be available—especially psychological features; these latter materials are rarely gathered unless the researcher has a specific interest in them and even then they are seldom related to adequate data on marital stability.

We must also ask whether we wish to test only already established theories and hypotheses or do we also wish to probe for new relationships that may not be available in the present literature. Cross-cultural survey techniques and methods are best suited for testing relationships already clearly stated and operationalized in data bank materials such as the Human Relations Area Files or the World Ethnographic Sample. To use such a method for probes produces results that are of very little interest or hardly capable of interpretation. Thus Textor's (1967) Cross-Cultural Summary data on divorce reveals almost nothing of theoretical interest, and the sample sizes are pitifully small. Given the rather disjointed collection of theory available on divorce and the paucity of good data, the wisest course of action would seem to be that of carrying out a field study to collect new data as well as making the study both a test and a probe. Thus older theories could be tested, new relationships could be sought, and much-needed data could be collected. Furthermore, there need not be any restrictions upon our methodological approaches to such data. Sociological, psychological, and any historical materials available could be collected. Only when a much larger set of such studies have been made—using specific quantitative techniques to obtain data on marital stability and its correlates—will a cross-cultural survey be feasible and in any way conclusive.

Methodology

The Site. Having decided that a partially open-ended field study is our best means of attacking the problem, we can still ask whether or not a one-society study or a controlled comparison of several societies would be better. Much of the theorizing about marital stability in anthropology has come from cross-societal comparisons in which structural features—especially those of kinship—have been varied, and the correlative effects on divorce have been observed and interpreted. A recent paper comparing two societies suggests that "factors that militate against divorce on an individual level are those that work in favour of a low divorce rate" [for the society as a whole] (Goody and Goody 1967). On a common sense level this statement is true and therefore if differences between societies can be operationalized to represent a set of differences within any one society, then comparisons can be made by observing variations within only one society. Unfortunately, the common sense quality of this logic only goes so far, and soon becomes questionable. Thus if fertility is shown to vary inversely with divorce, can we logically say that the greater the fertility of societies (compared as units) the lower will be the divorce rate (per society)? Of if matriliny is correlated with high divorce and we are studying a bilateral kinship system, can we say that in those exceptional cases where boys inherit goods from their mother's brother (i.e., matrilineal inheritance), the divorce rate will be significantly higher? I don't know the answer to all such questions, but I strongly suspect that some variables are best studied within a society, some across societies, and some can be studied using both settings or "levels." Thus in the case of fertility, most studies including the present one show an inverse relationship between divorce and fertility (Ardener 1962). Goody and Goody (1967) compare two West African societies—Lo Wili and Gonja—which are quite different in divorce pattern, but similar with respect to the fertility/divorce relationship. Thus to say that fertility predicts divorce rate when societies are treated as units is clearly unsupportable. On the other hand, some factors such as disjunctive social relations between husband and wife may predict to variation in divorce *both* within and between societies. Why this should be so with some variables and not others is a complex problem that we will return to in the concluding chapter.

Ideally, then, it would be better to study marital stability in several field situations controlling for major structural features and collecting both probe and test data across a wide spectrum of behavior.

Although I recognized the scientific superiority of the above statement before going to the field, only one society was chosen for investigation. The reasons for this were almost all practical. First of all, funds were limited so that the more grandiose plan of engaging the help of a team of researchers was simply not feasible financially. Secondly, the society chosen for study—the Kanuri of Bornu—was one that I had worked in previously, and this foreknowledge allowed for quite detailed research designing before field work began. Thirdly, because I was already familiar with the language, culture, and history of the area, I could more easily maintain the probing quality of the work as well as setting up explicit tests of available theory. Fourthly, the Kanuri were known to have a high rate of marital instability and the nature of family life within the context of such a system is an intriguing one. Fifthly, I was anxious after some years' absence to return to the Kanuri to widen my understanding of their culture and society, and the very high divorce rate seemed a good means of probing more deeply into the social structure. Thus for a variety of reasons—some practical, others more personal—it was decided to carry out the study among the Kanuri of Bornu, Nigeria, with whom I had already spent two years (1955-57).

The Logic of the Research Design. The research project called for two kinds of information: (a) data on the divorce rate or more precisely on marital stability, and (b) data on a set of correlates that would help to explain the rate. The analysis then had to both test the strength of relationships posited in theories already available and, if possible, provide avenues to new explanations through data not considered in other theories.

The major dependent variable in the study is marital stability. This refers to the strength of the husband-wife bond in terms of its durability and probability of dissolution. The two most important types of measures or indicators of this variable for present purposes are those dealing with divorce rates and marital durations. A rate is a measure of the relative frequency of an event and thus can be expressed as a fraction, decimal, or a percent. When the numerator of such a fraction has been drawn from the population of the denominator, the fraction is, properly speaking, a rate; when this is not the case, then the fraction is spoken of as a ratio. Thus the number of males over females in a population is called a sex ratio, while the number of divorces occurring in a sample of marriages is a divorce rate (Glick 1964). The difficulty with marital stability as a concept is that any one measure of its relative frequency tends to involve distortion or error. As Barnes (1949, 1967) has pointed out, we can count extant marriages or leave them out, count dissolution by death or not. It is at present difficult to say which of these rates is "better." Furthermore, divorce can vary drastically with age and duration of marriage. Therefore to control for these variables and to obtain the pattern of divorce and not just its lumped value, we must construct age-specific and duration-specifc tables from a large enough sample of unions so that such detailed partialling will still provide sufficient material for all cells of the tables.

But divorce rates alone do not tell the whole story. For example, if two individuals have had three marriages and two divorces each, then their divorce rate is the same. Let us say, however, that one of them has never remained married to the same woman for more than one year, while the other carried out his two divorces after more than five years of marriage to each wife. Then, although the divorce record is the same (i.e., two divorces out of three unions), the second has consistently longer marriages. Thus durability of a union is an important measure of marital stability; indeed it may very well be the most important indicator of variation in marital experience in a very high divorce society.

A careful look at the definition of marital stability used above shows that other indicators such as death or desertion could enter in to create comparable high and low amounts of instability. Although verifying such a notion is beyond the scope of this book, I believe this approach to the subject is useful for comparative purposes. Ultimately the stability of the union, no matter what the reasons for it, is important for family life, remarriage, husband-wife relations, and possibly many other aspects of social organization. Consequently, communities with an extremely high mature adult death rate (such as a number of arctic settlements of a few decades ago when tuberculosis was rife) have much in common with high divorce societies even though they have relatively lower rates. In both such societies there is much remarriage resulting in many half-sibling relationships and widespread genealogies. Children in both often lose at least one parent and sometimes both through death or divorce. In other words some common adjustments must be made to constant rates of dissolution at the same life stage no matter what the explicit causes of the break-up happen to be.

As already noted in Chapter 1, a number of variables have been significantly related in previous work to variations in the divorce rate. Some of these, such as membership in a different religious sect, can not be studied among the Kanuri who are all Muslims. Others, however, can be operationalized and investigated within a Kanuri context. Variables such as fertility, bridewealth payments, socio-economic status of the husband, kinship affiliation of each spouse, as well as possible kinship connections of spouses to one another, can be entered as items on a questionnaire along with the relevant material on marital stability.

Psychological variables require some systematic means by which such characteristics can be collected and related to the basic dependent variable. Ideally, those people already sampled for sociological characteristics should be given psychological tests so that our psychological data could then be geared in with and compared to the large array of sociological features we had decided to measure. In order to do this, however, we would have to clearly identify informants so they could be re-interviewed for psychological purposes. The question then arises as to whether it is more advantageous to advertise anonymity and use a new sample for psychological testing, or give up anonymity of informants in order to use the same individuals and thus deepen our ability to interrelate psychological and sociological variables. Field assistants were of the opinion that anonymity was much the preferred way to treat respondents, so we decided to carry out the psychological study on a separate sample of people who were identified with respect to a small set of sociological variables, including their divorce and duration records for each of their marriages.

This does not mean that it would have been impossible to obtain re-interviews—but the research team, and personal friends, frowned on such a technique. The subjects would have to be *re-interviewed* because the TAT cards were not ready during the time when the first sociological interviews were being carried out. From an administrative point of view it would have meant asking local authorities for a particular person, by name, rather than by sociological characteristics—something we did not do throughout the entire study. In other words, we did not have any clear-cut reason for wishing to speak to a particular individual and we wished to convey this idea to our respondents. Re-interviewing would, I believe, have jeopardized this anonymity.

In terms of historical materials or time depth, several avenues presented themselves. There is a large volume of traveler's materials going back to the 1820's which deals with the Kanuri of Bornu. This material can be culled carefully to see what light can be shed on divorce over the past 150 years. Secondly, sampling for all age groups can shed some light on change or the lack of it over the past twenty-five to fifty years. Thus if a younger age group has more divorces per person than an older age group—who have had longer to divorce—we may conclude that divorce is increasing. There is also patience and foresight. If we have carefully measured the marital stability in a specific sample during this field trip (time one), then a decade from now we can measure an identical sample (time two) and compare the results. Thus if all else fails, the present study can at least serve as a baseline for a re-study in the future and the two studies together will then provide the time depth required for an historical approach.

Finally, there is the logical possibility of examining those who will inherit the future, i.e., the young people who will in the next few years become young adults and begin to marry and divorce on their own. We decided finally to use young people, especially those who could be expected to change the most in the next few years. These are the young people at the secondary school level of Westernized education—the highest educational level provided in the Bornu area. We interviewed some of these students and had the rest write essays expressing their views on marriage and divorce and how they viewed their own future as husbands and wives. Although this is not a foolproof method, it does at least give us some indication of how these future elite members view their own marital futures.

These, therefore, were the basic design features of the study. We hoped to gather material relevant to divorce at the sociological, psychological, and historical levels. Besides this, we hoped to have some ability to analyze some of our major independent variables as if they were dependent ones.

Obviously, to do this fully with a large array of independent variables is impossible since it would require almost a separate research project for each independent variable we wish to fully analyze. However, some simple information on household composition, wife order, parents' socio-economic status, and a few other variables could hopefully shed some light on the nature of those variables that correlated to the divorce rate. We felt this might be quite important with psychological variables since we did not really expect to find startlingly high relationships between specific psychological qualities and the divorce rate. Our reasoning here is quite simple. If a very high proportion of the population experience at least one divorce, then psychological distinctions are less important because nearly everyone, no matter what kind of person he or she is, will in fact divorce. However, there is still the possibility that psychological data will discriminate between high and low divorcers. At any rate, a few variables such as age, sex, rural or urban residence, socio-economic status, fertility, and so on, may be more significantly related to psychological distinctions than is divorce rate and therefore we designed the study so that such an interpretation is possible. This also allowed for a replication on a separate sample of some of the major relationships in the sociological study thereby giving us some check on the reliability of the results.

The probe quality of the study, i.e., an open-ended search for new explanations, requires first that we include some variables for study that are central to this particular society, but which are not necessarily considered crucial in the literature on divorce. Elsewhere (Cohen 1967) I have suggested that the household is the basic unit of social organization among the Kanuri. Therefore it was decided to gather, systematically, and in relation to other marital data, material on the exact nature of the household organization.

Secondly, there is always the possibility that contextual features not even considered are more crucial than those variables included in the research design. In all probability the best way to obtain new and unlooked-for material on social institutions is simply to participate and observe. I had done this in my previous study in Bornu, but this time my interests were more sharply focused. I decided therefore to leave time every day for visiting friends in their households. At such times conversation often turned to marriage and divorce, and events such as marital break-ups, which occurred regularly. Thus, the actual stuff of marriage and divorce as it occurred in its natural setting was observed and has been used to add depth and understanding to the quantitative data.

Techniques

The research design worked out for this study required that we relate marital stability to a set of sociological and psychological factors and try to obtain some understanding of what effects historical factors in the past or future play on these phenomena.

The sociological materials are in general well adapted for inclusion in a questionnaire. Indeed, a glance at our questionnaire (see Appendix I) shows that most of the material asked for is already in numerical form. Such items as age, age of spouse, duration of marriage, cost of the two major bridewealth payments, numbers and ages of children, household members, etc., could all be entered onto a pre-designed answer sheet. Ages and time intervals were geared into an event calendar that had as its main date the time of Shehu Umar Sanda's succession to the Bornu throne in 1937. Almost everyone could relate his own age and that of others to this date. Other dates utilized were the various reigns of Waziris or chief ministers of the kingdom, and the beginning and end of World War II.

Non-numerical material such as the reasons for divorce, the image of a good and bad husband and wife, the genealogical relationships of members to their household head, or of cousins to one another in a cousin marriage, were written out on the answer sheet. These materials were then coded later in the analysis.

The pilot study carried out in the summer of 1964 on a sample of twenty-five urban men who had contracted just over 100 marriages led to one major alteration in the marriage questionnaire. In analyzing the data I found it difficult to assume that all informants were sociologically constant. Thus if an old man who had contracted twelve marriages said he was a trader doing "fairly well" in the city—could I assume that he had been the same sort of person when he contracted his first marriage? Thus in redesigning the questionnaire it was decided to divide it carefully into two parts. The first part reviews the informant's marital history and current sociological situation. Then a series of approximately twenty-minute interviews are given for each marriage ever contracted. In this marriage-specific section, major sociological characteristics of the respondent are asked for again, but projected backward into time so that we may record information on a particular marriage.

In the summer of 1965, the revised version was taken back to Bornu and a two-man team of Kanuri assistants translated the questionnaire, then back-translated it into English. These operations were continued through several rounds until everyone connected with the project was satisfied that the Kanuri words and phrases were in fact denoting, and as nearly possible connoting, the meaning we had originally written into the English version after the 1964 pilot study. For example, the last question (No. 47) on the general information questionnaire (for men) concerned (a) the ownership of a horse and (b) how it had been obtained. I had translated this into Kanuri as:

(a) *Furnum mbejiwa?* Is there your horse in this place (or with you)?—which eventually became the more colloquial and (to me) controversial, *Furnum wa?* (Do you have a horse?). There was nothing particularly wrong grammatically or semantically with my own phrasing, but the native Kanuri speakers simply felt more at ease with this second choice. My suspicion here is that my own unconscious structural biases are against such a shortened form as *furnum wa* which is literally translated as "your horse?" Instead, I tend to use the Kanuri *mbeji* rather like the French word *chez* to mean "at your place" or "with you" which is grammatically correct Kanuri, but evidently a little awkward in conversation. The new phrase was controversial because I thought the curtness of the shortened question could be interpreted to mean that the questionnaire was using the language of a social superior and thereby *demanding*, not politely *requesting*, an answer. I was assured by both the assistants and close friends that this was not so, and after checking the point further with people who knew the subtleties of rural-urban distinctions in language usage, I decided to accept the shortened phrasing. However, this one phrase serves to show how delicate a matter the construction of a questionnaire can be, even when the researcher believes he knows both languages.

(b) *Ndaran fandimin?* Where did you find (or get) it? After much discussion, this question was judged to be slightly impolite because it would be "nicer" to infer that someone had given the informant the horse. If this were not so, the person could then say, "No one, I purchased it in the market." So the question became: *Ndu nyiro cho?* (Who gave it to you?). A large number of the responses on this question (76%) are denials of gift in which the respondent reported that he obtained the horse in some other way. Thus, what a Westerner would consider a "leading" question seems to have been a perfectly neutral and indeed a more polite way of speaking.

An easy conclusion from the above example is that no foreigner should ever construct a questionnaire without the help of a group of native speakers. I consider myself a quite good, even fluent, Kanuri speaker, but not a sophisticated one. Indeed, the construction of a questionnaire is a good test of one's own degree of deviation as a foreigner speaking the language, and in the end helped me to understand the language much better.

When the questionnaires were finally ready, they were administered during the summer of 1965 and 1966 by myself and a graduate student in anthropology (David Spain) to a sample of 116 men who gave information on 504 marriages. The student and myself each worked with a Kanuri-speaking assistant. Statistical tests indicate no significant differences in our results when his materials are compared to mine. The female questionnaire was administered during 1965 and 1966 to 99 women who reported on the details of 237 marriages. The 1965 interviews were done by Mrs. Catherine Spain, and those in 1966 by Norma Perchonock, graduate student in anthropology. Both of these American women used the same Kanuri-speaking assistant. There are significant differences between the two women interviewers which disappear when their interviews are controlled for rural/urban distinctions among respondents. Unfortunately we do not know what differences, if any, would appear between interviews with the same sex of respondents as recorded by both men and women researchers. It was assumed instead that women would react "better" or more comfortably to a woman researcher and vice-versa. In general, Kanuri informants, friends, and research assistants agree on this point.

The psychological factors that might be associated with marital stability required some systematic technique for collecting such data. Depth interviews of high and low divorcers by a psychologist would have been ideal, but we did not have the resources. On a previous occasion, I had administered a few Rorschach tests. This produced a plethora of exotic folklore material as well as many references to plants, animals, birds, insects, and fish—that I had never heard of. It soon became clear that a proper evaluation of the results would require a detailed ethno-botanical study as well as more intensive research on folklore. The reason for this was the symmetry of the blots and their lack of clearly identifiable form. It was therefore decided to reduce the stimulus ambiguity drastically, and increase the directedness of the projective material, i.e., focus the test on a pre-set group of topics concerned with matters that might be related to marriage and other types of human interaction.

The ideal format for such material is the TAT (thematic apperception test). It was therefore decided to create a set of pictures from drawings of Kanuri men and women interacting sometimes with their own sex and sometimes heterosexually. Almost all of the pictures finally chosen (see Appendix II) involve the potentiality of conflict between persons or groups. However, each card is ambiguous, so that a non-conflict interpretation is also possible.

It can be argued that the best course of action would have been to use the standard TAT cards, or to adapt these standard cards to a Kanuri setting. After all, the standard cards have been widely used for personality assessment; why invent a new set that cannot be systematically compared to findings in other societies? The methodological rejoinder to this criticism is important for comparative research. First, my main interest in this study is *not* Kanuri personality. I only wish to include in the research design the possibility that psychological differences among Kanuri adults may be related to variations in their marital histories. Therefore, psychological data pertaining most closely to my own topic has highest priority. In this regard, Spain and I have both carried out TAT research among the Kanuri with widely differing results. Spain is interested in achievement motivation and has presented pictures which could have a possible achievement theme. His results (Spain 1969) indicate many such responses, while I obtained very few. On the other hand, my cards were designed to elicit interpersonal conflict data, which they did. Conversely, Spain did not get much material on this theme. Thus the TAT is in fact a semi-directed interview and, like all semi-directed interviews, it should be pointed in the direction of the researcher's interest in order to obtain the best results for within-culture comparisons.

Secondly, even for cross-cultural comparisons, it should be remembered that a culture-specific indicator and the variable it is designed to measure are quite different phenomena. Thus variables taken from my TAT's such as "flexibility," "subordination," "hostility," or "cooperativeness" may still be quite useful if and when researchers devise comparable means for obtaining indicators of these variables in other societies.

The original group of eighteen pictures were photographed and developed in three different degrees of vagueness. These 54 cards were reduced to twelve in a pilot test and administered to 93 men and 68 women during 1966. Difficulties emerged immediately over figure-ground distinctions and responsiveness. Pictures are not part of traditional Muslim Kanuri culture. Thus the black and white shapes on the card often made no sense whatever to the respondent, who if pressed might then try to pick out something, often quite exotic in its form, from the shapes on the card. In order to avoid this quality which made the test more like a Rorschach, and in order to standardize the stimulus—which is what it is designed for—we instructed the informant that there were *people* (no sex indicated in the instructions) on the cards. We then pointed to feet, hands, body, head, etc., in order to outline the figure(s). The informant soon learned (one or two cards) to look for the people and "saw" the ones we had drawn.

The experience was still quite strange and often the productivity was very low, out of shyness and fear of making a mistake, rather than a desire to reject the test situation. In order to obtain maximum productivity and to obtain more clarity in rejection responses, we prodded the informants with questions such as, "What are they doing?" or "Why?" after one of their statements. Most often such prodding led to an extension of the story. In a minority of cases, it could lead to a codeable rejection such as "I don't know such things," or "Only God knows such things," etc.

The tests were administered by myself and a Kanuri-speaking assistant to the 93 men, and by Norma Perchonock and a Kanuri-speaking woman assistant to the 68 women. Besides a number of content differences between the sexes which we believe can be interpreted, the productivity of the men is higher than among the women. This means that their results cannot be directly compared since the incidence and frequency of any variable in such material is a function of the productivity or length of the protocol. Although this may be a sex difference, it is more likely a result of the fact that I speak Kanuri and Miss Perchonock does not. Thus in the projective situation, I, as well as my assistant, prodded the informant without using translation, and very likely the longer male protocols are due to this difference in the interview situation. It should be remembered from above that Spain and I do not differ in our sociological divorce data, even though he was not a Kanuri speaker at the time of these interviews.[1] Thus, for demographic data, language does not seem to be crucial, while for more open-ended situations such as a projective test it may be a significant factor affecting the results.

The historical approach is much the most difficult of the three being used in the study. Ideally, the present study must be repeated in a decade or so in order to plot the changes that have occurred over time. Historical documents have been studied and these will be discussed in Chapter 8 along with the rest of the "historical" data. As already noted, some time depth can be obtained by comparing the old and the young members of the samples—this too has been done. However, in common sense terms, the most significant historical factor in Bornu is that of Westernization. We know from studies carried out elsewhere in the Islamic world that modernization is correlated to a drop in the divorce rate in Islamic societies (Goode 1963). This has happened with such regularity as to have almost the logical status of a "law." Therefore, it becomes important to try to gauge the effect of Western education on the people of Bornu with respect to marriage and divorce.

For a number of reasons, explained below in the discussion of sampling, it was impossible to do much formal work with married people who had Western education and were usually members of the civil service elite. As a compromise, we decided to gather data from the post-primary school population of Bornu. Two out of three types of schools were chosen—the secondary school and the teacher training colleges for boys and girls. This gave us four schools in all, since the sexes are segregated. The craft school was omitted because there was no female counterpart.

In terms of our problem, it was reasoned that although these students are not yet married, the men are nearing the traditional age of marriage and the girls have generally passed it. They think about marriage a great deal, discuss it among themselves, and have views on what should and should not be changed. Although not all, or possibly any, of these views will be actually practiced when they are married, still this is the one group in the entire area more influenced by Western culture than any other. Thus we decided that tapping their views on marriage and divorce would be a useful guide to the future, even though it was not in fact the future itself.

One other useful purpose could be served by this population. The sociological interviews on marital history obtains very biased answers to the question, "Why did this particular divorce occur?" Almost to a man and woman, informants explained a particular divorce in terms of the transgressions of the spouse; never are they themselves at fault. Thus we decided to ask the secondary school and teacher training school students to explain the reasons why divorces occur. This would at least tell us whether men always feel that divorce is the fault of the woman and vice versa. Beyond that, it provided us with a large body of data on local "social theory" or if you like, the folk view of marital stability.

The form of the data was that of a school essay or "composition." This resulted in two essays each from over 600 young men and women ranging in age from 14 to 25. Unlike our other data, these students also represented over 50 different ethnic groups in the Bornu area. Along with each essay, the students were asked to write in information on their ethnic membership, religion, age, name of their home town, village, or hamlet, and family background. (See Appendix III for some sample essays.)

The material to be used for general probing was spread throughout the three systematic data sources: the questionnaire, the TAT, and the school essays. In the questionnaire, some questions were inserted for purposes of pure curiosity, although it was considered possible that they might shed light on marriage and divorce. Thus question No. 74 on the marriage specific interview is concerned with *bənji* (a child in the womb that will not come out). The Kanuri believe that such a phenomenon can occur and can subsequently last for years. I wished to know how often this phenomenon actually occurred and what else it might be related to, such as wife order in a polygynous household. Thus it was entered as a "probe" item.

Similarly, the TAT data as a whole could very easily turn up nothing of significance in relation to divorce. Indeed, there are good theoretical reasons for saying just that. Nonetheless, such detailed psychological data, along with a few sociological correlates could shed new light on Kanuri culture and society as a whole and point the way toward more specific psychological research in the future. The same can be said for the school essays with respect to the study of modernization and social change.

Finally, as already mentioned above, participant observation was carried out consistently throughout the entire time in the field. In general, systematic interviewing with either the questionnaire or the TAT began at about 7 a.m. and continued through until 12 noon or 1 p.m. every day. After lunch and a short rest during the heat of the day, I would visit friends or they would visit me. During the first summer of 1964, formal interviewing was held up for nearly one month. During that time a complete review of early work done on Kanuri kinship, marriage rules, and customs was carried out with some former friends serving as major informants. These men were well aware of the nature of ethnography from my previous field trip. As a group we worked each day from early morning to noon, and again in the afternoon from approximately 2 to 5 or 6 p.m. talking, discussing, arguing, while I wrote down as much of what was said as possible.

At the same time I participated in marriage ceremonies, often serving in some special capacity because of my ownership of a car. I also participated once, as noted above, as an intermediary for a husband whose wife had left him. It was my job to go to the girl's relatives, to whom she had run, and talk "softly" to them, and her, about the possibility of her return to her husband.

To some extent, but not as much or as systematically as I had planned, I also visited respondents who had answered the marriage questionnaire. During the interview or just after it, I often asked, "Where do you live? I may come to greet you soon." When this did occur I attempted to obtain an independent check by observation of the household on some of the data given by this respondent in his questionnaire interview. In only one case out of a dozen or more did I come upon serious discrepancies between what the informant said in the interview and what I learned about his married life later on a more informal basis.

Participant observation also told me something about my changing role in Kanuri society. When I first went there in 1955-57, I was a young pre-doctoral student getting a degree. I was, in the eyes of many, still a *fugura* (student) or a young *mallam* (teacher in training). My wife and I were accepted and generally liked for "braving it" out in our mud hut in a small rural village, and for learning the language. Now, I was "*rashidi*," a mature man with a rented house in the city. I had finished my degree—a question many old friends asked immediately; I had three sons (a great blessing from Allah); I was an associate professor—a title that I explained endlessly in relation to the ranks above and below it—and I had a good salary. Friends told me they always knew I was a "comer" and bragged to others about how *they* knew me when! In other words, my status had risen in Kanuri terms. It meant that I could be more serious, more demanding if I wished, and should be more careful about not doing silly things like the young men. In other words, I was older and more responsible in their terms, but so was I in my own view. Where the last trip had been almost totally carried out using participant observation, I was now gathering statistical data. The greater formality of the research techniques seemed appropriate to my age which is also associated with more formality in Kanuri culture. The endless chain of interview appointments, dealings with officials, getting the materials printed, and so on, added to this effect and indeed validated my status as a "busier" man than the one they had known in earlier days who could sit around for hours just listening or talking to the assembled company. In summary, my status had changed but it all seemed understandable and even predictable in Kanuri terms. To me, my field time seemed freer and more personally independent than had the first trip in which the largest portion of my time was determined by events rather than any particular research schedule.

Sampling

In general, sampling procedures in a non-Western area are a complex result of ideal standards, the exigencies of the field work situation, and the specific goals of the research design. Several writers (Barnes 1949; Ardener 1962) suggest that divorce studies can be carried out reliably only if large random samples of the population are chosen for study. Intending to follow such advice, but wishing to make sure of adequate quotas of both sexes as well as rural and urban areas, I used the pilot study in 1964 to investigate sampling with research assistants and local leaders who would be affected by the technique.

The first plan was to select a number of research sites in rural and urban areas on the basis of representativeness and accessibility and then obtain respondents within each site on a random basis. To a man, research assistants and local leaders were against such a plan. Local leaders stressed the fact that it was too arbitrary and could turn up many unreliable as well as reliable respondents. The research assistants insisted that any random method of selection public or private would create great suspicion. Any one chosen could (and would, they said) ask, "Why me?" It was finally decided therefore to use local leaders, who promised cooperation, to choose twenty-five respondents of each sex from each research site. The men chosen were to be of three categories; eight of them would be "wealthy," eight "poor," and nine "not rich-not poor." This was to be the basis of the questionnaire sample.

Advice was also unanimous on the choice between anonymity and using the respondent's name so that he could be located again for other types of questioning such as TAT or for a re-study in the future. It was suggested that by not even asking for the man's name in the interview we would be imparting evidence of anonymity which would be a great asset to the study.

The above decisions led to the choice of four major interview sites, two (Shehuri and Maifoni) in the capital city and two (Konduga and Delori) in the rural areas. The two urban sites were well known as a traditional urban one (Shehuri) near the royal palace of the Shehu, and a newer commercial one (Maifoni) that was strongly Kanuri but less connected to the political elite.

The two rural areas were both to the east of the capital near to a good motor road. One (Konduga) is approximately 30 miles from the capital and is a village of approximately 2,000 people. The other (Delori) is fifteen miles away from the city and is much smaller, about 600 people. Konduga is a district capital with a weekly market, a school, a nursing station, a district head, and a courthouse as well as a head man for the village. Delori used to be a district capital, but is now simply one of the villages of a district. There is a school and a village head man. Around both of these towns there are numerous small hamlets considered part of the jurisdiction of the village head. Informants were to come from both the village and the surrounding hamlets and be identified as such. Thus respondents of both sexes would be coming from the three tiers or levels of settled population in Kanuri society—the city, the villages, and the hamlets.

The TAT sample was not the same one as that used for the questionnaire. It was decided therefore to ask local leaders to bring people of all ages equally from two groups: those who had divorced very little or not at all and those who had divorced a great deal. Thus the psychological study was to be divided by an indicator of the dependent variable. It was also divided to represent both sexes, rural and urban areas, and to some extent, at least for men, to obtain some representativeness of socio-economic status (as with the marriage questionnaire).

The technique for obtaining a quota of sub-groups *per* interview site was simply to rely on the judgment of the local head man and his followers. By checking a few sociological features at the beginning of the interview we could tell which category the respondent belonged to. As it turned out, this was of little importance near the beginning of the interviewing at each site unless the person had never been married at all—a basic prerequisite for inclusion in the sample—in which case he was rejected. Respondents were also chosen to vary across all ages so that each age group could be represented in the sample. But toward the end of the work at each site it was necessary on rare occasions to send an informant away because we already had enough of his particular category and needed others instead to fill our quota of twenty-five persons of each sex. This was not usually necessary, however, because we generally let the head man know where we stood in our sampling and suggested therefore that tomorrow such and such sort of person be sent because we had completed our requirements for the others. Most often this was sufficient.

In all research sites, a quiet place, sometimes an entrance hut or some closed hut within a compound, or a meeting room, was made available by the local head man for each interview. Informants and interviewers both came to the interview site and other persons were kept away from the site. The one exception to this was in Shehuri where interviewing took place inside the ward head's compound at the spot where cases were usually brought to him. On a number of occasions interviews at this spot were broken up because an important case was to be heard. At such times my general ethnographic curiosity was too great and I preferred to listen to the case rather than ask for a new interview site.

Despite all of this helpful cooperation, it was almost impossible to obtain very many exceptionally high status people, and almost as difficult to find people of very low status who would come to the interview. Thus our distribution of statuses is lumped toward the middle ranges as it is in the population as a whole. However, this means that the sample is biased toward these middle statuses. The only serious problem here is that this excludes any members of the Westernized or partially Westernized elite who may very well have qualitatively distinctive life-styles. There is only a very small handful of such people in Bornu and thus I assume that the sample is not seriously biased by this absence of status extremes. What it does mean, however, is that any findings on status distinctions should be qualified by these exclusions at the "ends" of the curve.

Very little need be said here about the school sample or that used during participant observation. The schools were chosen because they represented the most advanced Western education available in the area. Participant observation with a comparable age group outside this level of schooling indicates very little differences in marital attitudes and behavior between the non-schooled generations whether they are young or old.

Participant-observation was carried out with old friends at first, then moved to new friends made by contacts with older friends, because of my urban residence, or through the questionnaire interviews themselves. I also tried to expand into the civil service and the schools so that these elements, represented very poorly if at all on the questionnaire, would at least be contacted and I could discuss marriage and divorce with them.

From the above discussion it is obvious that the sample is not good enough to make simple generalizations which could then be applied in strict terms to the population. *But it was not designed for this purpose*. What is represented in our sampling is not the Kanuri people but a set of variables. Thus we have tried to stratify the sample by age, sex, rural or urban residence, and socio-economic status. It is about these qualities that we hope to make our final generalizations.

The technical difficulties that distinguish a strictly random sample and a stratified one can easily be seen in the comparison of urban and rural differences. From previous field work, as well as from research in other parts of Africa, rural-urban distinctions are known to be very important. In Bornu, these urban distinctions are represented most clearly by the differences between Maiduguri and the rest of the emirate. Maiduguri is about 10% of the entire population. In a truly random sample of the entire area, therefore, Maiduguri would make up about 10% of the sample. To test for rural-urban differences would require approximately fifty cases in the urban category. This means the total sample would have to be much larger than the present one if the sampling were to be random. The utility and parsimony of stratified sampling is thus quite obvious when there is some awareness of which variables are important for a particular study.

Nevertheless, even though we cannot be accurate, descriptively, some transformations from our sample to the populations at large can be made by using census material to obtain proportions. These proportions then become simple correction factors for estimating the population values for our findings. Thus our rural-urban proportion is 1:1. This can be "corrected" by weighting the findings in terms of the census proportions of rural to urban in Bornu as a whole.

These then are the methods and techniques used in this study for the collection of data. We have not discussed at this point the methods and techniques used in analyzing the data because it is felt that they can be presented more clearly and meaningfully along with the materials themselves. Suffice it to say at this point that as many or more decisions and compromises have to be made for purposes of analysis, as for the field work. None of these at either level has been totally acceptable; some worked better than others. On the end, methodology, especially in anthropological field work, is a compromise in and of itself. The researcher is as far from the controls of a laboratory situation as it is possible to get. Not to recognize this and not to adjust to what *is* possible rather than ideally desirable is to make all meaningful work impossible.

PART II
THE SETTING

Chapter 3
Larger Scaled Socio-Cultural Environment

This chapter is essentially a summary of Kanuri culture and society designed to provide an understanding of the environment in which marriage and divorce take place. More detailed descriptions and analyses of these materials can be found elsewhere especially on the political organization and its historical development.[1] Kanuri society, culture, and history are extremely complex. Consequently we must choose from the large amount of material available those aspects that are required to illuminate the specific problem at hand, namely marriage and most particularly divorce.

The criterion I have chosen to apply is that of value orientations. Marriage and divorce take place within an overall social system in which persons are taught by upbringing and experience to strive for a finite set of desirable ends. This finite set of culturally shared values, sometimes referred to as *ethos* or *cultural goals*, has its origin in the social, economic, political and religious institutions of the society and the historical development of these practices. When we understand this set of goals we can appreciate the shared set of values that Kanuri bring into a marriage, or indeed into any kind of relationship. Obviously, there are individual differences in the intensity with which such values are held and even idiosyncratic values that are not shared. Nevertheless, it is assumed here that a set of culturally distinctive Kanuri value orientations do exist and that they can be distilled from the institutions and organizations that form the basic means for achieving such ends.

Physical Environment

Up until 1903, the term Bornu referred to the political system of the Kanuri people, that is, to an emirate nation-state in the Chad Basin to the south and west of the lake. After the inception of the colonial regime, there were in effect two entities with the same name. One was Bornu Province. This included Bornu Emirate, Biu Division, Bedde Division, Potiskum Emirate, and informally Dikwa Emirate in the Northern Cameroons which was administered from Bornu Province. In previous work, I have reserved the word Bornu for the emirate or kingdom and if necessary used the term Bornu Province to refer to the larger unit. As of 1968, this distinction is unnecessary because Bornu Province has now been abolished and replaced by an even larger unit, that of Northeast State—of which Bornu Emirate is a part; Maiduguri, the capital of Bornu, is also the present capital of Northeast State. Thus, when the term Bornu is used here, it refers to an emirate or kingdom in Northeast State, Nigeria, the homeland of the Kanuri people.

The area lies in a sub-Saharan savannah zone which is generally flat and tilted gently toward Lake Chad. Hence the name Chad Basin which reflects the inland drainage of this large body of water—one of the largest fresh water lakes in the world that has no access to the sea. The lake does drain, underground, toward the northeast since the basin continues to tilt in that direction reaching a low point in the Bodele Depression some five hundred miles into the desert. Presumably this entire area ranging from Lake Chad right up to the Tibesti Mountains was under water, or at least was very wet, only three or four thousand years ago. At that time the southern and western boundaries of the lake were extended into present day Bornu and these old lake shores can still be seen today in the form of low ridges running across the flat Bornu plain. As dessication occurred the lake retreated to its present site, leaving the Yo River flowing in from the west and its two main suppliers, the Shari and Logone, running northward from the Cameroon Mountains. These barriers and the lake form natural boundaries to Bornu on its eastern and northern flanks and have served this purpose for centuries.

Rainfall in the area is generally low, not exceeding twenty inches for most years, and falls almost completely between June and September. This basic quality determines a great deal of the rhythm of life in the area. Crops are sown and tended during these months, and then harvested in the autumn months right up to December. Cattle nomads take their cattle north to new pastures during the rains and south in the long dry season where waterholes are more permanent and fodder can be obtained. Craft production and trade flourish during the long dry season and decline somewhat during the growing season because people are working on their farm plots. In general men have two occupations, one during the dry non-farming season and then they cultivate their plots during the rains.

This rainfall distribution plus Bornu's latitude and proximity to the Sahara determine the seasonal shifts in climate. Basically, there are two distinct divisions in the seasons: wet and dry. However, the dry season can be further subdivided into (a) the "little" hot season, from late September to December; (b) winter, from December to March; and (c) the hot season, from March to June. This subdivision is basically a function of the winter season in the northern hemisphere, which cools the area somewhat, and the northeast trade winds known locally as the Harmattan. These winds blow daily in the winter season bringing dust from the desert and creating the basic condition for all village houses to face west and/or southwest, away from the wind. Often, as well, the butcher's section of town, or the meat stalls in a market, will be situated in the extreme southwest corner of town or of the market. Thus the Harmattan takes the smell away from the populated area rather than into it.

The supply of water has been ameliorated and partially controlled in the last decade by the drilling of deep bore holes throughout the area which have tapped a large underground source of water. This water is clean and less dependent upon seasonal variation, which has meant that cattle can be watered more easily in one place and cities are supplied with clean running water from taps rather than wells. The latter has traditionally been a good place for the propagation of guinea worm and other parasites.

Soils in the area are sandy, easily worked, and easily leached. This means that hoe agriculture is not difficult but that fields deplete in productive capacity rather rapidly and must be left to fallow every four to six years. Although there was resistance at first (Cohen 1961), more recently the population has accepted the use of super-phosphate fertilizer which has increased local productivity for both subsistence (millet and guinea corn) as well as cash crops (mostly ground-nuts).

In general, then, climate and soil combine to provide a fairly secure and easily obtained livelihood for the people. In the present period, this base-line is being improved through greater control over water resources and increased productivity by chemical fertilizers. On the other hand, droughts are not unknown and can be famine-producing. Disease is rampant in the area and death rates, especially for infants, are those typically associated with underdeveloped areas of the world.

The People: Population Characteristics

The two most recent censuses (1952 and 1963) were carried out under the old political divisions when Bornu was part of Bornu Province, which was in its turn part of the Northern Region of Nigeria. Thus any description of the population must be limited to this older frame of reference. Furthermore, there is the problem of validity. The 1952 census is in all probability an underestimate of the population, since people generally felt it might have something to do with taxation which is partly a function of numbers of dependents per household head. On the other hand, the 1963 census is generally suspected of being inflated. It was taken at a time of intense north-south competition in Nigeria and the continued dominance of the North was dependent to a great extent upon its ability to demonstrate its numerical superiority in the country at large. Thus it was locally patriotic in 1963 to inflate the census. Whether this was in fact done or not is unknown. However, the possibility that northern self-interest may have led to numerical distortions upwards is a fact of life in the area that must be taken into account by researchers using these data.

Bornu Province has a population of approximately 2.9 million which is 10% of the former Northern Region of Nigeria. Since the emirate has about two-thirds of this population, it alone accounts for approximately 80% of the region. In ethnic terms, the Kanuri are the third largest group in the former North and the dominant group in Bornu Emirate where they make up approximately 73% of the entire population. This information, at both the regional and Emirate level, can be seen in Tables 3:1 and 3:2.

TABLE 3:1. ETHNIC COMPOSITION OF MAJOR GROUPS IN
NORTHERN NIGERIA (IN MILLIONS)

Ethnic Unit	1952	% of total	1963	% of total
Hausa	5.5	32.7	11.5	38.5
Fulani	3.0	17.9	4.8	16.1
Kanuri	1.3	7.7	2.3	7.8
Tiv	.8	4.8	1.4	4.7
Yoruba	.5	3.0	1.1	3.7
Nupe	.4	2.4	.7	2.3
Igala	--	--	.6	2.0
Idoma	--	--	.5	1.7
Gwari	--	--	.4	1.3
Igbirra	--	--	.4	1.3
Ibo	.2	1.2	.4	1.3
Total Population	16.8		29.8	80.7*

*All others, 19.3%

TABLE 3:2. ETHNIC COMPOSITION OF MAJOR GROUPS IN
BORNU EMIRATE (IN THOUSANDS)

Ethnic Unit	1952	% of total	1963	% of total
Kanuri	626	62	1446	73
Fulani	111	11	223	11
Hausa	53	5	162	8
Shuwa	45	--	47	2
Karekare	--	--	23	1
Babur	7	--	13	.7
Other named groups	--	--	58	3
Total Population	1005		1972	98.7

The distribution of Kanuri in Northern Nigeria shows them to be concentrated heavily in their emirate homeland. Thus there are 1.5 million Kanuri in the emirate and .8 million (about one-third) live elsewhere in the North. Those outside the emirate tend to cluster in the large urban areas, especially Koro Province (248,000), Katsina (102,000), and Bauchi (171,000). Only 200,000 Kanuri live in what was Bornu Province, but outside their own emirate. Thus as a people they do not diffuse or spread outward evenly from the homeland but tend instead to migrate to other large urban centers of the North. The remaining 200,000 are to be found in Dikwa emirate to the southeast of Bornu and throughout the rest of Nigeria, especially the Muslim north.

The emirate itself where this study was carried out is approximately 24,000 square miles in area. This means that population density was 42 per square mile in 1952 and using the 1963 census it has increased to 82 persons per square mile with a mean value for that ten year period of approximately 60 per square mile. The people live in hamlets and villages spread out over the entire emirate. There are approximately 300 named and variously sized settlements ranging from Maiduguri (called Yerwa locally), the capital city (57,000 in 1952; 88,000 in 1963), to very small hamlets of only a few households. The bulk of the people, about two-thirds of them, live in 250 named village units that range in size from 1000 to 5000 (1952) or 1500 to 8000 (1963). Named villages, however, are in fact village area units which include a central village and a group of surrounding hamlets under the jurisdiction of the village area head. Often as not these hamlets make up half or more of the population figure attributed to the village. It also means that outside the cities the population is spread rather evenly across the countryside. By contrast with the smaller villages, there are about 60 settlements whose populations are over 10,000. The 1963 census gives a figure of 201,000 as "urban" and 1,771,000 as "rural," making the rural:urban ratio 8.81:1 for the emirate as a whole.

The age-sex distribution for the emirate population shows that for both the 1952 and 1963 censuses between 35% and 40% of the population is under 15 years of age. When the sex ratios are broken down into rural and urban residence a reversal of the folk image appears in the data. Informants generally believe that there are more women (especially young ones) per man in the cities as compared to rural areas. The census material indicates that in the age range 15-24, the proportion of women to men is 13:9 in rural areas and 14:13 in the urban centers. In all likelihood the stereotyped judgment which reverses these facts results from there being more *divorced* women in the cities, i.e., free to roam about in the streets, which makes it seem as if women are greater in absolute numbers.

Vital statistics on the Kanuri are not available, and the sample used in the present study is too small for any firm conclusions about actual rates of population growth or decline. However, the overall impression gained from what material is available strongly suggests that fertility per woman is very low.[2] This agrees with estimates made by local medical authorities and with information collected in my first field trip in the 1950's. In the sample of women questioned about marriage there were 133 live births reported per 100 women, 46 of whom were dead by the age of two and 61 of whom were dead at the time of the interview, leaving 54% of the progeny still alive. Given the fact that all of our respondents have been married, it is significant that 33% report never having been pregnant in any of their marriages. The nine women in the sample over the age of forty-five had produced sixteen live children. Since all of these children were reported to be over five at the time of the interview, we added in nine more women who made up the 40-44 year old category. This total group of eighteen women near or at the end of child-bearing had given birth to twenty-six live children or 1.4 live births per woman. If these figures are in any way close to describing the area then the population would be in decline if it were solely dependent upon its own reproductive resources.

Explanations for this low fertility vary from discussion of local diet, to venereal disease, to contraception. Although physical reasons cannot be pinned down as yet, it is quite clear that the Kanuri do not practice any form of contraception or abortion beyond the use of prayers and charms. This leaves us with the biological properties of the population in its present environmental adaptation as the likeliest explanation. When such features are changed through increased health facilities, the population will expand rapidly. Meanwhile, in socio-cultural terms, fertility is a scarce value distributed unevenly throughout the population and highly desired by both men and women.

Historical Background

The Kanuri Kingdom of Bornu is a successor state to an earlier one which began sometime in the first millennium. This early society, known as Kanem, grew out of a mixed group of peoples and clans in the central Saharan region who had probably retreated southward toward the lake as water supplies dwindled between the Tibesti region and present day Lake Chad. From these congeries of peoples, there emerged a dominant clan, the Magumi, and within it a chiefly or monarchical lineage, the Sefuwa. By the thirteenth century, this state was well known throughout the Near East as one of the great Islamic kingdoms of the southern Sahara. Contacts were maintained through trade, diplomacy, and the pilgrimage which sometimes took peoples of the Sudan to North Africa and Egypt first before Mecca. This means that Islamic ideas of family law, divorce, inheritance, and property were well established in the area before the founding of the Kanuri state of Bornu.

For a variety of reasons this early kingdom was rocked by a series of internal conflicts from the mid-thirteenth to the late fourteenth century.[3] In the end a rebellious clan-cum-ethnic group,[4] the Bulala, succeeded in their attempts to upset the ruling Magumi Sefuwa rulers of Kanem. This group and its followers then fled to the southwest of Lake Chad where they eventually established the kingdom of Bornu. Although little is known of the means by which Bornu was founded, somewhere during the reign of Ali Ghajedemi (ca. A.D. 1470-1500) a capital city, Birni Gazargamo or "the walled fortress," was built near the southern banks of the Yo River in northern Bornu.

The kingdom then entered a period of great power and prestige, whose effects are still felt today throughout the central Sahara and the Sudanic belt of the southern desert rim. Kanem was recaptured and tributaries were established to the north of Bornu and to the east and west, along the major trade routes. Bornu vied with the other great Sudanic power, Songhai, to the west, for hegemony over the Hausa states, especially the trading city of Kano. Documents that have survived from this period tell of highly organized warfare with cavalry, musketeers, bowmen, foot-soldiers, and well-developed combat strategies as well as a complex political organization for maintaining the state, its power over tributaries, and diplomatic relations with other Islamic nations (Ibn Fartua 1928; Cohen 1967). It was during this period that Bornu was first mentioned on European maps of Africa and from that time forward it numbered among the great interior kingdoms of Africa known only by reputation to Europeans.

The Bornu plain was not empty. In it lived a number of pagan peoples lumped together in oral traditions as the So (Cohen 1962). They are reported to have been giants who opposed the rule of the Magumi and their followers. The Kanuri,[5] as the invaders now (fifteenth century) came to be called, fought to conquer these folk throughout the fifteenth and sixteenth centuries and possibly even later. Eventually, however, they were subdued and began to be absorbed by acculturation and political control into the dominant Kanuri culture—a process that is still going on. On their side the Kanuri organized their conquest state from their fortress capital Birni Gazargamo.

From the late fourteenth century forward, then, there existed a "great" and "little" tradition in Bornu.[6] The urban capital housing the ruling group acted as the center of trade, government, law, power and Islamic sophistication. The rural areas with heterogeneous non-Islamic cultural roots adapted to this "great" tradition while maintaining some of their own local identity and memories of separate origins. To this day the rural-urban distinction is a significant and easily observed one throughout the emirate.

Bornu traditions refer to the periods after the sixteenth century, for at least the next two centuries, as times of steadily declining power and vigor. Tributary states defied Bornu, trade declined, and internally the central administration at the court of the *Mai* or ruler is said to have been weighted down in excessive ritualism. On the other hand, there are also traditions of successful military campaigns to subdue tributaries while the state and its ruling dynasty continued to control the Bornu plain. Comparing this period with all others there is no significant increase in usurpation attempts or royal assassinations, nor are royal reigns any different in length or type of succession. Thus if the period was in fact one of decline, it was either not recognized by those near the center of power, or if they did perceive the weakening, there is little evidence that those groups most benefiting from the power of the state (i.e., the nobles and royal heirs) ever did anything to correct the situation (Cohen 1966a).

On the other hand, from the end of the sixteenth century onward the entire southern Sahara was very unstable politically. The fall of Songhai in the 1590's was not replaced by a similarly well-organized successor state. Instead, many nomadic groups, especially Tuaregs, were free to pillage and raid right up to the borders of Bornu. Where previously Bornu and Songhai had been large imperial nations which could control smaller, less powerful peoples in their orbit of power, now there was only Bornu and the relatively smaller Hausa states. Thus even if Bornu remained as strong in the so-called period of decline during the seventeenth and eighteenth centuries as before, the numbers and strength of her enemies increased. And this increase occurred in the Sahara, which contained her most important channels of trade and communication.

Into this vacuum of the late eighteenth and early nineteenth centuries came the rising power of the Fulani empire of Sokoto, which soon threatened Bornu and led to the rise of the second dynasty of the kingdom (Last 1967). In the process of helping Bornu to protect itself against the Fulani uprisings a Kanembu sheikh or Shehu rose to obtain the dominant power position in the Bornu state (Brenner 1967; Cohen and Brenner 1970). Although he did not usurp the royal power formally during his lifetime, this leader was able by the end of his life (1837) to be recognized as the highest authority in the state. Later, in 1846, his son killed the last of the royal heirs to the Magumi Sefuwa throne and set himself up as sole, now royal, ruler of Bornu. It is this family that rules in Bornu today (Cohen 1970).

At the end of the century, in 1893, the kingdom was attacked and defeated by Rabeh, a marauding slave trader from the Sudan to the east of Bornu. Rabeh took over the kingdom and was about to set up a third dynasty, but was interrupted by the inception of the colonial period. He was killed by the French in 1900. By 1903 the British had entered present day Bornu and enticed the Shehu from French hands back into Bornu by promises to rebuild the nineteenth century capital of Kukawa, destroyed earlier by Rabeh (Brenner 1967), and protection from French claims for money in payment for their having defeated Rabeh.

From 1903 to 1914, the British colonial officials experimented with a number of organizational changes in the Bornu government structure and by 1914 they developed the system that has, with only minor changes, existed until the present day. The slave trade was abolished even though it continued sporadically right into the early 1920's. As roads and communications were constructed and border tolls applied, the entire trading pattern of Bornu changed from a trans-Sudanic and trans-Saharan one to one in which Bornu was an integral part of the economy of modern Nigeria. This was aided by the coming of the large European trading companies who carried the bulk of exports and imports as part of the Nigerian economy (Cohen 1970c).

World War II brought the next significant change to Bornu. After the war, export prices rose very rapidly and local tax revenues increased enormously. The late 1940's and 1950's witnessed a rapid increase in emirate government services and in the number of paid civil servants working for the emirate (or Native Authority; NA as it is called locally). This period also witnessed the rapid growth of the nationalist independence movement in Nigeria as a whole and the inception in Bornu of political parties. One of these (the NPC) represented the unity of the traditional emirate governments of Northern Nigeria; the other (the BYM) was linked to an opposition movement in the region. These two eventually clashed seriously in 1958, and the BYM was destroyed as an effective party. For our present purposes, however, the most important quality of this post war period was the rise in income that brought increased buying power to the entire population and stimulated the development of local Bornu trade.

After independence in 1960 these developments continued steadily although the price of exports remained stable, such that local incomes have not increased in nearly the same way as they did from 1945-55. Bornu people obtained jobs in regional and national civil services, and a Kanuri became the first Nigerian Governor of Northern Nigeria.

The most serious changes have occurred since 1966 in the aftermath of the two military coups and the civil war. After the setting up of the new states of Nigeria in 1968 and the abolition of Bornu Province, the emirate, now the only entity named Bornu, became part of Northeast State, taking part or all of three previous provinces. Thus the emirate is now only a minority among the minorities instead of being the dominant majority in what was Bornu Province.

Although this brief summary cannot do justice to the rich historical experience of Bornu, it does indicate the continuity and degree of autonomy enjoyed by this society through a number of significantly different periods (Cohen 1970a). Two major dynasties, a third unsuccessful one, colonialism, independence, and the post-independence civil war have come to the area; and yet Bornu as a distinct, clearly bounded society has persisted. For the smaller scaled social organizations, the villages, households, descent groups and families, it has meant that their socio-cultural environment—the political, economic, social, and cultural setting in which they operate—has continued for a very long time. Contacts with the outside world have always occurred, but their effects have always been filtered through a society that has been to some degree independent in the management of its internal affairs. As we shall see, only very recently have outside influences begun to affect the nature of attitudes toward marriage and the family and as yet only a very small group are involved.

Political and Economic Organization

The traditional pre-colonial political organization of Bornu was essentially that of a feudal state in which fief holders lived in the capital and administered a set of dispersed fiefs through subordinates in the rural areas (Cohen 1970c). The number of fiefs varied per titled noble and was a measure of his, and his patrilineage's, success in the government. This central government was presided over by the monarch who ruled through a complex administrative hierarchy of free and slave nobles.[7] As in many pre-industrial societies the hierarchy was made of a series of great households (the greatest of which was the royal palace) whose heads formed the various councils of state. These households contained the family of the lord, ideally a polygynous extended one, his clients, slaves, and dependents who were often agnatic relatives, plus his mother if she was alive and single.

In the rural areas, two distinct ways of life were practiced. The Kanuri and other settled ethnic groups lived in permanent or semi-permanent villages, while a number of ethnic groups such as the Fulani, Shuwa, and Budduwai were pastoralists practicing a more or less fully nomadic way of life (Stenning 1959). The nomads were linked through their own headmen of large descent group segments to the central government of the state. The settled people lived in villages and hamlets of varying size. Each of these villages and their surrounding hamlets were separate fiefs. Local headmen were under the jurisdiction of fief-holder's representatives, who served as an intermediary between the rural areas and the central government.

Under local headmen were the heads of households, who served as the political leaders of the households and representatives for their members to other households and to the political hierarchy. Thus the household was the smallest localized unit in the political organization.

Most of the essentials of this traditional system are still practiced today. However, there have been some significant changes in the state structure. The British consolidated the multitudes of small fiefs into twenty-one districts named after the leading village of the area. Each district contained what before had been a number of fiefs. The district head represented the central government in the rural area and ruled through his own following of clients and kin, as well as headmen of each village in the district. At the center, a Shehu's Council under the chairmanship of a *Waziri* or chief minister has slowly taken on the attributes of an emirate cabinet with each Councilor in charge of a Native Authority department within the emirate. These departments have central offices in the emirate capital and representatives stationed in the district capitals throughout the state. Local district officials—teachers, sanitary inspectors, dispensary attendants, etc.— form a local urban upper class living out in these major rural towns along with the district head and his retinue of followers.

The Bornu Emirate was placed under a Bornu provincial government, under a Northern regional administration, until 1968. For most of this century, until independence in 1960, this higher administration has been a colonial one. The structure was quite simple. At the head of the administration was a Resident Officer, called Provincial Commissioner after independence, under whom the general administrative officials, called District Officers, and technical personnel, carried out their duties. These latter operated in such fields as roads, schools, forestry, veterinary services, etc. District Officers were assigned to a particular emirate or division and were responsible for its activities, especially in areas where chiefs operated, such as taxation, adjudication, and new appointments. Technical personnel ran provincial departments, which were responsible for the success of programs run by each of the native departments in the emirates and divisions of the Province. Thus a Provincial Education Officer would have under him all Native Authority departments of education in the Province, the largest of which was that of Bornu Emirate. The situation today is essentially the same, except that Northeast State is much larger and therefore the number of local NA departments under the State administration is much greater.

The basic effect of this colonial organization was (not too surprisingly) a decrease in the independence and autonomy of Bornu Emirate. Demands could be made upon Bornu from outside, such as an increase in taxation, and the emirate was under compulsion to accept and comply. Local people realizing the superior authority of the colonial administration could on occasion complain to the British against their own leaders. And the system of technical departments in the emirate under a provincial authority meant that institutionalized means for development and change had been created within the Bornu hierarchy (Cohen 1964).

On the other hand, many essential features remained. Officials of the Bornu Emirate are still appointed by the central government of the emirate, and no change toward elective office is contemplated as yet. Women rarely participated in politics and even today they do not vote. The monarchy has lost authority to the NA Council, but this office is still the central symbol of statehood and of the cohesiveness of the Kanuri people. Local leaders still adjudicate disputes and serve as an appeal court hierarchy from household head through ward and hamlet heads to village area heads up to the district head. Indeed, at the local level, whether it be in the city or the rural areas, local political organization has changed very little in the past fifty years. For the individual, political authority starts with the household head and continues up the hierarchy through the district head to the central government of the emirate. With the few changes in structure noted here this is not very different from the system which operated not just fifty years ago, but a century ago as well.

The organization of economic life in Bornu is similar to the political in that the most significant changes have occurred at the macro or society level, while the local level of the village and the individual householder has changed but little in the past half century. This does not mean changes have occurred only at the macro level, but that persistence rather than change is the most overwhelming quality of local life, especially in the rural areas.

Traditionally, Bornu had a semi-subsistence economy in which partial specialization plus feudal tributes in kind provided the institutional basis for the transfer of goods. In the rural areas, people produced grain and craft goods in the settled villages, while nomads produced meat, hides and milk among the nomads. They exchanged these goods either by barter or with locally recognized currencies at weekly markets distributed throughout the area. In the urban areas, many people owned farms or used their craft specialties to obtain produce. The nobles obtained food from their fiefs in the form of annual tributes.

Foreign trade was carried on primarily by the urban upper class using their own subordinates or traders who came from Kano, Tripoli, Zinder, Murzuk, etc. Slaves, ostrich feathers, locally produced Korans, ivory, leather, and other locally produced goods went out of Bornu, especially to the north. Minted currency, guns and gunpowder, cloth and clothing, horses, camels, rugs, perfume, glass, swords, and a host of other items known on the Barbary coast came south. Indeed it was a mark of upper class membership in nineteenth century Bornu to have as clothing an object of foreign manufacture.

With the beginning of the colonial era, foreign trade was turned around toward the south and to the rest of Nigeria. Roads were built from Maiduguri to Jos and Kano as well as being continued on this route to Fort Lamy in Chad. Maiduguri also served as the hub of a wheel, with roads constructed outward to all of the district capitals of the emirate. By 1966, the railway reached Maiduguri, linking Bornu to the rest of the Nigerian rail network. Thus Maiduguri serves as the central entrepôt for the emirate. In like manner, each district capital is connected to Maiduguri and serves as a distribution center for the surrounding villages. Because of the upper class urban group of officials living in each district capital, its local market must also serve the needs of this non-agricultural group who can afford also some luxury goods, such as expensive clothes. And so the political changes of the recent times are reflected in the economic sphere as well.

Again at the macro level most of the significant changes have occurred in and around Maiduguri in the last several decades. The city is witnessing a building boom that has brought in a small scale cement block industry, as well as a group of contractors, many of whom are very successful. At the northern edge of the city there are two large industrial developments, a groundnut oil mill and an abattoir, as well as several smaller scaled producers such as a tannery and a bakery. More are promised for the future. To the east of the city, a few wealthy men have purchased farm plots and are setting up large acreage citrus fruit farms. And even more recently, a group of wealthy men have formed a general investment corporation for developments in building, real estate, and small industry.

In the rural areas, the most significant change has been the development of bore holes for water which has helped to increase the number of cattle, the amount of irrigated crops, and decreased disease from the parasites found in well water. The government still (as it always has since World War II) sets the price of export crops and controls the licensing of buying agents in order to encourage local traders.

Not a great deal is known of the economic life of the individual household during the pre-colonial period. From descriptions of markets, fields, and other local scenes in the urban and rural areas, we can assume that basic crops and crafts were essentially the same. A few, such as native weaving, have died out and in some cases, such as imported enamelware or wooden matches, a new product has become ubiquitous. From all accounts, slave labor in households and in the fields was extremely common although the number per household, at the commoner level, was probably very low—not more than one or two per household (Barth 1968). This latter figure was probably higher among urban households, particularly those specializing in craft production. For nobles, the numbers must have been much larger.

The division of labor was a function of sex and occupation. The sexes lived separate lives economically, only cooperating in the farm work in the fields. Otherwise, men carried on their semi-specialized or specialized activities such as craft work, trade, or more full time work such as religious teaching or local administrative duties (such as those of a village head). Crafts were organized into local guilds under headmen, who were in turn rather loosely subordinate to the head of the same craft in the capital. Divorced women were organized in the same way and could be called, through local head women, to help provide hospitality and entertainment for officially sanctioned strangers passing through the town. Ordinarily, either the monarch's father's sister or some other of his agnatic female kin was the titled head of these women, although her exact power and authority over the group are not clear.

Female slaves worked in the fields or the household as extra labor for the wives and daughters of the compound. In addition, they served as extra sexual objects for the head of the family who consequently had greater chances of having more children of his own (Cohen 1967b).

The greatest differences between local economic life today and that of 50 to 100 years ago are (1) the near abolition of slavery, (2) the acceptance of a universal currency, and (3) the increased number of occupations and objects available as a result of Western technology.

Except for a few men who obtain some personal gain from the role, slavery and slave trading have been abolished. For those who can afford it this has been replaced by wage labor or, more commonly, by clientage in which non-kin are absorbed into a household in the role of a diffuse subordinate (*tada*) to the household head. Clientage has always existed in Bornu, but has become the dominant means of expanding household size today, whereas it was only one of several ways in the traditional pre-colonial society. Female "slavery" has died a little more slowly and is still practiced by a few upper classmen who use them for extra help in the women's work of the compound. They are, however, indistinguishable in every way from "free" wives except that they are not married to their consorts.

Although currencies have existed heretofore in Bornu, the colonial period saw a change from special purpose monies to a more general all-inclusive type of currency. Thus peasants would often not sell grain in the nineteenth century urban markets unless paid in cloth or clothes, even though Maria Teresa dollars and cowries were widely used. By having everyone accept one all-purpose currency, the colonial government enabled people to trade more widely afield and gave everyone access to much wider markets of goods and services. Add to this the increased cash income since World War II and the result is a wide distribution of transistor radios, manufactured cloth, flashlights, and other imports.

The traditional political and economic organization supported a complex system of social stratification which cross-cuts and sub-divides a basic two class system made up of nobles and commoners. Nobles were slave and free titled persons connected in some way to the centralized political system. At the top of the free noble class are the royals who claim some genealogical relationship to the royal dynasty. Commoners are divided by a series of status criteria such as occupation, sex, ethnic origins, rural or urban status, wealth, etc., which make them more or less important within their own sub-grouping of the society.

The primary mode of upward mobility and success is and always has been that of creating or maintaining client or kin relationships to powerful people in the society. Clientage is indeed a basic means by which people create a rewarding existence in Bornu (Cohen 1965). This is accomplished by various types of alliances between people at differing levels of the political and economic hierarchy which are modeled upon or use the idiom of the father-son relationship. To get ahead in Bornu is to become the trusted follower of an important man who has become successful in the field of endeavor that the individual wishes to follow. No wonder then that *barzum*, or respect, or discipline-respect (the essential behavioral norm of the father-child dyad) is considered to be the most highly valued behavioral quality in the entire social, economic, and political life of the society (Cohen 1967a).

Religion

Islam has been the dominant religion of Bornu since the fifteenth century, going back to Kanem before that time. The monarch is commander of the faithful and monarchs are known to have taken the pilgrimage since sometime in the eleventh century. Thus the people are all Muslim. They know and accept the basic tenets of the faith and almost all young men are given some religious instruction. Certainly all ceremonies, public meetings, and even written correspondence reflects this awareness of Islam.

In contemporary Bornu there is an Islamic court system with a high court presided over by a chief judge or Alkali, for the emirate with a formally recognized court in each district. In addition political leaders keep religious practitioners in their entourage as legal and religious advisers. Below this level are many *mallams* or teachers-priests who have elected to become specialists in religion. They officiate at ceremonies and teach the young. They also carry on some simple medical practices, write charms, and in some—but not all—cases they also practice divination. Some are also rumored to be amenable to doing "bad" things, i.e., carrying out sorcery for a fee.

To the Kanuri, the supernatural world is populated with a hierarchy of entities. At the top is Allah or God—a vague, non-personal being that rules despotically and ultimately over the entire universe. Prayers are addressed to Allah who is ultimately responsible for the Final Judgment which will come on a fateful Friday at the end of the world when right will triumph, and guilt be punished by eternal hellfire. Below God are the angels, his assistants, who aid him in the complex task of governing the universe. There are also bad angels, the chief being Shetan (Satan) who rules over evil in this world and the next. The non-empirical world is divided into seven levels of heaven, above the flat earth, and seven below in Hell.

On the earth are local spirits, or *jindi*, who live in trees, ponds, fields, stones, and wells. They are both good and bad and merge sometimes, in ordinary parlance, with angels—especially Satan and his helpers. When these spirits interact with human beings, male spirits attack or help women and female *jindi* appear to men. They resemble humans, but may also have wierd physical features such as exaggerated sexual characteristics or long necks or many arms. There are also witches (*karama*) who alone or with the help of evil spirits produce malevolence for others. Witches are distinguished from sorcerers who for a fee practice magic on others. This ranges from providing a love potion for an anxious young swain to sickness and even death. The latter is believed to be accomplished by needles which the sorcerer sends in the night into his victim—one variety for males, another for females. Sorcerers and religious *mallams* cure such illness by removing the needles which are then shown to the victim and his family.

This must not be taken to mean that Kanuri live in a world full of magic and religion in which fear of supernatural malevolence is always present. In nearly two years in a rural village I witnessed only one true case of witchcraft accusation. There was much supernaturally oriented medicine practiced, and quite a lot of sorcery, especially of the rather gentle variety having to do with love potions. Only when my house walls fell down a third time was it considered necessary by the builders and the villagers to exorcise the evil spirit who seemed to be responsible and a proper ceremony was carried out. Certainly people wore charms against disease, thievery, snakes, financial ruin, but these are more akin to the Western concept of insurance than supernaturalism.

The same holds true for Islam. Mosques are well attended, the annual fast of Ramadam is universally practiced, all males are circumcised, many people pray five times a day, and Muslim law holds sway in the courts. Men can often be seen telling their prayer beads and conversational expressions such as "If God wills it," or "Only God knows," or "The blessings of Allah upon you" are common in everyday language. However, unless the issue is one of Islam versus non-Islamic belief or practice, then religion is not an ever-present or even highly noticeable part of life. Islam indeed is not a "Sunday" religion; it is instead pervasive in all aspects of life and therefore not easily separable as a special category in the culture of Bornu. Add to this the fact that spirits, magic, sorcery, and other supernatural phenomena are not common topics of conversation and the result is that everyday life in Bornu is concerned with what Westerners generally call secular concerns. Economic, political, and general social affairs are the dominant elements of interaction and communication, although they admittedly take place within a framework or basic set of assumptions, often unspoken, that are ultimately religious in their origins and justification. In other words, Islam itself pervades all of organized social life, yet it is everyday affairs rather than the supernatural that is emphasized.

Dominant Values

The dominant values expressed by the larger scaled social and cultural environment of Bornu can be obtained by asking some simple questions concerning the material presented above on this setting. What are the most desirable behaviors and attitudes in such a social system? Do they form a coherent whole or are there basic conflicts between values in various sectors of social life?

The most pervasive quality in Kanuri society is that of the socio-political hierarchy, and the values that surround this structural mode are the most dominant in the culture. Such values reflect the value or identity of the society itself and its long well-known history as a great power of the Sudanic area. In everyday terms, this means that membership in the society is highly valued as is the idea of hierarchy upon which the society is based. Who is senior to whom in a household, a ward, a village, a district, a faction, or an economic organization, defines the manner in which people can interact with one another. To come into a Kanuri village and not greet the chief is a gross insult. Indeed, special modes of greeting are used which reflect whether the people are of similar or different social status. Not to know such things is not to value the nature and history of the Bornu state and its people.

As already noted above, the concept that most clearly incorporates such values is that of *bərzum* or discipline-respect. For the Kanuri, this is the essential quality of all superior-subordinate relationships including such diverse dyads as father-son, patron-client, chief-someone under his jurisdiction, employer-employee, teacher-pupil, *and husband-wife*. The essence of the relationship is loyalty and obedience by the subordinate which is given to the superior in return for political and economic support. The interaction is basically diffuse or feudal rather than specific or contractual and involves a high degree of mutual trust (Cohen 1966b). The subordinate has faith that he will be supported by the superior, and, conversely, the superior feels that all activities of the subordinate are in the interests of the superior. If this is not the case then the trust begins to diminish and the bond weakens. One of the ways to say that a person is untrustworthy, indeed the most common and most telling, is to say he is *bərzum ba*; i.e., he has little or no *bərzum*. Another way of saying the same thing is to describe a person as having no proper sense of shame (*nungu ba*). To say this implies that the ordinary social pressures for conformity to norms have little or no effect on the person and therefore he cannot be trusted to live up to his obligations. And in Bornu primary obligations are carried out in superior-subordinate dyads. Thus a shameless person is also one who does not have a well-developed sense of respect for superiors.

All of this is not meant to imply that social position and mobility is not present or valued even though the society is organized into a complex hierarchical network of social relationships (Cohen

1970i). What is apparent, however, is that the Kanuri view individual achievement as taking place within an organization. Introduce a Kanuri to someone he does not know and he immediately asks about the person's membership in a kin group, a household, a town, and any client relationship this person might hold to more or less well-known patrons in the area. Within such social relations the person succeeds or fails in achieving material and social benefits for himself and those who are in turn dependent upon him for their place in society. A man completely on his own, striving individualistically for his own goals, is thought of traditionally not as an entrepreneur but as "just a person," a man who cannot be fully trusted since there is no easily identifiable group to whom he is responsible or who will share responsibility for him to other similar groups in the society.

In order to get ahead in Kanuri society, then, a person can advance within the organizations he belongs to, attempt to join new ones that provide more rewards than ones he now belongs to, and create new organizations with himself as the senior authority. The details of how this is done will become clear in the discussion below on household organization. However, an important feature of this system is the easy transferability of the ingredients of hierarchical relations which is allowed for in Kanuri traditional values and practice. Elsewhere I have spoken of this as being a type of currency in which superiors, but more especially subordinates, bargain with their allegiances to obtain the most rewarding memberships they can find in the society (Cohen 1965). Thus there are always persons who are ready to become new clients if they see some advantage in the arrangement. Conversely, superiors with benefits to offer for allegiance can quickly expand the numbers of their following. —

Enhancing this malleable and dynamic quality of hierarchy are those values concerned with the proper validation of status. The Kanuri believe there are better and worse ways of enacting the roles associated with status in the hierarchy of their society whether these are in the family, the household, the community or the emirate as a whole. The most widely accepted values in this regard are those already discussed concerning *bərzum* or discipline-respect which deal with proper loyalty and obedience, and those dealing with the proper dispensation of material goods.

The use of property is seen principally in three separate categories. First of all it is used for subsistence. To be successful, a man must be in a position to take care of himself and those dependent upon him. Second, he should be able to reciprocate gifts to those who attend his ceremonies (birth, marriage, naming, circumcision, death, etc.) when he attends theirs. Third, he must be able to reward dependents (sons, wives, clients) through gifts of property in return for their subordination. Since they also act as a work force in producing his wealth, this may be called a redistributive use of property which, as in other parts of the world, validates the status of superiors in hierarchical organization.

However, the exact balance of subsistence, reciprocity, and redistribution is not an easy one and there is constant tension over it for all but the most powerful members of the society. Even at the highest levels, tension still exists. Thus people often say the Shehu (emir or king) is a "poor man" even though his salary and tributes are very large. This expresses their understanding of the constant generosity which his royal office demands.

In value terms, this tension is expressed in three terms—generosity (*kare*), stinginess (*bayil*), and the spend-thrift (*wujirma*). The properly generous man is one who takes care of his own needs first and those of his dependents, and then fulfills his reciprocal obligations. If anything is left over, he may use it to obtain more dependents or provide bonuses for his dependents. Such a man cannot be pressured into giving more than he is able, nor would he withhold wealth simply for purposes of accumulation. However, the pressures to spend more than one can afford are constant and intense. Would-be clients, wandering praise-singers, demanding wives, and indigent neighbors are constantly asking for gifts. To respond is to enhance status; to refuse is to show publicly the limitations of one's own capabilities. I have seen men hide for several hours rather than walk homeward on a path where a man they know only slightly is waiting to request a gift of money or goods—and they would rather avoid this situation than make an outright refusal.

On the other hand, to actually own the requisite resources and not distribute them to followers, dependents, and would-be followers is considered strongly anti-social behavior. Such a person is like a man who sits down to eat in the presence of others without asking them to join him—in other words, he is vulgar and irresponsibly self-serving. To give and to receive are equally important, for they indicate what capabilities a man has achieved within the status positions he occupies in society. Giving more means more has been received, and success is demonstrated. To be recognized as having much more and not giving significant proportions to others, especially among his own following, means a man does not value his following sufficiently to maintain their subordination. They in their turn are stimulated to shop elsewhere with their loyalty and obedience where the returns may be more rewarding.

Finally, there is the case of the spend-thrift (*wujirma*). He has a strong desire to rise in the world but does not have the means to do so. He wishes to obtain the respect of his fellows as a man who is moving upward in society. Such a man not only reciprocates when necessary but gives more at the ceremonies of friends, relatives, and neighbors than he can afford. By so doing he is advertising his "success" even when it does not in fact exist. *Wujir* is a word that refers to ceremonies and *wujirma* means a "ceremonies man" or one who attends many ceremonies. He goes even when it is not his duty to go, gives when he needs not do so, and then gives more than necessary. In other words, he tries to turn many of the reciprocal obligations into redistributive ones, showing that he is in fact superior by virtue of having superior means. If the means are in fact available he is simply demonstrating his new found wealth; if not, he is making a fool of himself by trying to achieve more status than he can in truth validate within his present capacity.

With increased means, a man can increase the number of his dependents, wives, clients, children, and followers. He can deliver more gifts and tributes to superiors in the hierarchy and become, thereby, a more important subordinate in the overall hierarchy of the community. Ultimately, then, these concepts (*kare*, *bayil*, and *wujirma*) have to do with the way in which power and authority are activated and desired through the use of property. And power as well as its recognized and legitimate component—authority—are what Kanuri strive for above all else. In a hierarchical society, it is not surprising that the values of superior-subordinate relationships are what tend to dominate the culturally derived motivations of individuals.

There are other values that derive from history and the social evolution of the society. Islam itself is a very important criterion for membership in Kanuri society, and aspiring non-Kanuri take on the religion when they wish to assimilate (if they were raised in an indigenous belief system). On the other hand, within the society, Islam does not distinguish between people except that religious practitioners can demand a general respect from their fellows, and some men work hard to gain such status.

Related to this, but separate from religion, is ethnic pride. The Kanuri are fully aware of their long history and the independence as well as power wielded by the Bornu state throughout the entire history of the Sudan. They value this ethnic background and consider many other peoples less worthy than themselves since others cannot point as easily to such an eventful, successful, and well-documented history. This leads to a high evaluation of Kanuri culture, its language, stylistic uniqueness in arts and crafts, and its inimitable women's hair styles and dress, all of which are considered important and worth preserving.

But there have been a number of significant changes in Bornu, especially in the last two or three decades: post-World War II economic development, independence, incorporation into a new state under a military government, Western schooling, and the coming of modern communications and transport. However, the values I have described as well as the social structure—including that to be described in greater detail in the next two chapters—have changed but little since 1955 when I first started studying them. By this, I mean that for the bulk of the people the great changes of the mid-twentieth century have had little if any effect. However, there is some change and it can be seen among those attending Western style schools, especially at the post primary level. Later we shall look at this group as an augur of the future. For the present, let me summarize by saying that as yet there have been very few fundamental changes in the nature of traditional Kanuri society, although an accelerating pace of economic development in the area could revise this statement fairly soon.

Let us now apply the major values described in this chapter to the central focus of this book—that of the husband-wife relationship. The Kanuri are a proud and ancient people whose history has developed for them a culture of hierarchy. The most useful and important relationships in a person's social existence are hierarchical ones and he or she must utilize these superior-subordinate relations to obtain the social, economic, and psychological satisfactions necessary to an ordinary life cycle. There are value terms which describe how well a person is carrying on the necessary activities of such a life cycle. First and foremost, he or she must understand respect or discipline-respect—the operative behavioral quality of hierarchy. Secondly, they should know how to gauge the degree of their own participation in a system that is constantly making demands on both superiors and subordinates.

The husband-wife relationship is therefore not simply a sexual one used for subsistence purposes and the raising of children. In Bornu, it is set into the context of the social structure we have discussed briefly above, and in more detail elsewhere. Husbands are superiors and wives are subordinates; in Kanuri terms, this means they can expect a range of obligatory responses from one another as well as a number of tensions and conflicts. Because this is so—that is, because the husband-wife relationship shares many of the fundamental qualities of all Kanuri social relations—we are in effect looking at the entire social system by looking at its most elemental quality, the superior-subordinate dyad as it is exemplified in the husband-wife relationship. This does not mean that there is not more to Kanuri marriage than differences in authority. It does mean that authority is possibly the most important quality of all Kanuri relations and therefore a marriage as well.

Chapter 4
Social Networks Surrounding Marriage:
Kinship Groups

The previous chapter summarized the larger scaled socio-cultural environment of Kanuri marriage and divorce. The next two chapters focus on this topic by describing and analyzing the social structural setting in which marriage and its dissolution are enacted in the society. The assumption here is that marriage must be understood within the context of social networks which form the major role sets for husbands and wives beyond the range of the immediate family. This range is defined by birth into a kinship system and one or more communities. The latter can then be further divided into household groups and wider (i.e., extra-household) social relations having to do (for the Kanuri) primarily with the political and economic relations incumbent upon normal adult roles. This present chapter deals with the kinship units, while the next one uses this material to describe and analyze the local residential groupings and wider organizational settings.

Genealogical Relations

As used here, kinship refers to three categories of socio-cultural information regarding bio-logical relationships among individuals. Although these categories overlap, they almost invariably differ systematically from each other, and therefore as empirical phenomena they are capable of varying independently. By name, these relationships are based on genealogy, descent, and affinity. The first, genealogy, is defined as the linkages between individuals which are based solely upon biological reproduction. Secondly, descent refers to the links between individuals based upon the allocation for specified purposes of members in a genealogy to a socially and culturally recognized kin group. On occasion, there are legitimate ways and means by which non-genealogical members or their descendants may be incorporated into the descent group. Thirdly, affinity refers to the links between persons based upon marriage ties between spouses.

Genealogies as defined above can also be divided into effective, recognized, and unrecognized types of networks. An effective genealogy is one in which there is some meaningful interaction between ego and all other members in a group to which he is related biologically. Most people know of more kinsmen than they interact with in some meaningful way; these are the recognized genealogical members. Finally, there are always people who are unaware of their genealogical connections to one another but who may, on closer scrutiny by themselves or by an anthropologist, turn up in the same genealogy; these are unrecognized genealogical links. It is possible to change or move from one of these types of networks to another through time. Indeed, the dynamics of kinship make such a progression inevitable. Thus descendants of effective kin may become recognized only, and descendants of recognized kin may lose even this quality and have an unrecognized biological relationship with one another. On occasion, the reverse process is also possible, as when a "long lost relative" turns up and wishes to interact effectively with people, some of whom may have been unaware of him as a kinsman.

With a few significant exceptions among the nobility, Kanuri genealogies are broad and shallow. Most people cannot name their great-grandparents or great-grandchildren. Thus, for most people, the recognized genealogical connections are at most five generations deep, from grandchild to grandparent. On the other hand, the breadth of recognized relationship goes to the children of parents' first cousins and possibly their descendants, which can produce a genealogy of several hundred persons, most of them still alive. The break between a recognized relationship and an unrecognized one is variable. For the majority of the population, it is difficult to obtain the name or location of a grandparent's sibling. Nevertheless, a significant minority of persons can name one or more siblings of their grandparents who are always reported as full or half siblings rather than classificatory. However, on the parent generation level, parents' siblings are usually recognized to be both real and classificatory (cousins of parents) even when the person cannot remember the name of a grandparent's sibling. Thus ego's cousins are children of his parents' siblings or their cousins, and only detailed descriptive questioning can get at the distinction between first and second cousins. Furthermore, since parents' "siblings" are both real and classificatory, there is no reason to believe that grandparents' siblings are not of both types as well.

This merging of "siblings" may be illustrated by examining cousin marriage. In a number of these marriages, the union is reported as being between the progeny of two full or half siblings. In other cases, it is between the grandchildren of two (so-called) full or half siblings, i.e., between children of two cousins. In one case, a man discovered that his and his wife's grandparents were half siblings only after he and she were married. In other words, he and his wife were unrecognized kin, genealogically speaking, before marriage. In this case, as we have already noted, recognized kinship had stopped at the distinction between grandparents and their siblings, plus the descendants of these siblings, while in other cases such kinship is recognized.

As implied by our definitions, the distinction between effective and recognized genealogical relationship is based on the nature of interactions among members. To the Kanuri, the distinction between such relations is determined by whether the persons involved come to each other's family ceremonies, at *rites de passage*. If they do not, then such kin are referred to traditionally as *dəkta dərenji* or far kin. The expression is metaphorical and refers to a vine that spreads all around a compound wall, often creeping over into the next compound, but originating from the same root. Informants point out that, although there is some correlation between genealogical distance and being *dəkta dərenji*, it is the interaction and mutual reciprocity that determines the distinction. Ultimately the distinction is most often determined by common residence in the same or nearby villages and towns. This means recognized kin can become effective ones if proximity is established and vice versa if it is lost. Other factors turn on the rewards to be gained by one or both parties to the relationship which is more properly discussed under household organization.

Descent Relations

The Kanuri word for kinship or "relatives" is *dur*, meaning cognatic kin. Within this inclusive term a person has descent relations with his father's (*dur bube*: family of the blood) and mother's (*dur chambe*: family of the milk) cognates. In-marrying affines are excluded from one's own descent group. A Kanuri speaks of his relationship to descent groups, therefore, through his own birth into cognatic groups related to him through his mother and father. He is also related to another cognatic group through his own marriage and to still others through the marriages of his cognates. This gross egocentric set of relations is shown in diagram form in Figure 4:1.

I have placed ego under his own cognatic group because of the much greater durability of this network membership. Similarly the instability of ego's relations to other cognatic groups through marriage is depicted by the dotted lines. It should be noted that the five cells of the diagram represent a variable number of descent groups to which ego might be effectively related. Thus each affine of mother's and father's cognates is a possible link to still another set of cognates, which means that it is possible for descent relations to unite with affinal ones to proliferate relationships in a widely ramifying manner. For example, in one actual case, two men were entering into an economic relationship. While doing so, they discovered they were related to each other through a mother's sister's husband's brother's son. Although the relationship was a distant one linked by marriage, and unrecognized until that moment, it still helped to add some greater validity and legitimacy to their economic relationship. On the other hand, marriage links, unless they are stable and long term, are tenuous compared to those established by birth alone. Consequently, the most effective descent group relations for ego are those he is born into which cannot be dissolved when a marriage link is terminated.

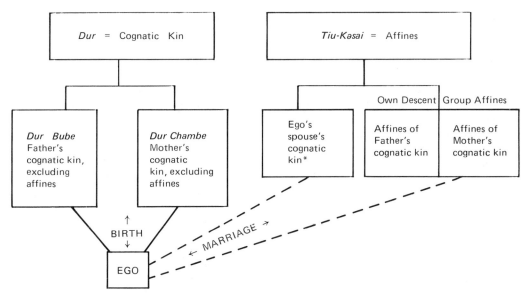

*Descriptive terms distinguish the different varieties of affines; e.g., wifely in-laws, fatherly in-laws, motherly in-laws.

Figure 4:1. Kanuri Descent Groups by Birth and Marriage.

An analysis of kinship terminology does a similar but more detailed job by expressing the cultural categorization of roles in the genealogy and indicating the possible distinctions between one's own descent group members and those related by affinity. However, by using specific criteria or principles of classification, the terminological system also expresses the types of values used now and in the past to order social interaction among kinsfolk.

Kanuri kinship terminology is given in Appendix IV. The most striking thing about these terms is the way in which a single term can be used to refer to each of the seven generations in the system except the parent (+1) generation. If this is added to the way in which suffixes and special terms are employed in ego's own and in the plus one generation to denote junior and senior (same sex) siblings of ego's parents, then the most important criteria used in distinguishing kin are generation and birth order. Both of these criteria reflect the significance of age differences, which in turn express the importance placed on seniority, whether such seniority is defined by generation level or birth order within a generation. This explains why in-laws are grouped terminologically into two categories—junior and senior.

Terminological reciprocity is a possibility that is often practiced. This occurs only when there is at least one intervening generation between the actors in the system, such that grandparents and great-grandparents can address their grandchildren and great-grandchildren by the same term as they are called by their younger relatives, although there is a recognized term for grandchild which is different from grandparent. This principle is so strong that it applies as well to grandparents and grandchildren, great-grandparents and great-grandchildren of ego's spouse, thus overriding distinctions based on affinity. In other words, reciprocity can be expressed terminologically between ego and his own or his spouse's relatives who have at least one intervening generation dividing them. As we shall see, this is also reflected in the behavior of members of these generations toward one another.

Sex is used as a criterion for classifying relatives among the first descendant generation (boys and girls) who are lumped together as an entire generation. Young girl cousins, especially if they are possible mates or under ego's jurisdiction and protection, are also called by the same term as daughter, or female progeny of ego's real and classificatory siblings. The only other sexual distinction is made at the parent generation where there are two male and two female terms. Thus sex differences are less important than generation or seniority within and between generations.

The only generation with clear-cut internal differentiation is that of the parents. Within this grouping of relatives, bifurcation is the most important criterion for classification. Thus mother is merged with mother's sisters and father with father's brothers, while father's sisters and mother's brothers have separate terms. In other words, there is an emphasis on the sex of the relative, and the sex of the connecting relative. The latter criterion (bifurcation) emphasizes the differences between patrilateral and matrilateral kin, while the former usually creates groupings among kin who are unilineally related to one another by making parallel cousins the progeny of "parents" and cross-cousins the progeny of "others."

The fact that the Kanuri do not distinguish terminologically among cousins, lumping all of them with siblings, produces what one writer (Dole 1969) has called a "bifurcate generation" system.[1] This same writer claims that such a system results from a unilineal past in which cousin terminology has been changed through one of two possible types of group endogamy. For the Kanuri, this evidence of a previous unilineal system is strengthened by the bifurcate merging pattern of the parent generation and, I would add, the symmetrical arrangement of the other terms used at the parent generation which further divided people into a "we" group and "others" separated by marriage. Thus terminologically *Bawa* = father's sister = mother's brother's wife = father's brother's wife and *Rawa* = mother's brother = father's sister's husband = mother's sister's husband.[2] The inference to be made here is that *Bawa* equals our women including those, such as father's "sisters" whom they get from us and whom we get from them as wives for my father's brothers. A special sub-category of these outside women are my own mother and her "sisters," the latter of whom also marry men of other groups (*Rawa*) in line with the Kanuri prohibition on sororal polygyny. The system as seen in Figure 4:2 and Appendix IV is consistent with exogamous unilineal descent groups that probably operated in the past to regulate intergroup relations including marriage.

All of this boils down to the idea that at some unknown time in the past the Kanuri very probably distinguished among cousins and then changed their kinship patterns such that these distinctions disappeared. But how, why, and when did such a change take place? This is not easy to answer at this point. Islam brings with it parallel cousin marriage which involves endogamy. Progressive shifts from more nomadic to more settled village life does the same thing. These changes provide evidence consistent with Dole's (1969) hypothesis in which she posits a causal relationship between group endogamy and the development of generation cousin terms equals sibling terms. This points to the process having taken place between the eleventh and thirteenth centuries when the Kanuri were adopting Islam and becoming progressively more sedentary.

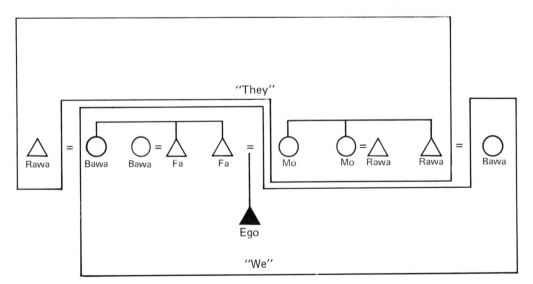

Figure 4:2. Relics of "We" and "They" in Kanuri Kin Terms of Parent Generation.

On the other hand, Goody (1970) has theorized that Sudanic bilaterality results from one patrilineal people conquering another and setting up a centralized state. The conquerors marry women of the conquered but not vice versa. Therefore, among the conquerors it often occurs that a man has access to rights in land and other valuables through his mother and her group of indigenes. It is quite likely that just such a conquest occurred in Bornu during the fourteenth and fifteenth centuries. This helps to explain the increased importance of matri-kin but it does not, like Dole's (1969) theory, explain the cousin terminology. Probably all of these forces— sedentarism, Islam, and conquest—helped to shape the present system with the major changes occurring in the first half of the present millennium (A.D. 1000-1500).

In summary Kanuri kinship terminology expresses the importance of seniority in the parent generation and birth priority within one's own and the parent generation, matrilateral as distinct from patrilateral kin, bifurcation which puts parents together with their siblings of the same sex and distinguishes siblings of the opposite sex, and finally reciprocity between alternate generations. In terms of values attached to various types of descent group members, these usages reflect superior-subordinate relations where seniority involving differential authority is stressed. The distinction between father's and mother's kin indicates some differentiation of these kin based on the nature of the relationships and/or the sentiments involved. Bifurcation linking father to his brothers and mother to her sisters, while differentiating mother's brother and father's sister, produces an emphasis on the filial ties connecting ego to his relatives. Reciprocity between alternate generations is more difficult to summarize easily, but for the present let us suggest that it emphasizes the authority between the intervening generation (i.e., the plus one) and ego, as well as serving as a possible tension release for the great restraint, subordination, and conformity necessary between these adjacent generations.[3] Sexual distinctions are important only at the parent (+1) and child (-1) generation levels, being submerged by generation distinctions every where else. Finally, there is strong evidence of a past system of unilineal descent (in all likelihood patrilineal, from the behavioral evidence given below) which has been eroded by forces of endogamy, sedentarism, Islam, and conquest.

Behavior Norms

In Kanuri, there are four terms which are used to describe the types of behavior appropriate to specific categories of kin with whom people interact. These words are also used to describe relationships outside the kinship system, but in general the kin relations are conceived of as the cultural model or idiom for the non-kin relations included under the behavioral category. The question arises then as to whether the wider societal relations have determined the kin behavior or vice versa, or whether both kin and non-kin relations should be subsumed under more general sets of relations that arrange groups of kin and non-kin together as people toward whom ego should interact in similar ways.

In all probability, the question of *extension* of kin terms to other basic groupings to which similar interactive terms are applied is a spurious one. On the other hand, the Kanuri themselves are clearly of the extension persuasion. For example, informants speak in similes of non-kin persons to whom kin categories and behavior are also applied. Thus a butcher, in describing his relation to an older Fulani herdsman who sells him cattle, says that the Fulani is *like* a grandfather to him and therefore they joke with one another. Or another informant says of the respect given to a Koranic religious teacher "He is *like* your father." In other words, they see non-kin interaction in kin-like terms and feel that the person learns these behaviors in his early relationships to kin members then *extends* such learning outward to non-kin when attempting to explain the quality of non-kin relationships. As we shall see in the discussion of household and community, the actual situation is more complex than this because many of these interactions are entered into or understood from the very beginning of socialization onward.

The four words used by the Kanuri to describe norms of interpersonal behavior in kinship and beyond are *nungu*: shame or shame-avoidance-respect; *barzum*: discipline-respect-friendship; *suli*: joking and reciprocity; and *numkam*: related or known by and interacting with in an unspecified way. In previous work[4] I have used these as separate categories of analysis without testing for overlap. Thus shame-avoidance is an intense form of discipline-respect rather than a completely different and separable quality. To indicate shame-avoidance the interacting persons must never eat food together or in the presence of one another. People having such a relationship are rarely ever alone together under any circumstances. Shame-respect is a trifle less stringent. Such people can eat together, if they are of the same sex, but only the most necessary conversation passes between them. The junior in the relationship must sit or stand with eyes downcast and always avoid looking directly at the senior. Respect itself deals with all situations in which there is difference in status between the parties concerned, ranging from greeting a person of senior status properly to the correct manner of behaving within a superior-subordinate relationship. In other words, all behavior associated with difference in status can be described as coming within the purvue of *bərzum*. This ranges from greetings, to juniors visiting seniors, to modes and topics of conversation, and to loyalty and obedience. At one extreme, it involves shame, while at the other end it can involve some friendship and intimacy, with discipline being somewhere between the two. Factors of personality, age, generation, sex, and more widely of general status differences, determine where on the scale any particular interaction will fall at any given moment in its development.

Joking relations are in one sense the lowest level of the respect scale. In such relationships the customary restrictions and demands upon behavior based on seniority, generation, sex, or any other status differences, are relaxed. They are instead replaced by formalized patterns of permissiveness in which the junior becomes the equal of the senior, and therefore a putative and formalized kind of reciprocity can be established.

Finally, there is *numkam* or relatedness. At first I took this term to mean friendship and an egalitarian relationship between social equals. Informants claimed that for relatives with no special request, or joking, and no shame, there is *numkam* "and therefore they are friends." Although there is a perfectly good word for friendship (*soba*), this seemed to be a synonym. Later, however, I realized that such people are friends *because* they are related. Relatedness (*numkam*) can consequently be used in a number of ways. First, it can refer to any kind of relationship, next it can refer to kinship connections, and more restricted yet, it can be used to refer to relationships within the kinship network that are not necessarily governed by the respect scale. This leaves only

TABLE 4:1. BEHAVIORAL NORMS FOR COGNATIC KIN
IN 0 to +3 GENERATIONS*

Kin type	Shame		Respect		Joking		Friendship		No Data		Total
	#	%	#	%	#	%	#	%	#	%	Responding
Father	47	96	48	98	0	0	0	0	0	0	49
Mother	47	96	48	98	0	0	0	0	0	0	49
Fa Sis Chi	14	31	5	11	1	2	33	73	4	8	45
Fa Bro	14	29	47	96	2	4	9	18	0	0	49
Mo Bro	13	27	43	88	1	2	10	20	0	0	49
Mo Sis	12	24	46	94	2	4	7	14	0	0	49
Fa Sis	12	24	46	94	1	2	7	14	0	0	49
Mo Bro Chi	11	24	7	15	2	4	33	72	3	6	46
Ol Bro	8	18	35	80	0	0	21	48	5	10	44
Ol Sis	8	18	35	80	1	3	20	45	5	10	44
Mo Sis Chi	6	14	10	23	3	7	27	61	5	10	44
Fa Bro Chi	4	8	5	11	2	4	40	87	3	6	46
Yo Bro	0	0	1	3	3	8	31	86	13	26	36
Yo Sis	0	0	5	13	4	10	28	72	10	20	39
G+/G/Parent	0	0	8	17	47	100	0	0	2	4	47
G/Parent	0	0	7	14	48	98	0	0	0	0	49

*Columns headed # indicate the number of persons claiming such a relationship. Columns headed % indicate the percent of the total sample who answered positively.

those relations not defined by seniority and status distinctions, i.e., egalitarian ones—usually between age-mates. Therefore, when the term for relatedness is used to refer to relatives without any other qualifications then there is an implication of mutuality, egalitarianism, and friendship.

Table 4:1 gives the responses by forty-nine men to a group of their cognatic kin in terms of the behavior norms discussed above. The men are mostly from Maiduguri, the capital city, and ranged across all ages and status distinctions, although the largest portion are from middle to low status occupations.[5] These men responded to questions concerning their behavior toward a number of kin. The interviewer was instructed to ask people *how they acted* toward each of the relatives in question. In the opinion of the field assistant, this was in fact the major consideration in determining responses. This is corroborated by observational data and by the explanation given for missing data in the original field interviews. In all cases, missing data is reported as refusal by the respondent to answer on the grounds that he did not have such a relative and could not therefore report on such an interaction. However, it is inconceivable that ideal patterns have had no effect on the interview situation, especially in masking any cases of extreme deviancy, if any such exist. On the other hand, the presence of variance among many of the responses per kin category indicates something more than simple conformity to widely known norms of behavior.

In general, the table shows the highest amounts of shame and respect responses in interaction with parents and their siblings and an absence of this feature with ego's own generation. Friendship shows a reverse patterning. The most obvious exceptions are between ego and his cross-cousins who, although given the same kin terms as parallel cousins, have nearly double the number of shame responses. Combining participant-observation materials with these interview data, we can analyze these interactions into blocks of kin with whom ego interacts, using the behavioral norms as guides to description and interpretation.

Relations to Parents and Their Siblings

As indicated in Table 4:1, the most stringent shame and respect relations among cognates are with one's own parents. Men and women are highly restricted in their relations to their own father. Although a man may eat with his father, he does so with a show of great restraint. Conversation as well is restricted, although ego may appear before his or her father in order to receive instructions, bring a message, or make a request, especially if this requires some material goods over which the father exercises his authority. One male informant put it very well when he said:

> If I have matters to discuss concerning my needs, I talk to my father; but if I wish to speak of marriage then I must not talk to my father or mother—there is shame in this. I will instead speak to my *abagana* (Fa Yo Bro) or my *abakura* (Fa Ol Bro) if I have one. I will then tell my sister or brother (real or classificatory) or my friends to go and speak to my father and mother for me. I must never speak directly to my father and my mother about my marriage or anything connected with it.

The net effect of these restrictions is to enhance the authority of the father and create highly formalized relations between children and parents, especially the father. Although the responses in Table 4:1 do not reflect the difference, there is much more warmth and affection between a child, especially a son, and his mother. Girls are raised in the women's section of the compound and come under the direct authority of their mother or her surrogate while they learn the adult role requirements of womanhood. But men are outside this hierarchy, learning and working with other men, often under the authority of their father. This does not mean there is no "shame" between a man and his mother. He will not eat with her, or indeed any woman, nor would he ever refer to sex or marriage in her presence. But of all the dyadic relations within the kinship system, the mother-child, but especially the mother-son, is the warmest and most openly emotional. One young man recounted how he simply walked away from a good salaried job one day because he was thinking about his mother 300 miles away and wished to be with her. In general, the Kanuri do not use emotional terms or refer to affect, especially positive affect, in everyday conversation. Here again the mother-son relationship is a rather striking exception in that a person is entitled to and should feel positive affect toward mother and can admit to such feelings without embarrassment. Thus, although shame and respect responses are similar with reference to father and mother, the affective content of the two dyadic relations is quite different.

The relations to parents' siblings is strongly associated with the distinctions between father and mother, although other factors of birth priority, sex, and personality enter to vary the ultimate result. In general, father's brothers (real and classificatory) are equivalent to a father, although as we have already seen some of the shame is reduced and ego can speak to his father's brothers of sexually-related topics such as marriage. On the other hand, respect for father's brothers as senior people who can demand subservience is almost equivalent to that of the father. Table 4.1 bears this out. Thus 98% of the respondents claimed respect relations with their father's brothers, although shame responses fall from 96% to 29%. When asked about this, informants say that the 29% represents father's older brothers, especially in situations where this person is head of the household and the respondent's own father is his subordinate. Other situations represent dyads where the father's brother (older or younger) is a very proud, haughty, or important person. In this case he demands more respect and ego practices more shame behavior in his relationship with him. The lowering of shame responses toward parents' siblings in the majority of cases is associated with a rise in interactions expressing mutual friendship and fondness. This friendship response is shown in Table 4:1 by 14% of the men in their interactions with mother's sister and father's sister and 18-20% of the sample in their interaction with mother's brother and father's brother while such responses are lacking for own parents.

These results are also obtained through participant observation, with one important difference. Informants claim that ego has a greater fondness and friendship with his mother's sister and her brother "because they love you, like your mother, and you like them in the same way." The data in Table 4:1 on father's brother and mother's brother indicate only a slight tendency in this same direction by having father's brother 2% higher on shame and 2% lower on mutual friendship and fondness, while mother's sister and father's sister are identical in the table. In practice, however, ego's relations to these two groups of the parent generation is significantly different. As the Kanuri say, if a man is threatened he thinks of his *bu*, i.e., his father's cognates, most often in practice his agnates; if he needs a loan of money he thinks of his *cham*, i.e., his mother's cognates. This is explained by the fact that a man's patrilineal kin are corporately responsible in court for the acts of any one of them. The *dia* or blood compensation money for physical injury, manslaughter, or murder is paid jointly by a man and his *bu*. Major, indeed most, meaningful inheritance such as land, household, liquid capital, and prerogatives to public office comes from a person's agnatic kin, although some movable goods can be obtained through matrifilial connections; the same is true of bridewealth. As one informant put it:

> It is the father's family that is responsible for the *dia*; they support you if you are in trouble; it is from them that you get your property; if you marry and have no money they collect it for you, and you don't have to pay it back—but you must help them when asked to contribute for others; they are the *mai durbe* (king of the kin).

On the other hand, matrilateral kin are said to be more affectionate and ego feels he can borrow money more easily from them because "they will not refuse you anything." Jealousy, too, is reported to be greater among agnates. This results from the fact that agnates form an inheritance unit.

> If you try to take *kare* (possessions, property, material wealth) from your father's family as a loan, or for any purpose at all, they may feel that it will not be returned and that you are trying to get some of the family property which by the rules of inheritance is not supposed to come to you. . . .
> But the mother's family like you very much, they give you things, and if you promise to pay back a loan, they will trust you and wait patiently.

Obviously, personality and character can vary such generalizations and the Kanuri recognize this. Thus people are always ready to qualify their cultural expectations with stories about some kind and generous man who is or was a paragon of faith and trust. Conversely, no one can expect credit repeatedly who defaults on loans—kin or not.

Relations to Siblings and Cousins

Kanuri kinship terminology does not distinguish own siblings from cousins, although such distinctions can be done by descriptive terms that refer to a common ascendant relative. Full siblings are described as "same father same mother," half siblings are "same father" or "same mother," while cousins are (a) "same grandparent," (b) his or her mother or father and my mother or father had the same father and/or mother. Wider relations, although rarer, are found and can be described by referring to the exact type of sibling relationship of grandparents.

These same distinctions can be made at each generation level, although from ego's point of view they are clearest for his own generation and downward toward the descendant generations, somewhat less clear at the parents' generation, and generally unclear for his grandparents'. Thus informants will on occasion refer to a mother's sister as mother's full sister when she is in fact a half sister or even a cousin. Such collapsing occurs even more often with grandparents and their "siblings." This means that, although there is no terminological distinction between siblings and cousins, the actual genealogical relationships are kept clearly in mind for one's own generation, somewhat less so for parents' and rarely for the grandparent generation.

The general relationship to siblings as indicated in Table 4:1 is one of mutuality, friendship, and fondness. Shame-respect is low, so is formalized joking while friendship is high depending upon age, sex, and descent. Although there is one term for all siblings and cousins (*yanyiana, ya'ana*) a special term can be used to distinguish any of these, of either sex, into those younger than ego (*kərami*). If the "sibling" is older, then respect and a little shame can be applied to the relationship which can become quite extreme when an older "brother" is the head of the household in which ego is living. It becomes much less stringent when the age disparity decreases, especially with two men who call each other brothers. With girls, the birth order is more formally expressed in everyday life, since the younger must walk behind the older on the way to the well, or any other work task associated with the household. On the other hand, relations to a younger brother lack any shame-respect and is one of protection and care which becomes more intimate and open as the age disparity lessens. The fact that relation with a father's brother's child parallels that with younger siblings in Table 4:1 reflects the fact that many of these respondents were referring to persons younger than themselves. In practice, such cousins are divided into older and younger siblings and viewed as such. Although sex is hardly important in distinguishing own-siblings (i.e., ones with whom ego shares a real parent), obviously it is generally easier to be more friendly to one's own sex than vice versa and the survey data this out. Indeed, younger sister was said by 13% of the respondents to be treated with respect. Thus sex differences decrease intimacy and increase the formalities of superior-subordinate relations.

Descent ties among those called "sibling" are divided into siblings related through the same parent(s) or by cousin links. Among siblings who share one or both parents, there is a scale of proximity and stability to the relationship which makes full siblings very close, especially of the same sex. A special kin term (*shakik*) expresses this relation. Next most intimate and strong in their bond are siblings who share the same mother, and finally there are siblings who share the same father; although there is wide agreement on such differences, they are not distinguished terminologically. The latter relationship is in general more transitory or weaker over time. This scale results from ego's household membership and his relation to his mother in a high divorce society and will be discussed more fully below under household organization. These generalizations are from a man's point of view. Women, like men, have very close bonds to their full siblings, but unlike men their next closest siblings vary depending upon whose households they use between marriages, if any.

As noted, cousins are termed "siblings" and may be related as first or second cousins depending whether they are related through a common grandparent or great-grandparent. Besides being divided into junior and senior "siblings," cousins who are much younger, especially girls, can be referred to with the same term as that used for sons (*tada*) and daughters (*fero*) or all children of the first descendant generation. As already noted, any female cousin who is to marry ego (male speaking) is referred to as *fero* or *feronyi* (my girl, or my daughter, or my fiancee, who has never been married before). A full discussion of cousin marriage is reserved for the next chapter. Suffice it to note here that there is a general rule that cousins are to be treated like siblings except where marriage is a possibility which adds some reserve (shame) to the relationship. In Table 4:1 this reserve is most manifest between ego and his cross-cousins; 27% of those responding claimed a shame relationship to cross-cousins, while only 10% claimed such a relationship to parallel cousins.

Informants are at a loss to explain this increase in shame to a sub-group within a similarly termed generation. These are also the only kin categories (among 32 in all) in which informants gave higher shame than respect responses.[6] Although this could be a result of sampling bias, I tend to interpret such results as more evidence from the past for unilineal descent and cross-cousin marriage.

In this regard, it is interesting to note that not only are cross-cousins differentiated significantly by shame and respect responses in our questionnaire material, but informants speak of a cultural practice of joking between cross-cousins of the opposite sex which did not appear on the questionnaire because it is usually carried on between young people rather than by mature men who formed the bulk of the sample. The joking takes the following form. A young man or boy jokes with one of his junior female cross-cousins calling her wife, concubine, lover, etc., and she returns the joke calling him slave, husband, lover. She also begs "joking money" from him on *Sala Laya* (roughly the New Year). This brings on play behavior with the younger and older siblings of the girl who are now in the position of "wife's" younger sibling (*tiu*) and "wife's" older sibling *(kəsai)*. Because there is a joking relation in the "real" kinship system between a man and his wife's junior siblings (real and classificatory), this joking is extended to the junior siblings of the junior cross-cousin who is chosen as the joking wife. They, too, can ask for joking money on *Sala Laya*. Siblings older than the wife are treated jokingly as if they were senior in-laws, i.e., with respect and avoidance. The young man can change the joking wife from time to time among his junior cousins, and then re-order his joking senior and junior in-laws accordingly.

This practice is not universal. A number of informants claimed that such behavior was unbecoming and hinted at the idea of illegitimate pre-pubescent sexual activity being a possible concomitant. Whatever its frequency, as in the case of shame responses already noted, such a practice seems out of place in a kinship system in which *all* cousins are terminologically equivalent to one another and to siblings, and where patrilateral parallel cousin marriage is sanctioned and preferred as well as cross-cousin marriage.

Relation to Grandparents

As Table 4:1 indicates, there is almost total agreement among respondents that a joking relationship exists between ego and his grandparents or great-grandparents if these are alive. As already noted, such relations are present when the customary restrictions based on differences of generation, seniority, and sex are relaxed and a formalized pattern of permissiveness obtains between the parties.

Besides formal joking, a number of cultural practices unite grandparents and grandchildren. Kanuri generally give the children the names of their own parents, thus children are often linked to a particular grandparent by a namesake relationship (*chubuna*). Conversely, anyone after whom a child has been named has a joking relationship (albeit somewhat milder) with his namesake. Since there is a non-reciprocal name avoidance between children and own parents, many young Kanuri boys and girls are addressed and referred to as *Abagana* or *YaGana* (small father, or small mother). Furthermore, many children are given to relatives or friends for fostering after weaning (18 months) and a favorite fosterer is the grandparent. Informants state that it is a good thing to give children away for fostering. Some go further, explaining that very young children do not understand proper respect, especially for their father and therefore it is a good thing for them to go away and learn such behavior elsewhere. When they return, they do so as more fully socialized members of the family who can understand the proper relations between children and parents. Again, an ideal person or couple to carry out such training is said to be the grandparent. On the other hand, people say that a child being raised by grandparents should return to his or her parents before puberty because there can be no real or proper respect where there is so much joking.

It is not uncommon to see a grandparent visiting his or her friends always accompanied by one of their little joking partners. As the friends sit down to chat, the grandchild may play nearby, then a little later comes over to nestle in the grandparent's arms. He pulls at the grandfather's beard, or grandmother's beads, and acts in a generally affectionate manner. The observer is struck more with the genuine fondness and affection of the relationship, at its early stages, than with any patterned joking. However, this latter quality becomes more marked through time. The grandparent may point out a young playmate of the opposite sex and say "There is your wife, or your husband, eh?" One informant summed up neatly:

> You may pull your grandparent's beard, or go into his house and take his possessions, and he does not mind; he is happy because his children have borne children. If you have a great-grandparent alive it is the same with him.

In general, none of the restrictions placed on parent-child relations are supposed to be present. Nevertheless, there must be some discipline because much socialization is carried on by the grandparent. Thus one grandparent was observed patiently and continually taking the left hand of his little namesake out of the food bowl every time the child tried to use this forbidden way of eating. This discipline is expressed in Table 4:1 by the fact that approximately one-third of those responding claim a respect relationship as well as a joking one between ego and his grandparents or great-grandparents. Thus there is an attempt to override age differences among alternate generations, which is expressed in the universality of the joking relationship. However, in a significant number of cases, the importance of age distinctions is recognized such that respect is given to the senior by the junior within the context of this cultural attempt at reciprocity.

Relations to Other Descent Groups

Another indication of the importance of unilineal descent groups in the Kanuri past is the presence among them of nonfunctional named patrilineal clans. As late as the early nineteenth century, Denham (1826) observed soldiers in the Bornu army who, among other criteria, were also organized by their common clan memberships. Practically no memory of any clan functions remains today among ordinary people except the name itself and the general practice of obtaining such an identification by agnatic descent. Even this feature shows some variation, however, since there are informants who, when pressed, simply replied by saying they are Kanuri, or by giving the name of the village or city of their birth. A number of informants also comment that originally one's clan membership determined the type of hair styling to be worn among pre-pubescent boys. Today, people simply choose the one they like, or shave the heads of young boys in the adult style.

Another problem with clans stems from the word itself. There is no separate Kanuri word for clan. Instead, a general category meaning "variety" or "species" or "type" (*jili*) is used which, depending on the context, could mean ethnic group, village, race, or clan. Furthermore, ethnic groups or parts of them have been incorporated into Kanuri society for centuries and the process is still going on. Thus a man may respond to questions about *jili* by saying he is *Manga*. The Manga are an ethnic group of northwest Bornu and southwest Niger who were absorbed by Kanuri social and cultural practices—but they are not a Kanuri clan. On the other hand, some people give Kuburi as their clan and Kanuri as their ethnic group. Kuburi is a leading clan group among the Kanembu people north and northeast of Bornu. When the first Shehu, a Kanembu, came to Bornu in the early nineteenth century, he brought many of his fellow Kuburi clansmen with him, as well as their slaves and followers. Today, 150 years later, Kuburi is often referred to as a Kanuri clan; however, it is in fact a Kanembu group and today many Kanembu as well as Kanuri identify themselves as Kuburi.

Some clan names seen to have diffused outward from the Kanuri to others in the region. Thus *Tɘra* is a widespread Kanuri clan, as are Ngala'a and Ngima. Nevertheless, all three of these names turn up among the northern Marghi peoples who have been in contact with the Kanuri for some time.

In general, people seem to know that all clan members are descended from a common ancestor about whom there is sometimes an origin story, often associating the founder with the Prophet Mohammed. Thus the *Tɘra* clan are said to have descended from a barber who shaved the Prophet's head. One day this barber is said to have made a mistake and cut the Prophet's scalp. When the blood appeared, the barber, realizing whose blood it was, drank it. This gave him a special power so that everyone who descends from that barber is not only *Tɘra* but also *sherib* or *sherif* (fire will not burn them). They are said to be common folk—not connected to chiefs or kings—which is symbolized in the low status occupation of their mythical founder.

Some informants feel that in pre-colonial days there may have been tendencies for clan endogamy, especially in areas where single clans were dominant, such as the Kuburi areas of western Bornu. Others, indeed most, claim no knowledge of such tendencies. Certainly no one today has ever heard of any exogamous rules or of stories which connect the clans to natural phenomena, i.e., to totemic symbols.

In functionally significant terms, this means that for most people clans have very little meaning today. Some people give two clan memberships, one from their father and the other from their mother. Others associated the idea with residential identification. Many people, however, know that the Magumi clan founded the present day Kanuri nation and that the ancient dynasty was always drawn from the Sefuwa lineage of that clan. Fewer know that the Kuburi was a leading Kanembu clan from which the present dynasty is taken. Instead, many informants in rural areas claim mistakenly that the present dynasty (the second) was of the Magumi clan (i.e., of the first dynasty). Clans, then, are the relic remainders of a past in which patrilineal descent groups were more important than they are today. A few upper class Kanuri, whose status it partially depends upon, keep the recollection of their patrilineage and its clan connections.[7] However, for most people the information is of minor importance. A third or fourth generation American of Russian descent might know that "his people" came from Minsk, but the fact would not be of much significance—such are Kanuri clans today.

Another problem is even more fundamental—what are clans in general? Chapelle (1956) says that clans are born, they live, and then die. He is speaking of the desert people of the central Sahara—the ancestral area from whence came the Magumi Sefuwa who founded Bornu and the Kanuri ethnic group. In the desert, people wander and control territories, and are related through real and putative unilineal descent. As groups, they separate and form new clans, or old ones may be absorbed. In Bornu, the Magumi Sefuwa of the fifteenth and sixteenth centuries conquered and finally absorbed a congeries of peoples they called by the collective name So. Are contemporary clan names relics of these original pagan peoples—names of particular ethnic groups among them? Or are they more recent? In pre-colonial times, large fiefs could develop out of a small settlement started by a lineage head. Over the generations, this original settlement could, theoretically, expand into a series of adjacent settlements in which a core group were still related patrilineally to the founder (Cohen 1970c). Others could have come into the area by choice or by force and through the years have been absorbed. It is not inconceivable that such a grouping could take on the attributes of the Kanuri clans as we know them. Is only one of these possible theories correct, or does the present situation result from a mixture of both? Only specialized historical research can answer such questions.

As noted above in Figure 4:1, ego is related to a consanguineal descent group by birth and to others through marriage. Without going into the details of marital relations themselves or how they are created and dissolved, it is appropriate here to discuss ego's relations to these various in-laws since they form part of the setting or network of relations into which marriage and divorce are placed.

The affines of ego's cognatic descent groups are differentiated by terminology and behavior. In the second descendant generation, they are placed in the general category of "grandchildren," while in the first descendant and in one's own generation they are my junior and senior in-laws, using the same classification as ego uses toward own spouse's cognatic kin. In the parent generation, affines are placed terminologically with father's sister and mother's brother, depending upon their sex, with an alternative form for father's younger brother's wife which puts this woman in the same category as mother's younger sister.[8] Father's other wives or mother's other husbands (divorced or present) can be referred to descriptively as "far mother" or "far father," but such a term is somewhat derogatory and could never be used to the person's face. It therefore is more common and polite to use father's sister and mother's brother terms for parents' other spouses. The general rule then is as follows: all men (except own father) married to women of ego's cognatic descent group members at the parent generation level are referred to as *rawa*, the term used also for mother's brother. Conversely, all women (except own mother) married to men of ego's cognatic descent group members at the parent generation are referred to as *bawa*, the term also used for father's sister. Cognatic descent group members of the parent generation's affines can be referred to as junior and senior in-laws, depending upon whether they are younger or older than ego. Beyond the parent generation level, the term for grandparent and great-grandparent is used for all affines.

The terms for ego's own in-laws are senior *(kəsai)* and junior *(tiu)* affine. In general, all of ego's cognatic kin who are senior by birth priority are *kəsai* to his or her spouse, and all who are junior to ego are his or her *tiu*. In practice this may vary. Thus if a fifty year old man marries a fourteen year old girl, her eighteen year old brother is, properly speaking, this new husband's senior in-law. However, the status differences may be so great on other grounds that the terms get reversed and the older man becomes *kəsai* while the younger is *tiu*. Parents, aunts, and uncles of a couple refer to and address each other as senior-in-law.

The data in Table 4:2 were gathered along with those in Table 4:1 above. It can be readily seen that the most stringent shame and respect relations are with spouse's own parents. When sexual differences are added (i.e., son-in-law to mother-in-law; daughter-in-law to father-in-law) the restrictions and avoidances become the most severe in the kinship system. These in-laws should never be alone together; only the most necessary conversation should pass between them. The junior in the relationship should avoid any direct confrontation with the senior. Thus if a daughter-in-law is on the way to the well for water and meets her father-in-law, she should pass quickly by with eyes downcast, or even move to one side so they will not have to pass side by side on a path. Indeed, communication is better handled between such persons through intermediaries related to one or both of the parties. Although less restrictive in practice, such relations are supposed to be extended to siblings of spouse's parents. Thus a wife's mother's younger brother might be on somewhat friendly terms to ego and could on occasion act as an intermediary between ego and his mother-in-law.

TABLE 4:2. BEHAVIORAL NORMS TO AFFINES

Kin type	Shame		Respect		Joking		Friendship		No Data		Total Responding
	#	%	#	%	#	%	#	%	#	%	
Wife's father	47	98	49	100	0	0	0	0	0	0	49
Wi Mo	49	98	49	100	0	0	0	0	0	0	49
Wi Ol Sis	36	78	39	85	2	4	12	26	3	6	46
Wi Ol Bro	35	73	45	94	3	6	16	33	1	2	48
Mo Div Husband	16	42	35	92	1	3	1	3	11	22	38
Yo Bro Wi	16	40	26	65	5	13	7	18	9	18	40
Yo Sis Hu	14	36	27	69	5	13	16	41	10	20	39
Fa Bro Wi	15	33	43	93	0	0	0	0	3	6	46
Mo Bro Wi	14	33	26	60	6	14	7	16	6	12	43
Ego's Div Wi	11	30	23	62	16	43	1	2	12	24	37
Fa Sis Hu	10	23	40	91	2	5	5	11	5	10	44
Mo Sis Hu	10	22	43	95	2	4	6	3	4	8	45
Wi Yo Bro	3	6	5	11	40	87	13	28	3	6	46
Ol Bro Wi	1	2	29	64	41	91	8	18	4	8	45
Ol Sis Hu	1	2	27	60	39	87	14	31	4	8	45
Wi Yo Sis	1	2	8	16	42	86	11	22	2	4	47

Given the importance of seniority to the Kanuri, it is not surprising that the next most restrictive affinal category is spouse's older siblings. These are given the same term *(kəsai)* as wife's parents. Although somewhat lower in shame-respect and higher in friendship than spouse's parents relative to ego, they are still classed for many purposes with spouse's parents, and many or most of the same avoidance can apply to them as well. Nevertheless, such restrictions are dependent upon age, sex, and status differences such that the greater the distinction socially between ego and his spouse's senior siblings, the stronger the restrictions, avoidances, and respect between the parties concerned. If this relationship is turned around and we view it from the senior's position looking at a younger sibling's spouse, the shame responses are cut in half and the respect responses decrease significantly as well.[9] Thus 76% of those responding claimed a shame relationship to their older siblings' spouses while only 38% claimed a shame relationship to spouses of their younger siblings. Similarly, 89% felt respect with an older sibling's spouse while only 67% felt this way with a younger sibling's spouse. In other words, it is the junior who feels the greater restriction on his behavior. Indeed, in a minority of cases (13%) there are joking relations between the older sibling and his younger sibling's wife, while hardly anyone jokes with wife's older sibling. Similarly Ego (male speaking) feels quite friendly to his younger sister's husband (41%) and this is paralleled by a warm feeling close to his younger brother's wife. In the cases, where wife's older brother is head of the family and the spouse's father is dead, then wife's older brother is treated with the same shame and respect as wife's father.

Although mother's divorced husband, mother's brother, mother's sister's husband, and father's sister's husband are all *rawa*, there are significant differences in behavioral interactions reported in the tables and by informants in discussing kinship. Thus mother's brother and father's sister's husband are reported as having a similar relationship to Ego, but this is quite different to that with mother's divorced husband. In general, respect is high with all persons called *rawa*, while joking is low, and as would be expected from our discussion above, friendship and fondness responses are somewhat higher for mother's brother than the others. On the other hand a higher proportion (42%) report shame-avoidance relations with their mother's divorced husband than with all other persons termed *rawa*. Kanuri informants explain this by saying that it is shameful to have anything to do with a man who has had sexual relations with one's mother. The same in reverse is true for all relatives called *bawa* (father's sister, father's brother's wife, father's other wives, or father's divorced wife). However, besides increased shame with father's other wives, there is suppressed tension between Ego and such women which can be alleviated or enhanced by personality factors.[10] There are formal joking relations between ego and his or her spouse's younger siblings. Ego jokes about who his spouse's younger sibling is going to marry, or have sexual relations with, or about possible affairs that the younger one should or might have. However, the younger person is still respectful toward the older sibling's spouse, as indicated in Table 4:2, while the joking is mostly directed toward the younger partner. However, it is impossible even in a joking manner to refer to spouse's younger sibling as "wife" or "little wife" as do the Hausa. Marriage with wife's younger sister is forbidden by custom unless the present wife (her sister) is dead. The sororate is possible but sororal polygyny is not. To even jokingly call wife's younger sister "wife" implies the death of one's present wife. Exactly the same conditions hold for a woman's relations to her husband's younger brother.

Kinship as Setting and Value

In summary, the Kanuri have what Dole (1969) has called a bifurcate generational system of kinship terminology. Such a system reflects a unilineal past in which local endogamy has blurred the distinctions between cross and parallel cousins. If we add Islam to this, which allows patrilateral parallel cousin marriage, the blurring is aided by Kanuri religion. Endogamy resulting from progressive sedentarism, and probably class stratification as well,[11] have worked together with Islam to change the original Kanuri kinship system seven to eight centuries ago when these features began to appear in the society.

The change was from a system that emphasized a we-they distinction to one in which generation levels and seniority are the primary means of distinguishing among relatives. The complexity and regularity of the parent generation distinctions among kin reflect the early system, while all other generations reflect the more recent values.

Given the accuracy of this reconstruction and therefore the correctness of my thesis that the present system reflects a unilineal past, what kind of unilineality was it? Unequivocally the answer has to be patrilineal. The people say that agnatic kin are the most important among all kin. Patrilineal kin give a man his place in society, his most important rights to fixed property; they must help a man with his bridewealth, and agnates are mutually responsible for one another in legal disputes. Indeed, in court the agnatic group is a corporate entity. In practice, people do obtain help from matri-kin for bridewealth, for rights to land, and even for court fines. The obligation to help is more voluntary on the matrilineal side and more compulsory among agnates.

Even though some of these ideas are Islamic, such as agnatic legal responsibility, I would argue that they pre-date Islam and sometimes even contradict it. Thus although everyone knows the rules of Islamic inheritance, which include women, very few if any ever practice it with fixed assets such as households and land. The older agnatic emphasis is strong enough to override more recent tendencies in other directions. Contrarily, however, the people themselves say that they are equally related to all four grandparents, giving the system its cognatic quality. Cousins on both the matrilateral and patrilateral sides are equally "siblings" as are members of all generations, except that of the parents, again emphasizing cognation.

In cultural and jural terms, then, the Kanuri have a cognatic system with a patrilineal emphasis which reflects their original nomadic or semi-nomadic existence. In practice today, patrilocality and high divorce combine to give ego a set of stable agnates to whom he is related through his mother and his father. Variables affecting residential stability and ego's relationship to each of these agnatic groups produces his individual feelings of closeness to one or both of them.

All of these difficulties of standard kinship analysis reflect another important Kanuri value. As a people, they value relationships as the most useful resource in the social and physical environment. To be hemmed in by a system that clearly assigned them to one part of the genealogy, but not another, would rule out a large and potentially useful set of friends, patrons, clients, and allies. Thus whatever the unilineal tendency among them, the strain for constantly increasing the scope of their relationships is also a constant tendency for cognation to override agnation as a principle of descent.

As a setting, kinship places a person within a system of relations. Traditions and current practices teach him that seniority is a dominant feature in this system and a highly valued principle of the society itself. Seniority means deferential respect and authority—the dominant theme of all Kanuri social structure and, as we shall see, of marriage itself. Because seniority and its behavioral expressions, power and authority, are the most important values of the kinship system, it is difficult if not impossible to contain the search for these values within any strictly defined descent group. Thus Kanuri kinship, like Kanuri society as a whole, is a search for meaningful superior-subordinate relationships, and these can and do range over the entire genealogy, creating strong tendencies for cognatic as opposed to patrilineal descent.

Chapter 5
Social Networks Surrounding Marriage:
The Household and Community

As already noted, the chapters of Part II form a description and analysis of the setting within which marriage and divorce take place. Although kinship describes an important set of relationships which a person brings with him or her into a marriage, other groupings are of more immediate significance since they are the actual behavioral settings for marriage on a day-to-day basis. Kinsmen are important and many everyday interactions in Bornu are either actual kinship relations or are so similar in form and content as to be difficult to distinguish, at first, as non-kin relations. Nevertheless, other organizational forms, especially that of the household, are more relevant to marriage and divorce because they provide the actual theater within which the dramas of family relations are carried out. As we shall see, many of these forms include or are even at times congruent with kinship groups. However, just as often they are different.

Theoretically, at least, we could treat all aspects of primary relations surrounding marriage under the rubric of kinship. But this would mean that theories concerning such relations would be kinship theory; i.e., dependent to a large extent upon the factors that determine the nature of kinship. On the other hand, by separating household and community as separate structures, we can get at the most important determinants of social relations—namely, the political and economic factors affecting interaction.

The reasons for such distinctions are simple but significant. Kinship by itself is a function of ascription. People are born into kin groups and their roles in these groups change and develop primarily as a result of births, deaths, and aging in the system. Marriage produces some choice comparatively, but very little for the Kanuri case, since everyone in the society marries at one time or another unless there is some very serious impediment such as insanity or an incurable and noticeable disease such as leprosy. On the other hand, household and community relations are the result of kinship plus choice; that is, of ascription, aspiration, and achievement. Which kinship relations are to be strongly maintained; which non-kin relations are to be created, cultivated, and strengthened? The answers to these questions take us into a consideration of the set of variables that determine group formation and change among primary groups within the society. It is within such units of social interaction that marriage and its dissolution are set.

Kanuri Households: The Atoms of Social Structure

The stranger entering a Kanuri village or city ward is confronted immediately with a series of walled compounds. These are the basic units that make up the settlement. As I have noted elsewhere (Cohen 1967), they are also the basic political and economic units of the society. Compounds, or households, have mud or grass mat walls running from 5½ feet to 10 feet high, depending upon the wealth and social position of the household head. The greatest household, that of the emir (*Shehu*), has walls at least 20 feet high, while a simple rural peasant surrounds his home with grass mats and sticks. Most compounds have only one entrance, which is usually in the form of a large hut with one opening leading into and one out of the household. Traditionally, the entrance hut is the place where much of the visiting and business is carried on with the rest of the community. Unless a man is a close friend of the household, he does not go beyond the entrance hut without being invited. This sense of privacy is so great across all of Muslim Nigeria that in a number of cases in 1966 it is said to have saved the lives of Ibos who were taken into the houses of religious leaders for protection. Mobs, even though they knew of the harboring, would not break the privacy rule when the household head refused them entry into the compound.

Inside the compound are the huts or "rooms" of the occupants, which are often walled off as well. Thus the inside of a compound is more or less open. A very small, poor one has few if any interior walls; as the resources of the household head increase so do the numbers and quality of his inside walls. Thus a fairly well-to-do Kanuri household leads from an entrance hut into a series of passage-ways. Doors or openings in the walls lead into the private courtyard of household members. Huts or sleeping rooms are usually windowless and have small doorways facing west.[1] Today these rooms vary from grass mat walls with thatch covers to cement block buildings having electric fans and lights. Traditionally, beds were generally on the right side of the door and in traditional women's huts a raised area at the back of the hut (*fannaram*) is used to store her possessions, pots, calabashes, boxes for clothes, etc.

Beyond the entrance hut is the living space of the males of the household and beyond that, often separated by a wall, are the women. Men, even when invited into the male sections, rarely ever go into the women's sections. Female visitors pass quickly through the men's section into the women's quarters. Pre-pubescent children are allowed free access to all parts of the household. The women have their own sleeping huts and generally a small shaded area attached in which they cook. If there is room, a small garden space is left behind the women's huts to grow vegetables and grains, especially maize, which matures faster than the staple crops of millet and guinea corn. Exceptions to such an overall plan occur in extremely poor households or in urban locations where housing is scarce, where the man and his one wife share the same (and only) sleeping hut. Another exception occurs among groups of interrelated adjacent households in which a doorway may be left open between them so that there is another entrance to the compound besides the front one.

Spotted throughout the household, sometimes in miniature huts above ground, sometimes in mat-lined pits below ground, are the storage granaries of the household. The contents, especially the underground storage, are considered confidential information within the compound, in order to avoid pressures to share from more indigent members of the community.

Figure 5:1 gives a diagrammatic outline of a large Kanuri household in which a number of ideal goals are represented. Thus it is polygynous, patrilocal, and an aged mother of the household head lives here as well as a client follower.

The most important variation from this traditional household plan occurs in the city among divorced women. Many of these women have no family compounds to return to in the city itself or, if they have, they may wish to remain independent. Therefore, a practice of renting single huts or sleeping rooms to single women within a compound has developed. Generally such quarters are *not* in the very back of the compound, i.e., the women's section, but rather nearer to the entrance making access easier and less restrictive.

Western style building technology has not changed the house plans to any serious extent. Instead of mud and mats, cement blocks are used, but entrance houses, men's sitting and sleeping rooms and then women's quarters, are built as separate buildings within the modernized compound.

Household Size

Household size is larger and more variable in the urban setting. In a sample of fifty households taken from two urban wards of Maiduguri, the size varied from one person to forty-five, with a mean of 8.5. In 115 rural households from two villages and their surrounding hamlets, households varied from one occupant to fifteen with a mean of 4.1.[2] However, in this same group 67% of the rural household heads report having kin members and their families living in adjacent compounds, while only 41% of the urban sample claim this to be the case. Put in more extreme terms, 9% of these urban households have three or more kin members and their families living in adjacent compounds while in the rural areas 38% report living in such close proximity to three or more households of their kin. In other words, urban people put more persons into each household, but rural people tend far more to live among groups of their kin. Indeed most of the rurals who did

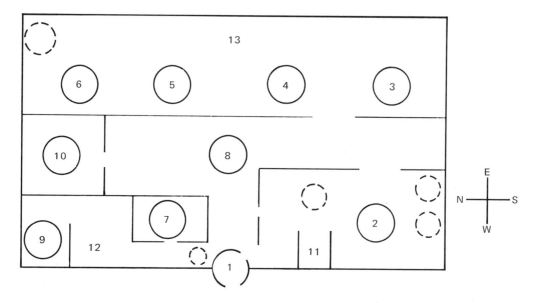

Legend
1. Large entrance hut (doors are never opposite one another)
2. Hut of compound head
3. Hut of senior wife
4. ⎫
5. ⎬ Huts of other wives
6. ⎭
7. Hut of son of compound head
8. Hut of compound head's mother
9. Hut of son's wife
10. Hut of client-servant
11. Horse's stall for household head
12. Son's horse stall and courtyard
13. Garden area

Dotted lines indicate granaries.

Figure 5:1. A Successful Kanuri Household.

not have kin in adjacent compounds report having some in the same ward. As one urban informant put it, "In the city everyone lives in the same compound because things are scarce and expensive here."

Besides rural-urban distinctions, there is a very strong relationship between socio-economic status (SES) and household size. A simple three point scale derived from earlier work was used to measure a respondent's status.[3] As can be seen in Table 5:1, there is a strong relationship between SES and household size. This reflects some of the most basic values of the society in that the number of a man's dependents are to himself and others a measure of his success and capability in adult life. The relationship is somewhat confounded by the fact that urban people are generally of higher status than rurals, and urban households are larger per se. However, when the data are controlled for rural-urban distinctions the relationship, although weaker because of fewer status distinctions in our rural sample, still shows the same trend especially for the urban households which show greater variance in terms of size and SES.

There is also a relationship between household size and age of the compound head such that larger households are associated with more advanced age. Table 5:2 shows that 95% of the younger household heads have medium and small sized compounds, while 76% of the middle aged and 81% of the older men head medium and large sized households.

TABLE 5:1. HOUSEHOLD SIZE AND SOCIO-ECONOMIC STATUS*

Household Size by persons	Socio-Economic Status		
	% Low (N=61)	% Medium (N=36)	% High (N=18)
1-3	36	8	22
4-6	43	25	44
7+	21	67	34
Totals	100	100	100

*X^2 = 27.62; p $<$ .01

TABLE 5:2. AGE OF HOUSEHOLD HEAD AND SIZE OF COMPOUND*

Number of persons in the household	Age of Household Head (N=113)		
	% young 20-34	% middle aged 35-49	% old 50+
1-3 (small)	32	24	19
4-6 (medium)	63	30	43
7+ (large)	5	46	38
Totals	100	100	100
	(N=22)	(N=54)	(N=37)

*X^2 = 14.42; p $<$ .01

Although these data understandably show almost no younger men who head large households, the data are much less distinct for both the middle aged and older groups. The reasons for this are complex. The bulk of the large households among older men comes from urban areas. As we have seen, rural people have smaller households in general, and rural old people often live as couples or with a young foster child. Furthermore, older city men are often wealthier than their rural counterparts, thus creating the necessary condition for larger units. Thus other factors of wealth and rural-urban residence enter to affect the size of compounds among mature and older men.

Household Composition

Membership in a Kanuri household results from kinship, fostering, clientage and/or apprenticeship, rental of sleeping quarters, and traditionally from slavery as well. The important point here is that all of these practices are not modifications of kinship or "extensions" of it; they are instead separate means by which households are initiated, develop, and either persist or disappear as specific organizations within the society.

Although analytically distinct, kinship and household are closely related. Among 250 men and women living in various urban and rural sites, we discovered only three (two old women living in a deceased husband's compound, and one man) persons living alone. In all other cases unmarried persons live as members of larger households. Of the total 113 male household heads interviewed, roughly half (49%) reported living in households having only conjugal families with no other kin or non-kin present. In other words, in about half of the sample households the conjugal family, both monogamous and polygynous, is co-existent with the household. However, when the sample is broken down, only 3% of the urbanites have this type of compound unit. As already noted above, this does not mean that rural families are more nucleated since most of them have kin in adjacent compounds. It reflects instead the greater difficulty of finding housing in the city, and of greater wealth there which allows for household expansion.

In households containing more than simple conjugal units, there are a number of different categories of persons. In our sample, 36% of all households included some patrilateral kin, not counting the children of the household head. Rural and urban residence makes no difference to this percentage. About 20% of all households included some matrilateral kin of the household head, again with no significant rural-urban differences. In absolute numbers patrilateral kin of the household head make up 13% of all persons and matrilateral are 5% of the total. Wife's kin are present in 9% of all sample households (making up only 4% of the total personnel) and this latter category is for the most part an urban phenomenon. In almost all cases (22 out of 26 persons), these were children of a wife's sibling, usually a real or classificatory sister who were being fostered by their mother's sister. The other four cases were old unmarried women who had found a more or less temporary haven in the compound of their female relative. Using old unmarried women as a separate category, 17% of our sample household had one or more of these ladies present. Sixteen (61%) of these were mothers of the household head, six (24%) were from his bilateral descent group, and four (15%) were related to a wife of the compound head. Twenty percent of the sample households have non-kin clients living in them. However, here the rural-urban distinction is important, since 34% of the urban and only 15% of rural households have such members. In absolute numbers, 11% of all household members in the sample are non-kin clients of the household head.[4]

It is difficult to give accurate figures on rentals of sleeping quarters except to note that it is an exclusively urban phenomenon organized in two ways. In some large city households, a sleeping room may be rented, usually to a single divorced woman. This woman often takes part in the social life of the women of the compound. In general, however, she carefully avoids the household head, maintaining a shame-avoidance relationship with him. This keeps potential jealousies between the "boarder" and the wives of the household to a minimum. Another system is what might be called living with a "pavilion of women." Here a household owner, often a man, rents an entire compound of rooms to divorced women who then live together in a manless house whose personnel changes as these women go in and out of marriages.

In our sample of 113 rural and urban household heads, 23% report having foster children living within the compound. There are, however, significant rural-urban differences; 37% of the urban and only 13% of the rural households had foster children living in the compounds. In terms of individuals, this is 5% of all compound members in the sample (13% in the city and 4% in the rural area). Corrected for the entire Kanuri population of Bornu, this means that 16% of all households have foster children which amounts to 4% of the total population or approximately 20-25% of all children. Fostering is thus a common institution in the area.

Processes of Household Growth and Decline

By rule, Kanuri marriage is virilocal, and in our sample three-quarters of the rural first marriages (male speaking) are reported to have been patrilocal as well. This figure is reduced to under one-half of all first unions occurring in the city. Patrilocality sets up the beginnings of a domestic cycle that is generally recognized by informants to follow, in many cases, a classic process of growth in which marriage brings in women as wives to expand the family into a larger household or group of adjacent ones. At the death of the father the organization loses much of its unity and often splits or fissions, at which point the cycle begins again (Fortes 1962). However, informants are much less clear or unanimous about forces which operate to modify this process.

As discussed by Fortes (1962), the domestic cycle is primarily determined by factors related to kinship such as maturation, marriage, and death. But in Bornu other factors enter which can alter the smooth or predictable path of such a cycle and thus affect the structure of household and family organization through time.

Turning first to children, we may ask what besides fertility and fecundity determines the presence of children in a conjugal family? A couple may be very young or only recently married and there has not been sufficient time for children to arrive, or in Bornu, children may be fostered elsewhere for the time being. In several such instances the husband had young children by a previous wife and the new young wife was considered too young to take care of these children. In cases where the couple is older and children marry and leave to live with their spouses, the cycle is more "normal." Where such children are girls it is fully expected that they may return between marriages if they choose to do so. These variant cases take up about one-third of all conjugal families while the remaining two-thirds are made up of a man, his wife or wives, and the children, if any, of such unions.

Another Kanuri household that on the surface resembles a conjugal unit in a normal phase of development is what might be called the childless unit. Many informants report never having had a live child, or only one, who has since left home. In many such instances children from elsewhere in the kinship group are found living with the childless household head. This is the receiving side of the foster relationship. As can be seen in case number two given in Figure 5:2 several of these involve situations in which a wife has imported children from her descent group.

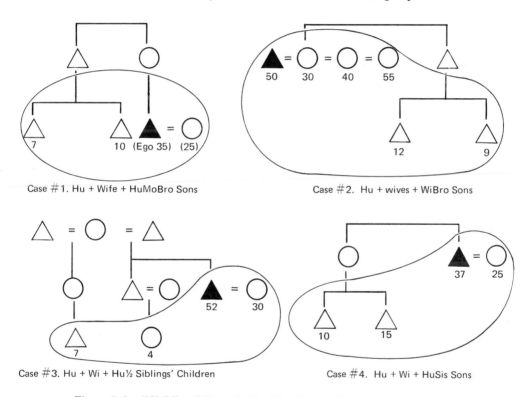

Case #1. Hu + Wife + HuMoBro Sons   Case #2. Hu + wives + WiBro Sons

Case #3. Hu + Wi + Hu½ Siblings' Children   Case #4. Hu + Wi + HuSis Sons

Figure 5:2. "Childless" Households (Numbers indicate age of persons).

Given patrilocalism, the problem of whether or not the unit remains together after the death of the father is a crucial one for understanding household organization. Thirty percent of our sample households contain people in them related by a sibling bond, real or classificatory, to the declared household head. If we trace these bonds to the common ancestor (all are connected at either the first, second, or third ascendant generation) and divide them up into subtypes, 81% of the relationships are either full siblings or traceable to a full sibling relationship; 17% result from half-sibling relations through a common mother and only 2% result from sibling bonds involving a common father but different mothers. I would conclude from this evidence that relations between full siblings and their descendants are by far the strongest, followed by half siblings through a common mother. On the other hand, links between siblings and their descendants based on a common father but different mothers have very little chance of being expressed in sharing a common residence.

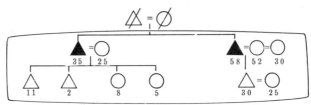

Case #1. Full Sibling Household (common)

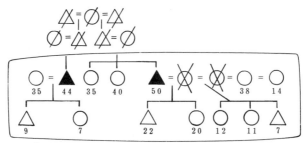

Case #2. Descendants of half brothers, same mother (uncommon)

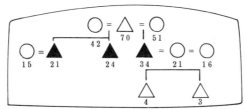

Case #3. Half brothers, same father, living in same house; note father is still alive (rare)

Figure 5:3. Examples of three types of male sibling bonds between household members.*
* ⟁ or ⌀, = deceased   ⟁ or ⌀ = divorced

Informants' statements corroborate these findings for full brothers. These are the very closest of all kin at one's own generation level. Several people claimed that although it is possible and generally practiced it is not really necessary to divide the inheritance among full siblings. They are so close they can use the wealth jointly for, ideally, they more than any others must trust one another. On the other hand, brothers with different mothers both feel responsible to take care of their mothers and compete for their share of the inheritance. Ex-co-wives have little to keep them together after the death of a husband, except possibly the memory of their rivalry and suppressed jealousies. The fact that each woman would like to enjoy her later years living in her son's compound is a force driving these half-brothers apart. Such tensions are absent in the case of brothers having the same mother but different fathers, so there is less competition and conflict in this relationship. These three types of sibling households are illustrated from case material in Figure 5:3.

As already noted, a common addition to Kanuri households is that of the single divorced or widowed mother of the compound head or other old woman related by some kin tie to the compound head. Many Kanuri women, after a divorce in their forties or fifties, find they cannot remarry because men favor younger wives. Such women then return to their kin to be sheltered by a son, brother, daughter's husband, other relative, or even in one or two cases by an ex-husband long since divorced whom the woman refers to as "my brother" (although there is no descent tie between them). However, as already noted above the majority of such cases are mothers of the household heads.

In effect this means that in a high divorce society such as the Kanuri, where women are valued and controlled for their economically productive labors in cooking and agriculture, their reproductive capacities and as sexual objects, (a) younger women are favored and (b) there is an age class of older post-menopause women who have been divorced and then remain single for the rest of their lives.

Such a result presents a problem which must be solved by some form of organization and the Kanuri handle it in a sensible and humane manner. There is a strong obligation for a son, or a brother's son, or a "brother" (classificatory and real) to take care of these women and provide a place for them within the household. The women themselves help in the compound, and also sell cooked and uncooked foods, grass mats, and other small sundries at the door of the compound or at a nearby small daily market place. In this way they can be somewhat independent economically and even make a small contribution to the household economy. Avoidance rules keep them from very much interaction with daughters-in-law, while grandchildren find them always pleasant and much less authoritarian than their own parents. When extreme old age and infirmity approaches they become more fully dependent members of the household in an economic sense. However, the very fact of longevity is in itself a contribution. For having achieved it the old woman indicates how powerful and blessed she is, and in so doing she automatically brings good fortune and blessedness to all those around her. Thus members of the household going on a trip or close friends of the household seek her out and receive her blessings before they depart. They feel that she above many others can provide a link to unseen powers that protect mankind from misfortune.

In summary, even though a great many women must ultimately leave marriage to spend their old age without a partner, the social structure provides them with a place in the household organization and in so doing keeps them within the family and its community setting.

One of the most common forms of expanding household size is through fostering and clientage. As already noted above, over one in every five Kanuri children live before marriage in compounds other than those of their own parents. For statistical purposes I define this as under twenty for boys and under fourteen for girls. Children can be fostered any time after weaning. Common places for fostering are kin who have no children of their own, or friends, or within the household of a namesake of the child. This latter practice is often used for purposes of upward mobility. Thus a child will be named after a wealthy or powerful person who is a mentor or relative or patron of some kind to the father. The family hopes that the child's namesake will help him or her to get a good start in life and hopefully a useful patron-client relationship will develop out of this namesake and fostering beginning.

Such hopes are best suited to situations where the fosterer has no children of his own and no competition or jealousies can develop. In one case, for example, a young namesake foster child was withdrawn from primary school because the child was doing better than his foster parents' own children. This could have led eventually to the foster child going on much further in school and thus outstripping the other children of the compound. On the other hand, there are many well-known cases in Bornu of important men who got their start in life by being raised in the compounds of foster parents who could help them.

How long do such foster relations last? The period varies from one or two years right up to the time of marriage. Often the child is in the same community as his own parents and can visit them regularly. In one case an informant has exchanged children with his own full brother. He has taken his brother's daughter (age seven) and sent his own two and a half year old son to his brother. He claims the boy's own mother (his wife) is too young to raise the son properly while the people in his older brother's compound know much more about child-rearing. His brother's daughter helps in the house and the informant feels she will remain until she marries. He has been appointed by her father to arrange the marriage which he will do when the time comes.

A common term for such arrangements, especially as applied to young foster girls, is *amana* or trust. In other words, the Kanuri view the foster relationship as one in which a child has been placed in trust into the hands of someone else. It means, therefore, not only that the child is raised in another household but that each compound head can by so doing advertise to the world at large his serious connection to other compounds.

For the child, fostering provides an opportunity to learn some of the most important lessons of Kanuri life. The father is not the only source of authority at the primary group level. That position is instead held by the head of the compound. All through life, a Kanuri must learn to react to nuances of differences in status and use the behavior norms of the kinship system easily and properly depending upon the situation. The foster child, by being raised in more than one compound, has the chance of learning such things at an early age. There are other ways of learning these skills, but fostering is perhaps the best means available.

A special kind of fostering occurs as a form of religious training. Some men give young boys of six to ten to religious teachers for a period of a year or two in order that the boy will learn about Islam. During this time the father helps with the expenses of keeping the child and may give the *mallam* something extra as well. In other cases, and for girls, children go to the house of the *mallam* during the day and return home in the evening. In either case the same lesson is being added—that of expanding one's use of *bərzum* (discipline-respect). As the Kanuri say, "*Mallamnum abanum kozəna*" (Your *mallam* surpasses your father; i.e., in fatherly qualities, qualities that demand respect and subordination, your *mallam* is as great or greater than a father). Unspoken, but clearly implied, is the idea that this relationship of *bərzum* between superiors and subordinates is the most important and highly valued in the society.

Given the fact that generalized acceptance and internalization of the superior-subordinate modes of behaving are one of the most highly stressed and often mentioned goals of child-training, it is interesting to speculate about the effects of fostering. Logically, fostering should aid such goals. If generalized reaction to authority rather than father-cum-household head is what is required, then using the general role of household head rather than a single person means that the child is learning to respond to the role not the person. The hypothesis here would be that fostering as opposed to non-fostering backgrounds creates a relatively easier adjustment to superior-subordinate relations in adult life.

Clients defined as non-kin subordinates are to be found in about one sixth of all Kanuri households at any one time. The institution is, however, much more pervasive than this figure indicates since it also defines relations between households. The present discussion will, however, concentrate on intra-household relations. A client is generally termed *tada njima* in Kanuri, meaning son-of-the-hut or less literally he is a "son" because he has a hut, or sleeping quarters, in the compound. In return, the client refers to the compound head as *aba njima* or father-of-the-hut, meaning head of the compound in which he lives. In both cases, the word *njima* also carries the connotation of a non-kin basis to the relationship (Cohen 1967a).

The client helps the household in the economic activities of the compound—on the farm and/or the non-farming activities such as trade or craft-work. He may serve as a messenger and general helper if his household has political duties in the community. Duties are general and diffuse, rather than specific. In return, the client receives subsistence and a place in the social, economic, and political structure of the community. The household head stands *in loco parentis*. If the client goes to court, his household head goes with him as protector, with or without the client's agnates. The household head may also help the client with his marriage and help to obtain land and an occupation in the community. In other words, as one informant put it, "Your *aba njima* is just like your father."

There are a number of methods for recruitment into the client role. The client may simply make himself constantly useful, perform small services for his potential patron, visit him almost daily to "pay respects," providing service whenever and however he can. In return the would-be client may ask for small favors, or gifts, hoping in this way to set up a relationship. If the subordination and its payment or hoped-for payment are satisfactory to both parties, the client may then move into the household of the patron to take up the recognized role of household member. In other çases, the client may be brought by a relative or friend, or he may be a namesake of the compound head so that the role of client and fosterer will then coincide and reinforce one another.

Apprenticeship in a particular occupation is carried out in the same way. Parents, or in some cases the young man himself, arrange that he come to live in a compound where the occupation to be learned is practiced by the household head. The client-apprentice (also called *tada njima*) carries out all the diffuse subordinate tasks of a client and at the same time learns the craft of the household. The length of apprenticeship varies with the occupation and the persons involved. Sometimes conflict can result because the compound head tries to hold on to the client-apprentice longer than is considered suitable by the subordinate. The following case illustrates how such an arrangement actually works.

Modu the Barber Apprentice

Modu is about nineteen years old. Previously he has been a wholesale seller of kola nuts using money advanced to him by his brother. He has decided to give up this occupation because the giving of credit to retail customers was a constant worry and he always seemed to end up a trading trip without any profit. His older full brother in Maiduguri, who had been his supplier of money and kola nuts, suggested he try barbering. The older brother advised him that one of the local barbers in the rural village where their mother lived needed a *tada njima* because his own son was as yet too young to help. Modu asked the barber about it and made his own arrangments concerning the apprenticeship. He moved into the barber's household and stayed for one year. He was able to visit his mother's compound during this time and to farm a plot of land for himself. He helped the barber on the farm, cut and gathered grass for his horse, carried water for the household now and then, and ran messages for his *aba njima*.

The barber taught him how to shave heads and cup blood (for medicinal purposes) and gave Modu a bag of tools with which the young man began working, sometimes with his superior, sometimes alone. By right, all receipts of Modu's work during that year were supposed to be given to his superior. Now and then he pocketed a fee, especially on market days when there were strangers in the town, but not too often; to do so would be to risk dismissal and an end to his career as a barber, at least in that village. The senior barber could, under the system, dismiss Modu at any time and take back the tools. During the year the barber fed and clothed Modu and gave him spending money. At special events—naming ceremonies or circumcision—he was given a small tip by the person running the ceremony, because of his role as the barber's helper.

The next year he moved back to the compound of his mother. He still does chores for the barber, and claims to give the barber some of his own receipts regularly. He still has to learn how to cut face-marks, remove uvula, and perform circumcisions. Only when all these skills are acquired will he be fully trained. Thus he still attends ceremonies with his patron-instructor and feels that he will be "like a son" to the senior for years to come.

In other cases, I have recorded clients who remained in their patrons' households for years as general subordinates. Others seem to move about a great deal looking constantly for a more lucrative or promising place to deliver their subordination. This latter quality is quite striking to the newcomer to a village who, if he is regarded as wealthy and/or powerful, can be deluged at first with offers of subordination by would-be clients.

Although clientage is, properly speaking, a non-kin relationship, there is a tendency, not universal but practiced, to refer to relatives, especially matrilateral kin, but even more so to affinal kin, as also being clients if they live in a relative's compound. The fact that such is rarely if ever the case with agnatic kin points up a major distinction between kinship and clientage. Kin, especially agnatic kin among the Kanuri, are all members of the same inheritance group, which means that they are potential competitors for non-divisible prerogatives such as the headship of the household or the best plot of land owned by a senior member. Furthermore, once authority has been structured, and after a death restructured, then the distribution of power, especially within the agnatic group, is stabilized. This latter point can best be seen in a quote from previously published work.

> I did not have a father and was now living in the house of my eldest brother who was head of the house. I therefore had to give my brother the same discipline-respect (*barzum*) as a father and keep myself continually under his command. I wanted a wife. All my brothers had married and moved out to form their own households by now, but my brother ordered me to wait patiently until I learned the occupation (butchering) properly. He said, ". . .continue to stay in my house and carry grass for my horse and learn the butcher's trade, and I will feed you and give you money for spending and I will buy your clothes." But I was not happy and saved my money in secret, saved enough to take a wife of my own. They were cheap in those days. My older brother was angry and did not agree to the marriage for he still wanted me to stay in his compound. But I did not wish to do that, and so I moved away to a house that X, the husband of my mother's sister in Maiduguri owned here in the butcher's quarter [Cohen 1967:50].

In this case, the informant did not wish to remain subordinate to his older brother and plotted his independence, thereby breaking up the household and reducing the numbers of his brother's subordinates. Clientage, however, has the advantage that persons who enter such a relationship do so knowing that it implied subordination and that without proper compliance they can be "fired."

Although I have recorded a number of cases in which households did not split up after the death of the father, most of these involve one of the brothers, often the eldest, taking over a very lucrative and powerful set of prerogatives from the father. Examples are political office or a large economic organization. Thus one counter force to household fission is greater than average power and wealth which is associated with the household headship itself. However, clientship (and slavery in pre-colonial times) is a much more common mode of increasing household size and ensures the corporate continuity of the household without having to rely on kin. Brothers may split apart, sons may marry and move away, but clients who are related only by subservience to a household head will remain as long as the conditions of their subordination are satisfactory.

The result for Kanuri society is a constant tension between the processes of domestic cycling, which are dependent upon the birth, maturation, and death of household members related by kinship, and processes of corporate group creation, maintenance, and expansion. These latter are dependent not on kinship alone, but on the political and economic power of the household head to run an organization and reward subordinate members, no matter what the origin or nature of their relationship to him. This means that the processes of household structure in Bornu are predictable if we combine two different sets of variables. Kinship by itself produces a patrilocal organization that ultimately splits upon the death of the father or even before with the marriage of the sons. This traditional type of domestic cycle accounts for a large number (about half) of conjugal families who occupy households. However, the fact that other than conjugal kin are present in many households results from the fact that Kanuri positively value large households and, through the proper manipulation of economic and political power, extra people can be attached within the household which negates the effects of the domestic cycle. As we shall see, this theoretical explanation can be extended to explain some of the relations between as well as within households.

Relations Between Households

As already noted in Chapter 3, Kanuri live in cities, villages, and hamlets all within twenty-one districts under the central government of the emirate. Hamlets are linked to villages within village area units, and within villages there are wards headed by men having the same status as hamlet heads. For large towns and cities, ward heads have the same status as rural village heads.

Within this framework, the household forms the basic unit of administration at the local level. Household heads pay taxes for their members and represent them to higher authorities and for purposes of dispute settlement. There is, however, a processual relationship between households as units and the next larger unit, that of ward and hamlet. In cities the process is much less distinct because of greater variability, land shortage, and less patrilocality. However, even in the city organization among groups of households it is not uncommon, especially among the wealthy and powerful.

The simplest situation of linkage between households is that illustrated in Figure 5:1. The son living in this household wishes to marry a second wife. If he does so, he will move out to form his own compound because he feels it is shameful to have two wives and still remain within his father's compound. If his wives should quarrel, both his parents would hear it and this would be embarrassing. His decision to move will involve the question of how far away it should be. To remain closer to his father means remaining more under his authority. In this case, the father is a wealthy and powerful member of their rural community. The son is an only child and stands to inherit his father's household and wealth. The father has younger brothers who live further away. If the son moves too far away then these brothers would begin to advance claims on the household. If the son remains, then he has first claim on it. He has elected to remain in a closed household several doors away from his father.

A group of households all near to one another and occupied by a group of brothers is quite similar to the case above. The degree to which the senior brother can maintain any power over his brothers depends on his wealth and power and their degree of dependence upon him for their own status. In one such case three full brothers live next to one another. The eldest brother has taken over the household of their mother's brother who raised all three of them. The next eldest has gone into trading hides and skins, using his brother as a contact among butchers. The youngest brother is a butcher and works under the direction of the eldest even though he has a separate household next door. These three men appear in court together if one of them has to go. They pay taxes separately and farm separate plots, although they help each other in farm work. The community thinks of them as a semi-separated unit within one of the wards of town.

In some cases, a small group of households such as this begins to expand. The senior person becomes wealthier and more influential in the community. He attracts clients and his sons and/or brothers do not move very far away when they set up their own households. When the clients get married, or if they are already married, they set up households near their patron. Again, the wider community begins to view this group of households as a unit. Such units may even split off and form new settlements. Elsewhere (Cohen 1967:93) I have described how groups of related households can create new hamlets-in-the-becoming by moving onto free land or farm plots outside the village.

In one rural area, a man was observed who asked permission of the village area head to move all fences of households on his street back about fifteen feet in order to symbolize his rising status as a ward head in-the-becoming. In Kanuri culture a political leader should by rights have his household facing west onto a plaza (*dandal*). This man lived on a street that ran east and west at the far southeast section of a village. Figure 5:4 shows what he wished to do and finally did carry out. Not all cases are so clear cut. This man lived among a group of households, all of whose heads had come to recognize him as their senior. Some of these household heads were senior to several of their own surrounding households. The new ward head was son to the man who first moved into this area. Others followed and always asked his permission to live there, as people still do today.

In the city there is always some attempt to have sons and supporters live close by, but housing density and shortages often mean that they live further afield in the ward, or even in another ward. Thus links between households in the city are often much more dispersed than in rural areas. Another phenomenon more easily seen in the city is that of ward factionalism. In rural areas,

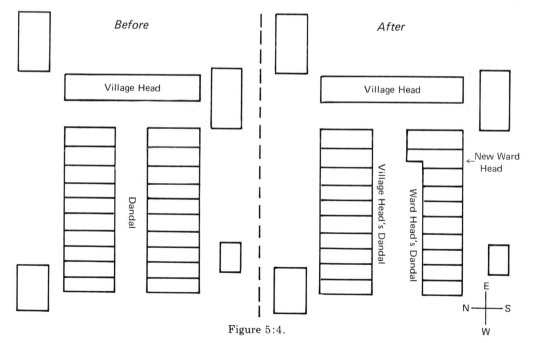

Figure 5:4.

people generally say, "We are the people of such and such a village area headman," when asked who their superior is. In the city they may say the equivalent, i.e., "We are the people of such and such a ward head." But sometimes powerful noblemen live in these wards or have a city residence in one of them. The ward head himself may be a client of this nobleman and he received his position for that reason. In such a case, a large number of the people feel they are clients or supporters of the nobleman. This seems to be a more traditional pattern and is less common today, although one or two wards of the city are well known for this kind of organization.

These groups of interrelated households give to many Kanuri settlements a socio-economic differentiation based often on occupation. The senior man of one of these was originally a calabash maker. His sons live near him and they are calabash makers, as well as several clients who are also calabash makers. Thus their craft is localized within one area of the village. The same is true of other occupations. Although some heterogeneity does appear after several generations, the original division of the community into such sections is remembered and a few, such as the blindmen's quarters where they make rope and the pagan quarter where they make millet beer, are strictly adhered to in most towns.

Although the major relations within communities are based on localized groups of households, a number of factors tend to create non-localized relations. Kinship links may or may not be localized and relations between kin are maintained by visiting, attendance at *rites de passage*, and the fostering of one another's children. Trade and weekly markets produce relations between non-localized households as well. Thus a man from village A may visit regularly at the household of a friend in town B on market days, then reciprocate the hospitality when his own village market is held. Similarly, men from rural areas who wholesale goods between the city and the rural areas may stay in the household of their urban wholesale suppliers when they visit the city. Men in the city often obtain, or retain from the past, land in rural areas. During the growing season, they move out to the rural area, or send some of their household members, or hire laborers in order to harvest a crop. During such periods, they stay in the households of relatives or friends, creating or maintaining links between the rural and urban setting. Because of a complex set of political forces, there is much mobility of political leaders from one post to another throughout the emirate (Cohen 1964). This sometimes means that client-followers of a political leader, especially those given local political offices such as village area head, may maintain affiliations to political leaders who are not part of the present political hierarchy in their area.

The result is that inter-relations between households is to some extent based upon local patterns of residence into hamlets, wards, villages, etc. However, these are cross-cut by a number of factors that produce relations between more distant households spread throughout the emirate. Relations between households are maintained for many reasons. Kinship, especially agnation and patrilocality, can produce a group of adjacent compounds that form the basis for a patrilineage. However, just as with relations inside the household, political, and economic ties among such households create the most important modes of stabilizing or maintaining some degree of working relationship among them. Because these functions, rather than kinship per se, hold households together, the ties between them can range from near to far across physical distances with little difficulty as long as the functions are being carried out successfully.

In summary, the actual organization within which marriages take place are those of the household and the community. Membership in these units is determined in a major way by kinship. Thus forces of domestic cycling based on birth, maturation, marriage, and death of household members does affect the structure of households through time. High rates of marital break-ups create a need for the care of post-menopause single divorced women who generally live with descent group members. Fostering, clientage, and apprenticeship tend to move people in and out of households on the basis of economic and political gains for the household head and the person concerned. These may or may not be kin. The consequence of these conditions is a tension between the forces of domestic cycling based on kinship and the political and economic functions that relate the members to one another and the household to other like units in the community and the emirate as a whole. A household is not just a place where a family lives; it is instead the basic corporate group in Kanuri society. Marriage is therefore only one among several social functions served by such a unit—and not always is it the most important one.

PART III
THE ETHNOGRAPHY OF KANURI MARRIAGE

Chapter 6
Marriage Inception: The Socio-Cultural Pre-Conditions

The previous chapters have attempted to provide an understanding of the social structural context within which Kanuri marriage and divorce take place. The focus of attention in Part III now shifts to a more concentrated description and analysis of marriage and its dissolution. More precisely, we now begin to focus in on the husband-wife dyad using the previous material as the context for understanding the social fabric into which the dyad is woven.

Marriage inception refers to the decisions, obligations, interpersonal and intergroup relations pertinent to the carrying out of a legitimized union between spouses. In this sense it is a crisis. Elsewhere, I have defined crisis as a decision-making situation which involves vital interests of the people concerned, and vital interests are rights and prerogatives over valued behaviors and objects (Cohen 1970g). In marriage, vital interests are radically changed; a girl or woman moves from one group to another; a husband is created who obtains new rights over a wife and takes on obligations to her and her kin; families are linked together through the spouses, and so on. Because the changeover is a dramatic one, interpersonal and intergroup relations are etched clearly in discussions over bridewealth and other marriage expenses as well as all the other preparations that are required before a marriage is successfully legitimized. This is the reason why anthropologists have always been so concerned with it—not because they are necessarily interested in the rituals themselves, but because the changes in the memberships and roles involved activate the social system at such times, and set it into a more easily recorded relief. Furthermore, because people of the related kin groups, residence groups, and the community at large have an interest in the marriage, the inception is a time when those outside the union-to-be indicate their relation to it. In this way, marriage inception is a bridge between the socio-cultural setting of marriage and a particular union between husband and wife.

Marital Prohibitions

Marriages among the Kanuri are deterred from occurring in two ways, by absolute prohibition (incest) and by being defined as shameful and to be avoided (*nungu*). Incest is defined culturally as *haram* or forbidden in the same way as pork is forbidden to all Muslims. It is thus a taboo which has the legitimacy and sanctity of religious law. For the Kanuri it is *haram* to marry or cohabit with one's full or half-siblings. This also applies to parents and their siblings (real and classificatory), and any one who has ever been married to parents and their real or classificatory siblings. The same prohibition applies to the grandparent generation as to that of the parents including grandparents' siblings and their spouses. By extension these rules cover ego's relations to the minus one and minus two generations as well. It is also forbidden to marry anyone, kin or non-kin, who nursed at one's own mother's breast. Finally, a man cannot marry the real or classificatory sister of his living wife or ever marry those he calls senior in-law.

It is considered bad or shameful to marry or have sexual relations with progeny of one's mother's sister. This is an extension of the prohibition against marrying anyone who nursed at one's own mother's breast. Some informants say that there is very little difference between own mother and her sister, and thus they are the 'same breast'. This point is somewhat complex but will become clearer in the discussion below on cousin marriage. Although not forbidden, there is great shame in marrying a live sibling's real or classificatory divorced spouse, although it is perfectly all right if the sibling is dead. It is not forbidden but shameful to marry a "pagan," i.e., a non-Christian or non-Jew. And, say the Kanuri, it is only allowable to marry Christians and Jews if they are white, because black men who profess these faiths are only recently converted and are therefore pagans underneath.[1] Again, it is considered shameful to marry illegitimate children, slaves or concubines, children of blacksmiths, leather workers, butchers, praise-singers, and street beggars. These are pariah groups with whom it is considered demeaning to be closely linked. It is also considered a bad thing and shameful to marry into an excessively poor family, relative to oneself and one's own family, because this leads to taking on a great many dependents. Finally it is considered shameful for important men, especially office-holders in one locality, to marry the same woman if one of them divorces her. Such women should marry ordinary commoners in the same locality, or if they have powerful connections, they should go away where their ex-husband is not known. Otherwise such unions can cause conflicts between important men.

Reports of incest among the Kanuri are extremely rare. In a number of field trips and for hundreds of unions, I have only recorded one case—that of a father who seduced his son's wife. This occurred in a remote rural hamlet and was gossiped about as a truly extraordinary, awesome, and horrible event unheard of in any one's memory. In my estimation, therefore, incest is so rare as to be negligible. On the other hand, some shameful unions do occur but they too are rare, accounting for less than 1% of the 741 marriages in our sample. Of these shameful unions, the only examples recorded are with matrilateral parallel cousins (discussed below) and with butchers. In the latter case, the somewhat wealthier status of the butchers overrides their pariah status.

TABLE 6:1. FREQUENCY OF MARRIAGE FOR MEN AND WOMEN

Number of Times Married	MEN (N=116)		WOMEN (N=99)	
	Frequency %	Accumulated %	Frequency %	Accumulated %
1	16.4	16.4	32.3	32.3
2	25.9	42.3	34.3	66.6
3	22.4	64.7	15.2	81.8
4	9.5	74.2	10.1	91.9
5	5.2	79.4	3.0	94.9
6	2.6	82.0	3.0	97.9
7	2.6	84.6	-0-	97.9
8	2.6	87.2	---	97.9
9	2.6	89.8	1.0	98.9
10	.9	90.7	---	98.9
11	1.7	92.4	---	98.9
12	.9	93.3	1.0	99.9
13	.9	94.2	---	---
14	---	94.2	---	---
15	---	94.2	---	---
16	1.7	95.9	---	---
17	.9	96.8	---	---
18	---	96.8	---	---
19	.9	97.7	---	---
20	.9	98.6	---	---
21	---	98.6	---	---
22	---	98.6	---	---
23	.9	99.5	---	---
24	---	99.5	---	---
25	.9	100.4	---	---
TOTALS	100.4		99.9	

Demographic Features of Marriage Inception

Muslim polygyny allows up to four wives; this and the high rate of divorce among the Kanuri means that both sexes generally marry a number of times, especially men. Thus in our sample of 116 men and 99 women, drawn equally from rural and urban areas, men married a total of 504 times or 4.4 per man, while women reported 237 marriages or 2.4 per woman. There are, however, rural-urban differences. The average number of marriages in rural areas is 3.2 for men and 1.4 for women, while in the city it is 5.8 for men and 3.1 for women. Corrected for rural-urban sampling biases, this gives a mean of 3.5 marriages for men and 1.8 marriages for women in the population as a whole.

Table 6:1 gives a more detailed picture of the frequency of marriages reported on in the sample. The fact that men marry many more times than women is obvious yet these results should be critically examined for their effect on the analyses to be reported on later. After the table passes approximately ten marriages per person, we are in fact speaking of very few people. When the data is analyzed per person, this is perfectly all right, but when it is manipulated per marriage, these few persons bias the sample. Nevertheless, it is possible to say from these data that under one-quarter of all men report having only one marriage, while nearly one-third of the women are in this category. Half of the men report having between two and three marriages, while half the women report having between one and two. Another way of indicating this same point is to note that 15% of the men report having more than eight marriages, while this occurs for only 2% of the women.

Kanuri marriages begin around puberty for young girls, sometimes earlier and after age 15 for boys, although only a few marriages (4%) take place for boys under 18. Women do not report getting married after they are 41, while men report marrying until they are 68. Table 6:2 gives the data on age at which marriages occur for both sexes. There is some tendency for urban men to keep marrying a little later in life, but it is not significantly different statistically and so I assume that the table is fairly representative of the population. However, respondents tend to report themselves as younger than they really are, and the table reflects this inaccuracy. On the basis of

TABLE 6:2. AGE AT MARRIAGE FOR MEN AND WOMEN

Age at Time of Marriage	% of Men's Marriages (N=504)	Accumulated %	% of Women's Marriages (N=237)	Accumulated %
9-11	---		1.8	1.8
12-14	---		43.4	45.2
15-17	4.0	4.0	12.7	57.9
18-20	13.9	17.9	14.0	71.9
21-23	9.8	27.7	8.6	80.5
24-26	11.4	39.1	5.9	86.4
27-29	7.6	46.7	6.8	93.2
30-32	11.6	58.3	2.7	95.9
33-35	8.3	66.6	2.7	98.6
36-38	6.6	73.2	---	98.6
39-41	8.1	81.3	1.4	100.0
42-44	4.5	85.8	---	---
45-47	3.8	89.6	---	---
48-50	2.0	91.6	---	---
51-53	3.8	95.4	---	---
54-56	1.3	96.7	---	---
57-59	1.3	98.0	---	---
60-62	.8	98.8	---	---
63-65	1.0	99.8	---	---
66-68	.3	100.1	---	---

participant-observation data, I would amend the table by claiming that there are more marriages among older men than is indicated, and a few older women beyond the age of 40-45 do in fact remarry. Thus the table reflects an overall trend for age at marriage but is not completely accurate. The pattern is none the less quite clear: women marry earlier than men, but men continue to marry well after women have stopped contracting unions.

A few cases of men's first marriages have been recorded over age 25 but none over age 30, and the bulk of them take place between 18 and 24. Some informants believe it is proper for a girl to marry before her first menstruation so she may learn to become a woman in the household of her husband. Certainly there is general agreement that all girls should be married as soon after the onset of puberty as possible. Puberty itself is unmarked ceremonially for boys, although they are circumcised (usually in groups) anywhere from age 7 to 14 giving a rough correlation to onset of physiological puberty. When a girl first menstruates, her cognatic female kin, plus the woman of the household she is living in at the time, come to her whether she is married or not. They cook millet cakes and distribute them as charity, often to small children training with a *mallam*. The girl, in the company of women only, sits on a wooden mortar used for pounding grain into flour. She is then daubed with milk and flour all over her body, with special attention being paid to her breasts and loins. People explain that this keeps evil spirits (*jinn* and satan [*shatan*]) from harming her during this change period when she may be particularly vulnerable to malevolent influences.

Symbolically, the ritual seems to stress the woman's role—cooking food and sexual maturation. Giving charity and the ceremony itself are part of a wider Kanuri belief that susceptibility to malevolent forces increases enormously at *rites de passage* or whenever a person stands out from his fellows.

Circumstances sometimes force young men to marry women who are older than they are. Kanuri believe that a husband should always be older than his wife no matter what his age. Seniority is believed to be a culturally derived correlate of age and therefore the husband's dominance is strengthened by his greater age relative to that of his wife. In practice, informants say that young men often marry women older than themselves—other young men, however, not they themselves. In reporting age of their own spouses, only six marriages out of 741 cases, all reported on by men, are with wives older than their husbands. All of these were by men aged 15-24 with women ages 25-34. Women, like men, speak of such age disparities in marriages other than their own, but report no such cases in their own marital histories.

The cultural norm of marrying a woman younger than oneself is therefore very strong—so strong that people tend not to report exceptions to the rule for their own marital histories even though they are quite willing to admit that such exceptions occur. Participant observation turns up such cases with little difficulty. Furthermore, older men report many marriages with young girls and young women. This indicates the value of such marriages for men of all ages and explains why some younger men with fewer resources simply must marry less expensively—i.e., among women older than themselves. Unfortunately, the strength of the norm means that an accurate quantitative measure of such deviations cannot be obtained.

An interesting distortion of age at marriage also occurs as a result of the sex of the speaker. This can best be seen by graphing marriages with young girls and women (see Figure 6:1). In both of these instances, data obtained from the men takes on the appearance of a log-normal curve while the women depart significantly from this pattern. In each curve men see themselves as "peaking" early then falling off slowly in the frequency with which they marry into each of these young age segments. Furthermore, they see themselves as peaking earlier for younger girls and thus Figure 6:1 (A) is highest at the youngest male age.

By contrast, women constantly see themselves as having been married to men not just older, but very much older than themselves. This is especially true at age 14 or under for the girl; women report that 13% of their marriages at this age were with men 55 and over, and 38% were with men 35 and over. Men, on the other hand, report on 175 such marriages altogether but claim that only 1 (0.2%) was with a man 55 and over, while 8% were with men 35 and over. This point is also made in Figure 6:1 which shows women very much higher in their estimation of marriages between young women and older men. Concomitantly, women and men differ as well in their reporting on marriages between young girls and young men. Women consistently report much less

6:1 (A) Marriage with Previously Unmarried Girls 14 and Under

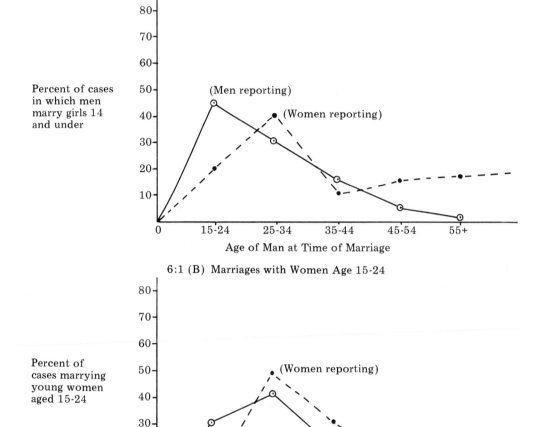

Figure 6:1. Marriage with Young Women as Reported by Men and Women.

of this. This is especially apparent in Figure 6:1 (B) where women report relatively few marriages between men and women both aged 15-24, while men report such unions to be quite common.

Men therefore see themselves as marrying young women, and report that although older they are close or closer to their wives in age. Women, on the other hand, see themselves as being forced by society and parents to marry very old men. They not only report many more marriages of young girls to men over 55, but give figures of 70, 75, 80, and even 85 in one case, for the age of their first, and sometimes second, husband. In no case do men ever report marrying anyone when they are 70 or over.

Thus the disparities in reporting by both sexes imply the same ethnographic fact. It is culturally valued for men to marry young women—no matter what age the men happen to be. This is not possible in all cases, and men therefore tend to "forget" or not report cases which do not approximate to the norm. Women make the same point when they underestimate marriages between young people of the same age relative to men, and see many men, especially older men, achieving the cultural value of marriage with young girls. The women are also in effect complaining—that for them early marriages often involve unpleasant unions with old men contracted because at that age they had little or no say in the matter.

Types of Marriage Inception

Girl-Marriage and Woman-Marriage. To the Kanuri the most important distinction in types of marriage is that between marriage with a girl who has never been married before (*fero*) as opposed to marriage with a divorced woman (*zower*). The first is referred to as *nyia ferobe* (marriage to a girl), while the second is called *nyia kamube* (marriage to a woman). Marriage with a *fero* or previously unmarried girl is more highly valued, and there is a cultural expectation that first marriages for young men should if possible be of this type. Indeed, all high status men report having carried out this expectation in their first marriage. The reason why such unions are more highly valued, especially for first marriages, are complex and will be considered later in the discussion on marriage ceremonies and the role of husband and wife.

In our entire sample of marriages reported by men (N=504), the greatest bulk of marriages (60%) are with previously married women. On the other hand, men report that 71% of their *first* marriages were with previously unmarried girls, while 29% were with divorced women, and there are no significant differences between rural and urban men on this point. On the other hand, urban men report that 34% of their subsequent marriages are also with previously unmarried girls, while rural men claim only 17% of their subsequent marriages are of this type.[2] This would give a figure of 19% for the entire population when corrected for rural-urban sampling biases. These differences can be accounted for by several factors. Urban men are in general wealthier than their rural counterparts and can therefore afford the more expensive and desirable unions with previously unmarried girls. However, the differences per man are not so large as these figures indicate, since our sample contains a few very wealthy men who have married many times. When some attempt is made to control for socio-economic status, the city man still marries previously unmarried girls more often than his country cousin, but the figures are much closer (25% for urban and 17% for rural men).

Although all Kanuri marriages can be classified into girl-marriage or woman-marriage there is a sub-category that describes a somewhat interstitial condition. This is called *njim suri* (she has seen the hut) meaning she is a young girl who has been in a man's (her husband's) sleeping hut but is still untrained into full womanly maturity. With girls marrying very young, it is possible at times to have divorced women in their early or mid-teens. These are technically *zower* or divorced women, but because of their inexperience they are often referred to by the special term *njim suri*. Such girls are highly valued because of their youth and beauty which is generally considered more attractive than previously unmarried girls who have not yet developed physically. Unfortunately the *njim suri* category was not included in the questionnaire. However, if we operationalize the term by saying it refers to all marriages with previously married girls seventeen and under who have had only one previous husband, then 17% of the marriages with divorced women are *njim suri*.

Ethnographic data from participant observation tend for the most part to substantiate these quantitative materials, except that the impression is gained that the numbers of men who marry previously unmarried girls at their first marriage is not quite so high as is reported on in the formal interview situation. Informants claim that a young man should have permission from his family and/or the head of the household he is living in at the time. These people invariably would like to have him contract a girl-marriage rather than a woman-marriage for his first union. However, this involves a much more expensive wedding and they often ask him to wait. The following case from field notes illustrates the kinds of factors that enter into such a decision.

> Momadu wanted a wife because he was living in a village away from his own cognatic kin where he was a stranger. He was eating at the house of a married villager and he was disturbed and ashamed about it. He felt that this made him obligated to the villager and he wanted very much to have his own wife to cook food for him so that he would be beholden to no one. He

sent a message secretly to his mother to ask if the family (cognates) would help him to obtain a wife. His mother sent word that the family would help but he must be patient and wait until they had enough money to carry out a girl-marriage. Momadu decided to reject this advice and told his mother he was going to marry Palmatta who had grown up with him in the same village. They were the same age (late teens) and Palmatta had recently divorced her first husband. The family discussed this idea, and through the mother sent word that they would give permission for the marriage, but refused to contribute in any way to the marriage expenses because they wanted Momadu to wait and marry a *fero* when they could afford it.

According to Momadu, his mother came to visit him secretly and gave him part (approximately one-fifth) of the new clothing to be included in the bridewealth. The entire wedding and bridewealth cost five pounds as opposed to five or six times that amount had he married a *fero*.

Other informants say that it is unusual for a family to refuse to cooperate when the young man decides not to wait for a girl-marriage, but all admit to experiencing such family pressure. The pressure to obtain a wife for her cooking services as in the case above, however, is a very strong counter force. In discussing this point among a group of young Kanuri friends, I asked each one to count up the number of men they knew who had married for the first time in the last two years. Among four in the group, they could remember eight to fourteen cases each, and figures varied from 40% to 60% for marriage with a *fero* which is a good deal lower than the results of survey interviewing. I interpret this to mean that many men have either forgotten, or do not wish to remember, that they did not marry a *fero* at their first marriage. Thus the cultural expectation has interfered with objective reporting. Another possible interpretation would be that *both* the quantitative and qualtitative materials are correct and that times have changed so that young men today are marrying *fero* less often for their first marriages. However, if this were so, then the incidence in the survey data would decline among young men when they are compared to older ones, which is not borne out by the results.

Charity Marriage. Another type of marriage, almost always performed with a *fero*, is called *nyia sada'abe* or marriage of charity. In such a union, most of the bridewealth and other marriage expenses are waived and the girl is given to the husband by those having authority over her marriage dispensation rights. In most cases, these marriages are with *mallams* or religious practitioners, and the marriage is considered an act of charity by the girl's family bringing honor upon the family. Or again, a man may wish to express his gratitude to a *mallam* for supernatural aid having to do with medicine, prayers, or divination used by the practitioner for the benefit of the group bestowing the girl. In the same way, most individuals having power to bestow a girl would hesitate before refusing the request of a *mallam* because of the general awe in which he and his supernatural powers are held in the public eye. This is also a reason for *not* giving girls to *mallams*. For if anything should go wrong with the marriage and produce dissatisfaction on the part of the *mallam*, his powers of retaliation are very great.

This does not mean that *mallams* receive all their wives through charity. One informant who was a *mallam* lived in a rural village. He farmed, wrote charms for the villagers, and officiated in a minor way at ceremonies in the village. He had been married six times. Of these only one had been a marriage of charity. He said he preferred to obtain his wives like other men; then he would owe no special obligations unless he specifically wished to create them.

The phrase "marriage of charity" can also be used to describe non-cousin marriages in which the family, usually through a senior male (*luwali*), who has marriage dispensation rights over a girl, gives her to one of his clients or apprentices. Since the senior male supports the client economically and is expected to contribute a large portion of the marriage expenses, the payments are often waived and the union is described as a marriage of charity. In terms of over-all social relations, this also strengthens the client-patron relationship by making the patron a father-in-law to this subordinate.

The reported frequency of such unions vary by sex. Women report that 13% of their unions were of this type, while men claim that only 2% of their marriages fall into this category. All of these latter cases except one were reported by men whose occupation was *mallam* or religious practitioner. Such disparity indicates a systematic variation by sex. Men marry about twice as often as women. This means that if these figures are accurate for men, then the women should report approximately 4%; if they are accurate for women then the men should be reporting about

6½% of their unions to be marriages of charity. That this is not the case means that there is under-reporting by men, over-reporting by women, or both. The disparity between the sexes can be explained in terms of attitudes toward bridewealth and independence in marital choices. Women generally feel that they have been ill-used by a society that forces them into their first marriage with very little personal choice on their part. Their reporting therefore of marriages of charity are weighted toward some exaggeration which is located at the time of their first unions. This is especially true when it is realized that few women know very much at all about the terms of their first marriage. However, these respondents were firm in their conviction that they had experienced these marriages of charity. Men, on the other hand, wish to feel, and have others believe them to be, capable of obtaining their own wives. Therefore, I would expect them to "forget" or not mention marriages of charity as often as they really do occur.

Cousin Marriage. Cousin marriage (*nyia durbe*: literally, kin marriage) among the Kanuri is considered "a good thing to do." Cross and parallel patrilateral, and cross cousins on the matrilateral side (especially the patrilaterals), are preferred mates. As noted above, it is considered wrong or inappropriate for ego to marry his (or her) mother's sister's children, but this involves some special problems of interpretation. Informants say that cousin marriage is a good thing to do because such marriages keep a family close together and cannot, especially on the patrilateral side, disburse the inheritable wealth through bridewealth payments to other unrelated kin groups. Other informants say that such a marriage is a good thing because the girl is your *kerami* (younger sibling or cousin). Therefore, she can never tell strangers embarrassing things about you or complain about you outside your own kinship group. The people she is most intimate with are your relatives too. Thus intimate personal affairs are kept within one's own group, at least more so than when marrying a non-cousin. The idea of maintaining close relations to kin through cousin marriage not only involves using kin as affines but also dropping or weakening in-law avoidance. As one informant put it: "My father must never enter a hut alone with my wife. But now because my wife is his brother's daughter he can do so." In other words, both the quantity and quality of interaction changes to greater frequency and more intimacy and friendliness when marriage occurs within the kin group.

It is generally accepted that only one of a man's marriages should be with a cousin, although a few cases of men marrying more than one do occur. However, it is prohibited to marry more than one cousin at any one time. This is the same, to the Kanuri, as sororal polygny which is proscribed because of their belief that such a marriage would involve the sororate, i.e., a desire for the death of the older "sibling" among the wives. The fact that cousins could be taken from patrilateral and matrilateral sides and therefore not be classificatory or real siblings to one another is beside the point, say the Kanuri, because all girl cousins are still "sisters" to the man even if not to one another.

The traditional method of contracting a cousin marriage involves very little bridewealth because it is all within the family. This is more applicable to patrilateral cousins than matrilateral ones, although the norm affects both. This is still very much the custom in such marriages today. Cousin marriages can be contracted at any time, even at the time of the boy's circumcision. When the "coming out" ceremony is held after fourteen days of seclusion, the young man can ask an uncle or aunt for their daughter as his promised future wife. One informant described the ceremony in the following terms:

> When I was *kaja* (circumcised) the girl was given to me. She was only eighteen or nineteen months old at the time and had been weaned about one month. . . .My father's younger brother came and said, "Stand up!" We were thirty-five *kaja* boys at the time. . . .My father's mother was sitting very close to me; she had raised me as a child. She said, "Do not stand up for your father's younger brother unless he gives you his girl." All my kin and the friends of our family came and brought many gifts. Then my father's younger brother came and put two pounds in my pocket, and said "Stand up!" and I said to him, "No, you must finish our custom." After a while he said to me, "I give my girl Palmatta to you." Then my father's mother said, "We agree, and she is now our girl."

The informant said that his uncle really did not wish to give the girl away, but was forced to do so by custom. This now meant that all possibilities of using his daughter's first marriages for his own personal advancement were now out of the question for the uncle. It is no wonder, then, that under 10% of all cousin marriages are contracted in this way. The rest are carried out by mutual consent of the parties involved.

The frequency of cousin marriage is low in relation to all marriages, but significant in terms of numbers of people who have practiced the custom. In our sample of 216 men and women who have married 741 times, there are 37 cousin marriages. In other words, 5% of all marriages and 17% of all persons are involved in such unions.[3] These data were collected in the 1960's using a questionnaire. Genealogical material collected in the 1950's (Cohen 1960) yield almost exactly the same figures (approximately 5% of all marriages and 20%-25% of all persons). There are no significant differences by sex or by rural urban residence. Table 6:3 shows the types of marriages involved, indicating that most cousin marriages are first marriages for both parties, although cases occur where one or both partners is not marrying for the first time. The very rare form is that where the male cousin is previously unmarried but the female cousin is a divorced woman.

TABLE 6:3. PRIMARY AND SUBSEQUENT MARRIAGE AMONG COUSINS

Female Cousins	Male Cousins		
	Previously Unmarried	Previously Married	Totals
Previously Unmarried	20	8	28
Previously Married	1	9	10
Totals	21	17	38

The type of relative chosen for cousin marriage indicates that most such marriages are with first cousins. Thus 29 (78%) of all cousin marriages are with children of ego's parents' full or half siblings, while only eight (22%) are with grandchildren of ego's grandparents siblings or half siblings. In a majority of cases, the sibling link creating the cousin relationship is a full sibling relation, while in other cases (with one exception), the half sibling relationship creating the cousins is same father but different mother. In other words, in 36 of 37 cases the cousins are linked in some way through a male. In the one exception, a male married his mother's half brother's (same mother) daughter. The ultimate link here is a woman. However, the informant claimed the union was within sanctioned range because the relationship had to go through a male (i.e., mother's half brother). Others disagreed, however, and said this marriage, even though it was with a "mother's brother's daughter," was shameful because ultimately the relationship went back to a common woman. The point is made more strongly if we examine the ten cases of marriage with a daughter of Ego's mother's sister. By custom this is the one type of cousin marriage to be avoided yet 10 out of 16 matrilateral cousins turned out to be of this type. On closer examination, however, *all* of these turn out to be only one of two varieties. In the first variety, ego and his cousin are ultimately linked through a male. Thus ego's mother and her "sister" are really cousins linked by a male as in Figure 6:2(a), or Ego's mother and her "sister" are half sisters with the same father *but different* mothers as shown in Figure 6:2(b). This means, say informants, that ultimately the two cousins are not joined through a common breast. It turns out, therefore, that although many people can be called by the term mother's sister, only the cousin relationships diagrammed in Figure 6:2(c) are truly proscribed and avoided in practice. These include mother's full sister's daughter, mother's mother's daughter's daughter, and mother's half sister's (same mother) daughter. More than any other ethnographic material on the Kanuri, these data indicate how difficult it is to correlate behavior with kin terms. To speak in Kanuri using only the kin category, mother's sister's daughter will elicit answers showing that marriages with the cousin should be avoided. Yet marriages with a person of this designation do occur. The reason is simple, yet important. The Kanuri do not think of relationships as being defined by role terms alone. Indeed the role term is a minor quality. *What is the basis for the relationship?* That is the important question. Applied to cousin marriage, this means that they ask immediately how any particular cousin is linked to ego and it is that ultimate

6:2 (a) *Ego married mother's patrilateral female's cousin's daughter*

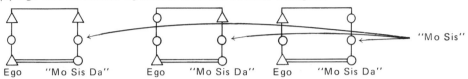

6:2 (b) *Ego marries mother's half sister's daughter (same father)*

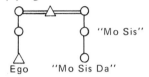

6:2 (c) *Ego's prohibited cousins*

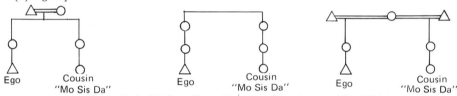

Figure 6:2. Mother Sister Daughter Marriage and Prohibition.

link that defined whether or not marriage is allowable, rather than the kin term applied to this particular cousin.

Theoretically, it is interesting to note here that two types of data both tell a story but neither is precise. Informants state the rule that one must not marry a mother's sister's daughter. In fact, cousins who are not married are mother's sister's daughters, terminologically—but statistically, some men do marry cousins to whom this term can be applied. The rules as given and the practice are thus in contradiction. But, we can create a generalization that does predict or "generate" both the culturally stated rule and its observed representation. This is as follows: ego (male speaking) can and does marry any cousin whose genealogical link to him goes through a male. The Kanuri say it by putting a hand on their breast, meaning that Ego must not marry a cousin whose apical relationship to himself goes back to the same female, i.e., whose ancestors nursed at the same breast.

If cousin marriage is preferred ("a good thing to do") then we must ask why 74% of all persons interviewed had never contracted such a marriage. Informants explain this by saying that cousin marriage restricts the independence of the married couple, especially the husband. The wife's relatives are also those of the husband; if there are difficulties leading possibly to a divorce, then the relatives enter the scene to patch up the differences and scold the husband for not being gentle and patient with his little "sister." In-law avoidance which draws a man to his wife, and she to him, as a social unit set apart from their own descent groups is much weakened in such a union, making it more difficult for a man to gain any independence from such a marriage. Men often went further and said that cousin marriage should be avoided because it is more difficult to divorce such wives, even when they are badly behaved.

Sororate and Levirate. The Kanuri know about sororate and levirate marriage and call it *fatoro ngawabe* (literally: he or she goes to his or her home). The cultural meaning can be translated as the younger sibling, real or classificatory, of the same sex, must go to the house of their dead sibling's spouse. This does not mean that an older sibling would not be an adequate replacement, or that there is a rule against such an event. Informants had simply never heard of such a case or thought of such an eventuality; i.e., there is a cultural expectation that a dead spouse's sibling replacement should be younger than the deceased. People explain it as a custom that preserves children within a family. Thus a man can marry his dead brother's wives and take on his nephews and nieces by moving into the dead brother's house, or having the wives and children move into his own house. On such an occasion, only the simplest of ceremonies are performed and no bridewealth is necessary. If, however, the sororate is being practiced and the dead wife's sibling has never married before, then the entire first marriage ceremony must be gone through, except that there must be no drumming or dancing, and bridewealth payments are very small or even nominal. To initiate the sororate, however, the father and mother, or whoever has marriage dispensation rights over the dead wife, must ask the husband to take a younger "sister" as a replacement. In the case of the levirate, the younger brother has the right to demand his brother's wives and children but must seek approval from her and her kin as a matter of proper etiquette and respect.

In practice, I have only heard of one case of levirate marriage. In 1965, a trader in Maiduguri died and his only younger brother moved into his house and took over his wives and several children. The sororate is a trifle more common. Most people can report having heard of two or three cases occurring in the past five years at the time of an interview. One informant remarked that he had had a wife who died and hoped at the time for a sororate union. However, the dead wife's father, who had several young girls (sisters of the dead wife) in his home, did not offer one as a replacement.

The extremely low incidence of the levirate puts it in a category we can label—known, but for all intents and purposes not practiced. This can be explained by referring to inheritance and the ownership of children. Upon divorce or death, the children "belong to," i.e., can be taken by, the husband or his agnates. Only if there is no agnate who wants them can they go to matrilateral kin. Thus if an older brother dies, his younger brother has the right to the children anyway. Thus there is no need to activate the levirate since its purposes are fulfilled by other customs. To take on an older brother's entire family is not a joyful task. Most men prefer to build their families and households as a result of their own decisions and ambitions. Thus, to a man, informants say they would not practice the levirate because it involves too many unwelcome obligations.

In the case of the sororate, the fact that it can only be initiated on the part of the dead wife's father means this man must give up the promise of large bridewealth if the sister is a previously unmarried girl. If she is a divorcee, she has a strong voice in the decision herself and would have to waive bridewealth receipts for herself in order to acquiesce in such a marriage. However, in a few cases, men have reputations for being extremely good husbands. In these instances, given the rather rare chance that all parties can agree, the sororate occurs.

Other Descriptive Categories of Marriage. The above categories are the major forms of marriage among the Kanuri. There are, however, a number of other descriptive expressions referring to varieties of marriage which are less important although they act as qualifiers of the marriage types already referred to. The most important of these is *kulle* or seclusion. In general, all men wish to have their wives remain in the compound as much as possible so that, in real attitudinal and behavioral terms, *kulle* is more a matter of degree than of kind. However, several indicators provide a watershed between one set of conditions and something quite different. If a wife does not sell things in public, and/or does no agricultural work, and/or does not go to the well for water either because others go for her, or because a water source is available inside the compound, then she is in *kulle*. All women leave the compound to go to ceremonies and to visit kin. But, operationally, the Kanuri use the term *kulle* to refer to an obligation to remain inside the household unless permission to leave is granted by the husband. As noted, such unions involve no regular duties outside the compound. Women know before entering a marriage whether any of these conditions will be present or absent and indeed the knowledge is easy because *all* urban marriages are reported as *kulle* and *all* rural unions as *non-kulle*. In all cases, the operational conditions above sort one type from the other.

Other terms used to describe marriage are descriptive of the types of relationships and contractual agreements upon which the marriage inception is based. Thus there are "marriages of wealth" which refer to marriage to a man of great status and especially economic power. From the woman's point of view, this refers to the status of the husband; from the man's point of view, it refers to his wife's relatives or his wife's personal wealth. In either case, the union is viewed as access through marriage to wealth and high status. In one such case, a man of high rank himself married a young previously unmarried girl who was the only heir of a rich old man of lower social rank to himself. The wedding foods and ceremony performed by the girl's relatives were looked upon askance by the groom's relatives and friends. However, all agreed privately that this was a true case of marriage for wealth.

The concept also refers, however, to political marriages. Thus a man in the official Bornu political hierarchy may wish to cement his relationship to some senior office-holder in the system. To do so, he asks for, or is offered, a daughter of the senior man as his wife. Such marriages may be ones of "charity" if the junior man is of very low status or a member of the senior's own household. However, more often the junior wife-receiver is an office holder himself and the wedding is a splendid occasion of great ceremony as the two men unite their households through marriage.

Two other phrases are used to describe ways in which marriages have been contracted with previously married women. The first, *nyia ardiabe* (marriage of agreement) refers to a situation in which the man and the woman have had some agreement or plan to marry and then follow through with it. The concept involves the idea of desire and strong affection between the spouses-to-be which motivates them to act together on their own as opposed to any wishes and desires of others of their friends and kin. As we shall see later on, the Kanuri consider such unions to be foolishly entered upon. For them, marriage is much too important a matter to be initiated and governed by emotional attraction as a dominant consideration.

The phrase *"nyia kolatabe"* (marriage of discovery) refers to the common idea that the man simply needed a wife at the time and came upon this particular woman. He then decided to marry her and began setting up the proper arrangements to do so. As one informant said, "There is no preparation, you just meet the woman somewhere and decide to marry her."

Getting Married

Decision-Making. As in many societies, getting married is a decision involving the spouses and those closely related to them. For the Kanuri, marriage per se is a positive value. It is better to be married than single if a person is of marriageable age. However, for everyone involved in the decision, there are both gains and losses. Each person then assesses these and decides on his or her own position regarding any particular marriage. For the groom, marriage means that he has someone to cook for him. Without such a person, he must eat and/or live in the household of another man, either a kinsman or neighbor. This creates obligation on the eater's part and is one of the operational ingredients in the creation of a patron-client relationship. To have this food-preparing capacity on his own, a man can be more independent and indeed start feeding others, thus creating obligation or social credit rather than expending it. On the other hand, as we have seen, others may wish to delay his marriage simply because they wish to maintain his dependence. In other cases, a man's family may ask him to delay because they cannot as yet afford their contributions to such an expensive ceremony. On the other hand, especially in rural areas, a family may see their son's wedding as an increase in the household's capacity to work. Even if the son moves out, he will still be close by and his new wife will be a new member of the linked group of households formed by a patrilocal pattern of residence association.

From the girl's or woman's point of view, marriage means finding a provider who can take good care of her needs. However, it also means great loss of freedom because the wifely role is so subordinated to that of the husband. Traditionally, all girls should indicate reluctance and even refusal to enter marriage. Not to do so is considered bad manners and interpreted to mean that the girl wishes to leave her kinsfolk. Although compensated by bridewealth, the family is losing a member, and many feel reluctant to consent, especially if the marriage means the girl will be taken far away from her natal family. Furthermore, there is dowry to be obtained, if it has not been prepared for over a long time period, and gifts to the groom. Even though these expenses are not as great as those of the groom, they are considerable and must be discussed, at least for the first marriage of a young girl. More practically, those responsible must also decide whether this is the "best deal" they can get. I have recorded several cases where the family of a young girl has broken off a marriage because they received a better offer from another man. Such cases always produce bad feelings and are avoided if at all possible. However, they are indications of the kinds of discussions that occur before a young girl is married.

The general cultural expectation for first marriages is one in which the close family of each spouse, especially the father, has a major voice in contracting the union. The data indicate that this is almost universally true for girls but only partially so for young men. Informants claim it is important to obtain the consent of the young girl. Indeed, it is said, if she runs away from the house of her new, first, husband three times in the first few weeks of marriage, then the marriage is legally annulled. However, no such instances have been recorded. Instead there are very few cases where consent of the girl is realistically sought; at least this is how women informants report on their own first marriages. The conclusion seems inescapable that young girls are told who they will first marry and most of them comply with this family directive. Young men are older at first marriage and generally more independent. Thus, many of them decide for themselves whom they will marry and then obtain aid, hopefully from their kin, in order to perform the wedding.

However, only part of this distinction is due to age at first marriage. Throughout her marital career, a woman must formally deal with marriage relations to society through a male who represents her interests in the marriage to other members of the male world, including her husband. This role, known as *luwali*, is most often taken by the father of the woman. If he is not alive or present, then a senior male of her cognatic kin group may fulfill the task, although there is a preference for such a person to be an agnate if this is at all possible. In the odd case where the woman has no kin available, a senior male of the household or ward she is living in may take the role and act as *luwali* for this particular union.

In the case of first marriage, the *luwali* is the senior negotiator to whom the would-be groom or his representative must go in order to create the necessary agreements. In cases where I am personally familiar with the details, the *luwali* has had most of the final decision-making power in creating a girl's first marriage. As we shall see, he also receives the bulk of the largest bridewealth payment for this first marriage.

In cases where there is trouble in the marriage, the girl almost invariably returns to the compound of her *luwali*. He and often his agnates appear as representatives of this marriage if adjudication is necessary and it is to him the husband first turns if he wishes to complain to any authority about the marriage.

As a woman goes through successive marriages, the importance of the role of the *luwali* declines. She may discuss it with him indirectly by sending someone to ask his permission or to get his opinion, but the decision comes more and more to be an individual's own choice. Nevertheless, the legal position of the *luwali* is still retained. In the eyes of the community of men, it is he, the *luwali*, who represents this marriage and he must be party therefore to all public negotiations which bear on the interests of the woman. It is important to repeat that in many, indeed most, cases the *luwali* is a senior male agnate of the woman in her role as bride and wife. He and his male agnates then form a corporate group which represents the woman's legal interests in her marriage. Should problems arise which can be settled or negotiated, it is the *luwali* and his group who deal with the husband and his agnates. This does not mean that a matrilateral kinsmen, e.g., a mother's brother, cannot act as *luwali*. I have observed a number of such cases. In these instances he may be joined for legal disputes by the girl's male agnates or his own. However, as already noted it is much the preferred pattern to use agnates for such purposes. This is tied to the idea that for purposes of legal disputation the agnates form a corporate group.

One more point needs emphasis in case the above description sounds too much like similar materials from peoples having unilinear descent groups. For most purposes, indeed nearly all, the *luwali* acts by himself as the male representative of the marriage. Since he is, again in many cases, the father of the wife and father-in-law of the husband, the latter generally deals with his *luwali* through intermediaries because of the shame-avoidance relationship between a man and his father-in-law. Even when a *luwali* is not the father this avoidance generally holds, unless the father-in-law-*luwali* is a relative to the husband (i.e., the union is a cousin marriage).

Premarital Conditions. Questionnaire material on the premarital circumstances of decision-making connected with getting married produced vague answers or avoidance of responses by about half of the male respondents. Women, on the other hand, produced short accounts of how each marriage came to be contracted. In 61% of their marriages, women report that mutual agreement between the bride and groom preceded the union. The 39% where this was not so are all first marriages in which the girl had no voice in the decision. On the other hand, women report that in nearly one-fifth of all their marriages close kin were involved in helping to arrange the union. All of these occur when she is under 25 years of age.

The length of acquaintance before marriage varies from a day or so to "all my life." If we divide these data into a short time (one month or less) and longer time (over one month) then two-thirds of the women's unions are reported to result from shorter acquaintanceships. No matter how these data are divided there is no relationship between type of marriage and length of acquaintanceship except with cousin unions (long acquaintanceship); all marriage varieties are therefore contracted on grounds other than the length of interpersonal relations between spouses prior to marriage.

Sexual relations before first marriage are proscribed for girls. However, some sex play between pre-pubescent boys and girls does take place, especially in "play" marriages in which children enact wedding ceremonies or play house.[7] However, such play must stop for boys when they can ejaculate, i.e., when such activity might lead to conception and possible illegitimacy. Premarital sex relations between a post pubertal man and a previously unmarried girl are generally felt to be rape, and the act is severely punished in the courts. I know of only three such cases in the period 1964-66, all between upper class men and young girls of lower class background. In all cases, the men received jail sentences. The girl's consent has nothing to do with whether the crime was committed—the act itself is the crime because it is her social status as a virgin unmarried girl that has been destroyed. Furthermore, the Kanuri share a wider Islamic view of the weak willpower of girls in matters of chastity. Indeed, in the stories of rape, the man is often credited with having persuaded the girl to act illegally. Thus such acts are viewed as a male crime.

The horror of the act lies in the fact that the girl, although not ever married, cannot go through a first marriage ceremony—in which her virginity is allegedly proven. Furthermore, only very low status persons would consent to marry her—and in all likelihood the wedding would resemble that of a previously married woman—with concomitant lowering of the bridewealth.

The point of view given above is that of the traditional culture in which unmarried girls are generally quite young. A special problem emerges under conditions of girls' secondary level education. These girls are previously unmarried but beyond the age of first marriage. They are seen as physically attractive and sexual activity with them is not seen as rape, albeit it is not sanctioned. Thus part of the seriousness of rape in traditional society is the very young age of the girl, and part of the widespread negative attitudes to post-primary education for girls is the feeling that they are sexually mature and should be married *before* any active sex life begins.

For once-married adults, premarital and extra-marital sexual activity is jurally a fineable offense. However, only adultery with a married woman has a very strong negative sanction against it. In the questionnaire there was no attempt to include premarital sex information. Men do not speak of such things except to close friends. Women, however, began offering the information gratuitously and therefore it was decided to collect data on the incidence and duration of premarital sex from the women. Of the 137 non-first marriages for women, 44 (32%) were reported as having involved premarital sex.[4] Frequency varies from only one act of intercourse to regular occurrences up to a year. Most, but not all, men feel there is nothing seriously wrong with premarital sex in the courting of a divorced woman although a few condemn it as being "against religion" and are vehement in denying they have ever practiced it. A number of women in discussing the subject say that although it is not supposed to happen, one should mistrust a man who does not try, because he may be sexually weak, incompetent, or even impotent, and is using his morality and piety as an excuse to keep such knowledge from a potential wife.

Almost all Kanuri marriages are contracted with a person living in the same locality. Given the data on length of acquaintanceship, this is what one would expect since men generally decide that they wish to marry and then look about them in their own locality for an available spouse. Thus women report that 84% of their marriages occur with husbands who live within five miles, while men say that 76% of their unions are within this perimeter. If we narrow this area to include the same settlement, be it city, village, or hamlet, then men and women both report 73% of their marriages are with spouses living in the same place. However, there are important differences between the rural and urban areas on this point as given in Table 6:4. These differences decline but are still present when the rural village settlement is expanded to include surrounding hamlets which form a marriage deme as well as a political unit. People in a village and its surrounding hamlets (most often under five miles from the village) see themselves as a single community, especially with respect to marriages, marketing, and the adjudication of disputes under the

TABLE 6:4. RURAL AND URBAN ENDOGAMY BY SETTLEMENT SITE*

	Yes	*No*
1. Marriages within same city	82% (272)	18% (60)
2. Marriages within same rural settlement	54% (153)	46% (132)
3. Marriages with same rural deme	71% (214)	29% (85)

*1. & 2.; $X^2 = 57.071$; p $<$ .01   1. & 3.; $X^2 = 11.100$; p $<$ .01

authority of the *Lawan* or village area head man. Nevertheless, although demes as here defined are 71% endogamous, the proximity of outlying hamlets to similar units in the neighboring village area, i.e., the neighboring deme, as well as the lower rural population density (making for fewer available mates), creates significantly more marriages into more distant units in the rural areas. In other words, both rurals and urbans tend to be endogamous, but rurals less so and they therefore go further from home to find a spouse than urbans.

If we forgot about local endogamy and exogamy and view rural and urban marriage as sub-variants of Kanuri marital unions, another kind of strong preference is shown. Urban marriages require no agricultural work and the wife is in much greater seclusion than her rural counterpart. In general, 90% of all unions are between spouses who are both urban, or both rural (93% for women; 88% for men). In those few (63) cases in which rurals and urbans marry one another, there are measurable differences by sex of respondent. Most (73%) of these mixed rural-urban marriages are practiced by men, and of this 73% (46 cases) nearly all are practiced by urban men importing wives from rural areas. Although this is only 11% of all male reported marriages, it means that men are aiding urbanization through their marriage practices. It also means that very few rural men ever marry urban women. Women, on the other hand, report almost the reverse situation, although there are very few cases (17) of exogamy in the 237 reported on by women. Most of these (11/17) are between urban women and rural men. Women are thus generally reluctant to move from rural to urban settings or vice versa and they say so. But urban men require more wives and so try to find girls or women in rural areas for about 11% of their unions. The ethnographic interpretation here is that with marriage being patrilocal and virilocal, it is women who must change the most in these mixed rural-urban unions. Their families are also loath to see them move far away. Thus the woman or girl and her family are not in favor of her marrying out of her locality. Men do not have this problem and therefore tend to find it easier to marry non-locals.

In discussing a spouse's previous marital record with informants, there is fairly wide agreement that one should if possible avoid marriage with women who have been married a great many times, since their propensity to divorce is high. Informants also claim that one should pay less bride-wealth for a woman "who has been used many times." The relation of previous marital record to divorce and bridewealth will be discussed later. Here, as shown in Table 6:5, it is sufficient to say that exact reporting on spouse's previous marital record is widespread although much less so for men. Thus in 37% of the unions reported by men to be with previously married women, men did not know (or did not wish to say) how many times the woman was previously married. Women, on the other hand, report easily and fully on a husband's previous marriages. In the case of the men, some of this 37% is undoubtedly valid. Many men do marry quite precipitously and never really discuss the women's marital history with her or anyone else. On the other hand, it is somewhat shameful to take a much married women so that men are probably not reporting all instances that have in fact occurred. There is little if any stigma in marrying a man of many marriages, quite the reverse if he happens to be rich and can therefore marry as often as he likes. Thus women have no reason to suppress such information to themselves or to others.

Supernatural Aids. In one case a man reported that one of his marriages was initiated by supernatural means. He was 38 at the time, living in a rural village with two other wives. According

TABLE 6:5. PREVIOUS MARITAL RECORD OF SPOUSES

Number of Previous Marriages	Men Reporting On Wives	Women Reporting On Husbands
0	205	71
1	90	53
2	47	43
3	26	22
4	13	12
5	5	10
6	1	4
7	0	2
8	0	4
9 and over	5	11
Previously married but number of times unknown	112	22
Totals	504	237

to the man, a woman of 25 who had been married "many many" times before took some earth from a place where he had sat on the ground. She then gave the earth to a *mallam* who prayed over it. He was then compelled by supernatural powers to marry this woman, even though he did not really wish to propose to her. The *mallam* discussed the affair with him before the marriage and told the husband that it would be a good thing to marry this particular woman—because it would bring the husband much good luck. The respondent claims the *mallam* did not tell him of the magic spell—that he found out from "someone else." Whatever the exact circumstances, he felt compelled to marry the woman for fear of the supernatural consequences if he did not heed the *mallam*'s advice. From a male point of view, the only cases I have ever recorded of supernatural aids have been "love potions" used by men to obtain the affection of a divorced woman. In these few cases, seduction rather than marriage was the basic intent.

Supernatural aid in getting married, then, is generally quite rare although techniques are known. For women these involve having the man ask her to marry him; for men the goal is one of obtaining sexual intercourse from which marriage may or may not result. The important point to be made here is that in actual practice the use of such techniques is statistically infrequent. As we have seen in this chapter, marriage inception is frequent and easy in Bornu for those of marriageable age, and practically no one is ever left out. The need for supernatural aid is therefore negligible and, as would be expected under these conditions, it is rarely practiced.

In summary, marriage inception in Bornu is a complex process above and beyond the necessary prestations and rituals associated with it that are dealt with in the next chapter. A number of factors such as age, sex, rural-urban residence, kinship, number of previous marriages, socio-economic status, and personal choice enter in to vary the type of relationship being established. Out of this amalgam of forces, Kanuri cultural experience has crystallized a set of specific marriage types. Each of these require somewhat differing modes of inception and represent different proportions of some or all of the determining variables. Thus zero versus all other numbers of previous marriages for the bride means a totally different kind of marriage; being a *mallam* or religious teacher means one can expect the possibility of a marriage of charity; being in a rural area generally rules out a marriage of seclusion for the wife; being over forty-five means a woman will probably not remarry; being one kind of cousin versus another means one can or cannot marry a particular cousin. When Kanuri discuss an upcoming marriage among themselves, the various sub-topics of this chapter serve as a check list of questions about the marriage that can be asked in order to identify what kind of relationship is being established—and what is its basis. For, as we were able to see most clearly with cousin marriages, it is the basis of the relationship that matters to the Kanuri not the term by which it is known. When questions concerning the relationship being established are complete, then a marriage is located among a culturally defined spectrum of possibilities. Within the spectrum, names or terms such as "girl-marriage," "marriage of charity," "woman marriage," "marriage of seclusion," and others are attached to constellation attributes which identify the kind of marriage being created.

For our present purposes, besides the ethnographic value of understanding marriage inception itself, it is also important to notice that earlier marriages, especially for girls, involve very little freedom of choice. Men who have authority over the marriage decisions negotiate the details of the union-to-be with the husband-to-be and his group, and then pass their authority over to the husband. Problems over the marriage, both before and after the wedding, are dealt with between men—her husband and the man among her male kin who represents her interests (*luwali*). However, as we shall see, when a woman goes through successive marriages and divorces she takes a progressively more active part in the decision-making and she keeps and/or dispenses the bride-wealth herself. Thus, increased numbers of divorces not only indicate a set of unstable unions, but they also create and support a system of increasing independence and less subservience for a woman to her husband and male kin who earlier in her life have almost full control of her social roles in the society.

Chapter 7
Dramas of Dominance: Kanuri Marriage Rituals

As in all *rites de passage*, marriage involves change. These changes may be within the person as it is at first marriage when the person moves from previously unmarried to married status in the community. Or it may also stem from the fact that marriage, like death or birth, changes the relations of persons to one another because a qualitatively new set of social alignments have now been created.

Bornu marriage rituals portray in symbolic form the collective perception and accumulated understanding that the people of Bornu have developed concerning marriage and the relationship of husbands and wives to one another. In this sense, I regard ritual as a form of art or expression which brings together in symbolic form the central features of the institution being celebrated by ceremonial. And the most salient point for this study of Kanuri marriage is the presence in these rituals of a recognition of the tension that exists in marriage concerning the dominance of the husband.

In general, the Kanuri wedding ceremony is strongly determined by the type of marriage being initiated. The most elaborate ceremonies are performed for the marriage of girls who have never married before. Thus a man may have several very elaborate weddings, one for each of the previously unmarried girls he weds. For a girl, such weddings occur only once in a lifetime, unless her first marriage is unconsummated. Later weddings after the first one, and marriages of charity, are much less elaborate, although even a marriage of charity when it is the first one for the girl requires much more elaborate ceremonial. The same is true of cousin marriage. Thus the basis ceremonial distinction concerning the bride's previous marital status cuts across all other types of marriages. In this, it reflects the fundamental importance of this distinction for the society as a whole. Indeed, in ordinary conversation, if two friends are speaking about a wedding, the first and most important criterion for understanding what sort of event is being discussed is obtained by asking simply, "*Fero gwojin?*" ("Is he taking a girl?"). This poses the question immediately, "Is it a wedding involving first marriage for a girl?" or (by implication) "*Kamu gwojin?*" ("Is he taking a woman?"). Once the answer to this question is known, the type of ceremony being planned is understood and the nature of one's own obligations (if any) are clearer.

The Virgin Wedding

At the outset, it is important to note that Kanuri ceremonies are modular. This means that parts can be attached and detached with varying amounts of ease. Ultimately there is a core that is essential, but beyond that there are options which form the basis for decision-making by those in charge of carrying out the activity. The most elaborate ceremonies are carried out by the upper classes who can afford the expense of these "extras."

The first part of the virgin wedding is one of these optional features not often mentioned by people reporting on their own weddings. In order to initiate the wedding discussions, a gift is sent to the parents of the girl and her *luwali* if he is a different person. This is called *ragaski* (literally: "I like or desire" meaning here a declaration of intention). The girl is generally not consulted. Instead, the fathers of the boy and girl come together accompanied sometimes by the senior male agnates on both sides. If the girl's people, and especially her *luwali*, decide they do not wish to go ahead, the matter ends at this point. The gift is a small one and is not returnable. In other cases a delegation arrives, or just the boy's father, or a messenger bearing a few kola nuts, and if the marriage is acceptable a date is set for the first formal meeting. Whether the first occasion is termed *ragəski* and is included or not the agreement at this first initial contact makes the boy and the girl *təmaji* (promised or affianced). In those situations where the girl was promised to someone much earlier in her life, a messenger (relative or friend) goes to the family to arrange for a formal meeting.

In the few cases where the girl herself is asked about the marriage, it is handled differently depending upon the age of the groom. With a young groom his friends speak to the girl's friends and they to the girl and a meeting between the boy and girl is arranged after which an approach is made to the parents. This method is favored in the city and among those with Western education. An older man sends for the girl and asks her. He may also wish to see her and watch her behave before he enters into negotiations with her parents or he may watch her at play and send her a message. How much power the little girl has in such a situation is extremely hard to say. Canons of good behavior demand that she, as a child, be polite and compliant with her parents' wishes and those of older people in general. Most women interviewed claim they had little or no say at all in the choice of their first husband.

The first formal meeting is known as the *kwororam* (the asking questions fee). A party of the groom's male relatives and friends go to the household of the girl and confer with her *luwali* and/or her father, depending upon whether these roles are held by the same or different people. Money, clothes, mats, blankets, and other valuables are brought as gifts. *Kwororam* expenses vary from two to three pounds in rural areas, to four or five in the city, although gifts and money totaling twenty to thirty pounds are not unknown. The gifts are given to the father and mother of the bride, the *luwali* if he is not the father, and close cognatic relatives who are present. In general, however, agnates form the majority. A small present is also included for the girl herself; perfume, soap, or a new item of clothing may be specifically purchased for the bride. The marriage is now seriously discussed. Of special concern are the major bridewealth payments and the date of the wedding. The period between this meeting and the wedding day now runs between two to three weeks, although it can run as long as a year, and all informants agree that it used to be longer.

The meeting is formal because there are witnesses—all men. The parents of the girl give these men a small token of money as a *shadaram* or witness fee and prayers are said to close the meeting. Under such conditions, a legally binding contract is entered into by both parties, and in front of witnesses. If something goes wrong, no matter where the fault lies, the *kwororam* payments must be returned to undo the obligation. Often the groom accepts return of only part and leaves the rest as a token that there are no bad feelings—however, there is no compulsion to do so even though it is as one informant put it "a gentlemanly thing to do."

Bargaining between the groom's and the bride's party is very polite, but each side tries to obtain a good contract and to impress upon the other side (a) what they can expect in the way of immediate benefits and (b) how expensive and burdensome the rest of the wedding cost will be, making the overall outlay very much greater than had been expected. Thus the bride's people (the *luwali* and male relatives) suggest that the groom will get many gifts in return from them which they have already planned for. They argue in turn that there is need of bridewealth money to finance these costs as well as the very fancy wedding foods which must be brought and prepared. The groom's party indicates how many pressures there are to make the groom's part of the ceremony expand into very costly performances. Women on both sides may want many drummer entertainers, while the groom had planned and budgeted for only one. The major item here, however, is the *luwaliram* which is the largest payment by the groom and his group to the *luwali* of the girl. Formally, this is *the* brideprice and should be paid before the wedding can take place. When all the bargaining is completed and a mutually satisfying set of arrangements is agreed upon, preparations begin for the actual wedding ceremony.

Between the *kwororam* meeting and the wedding, the groom usually sends small presents to the girl and her close household relatives. In this period as well, he appoints his "best man" and "best woman." The best man or *soba kura* (chief friend) will act as his chief intermediary in making all arrangements with religious practitioners and other community members, as well as with the girl's male relatives, especially her *luwali*. Both of these persons also arrange for messages to be sent to all relatives and friends of the groom telling the date and place of the wedding. Today in the city, this often means having invitations printed which are then sent out by messenger. The best man also arranges for the means of conveying the girl from her house to the groom's. In rural areas, conveyance is by horse or camel. In the city, it is almost customary today to rent a car. The best man must also arrange for a special ceremony (the *kolawa*) to be performed if this is the first wedding of the groom to a previously unmarried girl. The "best woman," usually a senior female relative, often a father's sister, acts as his intermediary with the women participants. The reason given for these aides is that the groom must maintain calm good relations during this period. To carry out all of the necessary negotiations himself could easily produce conflict on his part which might adversely affect the orderly progression of events leading to the completion of the marriage ceremony.

The day before the actual wedding, a series of ceremonies are performed. By this time, relatives from other villages have arrived and an air of festivity and preparation can be detected in both households. Early in the morning on the pre-wedding day, separately, but at both the boy's house and the girl's (for first weddings), the female relatives gather around a large calabash filled with water in which a smaller one is floating. The women beat the smaller calabash with sticks in rhythm while singing songs of praises to the parents. The bride or groom is referred to as a "monkey" and the ceremony is referred to as *da'al bota* (monkey calling). The implication here is that the bride and/or groom are like monkeys—they can only imitate what they see but have not the experience to act in expected ways. At the groom's house, they emphasize his authority and tell him he must be strong and properly control his wife. If not, she will control him and he will not learn how to be a proper husband. If he does learn this, he will be attractive and popular to her and to all women. At the girl's house, her female relatives tell her to be a good obedient wife who, for example, should not eat the meat from her husband's soup while preparing it. She is also told to respect and behave properly to the boy's parents and senior relatives. Thus both ceremonies emphasize the subordination of the wife. Interestingly, the boy's ceremony is performed, or should be, very early—before the one at the bride's compound. It is said that if the ceremony is held first at the bride's house she, and not he, will be the stronger authority in the marriage, and she, rather than he, will become more popular and attractive to the opposite sex.

This piece of lore and others like it always bring a smile to informants when they are asked about it.[1] And stories of henpecked husbands can be gathered in this context. The symbolism here connotes the social reality. Male authority and dominance are expected—their achievement, however, is not an automatic consequence of marriage.

In the afternoon at the bride's house, a new mat is brought by the mother of the girl or the woman who had the most to do with her upbringing. She is given a new set of clothes and henna is brought to dye her hands. The mat is lifted up into the air seven times and then the girl sits on it. The women of the girl's family then dip pennies in okra and henna and throw the pennies into a bowl of water over which the girl cups her hands. Then henna and okra are daubed on her hands and feet to bless her and her future life as a married woman. The girl cries all this while (it is rude not to) because she is leaving her home. The women tell her not to be sad for she is now going to be married. The ceremony dramatizes the difficulties involved in leaving home. She is still a very young girl and is facing an entirely new set of primary social relationships as well as the intimacies and obligations of married life.

Among wealthy people, in the evening before the wedding day, a ceremony called *betu* (advice) can be carried out. Praisesingers gather at the house of the girl. She remains inside or sometimes comes out heavily veiled to sit on a mat. The groom and his friends attend as well, and sit on mats, giving money liberally to the praisesingers, as does the father of the bride in his role as *luwali*. The singers remain all night singing advice on the proper behavior of spouses to one another.

More commonly, another advice ceremony takes place at the girl's household. The female relatives of the girl put a small calabash into a large one filled with water (as in the monkey-calling ceremony performed early in the morning). A brass pestle is also placed on the ground. Women beat the calabash and the pestle while singing songs of advice to the bride. These songs repeat over and over again the wife's role of obedience, but emphasize as well that she must not swear on the Koran (take an oath) to her husband because leprosy results if such oaths are broken.[2] The implication here is that wives very often must lie to their husbands and this practical necessity of the role should be recognized.

During these ceremonies, the young bride sits on a mat and her hands are dyed red in henna—a cosmetic practice among Kanuri women (men dye their hands blue). Young girl friends of the bride go to the groom's house and sell some of the henna to him. The symbolism here can be interpreted to mean that, whereas he did not need to make such purchases before, now as a married man he will have to supply his wife with her requirements. These young age-mates of the bride will also stay with her for a week after the wedding and they use this money to defray expenses. Primarily, however, this little ceremony symbolizes the change to come in the young man's life. Women as wives have special needs. Before marriage, these were looked after by her own descent group; now her husband should take on this responsibility.

Early the next morning, the formal wedding ceremony begins. Those related to each side gather at the household of the bride and groom. Often, especially in rural areas, both parties gather at the entrance to the village head's compound. The groom does not attend nor do the women of his household, but he is represented by a senior agnate referred to as his *luwali*. If the ceremony is not at a political leader's gates, the groom's party moves to the girl's household. When the two parties of men are together, either in front of a political leader's household or the girl's, the head of the *mallams* who have come to officiate asks for the *luwali* of the girl and of the boy. He then asks the boy's representative, "What do you want here, why have you come?" and the answer is made, "I have come for the girl." The *mallam* then turns to the *luwali* of the girl saying, "Do you wish to give your girl to him?" "Yes," answers the girl's *luwali* who is then asked, "What is this girl's *sada'ə* (wedding fee)"? And the answer is made, usually in *gursu* (= 5/- per *gursu*),[3] as was agreed upon at the *kwororam* meeting. Because many new unpredicted expenses may have occurred, a little gentle bargaining may go on, but it is over quickly. The *mallam* announces the name of the girl, the boy, and the amount of the *sada'ə* to all those assembled so they may be witnesses to the proceedings.[4] Prayers are said and the women inside the compound ululate to celebrate the creation of the legal bond. The *sada'ə* payment is a relatively small one and is by tradition always given to the bride herself, or her *luwali* asks her what she would like to buy with it and then purchases it for her.

Sometimes the entire *luwaliram* payment is not fully paid by the date of the wedding. Under such circumstances, the wedding can be put off, or cancelled, and the bridewealth already paid should then be returned. More common, however, is the practice of having the *mallam* announce at the wedding that such and such a *luwaliram* was promised, and a portion of it is still owing. Men informants say this sort of thing rarely happens; women informants say it happens quite often. It is as if the women are complaining that they are often short-changed, and the men are saying that they always honor their obligations.

Either before or after this *sada'ə* ceremony, the Kanuri ceremonial reciprocity custom (*nzaye*) is carried out. I have described this in detail elsewhere (Cohen 1965) so that a summary is sufficient here. Friends and relatives of a man or woman giving a ceremony come and make contributions to help defray the cost of the ceremony and to dramatize their reciprocal membership in a social network. Such a ceremony is quietly held at the groom's house, and outside the bride's house a quiet *nzaye* is carried out for the father of the bride. Inside the bride's household, a more elaborate *nzaye* takes place for the mother of the bride. This is explained as compensation to the mother for having contributed and worked to obtain the girl's dowry. Realistically, the girl's father has also contributed, but over the years the mother has saved and scrimped for this large outlay for mats, pots, jewelry, etc. Often, even the girl herself has been made to go out as a young child and sell cooked foods in order to save the money necessary for this expenditure.

At the groom's house, the best man and woman oversee the sending of the final gift to the girl and her family. This is officially seen as a gift by the groom's parents to the girl's people. Added to this today is a payment of several pounds for the girl herself, the *feroram*, which used to be paid to the girl on the wedding night and still is in many rural areas. The best man and woman then lead a party over to the bride's house where these gifts are given over to the girl's parents.

Then, at the bride's house, there is a heated and detailed discussion by the *luwali* and all of the other relatives concerning the entire bridewealth. How much was the *luwaliram*; how many other things have they received? How much should go back as a gift to the groom; how much goes to the *luwali*, and to all other relatives in attendance? Traditionally the *luwali* kept the largest portion for himself and distributed the rest. After this, men of the bride's house take over the special wedding gift (*fəfari*) to the groom. The best man then receives it in front of witnesses and gives a small gift to the men who brought the gifts as a *kəngayamram* (gift to a bringer of gifts). The groom, through his best man, then distributes some of these "groom's gifts" to his male agnates, usually trying to keep the majority for himself in order to allay personal expenses incurred by the marriage.

Tensions and difficulties can, however, occur. Thus one informant, after going into serious debt over marriage with a previously unmarried girl, received about half of the groom's gifts he had hoped for. Included in the gift was a horse. But his older brother who had helped him a great deal in life had no horse and demanded it. The informant complied but went even further into debt because he had been counting on selling the horse to pay off some of the marriage expenses.

In the afternoon at the girl's house, a *kolawa* ceremony is performed. Both the bride and groom, on the occasion of first marriage to a previously unmarried spouse, carry out the *kolawa* in the afternoon of the next day (after consummation). Thus the *kolawa* ("to be matured") is a *rite de passage* carried out only once for each sex. On her wedding day this involves blessing food and giving it to the girl. She then spits it out three times. This is to symbolize that she is now a mature person and must not as a wife "swallow bitter words" or let her husband make a slave of her. The *mallam* says she is free to leave a marriage if there is an insoluble disagreement. The ceremony thus emphasizes the fact that although husbands are dominant, authority rests on consent and (a) can never therefore be total, (b) it can be abrogated if the wife subordinate decides she does not wish to continue her subordination. Ultimately, then, a wife's consent is required if her husband's dominance is to be maintained.

Later in the afternoon, the girl is taught how to bathe herself after intercourse. This is done by her father's sister or mother's sister or a senior sister, but never her own mother. After washing the bride's hair, the suds are taken to the groom's compound and sold to him as proof that she is a virgin. It is said that if she is not a virgin it is impossible to produce heavy suds. The husband is then asked for grease for the girl's hair because they have now washed the grease of her father's house—and from now on he, the groom, must supply things for her. While dressing the girl in her final marriage clothes and replaiting her coiffure, a sugar lump and a date are placed in her mouth. Lore has it that if she swallows the date, or if the sugar melts before the dressing is completed, then she will be subservient to her husband's wishes whether these are good or bad, just or unjust. On the other hand, if she does not swallow the date or melt the sugar, she will be able to stand up to her husband and demand her rights when such behavior is appropriate.

About seven or eight o'clock in the evening, the groom's party, his best man and best woman, appear at the girl's compound. A *mallam* blesses the entire group of the girl's female relatives and emissaries of the groom. The girl, covered with veils, cries, saying she does not want to leave her home—and her mother tells her that it is time to go. In the city she is carried to a car, and in the rural areas generally to a horse, camel, or ox. At the groom's house she is carried into the household, and from there the *kususu* (best woman) takes her into what will be her own sleeping quarters. The *kususu* (often the groom's father's sister) leads her in and out of this door three times and then leaves her. Young age mates of the bride then come and "sell" mock foods of mud and henna to the groom and his male friends. This trade is animated and yet serious. The girls each sell their wares in turn and the men, led by the best man, try to joke with the girls and settle for a few pennies, even though asking prices are usually several pounds. This "small trade" is a prelude to the "big trade." Sometime later, the groom goes into his bride's hut and bargains first for her to uncover her head, then for her to open her mouth so she will speak to him, and traditionally he then bargained for her virginity (the girl fee) which is now (*feroram*), often being paid earlier in the day. Traditionally and in rural areas, this "big trade" is carried on after the girl is brought to the groom's sleeping room or hut. A white mat or blanket has been placed on his bed by his best man.

Both of these "bargaining" ceremonies are indicative of the tensions involved in man-woman and especially husband-wife relations. Men must expect to pay for what women give them. If not, then women may refuse to provide services for which they are valued—food preparation and sex.

Before going to the groom's hut, the bride's father's sister takes her out to urinate and gives advice about the consummation. She generally is said to advise the girl not to resist for too long, for if she keeps fighting off her husband, it may make the man impotent, which is very shameful, and people will say she is not a virgin because it was not proven on her wedding night. They will also gossip, she says, and claim that her husband is not a man, i.e., he is impotent.

The girl is then escorted to the groom's sleeping quarters by the *kususu* or best woman of the groom. Traditionally, the bride remained on a mat on the floor and the husband carried on the "big trade." The women, with the exception of the boy's mother, traditionally wait outside the hut. In the city many young men claim that everyone leaves the couple alone, but the traditional custom calls for the women to be witness to the man's potency. After the man has broken the hymen and blood is available on the white mat, the "consummation" is over. Most informants agree that it is cruel to finish intercourse on this first semi-public occasion. As one informant put it, "The man must control himself, he should not finish because it is too hard on the little girl." The groom then steps out of the house and either calls the women to give them the mat, or he shoots off a gun announcing the virginity and the consummation. Women of the girl's family then take the mat and parade about the neighborhood beating on plates, accompanied by drummers to tell everyone that the girl is a virgin.

Informants all agree that everyone likes to see blood on such occasions. They also agree that it is not always possible and this can lead to trouble so that various artifices are employed to make sure some blood is in fact shown.

The girl's father's sister (*bawa*) comes to take her back to the bride's quarters where she is bathed. A male agnate or mother's brother of the boy (but not his father) arrives and they show him how to bathe after intercourse. Most men already know, but the custom is carried out anyway because "it is the right thing to do."

The next morning, the women of the groom's family go to the bride's compound to collect her dowry. If she came from another town, then her dowry goods would have still been left outside the compound until after the consummation and proof of her virginity. These dowry goods are then arranged and set up in the hut or room of the bride during the seven days of her confinement. The groom and friends go to the house of the bride's people early in the morning after the consummation bringing a few gifts. Usually these have to do with lying down, such as a mat, a carpet, or a blanket. The girl's parents in turn give the groom a small gift of money or clothes. This is called "greeting the in-laws" but seems also to symbolize the husband's gratitude for the girl's sexual purity and his satisfaction with his own manhood.

The day after consummation is also the favored time for the main portion of the *kolawa* (to be matured) ceremony. In separate parts of the compound, special food is placed in the cupped hands of both the bride and groom. The central act involves throwing this food back into the bowl. Lore has it that the partner who throws the food with greatest force will be the strongest power in the marriage. Again, as in previous rituals, people are aware here of the symbolism. Such ceremonies are not believed to cause marital relations but to symbolize the way in which the sexes interact within marriage.

Later in the afternoon, food is cooked by the bride's female relatives and given out to friends, neighbors, and relations under the groom's orders. This food ceremony (*muskeru*) is another module that is often attached to many Kanuri rituals like the *nzaye* (money receiving). The girl's female relatives remain for one week to cook for the husband while the young bride is in strict seclusion. At the end of the week, a small "coming out" ceremony is performed to keep the girl safe from evil spirits, and she takes up normal wifely duties. In cases where the husband already has wives in the house, he must sleep only with the young girl for this week, then afterwards begin the custom of taking turns between wives.

Subsequent Marriages

When a subsequent marriage for a man is with a previously unmarried girl, everything is exactly the same as described above. The only exception would be the *kolawa* ceremony which the girl carries out, but he does not if he has done it before in a previous marriage. Informants claim that it now is not uncommon, and not frowned upon, for a young man to perform the *kolawa* ceremony at *his* first marriage whether it is a girl-marriage *or* a woman-marriage, rather than waiting for his first girl-marriage. However, in rural areas the traditional custom is still practiced and thus if a man never marries a girl (previously unmarried) he will not go through the *kolawa*.

The wedding of a previously married woman is less elaborate, and essentially a bilateral agreement between the man and woman in which relatives and friends are helpers but not decision-makers.

The manner of initiating such marriages may or may not involve premarital sexual relations or cooking of food for the man. Length of acquaintanceship varies enormously from a few hours to a lifetime. The relationship is established before either party tells their own kin. To discuss marriage, the groom either sends representatives (male or female) or speaks to the woman himself. Usually they are thought of as *təmaji* (affianced) at this point; indeed, in this regard, the word also has the connotation of "lovers." She then decides, sometimes with the help of the groom, who will be her *luwali*. This is preferably a senior male agnate if her father is not in the vicinity. If none of these is available, then a senior male agnate, the head of the household she is living in, or a local political leader (in that order) may fill the role.

Between them, the bride and groom arrange the bridewealth payments, the *luwaliram* and *sada'ə* The groom may send an intermediary to avoid any possibility of personal conflict with his intended, although most men do not. At this time, the couple also agree on what he will give, if anything, to her mother if she lives close by. The couple then inform their parents, and relatives, or the head of the household in which they are staying. The man sends or takes the *luwaliram* payment to the *luwali*, who turns it over to the bride. She distributes it to her relatives, and gives a small fee to the *luwali*, keeping most of it for herself. There is no *kwororam* (asking fee) and no *feroram* (consummation fee) payment.

In a week to a month, the wedding day arrives. People have been invited by the bride and groom. They gather in the morning just as they do for a first marriage to a girl. A small *nzaye*, or giving money to the ceremony-giver, is held at both the groom's and bride's compound to help with the wedding expenses. The *sada'ə* either at the *luwali*'s compound or that of a local political leader, is the same as for a first marriage. After this, the groom sends a few gifts to the bride through his *kususu* (best woman). As in the first marriage, these gifts are divided between the mother and the bride. The bride keeps hers and the mother distributes some of hers to close cognatic female relatives. No *fəfari* or gift to the groom is required, although some families and/or women send over a little money to the groom, but this is a new idea and was not practiced traditionally. It is called "something that dropped from the sky" to connote the fact that it is a surprise.

During the day before the wedding night, the woman's possessions are sent to the groom's compound, rather than the next day as in a girl's first marriage. This emphasizes the idea that a first marriage should, ideally, be dependent upon the test of the bride's virginity. If this is not confirmed then, again ideally, the groom may demand the return of the bridewealth and the girl's belongings cannot be moved into his house. By contrast, the marriage with a previously married woman cannot include such a test and therefore her belongings may be moved in before she herself enters her husband's household.

In the early evening, the woman bathes, dresses, and re-does her hair-do and puts on make-up (antimony around her eyes) and perfume. The man then, through his *soba kura* (best man), sends transport for her and she, along with her female relatives and the man's best woman and best man, come to his house. After a brief period of greeting at the man's house—during which the woman enters her sleeping quarters—the guests leave. The man then says to the new wife, "I am ready to sleep" and she comes to his sleeping quarters. She has sole sexual access to him for three days and is in semi-confinement for that period. Unlike the first marriage, the girl's female relatives do not cook for the man.

The next day, in the afternoon, the man distributes food cooked by the woman's relatives to his friends and relatives as well as hers.

None of the little drama ceremonies is performed that symbolized the tension and conflict between husbands and wives. In general, the ceremony is short and can be carried out quite cheaply if both parties agree. This accentuates the idea that first marriages are *rites de passage* while subsequent ones are not.

Obligations to Present Wives

Kanuri male informants admit that marrying a new wife may involve problems with wives already in the household. In order to allay some of the tensions resulting from the acquisition of a new wife, it is customary that these wives receive gifts from the husband. The most common expectation involves the giving of half of the female presents and money to each wife already in the compound. Thus all presents to the girl and her female relatives are totaled and half that amount goes to each of a man's other wives. If there is a concubine in the household, she receives one-quarter of all such gifts. A variant of this custom is to total up all clothing and provide half of this for each wife, leaving out the money payments; for a concubine, this arrangement involves one-quarter of the clothing.

This secondary bridewealth payment to present wives on the occasion of a new wife being added to the polygynous family forms is an area of potential conflict. Men claim that in special cases, where there is a good relationship between a husband and his wives or where the wedding is putting him into serious debt, a special agreement is made. The husband discusses the wedding and the expense and says that he will give his present wives one or two gifts and asks that they be satisfied. If they agree, he can then consider this obligation complete. In a few rare cases of a wealthy man married to a very high status woman, the husband's gifts to her may even exceed those to the new wife. Women claim in a number of instances that the lack of full payment, or any payment at all, of secondary bridewealth is the cause of many divorces. According to women, men always try to avoid these payments, while wives feel such compensation is their due, and become angry at attempts to have such obligations waived.

The Meaning of Marriage Rituals

In other types of marriages, various modules can be added or subtracted depending upon the marital status of the bride and groom and the agreements already made. Thus in marriage of charity, the distinction "previously married or not," especially for the bride, still defines what type of ceremony will be held. However, those parts of the ceremony dealing with payments are deleted or drastically curtailed and at the *sada'ǝ* ceremony on the morning of the wedding day it will be announced publicly that this is a *nyia sada'abe* (marriage of charity).

In Kanuri terms, this means that the basic distinction, that which predominates over all others in a marriage ceremony, stems from the bride's previous marital record. If she has never been married before, she is presumably a virgin. She has never had intercourse with a mature male—and almost universally this is true. Once this distinction is made, everything else follows, since the ceremonies are linked to this basic distinction.

The virgin marriage ceremony takes place at or before the girl has reached puberty. Thus for a Kanuri girl, marriage itself is part of her puberty ceremony. It is at her marriage that she is initiated into the role of adult womanhood, and the special ceremonies directed to this end all tend to symbolize and dramatize one of the great truths of adult Kanuri life. Men as husbands are dominant, but this dominance involves a tension, indeed a contest, in which women do not necessarily comply without trying to maintain their own rights. Not only must men be made to give women what custom says they have a right to ask for, but women may even try to reverse the dominance and take power away from their husbands. The one ceremony the groom goes through as a sign that he has entered the realm of marriage, the *kolawa*, which he can only practice once in his life, is seen as a contest over who is to dominate, and over who will spit out the bitter words rather than accept them—the husband or the wife. In other words, the girl and the boy are both initiated into adult married life by undergoing ceremonies of marriage which predict not harmony but conflict and entreat each to be careful of his and her rights in the situation.

It is only in this same framework that we can understand the great value placed upon a girl-marriage as opposed to a woman-marriage. Kanuri men do not value a very young pre-pubescent or pubescent girl for her sexual charms. To them, as to us, she has very few of these. Most men take care not to rush such a child into full sexual intercourse and instead wait patiently while she matures and then they train her as time goes on. Furthermore, the traditional semi-public defloration of the virgin girl can be a terrifying experience for some, and is certainly a testing time for any man. According to this custom, he must publicly show his potency. I have observed men actively engage in weeks of prayer over this event. Even so, a few fail to consummate their wedding night. In such cases, the man is given ninety days to consummate or the marriage is annulled.

In one exceptional case Modu,[5] a man of forty-five, was marrying a virgin girl and it was her second such marriage. Her first had been annulled because her young husband proved impotent (for the first time in his life, after two successful marriages). The young girl had been promised to one man (Ali) and the *kwororam* meeting had taken place. However, the girl's *luwali* changed his mind and gave her to someone else after returning all the *kwororam* gifts to Ali. It was this second man who then proved impotent. Modu worried over these events, for he knew, as did everyone in the village, that there were bad feelings over the breaking of that first promise. He went to Ali before ever contracting the marriage and asked his permission and blessings upon the marriage. Ali told him that the matter was now closed, and it was none of his affair any more.

Modu prayed at least several hours a day until the wedding night, but to no avail. He later admitted to intimate household members that he was at first unable to reach an erection. Therefore, in the middle of the night, he visited a senior medicine specialist in the village. This worthy told him that no one could ever impregnate this particular young girl because he, the medicine man, had "closed her up" for Ali when Ali had been rejected as her first husband. The matter was now closed and for a small fee he would "open her" again. He gave the anxious groom some medicine and Modu returned and consummated his marriage successfully.

In the cases of impotence over the same girl described above, both men knew there was a history of "bad feeling" over this girl. The possibility that malevolence might be involved was very much enhanced in such an atmosphere. Thus the normal anxiety over the semi-public display of one's manhood was heightened by the knowledge that someone had in fact not wanted this marriage to take place—and might have done something supernatural to prevent it. In such a charged climate, two successive cases of impotency are not surprising, and the medicine specialist did well to calm things down by admitting to the reality of the malevolence. Indeed, in taking credit for it, he created and enhanced his credibility to the point where he could believably withdraw the "spell."

Although this is an extreme case involving extra reasons for anxiety over potency, this fear is always a potential threat in the wedding ceremony with a young previously unmarried girl.

Then why suffer through such a ceremony? Why pay more for it? As I have explained elsewhere (Cohen 1967a: 39-40):

> A young girl has never been touched sexually by other men; he is the first; he can train her as he likes, and teach her to be a proper wife to suit his own personal wishes. Besides, it is a good Muslim custom, they always add, as they do about almost every custom when they are asked. In this case they are correct, for such young marriages are very widespread throughout the Islamic world. However, there is more to it than that—indeed it comes close to the heart of the Kanuri way of looking at things. Kanuri social life is a constant search for fruitful social contacts in which one man is superior and the other a subordinate to him. Between the sexes, the culture defines women as inferior in rank to men. Thus the place universally available to all men for the achievement of subordinates is the family and the household, and the ideal female subordinate is a young girl, one who has not yet been divorced, that is rejected her subordination to her husband, and one whom the husband can train to become properly obedient to his own personal wishes. Thus marriage to a previously unmarried girl symbolized what every man wants, not sexually, but socially; unblemished and complete obedience from docile subordinates who receive material benefits in return for subordination. Seen in this light the marriage with young girls then becomes more understandable for it represents some of the most profoundly important values in the society.

As women grow older they are less easily subordinated. For one thing, the added factor of extreme youth which always enhances junior status is gone. Secondly, the girl has learned how to interact with superiors (husbands) and how to compete for power where this is possible. As we have seen, this competition itself is "written" symbolically into the wedding rituals of first unions.

It can be seen again in the problem of secondary bridewealth. Women demand that as a good, ideal provider, a husband should give them their share of the bridewealth going to a new wife. Why should she have new clothes, and they receive none from the person responsible for meeting these needs in their lives? Such payments then proclaim the worth of present wives or, conversely, withholding such gifts may declare a husband's intention of discarding the present wife for a new one. Marriage rituals emphasize a matter of deep concern to all Kanuri social relations—namely, what is the basis of a relationship; what are the obligations and the possibilities in such an arrangement; what can each expect as his or her due; what room is there for maneuver between the superior and subordinate and what strategy will produce the most gratifying rewards? Marriage rituals dramatize the change in status of a man and a woman. Kanuri rituals carry out such functions, but as expressions of the culture and its society they also portray and dramatize the tensions inherent in all superior-subordinate relations as these are played out between the sexes in marriage.

Chapter 8
Images of Dominance: Sex and Spouse Roles in Bornu Society

Societies vary with respect to the nature of husband-wife roles and relationships. Anthropologists have been quick to see the relation between different types of descent group structures and the husband-wife role so that matrilineal systems affect the roles in one direction while patrilineal systems create other conditions resulting in still different husband-wife roles. We shall consider such factors a little later but first there is, from a descriptive and analytic point of view, something which precedes this kind of relationship. This is the cultural image of male and female and an understanding of how these conceptions are incorporated into the roles of husband and wife.

I do not mean that these images necessarily "cause" anything to happen in a scientific sense. As the new feminists in Western society have pointed out, the assumptions that culture provides about men and women come into operation when they have to live together as real flesh and blood beings—indeed, that is what creates all the problems—but acting upon this reality as a stimulus to guide perception and judgment is the image each has of the other as a separate sex and as husbands and wives.

The Islamic Background and Bornu

The Kanuri have been Muslim for many centuries and their views of men and women are very strongly influenced by Islam and its teachings. In Islam

> Men stand superior to women in that God hath preferred the one over the other. . . .Those whose perverseness ye fear, admonish them and remove them into bed-chambers and beat them; but if they submit to you then do not seek a way against them [Koran 4].[1]

In other words, men have greater authority as a caste and if women do not wish to acknowledge their inferior status they should be scolded and beaten. On the other hand, if a woman submits to male authority, her master-male must try to be good to her.

In traditional Islam, a woman has some rights but they are restricted. She is also relegated by law to a separate social existence, and intersection between the male and female realms should be handled with care and circumspection. Thus in matters of inheritance her rights to property are only half those of a male. In some areas this is reduced to zero, especially where corporate segmentary unilineal descent groups are strong and women are for the most part married outside the corporate group. As late as 1952, the Mufti of Egypt declared that women should not have the vote in national and local elections because there was no authority in Islamic thought and theology for such rights to be granted to women.[2]

The restrictions on women mean that they are barred from active participation in many sectors of social life. A thirteenth century Islamic commentator is quoted by Levy (1957:99) as saying God has created the world so that only men are capable of prophecy, religious leadership, sainthood, pilgrimage rites, the giving of evidence in law-courts, the holy war, worship in the mosque on Friday, electing chiefs, and discretion in divorce matters. The common theme running through all of the above activities is that of public or community affairs involving the interaction of people from differing families and households. That is the man's world.

In Bornu today, women do not have the vote and their rights to inheritance are limited by Islamic law (often simply avoided in practice). They take no part in public or legal affairs. Traditionally, there was a separate women's room beside the law-court and they spoke into the court through a small window. Today, however, Kanuri women appear in court (although not often) and they do go on the pilgrimage. Nevertheless, the restriction on women in classical Islam is strikingly parallel to the view of their position held by men in Bornu today.

Early Islamic writers explained this inequality by claiming that Allah has preferred men over women, making men mentally and morally superior in intelligence, in their ability to give advice, and in their capacity to perform public duties and carry out the divine will (Levy 1957:99). In other words, women are innately inferior to men in the psychological qualities necessary for successful activity in public life outside the home. Maleness as such is more valuable than femaleness; in some Near Eastern markets gold coins having the same weight are worth more if they have a male figure rather than a female (Austry 1967:26). However, the differences go much further than this. For, as one writer, (Antoun 1968:690-691) has recently suggested, Islamic thought conceives of women as being driven by

> inordinate sexuality. They are animalistic in their behavior. They manifest inordinate aggressiveness. They are informed by evil forces. They bring discord to the body social. For all these reasons women constitute a threat to the group and its honor. . . .

Men, on the other hand, although they can experience lust, can exercise restraint through superior powers of reasoning which is theirs by virtue of Allah's will at the time of creation (Antoun 1968:691).

Although the mental inferiority of women is not stressed in Bornu, there is a widespread belief that women, at least most of them, can be seduced with very little difficulty. As one woman informant said to me, "If the right things are done, then it is possible to have nearly any woman in Bornu." Why this should be so will be discussed in greater detail in the next chapter. Suffice it to say that in Bornu it is not thought to be due to an innate and uncontrollable sexuality on the part of women, but to the material and social gains she can obtain through the granting of her favors. In this sense, Bornu does not seem to follow the wider Islamic world as described by Antoun (1968).

In both the Islamic world in general and Bornu in particular, the most obvious correlates of these images of women as inferior, different, and sexually untrustworthy, are the ideas of purdah and of the "code of modesty." If a woman cannot adequately operate in the man's world outside the home, then she should be confined within the household where she can do those things (food preparation, reproduction, and care of children) for which she is ordained. Furthermore, if she is kept in the household and if all interactions between men and women are governed by rules of strict control in which any sexual content is severely limited, then possibly some of the opportunities for insubordination and sexual misconduct can be avoided.

Why go to such trouble to control man-woman interaction? In both the Near East and in Bornu a woman's sexual activities, her reproductive powers, and some stipulated parts of her economic potentialities are transferable to her husband at marriage (Patai 1962:ch. 4). The woman herself is not purchased, only these rights. But rights in a person cannot be locked away safely like jewelry, or even protected like land-use rights. They exist in an actor who may decide, or be persuaded, to act otherwise. Paradoxically, then, at the core of marriage lies a threat that the system will not work. By restricting man-woman interaction, and by giving men the dominant and women the inferior position in cosmology, in law, and in society, a complex of forces is released to allow men and women to view the woman as a transferable value between men who have the right to do so as the decision-makers of society.

In Bornu, there are many expressions in the culture that indicate the dominance and superiority of husbands over wives and men over women in general. Women walk behind men on the road, and move off a path when a man approaches, leaving the path for the man. Men going to market can be seen on horseback with their wives carrying loads behind them. Women must move to a man's household upon marriage and not vice versa, and women come to the man's sleeping quarters for the night. This reflects the more general belief that the subordinate in a relationship must always come to the place of his superior. In intercourse, all positions are permissible except having the woman on top of the man. This, it is said, will produce gonorrhea when the semen flows back into the penis. In wider terms, to be higher than someone in physical space is to be his superior socially.

This then is the overall ideology of sex roles that obtains in the Islamic tradition and in Bornu as well. Men and women are raised in a society and a cultural tradition that stresses over and over again the superiority of men and their obligations and right to dominate women as wives. Women are told that they are inferior and must submit to the will of their men-folk because that is the way the sexes are innately related by their very nature as this was created by Allah at the beginning of time.

Survey Results of Spouse Image

In order to get a broader picture of how each sex views the role of the married person, we asked each respondent in the questionnaire to tell us the characteristics of a good and bad husband and wife. Given the foreknowledge of dominance already available and discussed above, it was theorized as a working hypothesis that both sexes, but most especially men, would emphasize male dominance and female submissiveness as the most important quality of these ideal good and bad images. The question was also designed to increase the complexity of the images rather than simply having the respondent agree or disagree with concepts of male dominance. In this way, a wider set of such images could be collected and compared with one another.

Tables 8:1 and 8:2 summarize these data on the role of the "good" and the "bad" husband. It should be noted that although these are lumped categories taken from fifty-three specific statements concerning good husbands and seventy-four for the bad husbands, sorting them into these more general rubrics was relatively simple. The number of words used varied from one or two for most people to seven. There are no consistent relationships between numbers of such words used or their order and any of our other sociological measures in the questionnaire. We have therefore assumed that these results characterize the views of the population. The total set of words used by all respondents is, therefore, the sample being analyzed in the tables which follow.

Table 8:1 summarizes the results of the good and bad husband image as seen by both sexes. Although there are significant differences, the most striking quality is the general agreement of both sexes about the characteristics of a good husband. For both the good and bad husband, the correlation of men's and women's responses is over .9. In all cases and from both the negative and positive points of view, the most important quality of the husband is his role as a provider. He is good if he provides, bad if he fails at this responsibility, and it far outweighs any other consideration, accounting for two-thirds of all statements made by either sex. With one significant exception—sexual relations—both sexes agree that a good husband is a person who is personally pleasant, kind, gentle, patient, and morally upright. And both sexes seem equally unconcerned over the husband's treatment of the wife's kin, even though a small minority mention such activity as part of a husband's good and bad behavior. In two areas, the sexes diverge very markedly from one another—sex and male dominance. Whereas men mention adequate sex relations as being 4-5% of the qualities associated with being a good husband, women mention it from 17% (for the good husband) to 28% (for the bad husband) of the time in their evaluation of the husband role. Conversely, although both sexes rarely mention male dominance as a characteristic of the good husband, 23% of the men's statements about bad husbands were concerned with dominating a wife by excessive means, while only 6% of the women's statements contained such features. Men also mentioned personal character traits, such as "patience," "gentleness," "seriousness," "inspiring confidence," and others, significantly more often than women do when describing the role of the good husband; they also mention unkind, impatient treatment more often then women, especially in their description of the bad husband. Women, on the other hand, although similar to men when associating the provider role with a good husband, mention lack of providing as an attribute of the bad husband more often than do the men.

Certainly the open-ended quality of the question has produced a more complex image of the idealized husband role in Kanuri society than a simple ideology of male dominance. Respondents interpreted the question to mean "What is it that makes a good or bad husband?" Dominance by itself produces only discipline, and so both sexes get right to the point: a man's responsibilities to provide appropriate sustenance for his family is his fundamental duty as husband and later as husband-father. Although both sexes agree on this, women mention the failure to provide more

TABLE 8:1. THE GOOD AND BAD HUSBAND IN BORNU

Attribute	MEN % of statements		WOMEN % of statements	
	Good Husband	Bad Husband	Good Husband	Bad Husband
Husband a good provider	68.2	--	66.0	--
Husband fails to provide**	--	41.9	--	53.0
Husband treats wife gently, kindly and with patience	14.3	--	12.4	--
Husband treats wife badly, impatient, not gentle**	--	14.6	--	8.7
Husband has good sexual relations with his wife**	4.4	--	16.8	--
Husband has bad sexual relations with wife**	--	5.0	--	27.5
Husband has good personal traits other than those mentioned above—serious, dignified, religious, etc.	9.1	--	3.2	--
Husband has bad personal traits**	--	11.9	--	.7
Husband treats wife's kin well	2.9	--	1.6	--
Husband treats wife's kin badly	--	1.5	--	2.7
Husband marries and divorces too much	--	2.3	--	1.3
Husband dominates wife	1.0	--	--	--
Husband dominates by excessive force and cruelty**	--	22.7	--	6.0
Total	99.9 N=384	99.9 N=260	100.0 N=315	99.9 N=149

Asterisks indicate a statistically significant difference between men's and women's responses on this particular item: * = $p < .05$; ** = $p < .01$.

often than men. Women are also striking in their declared concern that sexual relations are important, while men are more concerned that attempts to dominate by extreme means can produce a bad husband.

Table 8:2 summarizes the statements made about the characteristics of a bad wife. Again, both sexes are highly correlated as to their views with some significant differences. Both mention obedience more often than any other characteristic, and women are significantly higher than men in their emphasis of (i.e., the number of times they mention) this quality. Next comes competence and trust, which both sexes mention and give about the same importance, except that women emphasize incompetence ("bad at her job") more than men. The other striking difference between men and women is the strong emphasis placed by men on immodesty (being brazen, loud, vulgar, unwomanly) as opposed to women who hardly mention such traits at all. Sexual behavior does not appear as a separate item here, although both men and women mention it in about 8% to 10% of their statements. It was decided instead that the sexual statements were semantically closer to other categories such as untrustworthiness (adultery) or disobedience (she is "proud"—i.e., refuses sex, in the hut or in bed). Both men and women agree that a wife should be cooperative, i.e., be committed to seeking some of the same ends as her husband and in helping him to achieve these goals. Again, both sexes agree that women should be trustworthy or at the very least not untrustworthy, and they should also be appreciative, i.e., they should react positively to whatever the husband has to give them no matter how poor such gifts or efforts are.

Here then is the Kanuri mode of idealizing the roles of spouses in marriage. The husband is above all else a provider. He is the person from whom the means for sustenance flows. He does not

TABLE 8:2. THE GOOD AND BAD WIFE IN BORNU

Attribute	MEN % of statements		WOMEN % of statements	
	Good Wife	Bad Wife	Good Wife	Bad Wife
Obedient**	34.7	--	45.9	--
Disobedient**	--	32.1	--	44.8
Good at her job (responsibilities)	31.8	--	25.1	--
Bad at her job**	--	19.6	--	25.2
Cooperative	14.7	--	10.1	--
Uncooperative	--	4.8	--	1.2
Good at sex, compliant and chaste, gives satisfaction (added on from disobedience and untrustworthy)	7.4	--	8.8	--
Modesty and respect to husband's kin**	2.1	--	6.2	--
Fertile—bears children	.3	--	--	--
Untrustworthy	--	17.3	--	16.6
Unappreciative	--	7.0	--	8.0
Total	100.0 N=309	100.0 N=219	100.0 N=295	100.1 N=156

Asterisks indicate statistically significant differences between men's and women's responses on this particular item: ** = p $<$ .01.

actively dominate, indeed trying to create superiority through force is associated with "the bad husband" role. On the other hand, the most prevalent theme in wifely behavior is obedience, or the acceptance of male dominance.

This is strongly analogous to the Kanuri conception of the superior-subordinate dyad as it operates in the social and political sector of the society as a whole. In Kanuri ideology, the superior supplies the needs of the subordinate for status, material goods, and support in the community at large—he is the provider. On his side, the subordinate provides loyalty and obedience to the wishes and goals of the superior. Informants say it is like a father-son relationship. Indeed, people often came to me in Bornu and either asked for a present or called me father. If I asked why I should grant requests for gifts, the person would often say, "Because you are my father"; that is, he wishes to place me in that position sociologically and establish a patron-client relationship or at the very least have me validate my superior status through being a provider for his needs.

In this sense, the ideal role of the husband-as-provider is the instrumental means, or operational definition, of superiority in the husband-wife dyad. To the Kanuri male, dominance and superiority are cultural givens of their Islamic, and probably pre-Islamic, heritage. However, as an ideology it must be activated by the dominant or superior male-as-husband. He provides material and social security to his wife-as-subordinate and she responds with her obedience. This leads to the important conclusion that obedience is conditional not only on the cultural traditions of Islam which preach of woman's inferiority and the need to control her. This may be true at the cultural level, but at the social level of interaction between spouses this analysis indicates that wifely subordination and obedience is also conditional upon the husband's role as a provider. Just as all Kanuri who are in the superior position in a superior-subordinate dyad must provide for the needs of subordinates or the relationship may atrophy, so too Kanuri as husbands face the same problem with their wives.

The next most often mentioned features can also be interpreted as deriving from the superior-subordinate interaction of husbands and wives. For husbands, there are statements about how he treats her—well or badly, gently, wisely. For the wife, they are about her competence—is she a good cook, does she waste resources, is she a capable skilled practitioner of the womanly arts? In other words, the husband is seen as "treating" her, while she is seen as meritorious or not in her responsibilities and skills. This, it seems to me, has about it the same quality as that of employer and employee. The employee sells his skills and the employer purchases them and should therefore treat the employee well—look after his or her needs and therefore *treat* them well. Thus the treatment by husbands is emphasized again and again because they are in the dominant position, while the service quality of the wife and her competence reflect the very opposite, i.e., her subordination to her husband.

This is also shown by the emphasis men place on modesty for women. Although Kanuri society is somewhat formal, it is interesting that women do not mention this as a good or bad attribute of husbands.[6] On the other hand, nearly 20% of the men mention female immodesty as a bad quality, indicating their concern to have women's behavior restricted within the formal limits set by cultural norms. The fact that such qualities have to do with willful acts on the part of the wife—loudness, vulgarity, etc.—leaves the question of the origins of control somewhat ambiguous. Obviously, if the husband is dominant, his wife will not behave in these negatively valued ways. On the other hand, if she controls herself, his job is less difficult. Thus the image of the obedient wife who is modest and competent also involves the idea that she should accept the cultural norms dealing with her subordinate status in society. Excessive or even overt authority by the husband is ideally unnecessary. That this is indeed the case can be seen by the fact that women are significantly *higher* than men in their mentioning of obedience and disobedience as the most frequent feature of the good and bad wife. They seem to be saying, "We know what the rules of the game are: we must be obedient and competent" (in 70% of their comments about both the good and the bad wife). The men also say such things are very important but then seem to say as well, "Yes, a wife should be obedient, competent, and carry all of this off with decorum and self control so that it doesn't appear she resents her position."

Finally, there is the complex problem of sex. Women want their husbands to be sexually adequate and faithful. Men hardly mention the subject when speaking of good and bad husband images, and both sexes mention it rather lightly in relation to the wifely role. This topic will be discussed in greater detail in the next chapter. Suffice it to say, speculatively at this point, that women may be using sexual activity to redress the imbalance of power between the sexes. If manliness is equated with dominance, then manliness in a sexual sense can be challenged through accusations of impotence or poor sexual performance which in turn challenges the entire structure of male dominance as a cultural ideology.

In summary, the Kanuri follow the general Islamic belief that men are dominant, and that men should by reason of traditional Islamic dogma take precedence over women in society. Women are weak, and in this ancient view they are easily seduced because of their innate lack of control over the more basic physical passions. Men, being more rational, are therefore more in control of themselves and can rule others, especially women.

In our questionnaire material, men as husbands are viewed as providers to the family of the material goods and services of the society. Women are seen as obedient subordinates who provide docile labor and (hopefully) children to the husband. The system works well when both sexes believe thoroughly in the ideology and women do not therefore require coercion. Instead, they become self-disciplined inferiors who accept male control over the family, the polity, and the economy.

Chapter 9
Married Life: The Playing Out of Dominance

The previous two chapters on various aspects of dominance ideology in Kanuri culture are meant to serve as a way in to married life itself. I do not mean to suggest that dominance by men is the only important quality in Bornu marriage—but it is, in my view, of central importance to our understanding. The real observable patterns and qualities that make up Kanuri marriage are of course much more complex—because married life itself is an intricate and complicated outcome of many factors. However, as we shall see, the theme of male superiority in marriage threads its way throughout family life giving meaning and substance to many specific customs and observable behaviors which otherwise seem incongruous to one another and to marriage itself.

Means of analyzing marriage and the family vary. Murdock (1949) suggested economic cooperation, sexual rights, reproduction, and socialization of the young as *the* universal functions of the family. Several objections can be raised to using these categories as the basis of our analysis. First of all, as I have already noted elsewhere (Cohen 1967a), the household is the basic unit of organization in Kanuri society and as such there are alternative means for fulfilling these functions outside the simple conjugal family. Secondly, we are presently focusing on the husband-wife relationship rather than the entire family. It is the stability and instability of this unit that concerns us rather than all of the possible dyadic relations in the family. These latter will be used as they help us to understand this husband-wife focus, and as they are in their turn affected by it.

In other words, I wish to organize the material within the context of relations between husbands and wives. To do this, we will look first at the division of labor and the daily work tasks that husband and wife have to carry out in the various kinds of settings they find themselves in. Next, we will look at the quality of husband-wife interaction, building on the role images outlined in the preceding chapter to the various kinds of expectations that husbands and wives are enjoined to carry out in specific types of situations, looking as well at some widely accepted Western expectations which are absent and/or disliked. We will also examine interaction by spouses with others in the household and beyond. These latter will show the strong utilitarian views of marriage held by the Kanuri as opposed to our Western view in which a primary requisite of marriage is that it be a satisfactory emotional relationship.

The Segregation of Everyday Married Life

Men and women live essentially segregated lives in Bornu. Men control political jobs, religious functions, and almost all gainful employment. There are a few occupations that are strictly feminine, such as female hairdressing, pottery, and the retail selling of cooked foodstuffs. Women's main work is seen as cooking, maintaining a clean household, fetching water, and the raising of young children, if there are any. The only major overlap between men's and women's work is in farming. To a variable degree, rural women help on the farm. Both men and women also engage in entertaining as traveling or local troupes of drummers and dancers, although even here the men perform some tasks the women others. Across the entire gamut of tasks necessary for the maintenance of social life, Kanuri culture ordains that there be as strict a segregation of the sexes as possible.

This segregation also involves evaluation. The entire set of possible tasks and activities to be carried out in life are then divided into two realms by their association with a particular sex. By definition, woman's work is unmanly, undignified, and lower in status than man's work. Overtly, at least, both sexes accept these cultural norms. In everyday life it affects job evaluation. Thus when discussing the possibility of a food processing plant with Kanuri friends, I quickly ran up against the idea that it might be hard to enlist a male labor force because as one informant noted "It is woman's work."[1] Again, this is a major reason why it has always been hard to find Kanuri cooks and stewards, even though the largest population of expatriates in northeastern Nigeria has always been in Bornu.

Variations in segregation are simple at a gross level of description. All wealthy men in either the rural or urban setting do not allow their wives to help on the farm or go outside the household for water. These tasks are accomplished through laborers and by having a water source inside the compound. Our questionnaire data on this point are quite dull in that there is no variation from this pattern at all. City women and wives of wealthy husbands, especially the latter, are the most segregated from their men folk in the conduct of daily tasks. *Kulle* or purdah varies along with these same qualities. In a sense, the exclusion of wives from society is the ideological end-point of sexual segregation, since the woman is segregated from all men except her husband and her kin. Put another way, purdah is the functional unification of men's and women's tasks by putting the man in control of the tasks. Then woman and her tasks become scarce values to control and hide from other men who also seek control.

But conditions vary. Rural peasants need help on their farms; water must be obtained from wells, often at some distance from the household. Even among the poor of the city, women must go out of the compound for water. Therefore, the poor cannot so easily keep women totally out of participation in overlapping activities and interactive areas in which they contact the man's world.

The following synthetic description taken from the accounts of several informants plus participant observation will clarify the ethnographic generalizations above by summarizing the typical daily activities of husbands and wives in rural and urban areas.

The City Wife's Day

In the city, a woman rises between 5:30 and 6:00 a.m. and, ideally, says her prayers. She then takes water to her husband for his prayers and his morning bath and prepares a small snack for him to eat (often a gruel of milk with sugar, and a little pepper and potash (*ngaji kulbuwa*). She either takes this to her husband or sends it with a small child or servant. The wife then sweeps the entire compound and draws water from the well in the compound or has water brought in. There are water taps spread throughout the town connected to deep bore-holes and it is widely accepted that this water is cleaner.

At 7:00 a.m., a city wife starts cooking the morning meal. As a part of this operation, she washes all of the plates and pots used for cooking and eating the previous night. When this meal is prepared, she begins pounding (in a large wooden mortar) the grain for the evening meal. Generally this takes anywhere from two to four hours, after which she spreads out the grain and chaff to dry on mats in the sun. Somewhere from mid to late morning (10:00 a.m. to 11:00 a.m.) she finishes this work, bathes herself, and rests for a while. After midday, the wife gets up and prepares bəlam (a gruel of rice, sour milk, and sugar). She draws or obtains water for her husband's afternoon bath and fills his prayer pot (often a small aluminum tea-kettle) in readiness for his return sometimes about 2:00 p.m. to 2:30 p.m.

After the husband has bathed and taken his gruel, he rests during the heat of the day. His wife should then fan him and keep the flies from him while he takes his siesta. (In some cases, the wife simply rests as well.) When the husband wakes (circa 3:30-4:30 p.m.), his wife may at this time groom him, picking his mosquito bites and taking out plant barbs, thorns, etc., from his skin.

After this task, she returns to her evening meal. The grain has dried and she starts grinding it into flour with mano and metate. This long and arduous task of preparing the grain can be reduced today by the small machine-driven grinding mills found in all quarters of the city and larger rural villages. This simple mechanization frees the woman from several hours of work each day, making her tasks a great deal easier.

In late afternoon (4:30-5:00 p.m.), water is again drawn for household use. The wife then begins cooking the evening meal. Pots and other utensils used in the morning and during the day are cleaned and the meal is readied. Drinking water is drawn, if it was not already obtained, and the wife prepares her husband's prayer mat for his return at about 6:00-6:30 p.m. Presuming he has returned, or has been home all afternoon, food is brought to him and set out in front of his sleeping hut. She retires to her own area and eats—in some cases she may eat before him, but never in his company—then she takes a bath and prays herself at 6:30 to 7:00 p.m. After this, she may have a visitor come to see her—some women or kinsmen, or she may ask her husband's permission to visit kin, or go to the kin for a special ceremony. If permission is granted, the wife changes into better, i.e., newer, clothes, lights incense near the garments to have them smelling sweet, decorates her hair and eyes, rubs her body with pomade and perfume.

She returns home by 8:00 to 8:30 p.m. and prepares her husband's bed. Sometimes she may send a servant or a small child to carry out this task but often she does it herself. The bedding is shaken out, replaced smoothly over his bed, and water is brought for bathing, prayers, and drinking. She then awaits his call.

The husband may have been out visiting friends or relations, or entertaining them at his compound. Somewhere between 9 and 10 p.m. he returns home and calls his wife to his sleeping quarters where she waits patiently. He says his prayers and afterwards disrobes and she then shakes out the robes and hangs them up. She undresses, leaving only one long cloth wrapped sarong-like around her body. The husband lies down on his bed nude while the wife massages and oils his body. (Informants are agreed that this custom is dying out and that only the older men like it. Young men, especially Western school boys claim they intend to discontinue it.)

When the massage is completed, the husband may, if he wishes, invite her into his bed. He may also send her back to her own quarters, or he may tell her to sleep on a mat on the floor of his hut. Intercourse may take place if she remains, but it is not always the case. Besides intercourse, this time in the husband's sleeping quarters is used for general discussions of household affairs, money matters, cooking, cleaning, the management of children, etc. If the couple is intimate, more confidential matters can also be discussed at this time: rivalries, ambitions, competition with others, and even more secret activities such as profits gained in trade or by other means. This is the one time during the entire day when husband and wife are fully alone and neither is required to be engaged in his or her economic or other social responsibilities.

The above description is the same for both polygynous as well as monogamous unions with a few significant exceptions. In the case of polygyny, the wife remains in the husband's sleeping quarters whether there is intercourse or not. On rare occasions, the wife might be asked to return to her own sleeping quarters; however, any repetition or patterning of such instructions brings conflict. The wife feels she is being rejected and that her husband wishes his room to himself so that he may bring in a woman from outside the household. The wife also feels it is her right to stay all night and, if this "right" is continuously abrogated, she feels the husband is being unjust, especially if such exceptions favor her co-wife who is then manifestly being favored over her. This idea of taking strict turns (*chi chi bojin* = he lies down [with them] alternately) is seen most strictly in the daily tasks of cooking. In the polygynous marriage, the wifely day runs from sunset to sunset. This means that the first task of a wife is to prepare the evening meal (whose preparation takes nearly all day) and ends with the last repast before the evening meal the following day when, as one English speaking informant put it, "She is off duty."

The Rural Woman's Day

In the rural areas, the early morning is quite similar to that of her city sister except that the water source may be quite a distance and often several trips are necessary so that enough water has been drawn for the day's needs. As in the city, the wife starts to pound grain after the morning meal (7:00 a.m. to 9:00 a.m.). During the farming season, she takes her husband his food out to the farm (9:30 a.m. to 10:30 a.m.). She obtains the nearest drinking water for him and works on the farming herself until about 2:30 or 3:00 p.m. Somewhere about this time (mid-afternoon) she leaves the farm. On her way home, she collects fire wood and various kinds of leaves for sauce to be eaten with the grain at the evening meal.

Upon her arrival at the compound, she goes again to the nearest well for water, grinds the millet (or has it ground if there is a small mill in the village), washes the morning's utensils, pots, etc., and cooks the evening meal. The husband returns from the farm plots circa 4:30-5:30 p.m. and often the wife gives him a small snack of ground nuts or leftovers from the morning meal. Afterwards, she brings water for his bath. The husband then rests or goes to visit friends or relatives in the village. The custom of fanning the husband while he rests is not practiced by rural wives. At about 6:30 p.m., the wife spreads out a prayer mat near the husband's sleeping hut and she takes his food and water there; on arrival, he prays and eats. After this, the wife retires to eat her own dinner.

In the city, the early evening is visiting time *par excellence* and women, unless they are very old, generally dress up at this time of day. In rural areas this is uncommon—instead, the good wife rests, or has female visitors until about 8:30-9:00 p.m. Then at circa 9:00 p.m. the wife cleans her husband's sleeping quarters, pours or carries water for his bath, and then she prepares his bed. There are no bed sheets in rural areas so the wife hangs up her husband's pants but uses his gown as a sheet, laying it on his sleeping place when he removes it. The woman then follows her city sister, removing her own clothes except for one cloth wrap, and massages and oils her spouse.

The City Husband's Day

Men are supposed to wake up at dawn (circa 5:30-6:00 a.m.) for prayers. Many do, but others may sleep longer and pray whenever they wake. Informants do not agree on who awakens first in the city and I interpret this to mean that the pattern varies with the personal predilection of each couple. If there is one sleeping room or hut, the husband and his one wife share it for the night. Some monogamous city couples have two sleeping rooms which means the couple may sleep together or separately. If they have slept separately and if there are other wives, the husband greets them, asking if they slept well, if they are well, and so on, through the rather formal greeting patterns of the Kanuri.

After the possibility of a light snack, the man goes to work, although salaried men (especially government workers) generally do not eat at this time, since they have a breakfast hour later on (9:00-10:00 a.m.).[2] The non-salaried men usually attend to household affairs or rest until about 7:00 or 8:00 a.m. and then go out about their business. For many people in the city, this involves going to a place of trade, often one of the marketplaces. They may remain away from the house all day, obtaining food from a friend or a food-seller sometime during the day or, alternatively, returning home. Salaried men come home about 2:30 p.m. and eat a light meal, or rest and wait for the large evening meal. They may also visit with men friends or relatives elsewhere in the city. However, the large majority of men in the city rarely see their wives at all during the day or, if they do, it is only for a short moment when the husband returns home for food and a short rest.

The evening meal is eaten alone or with men friends and relatives after sunset prayers. Afterward, men visit or are visited by male friends and relatives or go to some entertainment (there are two cinemas and many "hotels" or "clubs" = bars *cum* dance halls). It is acceptable to return about 10:30 to 11:30, but in general Kanuri retire early and going to bed between 8:00 p.m. and 10:00 p.m. is not uncommon. When he returns home, a husband may beckon his wife, or say goodnight. Men are in substantial agreement that one should take strict turns and, if there is more than one, always call the wife who cooked the evening meal. However, it is not necessary to take strict turns with intercourse or even to have the wife remain the whole night. The wise husband nevertheless does take turns with sleeping arrangements and also shares out his sexual favors. Skipping an invitation now and then is not uncommon. However, any continuation or patterning of such omission can lead to conflict and divorce.

The Rural Husband's Day

In general, rural men sleep a little later in the morning, while their wives get up earlier in order to get water for the household. After prayers and possibly a light snack the men go to work, which for some non-farming activities may mean staying in the compound, although trade, marketing, and farming take men out of the house quite regularly. As noted, women may come to the farm later with food. Men return late in the afternoon and may have a snack of leftovers at this time. After this, they rest and go visit with friends and relatives. At sundown, prayers are said and the evening meal eaten. Afterward, they rest and visit until 8:00-9:00 p.m. when they go to sleep.

Many poor rural couples have only one hut per compound and so a man and his wife always sleep together. If there are two wives and only the minimum of two huts, the man takes turns sleeping in each hut. Informants, both men and women, are agreed that in rural areas men sleep with their wives more often and take turns more strictly. This is because city men, they say, skip a turn more often so they can have other women from outside the household visit them at night.

In summary, rural men see more of their wives on the farms and in the household where the nature of everyday tasks brings them into more continuous contact with agriculture. Indeed, rural men estimate crop size in terms of how many wives they have during the growing season. Whether they have added or subtracted from the previous year's number through divorce or marriage helps them to estimate crop yield (Cohen 1960). The ideal for the operation of dominance is segregation of the sexes, which is ameliorated in rural areas and more stringently adhered to in urban centers.

The Interaction of Spouses

The above description, and to some extent the previous chapter as well, provides a framework within which the actual interaction of husbands and wives takes place. In a sense, the ideology of dominance and the press of everyday tasks are like a stage setting. All Kanuri men would like docile, obedient, competent wives and, if possible, they should also be fertile and beautiful. Ideally, wives should also be cooperative and help a man achieve his goals, besides being trustworthy, chaste, respectful of the husband's kin, and purdah-minded; that is to say, they should go out of the house only when necessary and never when permission is not granted by the husband. On their side, women hope for generous, kind, gentle, husbands, who are good providers, adequate sexual partners, and who grant them permission to visit friends and relatives whenever necessary. The husband's physical appearance is not so important, although physical deformity of any kind is very much disliked by either sex—so much so that such people often have to marry others with deformity in order to find a spouse.

These are the major values in marriage, and the everyday activity of spouses is the field of action within which these values are more or less achieved. Most Kanuri realize that in actual experience it is not always possible to satisfy all of these goals. Indeed, several informants commented that this was the basis for polygyny. They claim that no woman, and therefore no marriage, could ever be perfect because no one women can embody in herself alone all of the values men wish to achieve in marriage. Therefore, a wise man should look for one wife who can provide some of these and then get other wives who are capable of satisfying the remaining values. Some women are beautiful, some are good and efficient cooks, some are very trustworthy, and a man should strive to have wives who represent all of these talents so that his polygynous family satisfies the full range of values inherent in marriage.

What actually happens inside a Kanuri marriage is not as easily observed or recorded as these general qualities. First of all, as already pointed out, men and women lived segregated lives and the usual interactions of husbands and wives, especially in the presence of a third person observer, is always somewhat formal. This formality is again a conscious attempt by both parties to live up to the ideal roles assigned to husbands and wives. Only in cases of extreme tension or in the very few long term marriages can an outside observer actually penetrate beyond this formal barrier. This is why it is more usual to find anthropologists describing marital relations in formal structural terms. The field methods he employs simply do not penetrate far enough to provide a clear picture of the intimate dyadic relations of spouses.

The way to get beyond this is to look at the types of activities that form points of conflict between husbands and wives, realizing at the same time that they do not apply to all marriages with the same degree of frequency. Another way is to obtain some record of the actual interaction and conversation between spouses over an extended time period by having someone observe this interaction continuously so that an entire slice of time is in fact recorded. This last method has been carried out by Dr. Alan Peshkin (n.d.) for different purposes, but he has gathered material on family interactions in several Kanuri households over a period of one month in which Kanuri assistants recorded all interaction and conversation.[3]

As already pointed out, a chief quality of the husband's role is that of provider. But the expectation is not very explicit about minimal standards. In rural areas, all husbands try to provide their wives with some new clothes after the sale of the cash crop in winter. But some crops fail, others go untended, and still others may be sold (illegally) as future to pay off debts. Thus there is great variation in a husband's capacity to supply gifts to a wife. Similarly with market money. Some husbands are quite generous, others give very little, while still others do the marketing themselves and do not give their wives regular money for food purchases. In some patrilocal marriages, the husband's mother may be the one buying major supplies so that the wife obtains her share from her mother-in-law. Conditions in one marriage may be better or worse than in another so that the wife may feel her previous husband's gifts and market money arrangements make this present husband seem poor by comparison.

The possibilities of tension over the husband's provider functions can be exacerbated by the jural rule which maintains husbands and wives as separate economic property-owning individuals. In effect this means that a husband must share his capital because of the expectation of being a provider, while there is no essential need or expectation for the wife to do so. The following edited case material from Dr. Peshkin's field data in a rural household illustrates this point.[4] A wife has recently returned from a family wedding among her kinfolk. She acted as *kususu* "best woman" for the groom and was given a large calabash full of millet as a gift in return for her services during the wedding.

> In the late morning Musa sees his wife Isa leaving the compound with a calabash full of millet. He says, "Where are you going?" and she replies that she is off to market to sell her millet so that she may pay off some of her debts. He answers by telling her to bring the millet to him so he can buy it. (This would result in her not going to market, remaining in the house, and not having anyone see his wife selling millet to obtain extra cash.) However, Isa replies that her husband would not be willing to pay the market price; to which Musa replies quickly that he is prepared to pay well, if the millet is suitable. She brings the millet over to him, measures it out in nine small calabash units. Musa offers three shillings which his wife rejects, and he then tells her she may go to market and sell the grain.
>
> Isa, realizing that her husband is probably angry, says that the people in the village to whom she owes money must be getting impatient, to which the husband retorts "Well you even owe me five shillings." (Ideally, a husband would forget such a debt or not mention it so that this statement reflects his pique.) The husband measures out the millet with a larger measuring cup getting a smaller total quantity. At the same time he raises the price slightly but Isa still refuses to sell. He then suggests that they may be short of food and he alone will get enough to eat to which she retorts, ". . .that is not my business. A husband must always provide his wife with food," and Musa rejoins, "A wife must also help her husband," implying that she is not doing so by refusing to sell him the grain at his price.
>
> Musa finally agrees; in order to save some semblance of his authority he tells Isa to go to the market, but if the prices are no better than his own offer then she must return and sell the millet to him. He also asks her to buy him some cooked food (gruel and sour milk) for fourpence while she is in the market, implying that her absence from home means that he must go hungry; so he will have her buy food publicly because she is not doing her job letting the whole village know at the same time. She agrees to the errand but asks for money to buy the gruel (i.e., she won't use her own income) and he tells her to look in his robe inside the sleeping hut. When she calls out that she cannot find it, he retorts that he has hidden his money and she should buy the gruel out of the five shillings she owes him. (At this point the Kanuri research assistant gave the wife fourpence in order to cool down what was becoming a serious quarrel and the husband said he was only joking.)
>
> When she had gone, Musa began contemplating about his wife, Isa. He claimed to have helped some of her relatives during *their* ceremonies, but when there was a marriage later on in his family none of her relatives reciprocated by helping him with gifts. He commented that he would never forget this and it might bring an end to the marriage. Furthermore, Isa had been difficult about money before this. Recently, he said, she refused to sell him a bottle of ground nut oil at one shilling but sold it to someone else at one shilling and a penny.

This dramatic sequence and others like it illustrate the separateness of the economic activities of wives and the difficulties men have in adjusting to this fact. Although the ideology calls for male dominance, the wife may maintain areas of economic *independence* over which he has no legitimate control. This is what is angering Musa in the example above, making him behave in such irrational ways as sending his wife to find money when it is not in the spot he directs her to look. By telling her to *buy* cooked food for him, he is also insulting her competence since she is by definition supposed to supply these needs through her work. In effect he is saying, if you're so concerned with your own affairs, over which I cannot seem to exert any influence, then obviously you don't have time or don't wish to fulfill your responsibilities as a wife. This is why the research assistant stepped in at this point. The argument was escalating very rapidly to a point where one party or the other or both could possibly go to the limit and break up the marriage. Being Kanuri himself, the assistant foresaw this eventuality and moved, as an outside mediator, to take away or depress the immediate cause of grievance.

Implied in the above analysis is another major point of conflict—that of the wife's obedience. Ideally, a wife should be obedient, compliant, and modest (i.e., self-restrained), no matter what are the circumstances of her marriage. In practice, such compliance to cultural expectations are very rare. Instead, the actual interaction is governed by the socio-economic status of the husband, his degree of dependency upon his wife, her attitudes to the ideology of female submissiveness, and a number of other factors. Two examples representing extremes of variation will clarify some of these relationships. In one case, a middle-aged rural farmer and low status supporter of a political leader had finally, after a number of years, managed to find a wife. His status as a slave had meant that few women wished to enter into marriage with him. (Generally, people of slave ancestry can only marry others of similar descent.) His present wife is a middle-aged woman, younger than himself, and daughter to his father's full brother, i.e., his patrilateral parallel cousin. Up until this marriage, he was eating at the compounds of other men and had developed several of these relations socially, which obligated him to the compound heads who fed him. He now felt free from such encumbrances and indeed could invite others, including myself, to come and eat with him, thus reversing his subordinate status as a food receiver to that of potential leader through his ability to provide cooked meals for others.

His wife helped him on his farm, cooked his meals, and was personally quite a handsome women with a rather gay witty way about her that often spilled over the bounds of modesty into rather raucous and bawdy conversation.

On one occasion while interviewing him on a different matter at about 5:00 p.m. his wife came out of her sleeping hut and started out of the compound. He turned to her quickly and asked where she was going. "Walking" she answered tartly. Not to indicate a destination or a proper excuse was extremely provocative, since she was in fact proclaiming independence over a matter customarily and jurally under a husband's authority. The husband answered sharply "Stay!" and she simply said "I go," again defying him. This interchange was repeated several times until finally the wife said "I am going, and if you like I won't come back." At which point the husband fell silent. After she left, the now terribly embarrassed man complained bitterly to me about how wicked Kanuri women are today.

In recounting the outlines of this story in other places to Kanuri friends (hiding the identity of the man) everyone remarks on its extreme qualities. The husband has very low status and needs the wife. The wife, they say, sounds like an extremely nasty and immodest women. The height of her immodesty is in her retort that she is simply going for a walk, which means she is suggesting the possibility of meeting other men as if she were an unmarried woman. Almost all informants remark that such a woman should be gotten rid of, but they sympathize (rather contemptuously) with the plight of the husband whose dependence on his wife's functions has allowed her to play such a free role as his spouse.

At the other extreme is the case of Mallam. He is an extremely well thought of and respected member of his community. His regular monthly salary from his civil service post puts him at the bottom rung of the upper classes, while his older full brother's position as a senior member of the emirate civil service solidifies this upper class membership. His two wives, he says, are in strict *kulle* (purdah). Recently, one of his wives came out of the front door of their city household to buy some cosmetics from a street vendor. Mallam was siting under the shade of a tree across the street with friends and neighbors and he observed her purchase.

Quietly and with his usual dignity, he arose, went over to this wife and divorced her, telling her to pack her things and leave his house that evening. Explaining his action, he said that her disobedience was unforgivable. Had he not told her many times that she could always send a small child, or ask him, or a client servant living in the household, to make any purchases she required? Did she not know that in his household *kulle* was strictly enforced and his wives left only on necessary visits to their own kinfolk or other absolutely essential business, discussed first with him so that he could grant his permission? Certainly she knew that. Therefore, Mallam theorized, the only possible reason this wife could break such rules was because she was going "to start trouble in the compound." Better, then, to scotch it before it began.

When I suggested alternative hypotheses such as her desire to make her own purchases and therefore choices among the varieties of merchandise, or her boredom at being within the household all the time (she was seventeen years old), Mallam rejected such explorations. To him, such ideas were irrelevant even if true because his authority and its implied abrogation by her actions were too important as issues to look for rationalizations or excuses. And, for *me* to think of *her* welfare, rather than *his* authority, he said, showed that I was not a Kanuri! The conversation then turned to stories of how Europeans find it difficult to control their wives.

It should be emphasized again that these are extreme cases. Yet they point up relationships that go to the very heart of Kanuri marriage. In the first example, the husband is over thirty years of age and has had only been married once and never divorced. Mallam in the second example is approximately the same age; he has been married seven times and has had five divorces. The hypothesis immediately arises that the stability of a marital union is a direct function of socio-economic status and an inverse function of dependency by the husband upon his wife's contribution to his status. This will be expanded later when it is tested against the statistical data. It should also be noted that one of these unions, the more stable one, was rural—while the union ending in divorce was urban at the time of divorce.

Does this mean that in all upper class marriages men maintain dominance, while this quality is ameliorated or non-existent in lower class unions? Not at all. I have observed many lower class unions in which the husbands were strongly dominant, the wife compliant and modest. On the other hand, only under quite particular circumstances do higher status husbands ever appear or act in anything *but* a dominant position with respect to their wives.

In many marriages, the husband has some attribute of character and status that sustains or supports his authority. The most common of these qualities is the age of the person, especially the husband. The Kanuri say that a man is not fully mature until he is thirty-five to forty years old. Up to that time, he can be expected to be somewhat unstable in his judgments, hot-tempered, and sexually adventurous. Maturity, on the other hand, brings with it, ideally, wisdom, experience in dealing with conflict, more stable judgments and responses, and an ability to contain sexual activity within the bounds of culturally expected chastity. Thus spouse interaction that can escalate quickly to serious disputes among younger persons are treated more calmly when the husband is older. To some extent the same is true for women, but for different reasons. Women who are older have much more difficulty remarrying and therefore tend to see divorce as involving greater risks and fewer options. This means that we can hypothesize a relationship between age and divorce such that divorce decreases with age. Many older husbands have younger wives; if age is regarded as an isolated factor (without interference from other variables), then it is logical to suggest a linear relationship such that divorce is highest when both spouses are young, medium when only one is young, and low when both husband and wife are old.

The marriages in our sample are characteristically fairly short having a median duration of 3.8 and a mean of 6.2 years for all unions.[5] This means that longer durations are interesting and require closer study. From participant observation data, one of the most striking features of the few very long duration marriages is the preponderance among them of cases of high status, politically powerful husbands. Sometimes, such wives are even referred to as *wakil* or chief subordinate (second-in-command) as a nickname. In all cases known to me, such marriages are over twenty years in duration. These wives are the most trusted person in their husband's retinue of followers. She knows his career and the politics of that career intimately and can speak and act in his interests through her own social contacts, or as a virtual head of the household when he is absent. In one example, I observed the wife conducting a trial hearing interview on a serious murder case while her husband was absent. As a senior political leader, he had to hear the case and then take it to the proper authorities. She told the persons involved to come back later after she had told her husband the details. The husband-wife relationship in such cases is still formally that of a superior and his subordinate. But the longevity of the relationship leavens its authority distinction and the subordinate moves more and more into the position of a trusted and intimate colleague and ally. When such marriages occur elsewhere in the social structure, people often say of the spouses that they are not husband and wife but brother and sister to one another, and the wife may even refer to her very long term husband as her "brother," while the husband refers to her as "my sister."

Although these long term marriages are not common in the society as a whole, they are generally in my estimation the most satisfying and rewarding roles women can play in Kanuri society. Certainly, the women I have known in such roles have been among the most mature, intelligent, secure people I have ever met in Bornu. When they are also close associates of a man of power and authority, they come close to achieving the most sought after goals in the society. However, such a role does not happen by accident. These women know their husbands, they know the ideology of dominance, and they have fully accepted their subordinate positions. But they also know that continued service, loyalty, and efficiency produces—ultimately—trust and confidence. They therefore gain admittance to decision-making through the influence they exert on their husbands by virtue of his trust. The hypothesis such a description suggests is that the greater the degree of confidence or secrets shared by a husband with his wife, the more stable will be the union.

One additional point is important. The above discussion does not suggest that marital stability *per person* will necessarily be affected by such sharing of a man's secrets. Obviously, if the society is polygynous it will increase such stability for women but it need not necessarily have any effect on the men. Indeed, it is quite common to observe upper class families in which one wife is kept over a very long period while younger wives are turned over (married and divorced) at a fairly rapid rate. Thus a man can have stable and unstable unions at the same time.

Sexual life between husbands and wives can bring conflict and problems of adjustment. This is a difficult area to investigate directly, especially if it is considered a sensitive topic of conversation as it is among the Kanuri. Discussions with intimate friends lead to several conclusions—first, that there is a wide range of competence among men at sexual activity and, secondly, that women demand or at least desire high standards of performance. Indeed, women claim that although premarital chastity (for a previously married woman) is the culturally respected norm, men who insist on living up to this rule are suspect. Such men may claim propriety, religious zeal, and piety, but they may in fact be hiding their incompetence until after the wedding. Such interpretations do not go unnoticed by men who are therefore subject to anxiety about their potency. Add to this the fact of semi-public defloration enacted at a girl's first marriage, and the fact that there are often many years of difference between the older husband and his young wife, and we can begin to see the outlines of the problem.

Many polygynous unions and unions with younger girls are carried out by successful mature, but physically older, men. Not all such men are at their sexually most potent stage of life when they are socially and economically at their fullest capacity to marry these most attractive wives. On her side, the woman or young girl tends to value herself in terms of her attractiveness to men as wife and woman. It is a correlate of the dominance of men that the subordinate in this superior-subordinate relationship should value in herself those properties for which she is valued by the superior, i.e., the dominant male. Therefore, it is predictable that sexual intercourse be important to the wife as an indicator of her success in her role. It is only a small step from this analysis to the next logical step which is to predict much attraction for extra-marital relations, since this activity would enhance the woman's opinion of herself and provide her with an opportunity to find "better" partners.

However, the word "better" is a difficult one to isolate unidimensionally. When I ask women to explain Kanuri adultery, they generally remark that no husband ever gives his wife gifts, clothing, perfume, soap, jewelry, etc., all the time. A woman's desire for these material goods always outstrips their supply from the husband, for they are symbolic measurements of her self-worth and her success as a person. Therefore, all a man needs to do is to channel such gifts secretly to the woman he wants and ultimately, say informants, she cannot resist. Indeed, there is a special name *(sərsər)* for the intermediary, usually an old woman in the pay of the new suitor, who brings news to a wife from a male admirer. If she succumbs to these entreaties, she may either have an adulterous affair or move toward a divorce with her present husband in order to be free, or both.

Adultery for either sex is considered a jural offense for which a person may be taken to court and fined. In practice, however, adultery with a married woman is by far the most serious crime, punishable traditionally by the lash and even death. Marriage and bridewealth in both wider Islam and Bornu create for the husband sole rights to a woman's services, especially her childbearing and sexual activity (Levy 1957:95). Thus a man caught in an adulterous action is made to pay a heavy fine to the husband and the court for having infringed on these rights. General Muslim rules of evidence requiring four witnesses are difficult if they must report on the illicit intercourse. However, the Kanuri courts accept more indirect evidence which establish a series of boundary behaviors for wifely modesty, and these have jural significance, i.e., they can be upheld in court. Thus a woman outside of her husband's compound should not enter the compound of a single man, or a married one whose wife is absent. Indeed, to be observed sitting on the same mat with another man's wife is considered an impropriety which, under some circumstances, can produce a court case for those involved. Thus immodesty which is observable and can be reported in court signifies adulterous intention on the part of a wife and can be used as direct evidence in a court. No wonder, then, that most married Kanuri women are extremely withdrawn in public and careful in the presence of men other than their husbands and close kin.

There is a now famous Bornu story of such an occurrence which had profound political effects during the 1950's. The wife of a senior official returned home early from an extended absence by her husband and herself. The husband's most immediate subordinate in the official hierarchy was in his superior's compound because he was fulfilling the senior's official duties during the latter's absence and therefore felt he should be residing in the "official residence" associated with the superior's office. The wife, on the other hand, felt that she would be compromised if she were to live in the same compound with her husband's official deputy and ordered him out of her husband's household. Ultimately, using threats of police action, she made him leave. He on his part vowed to create political trouble for her husband—for this loss to his dignity—which he proceeded to carry out with serious results. Whether this story is true or not, it illustrates how strongly women feel about the appearance of modesty, as well as how offices and residencies are conjoined in peoples' minds.

One final point of wife adultery. Although it often does occur, there is no necessary connection between adultery and divorce, at least in a strictly legal sense. Many men, however, either collect this fine, and then divorce, or divorce unfruitful wives or even suspect ones. They reason that their power to control such a woman has been lost and she may very well try this same behavior again. Therefore, the rights they thought they paid for are not in fact available in such a union. To be continually cuckolded is a form of impotence which most Kanuri cannot tolerate.

Infidelity by husbands, especially in the urban area, is extremely common. Although it is known and accepted that extra-marital affairs by men are a type of adultery, it is also considered extremely common for married men to have sexual liaisons of shorter or longer duration with unmarried divorced women. Sexual liaisons with married women are, as already noted, a serious offense. However, having an affair with an unmarried divorcee is not considered, by men, to be a very serious breakage of the rules governing sexual activity and marriage. But there are two quite different situations under which such an affair can be described. In the first, the man has relations with the woman at her residence, and in the second he has her come to his own compound.

Unless there is definite evidence of wrong-doing, the Kanuri believe that a man's home should not be entered. Thus, if his present wife is absent, or does not know about it, it is fairly safe to bring a divorced women into his own household for sexual relations. Law enforcement authorities have no right to enter the house without the man's permission and, therefore, if his internal household relations are not disturbed, it is quite safe to carry on such activities in his own household. A very wealthy urban man may have several houses so that if he wishes, one can be used safely for extra-marital relations while his family and tenants use the others. On the other hand, to go to the residence of the woman involves the risk of being caught and fined. On several occasions, I have observed the results of round-ups in which the police made night-time visits to the rooms of known divorced women. The next morning a large crowd of men and women crowded round the police station to be charged with illicit sexual relations and pay fines. However, such "raids" are rare and do little except to make people a trifle cautious.

The fact that such extra-marital relations are not regarded as serious offenses can be seen in the following illustration.

> Baba is an urban person living in a rural village as the field representative of his emirate department. He is a young man of thirty-two, has one wife (one other recently divorced) and no children. He is well-known for his interest in the opposite sex and his joking remarks and gossip about sexual topics when in the company of close male companions of roughly the same age.
>
> Recently, word had reached him that a high status woman, wife of one of the leading men of the village, had warned another woman to be careful in her relations to Baba because he was quite capable of making adulterous advances, thus ruining her reputation with her husband and the village. Baba was furious and swore to his friends that he never had sex relations with married women. Such a thing is tantamount to thievery, he said, and to link him to such acts is to call him a thief.
>
> A few evenings later, a commotion occurred, at Baba's compound. His wife had gone to visit her kinsfolk in the city and Baba had brought a young divorced woman to his sleeping hut. He then rounded up witnesses, some of them officials of the local district court and brought them to his compound to show them the girl. He said that rumors were going about that he, Baba, was an adulterer who sought after other men's wives. Not so and we were instructed to look closely at the girl to see if she were anyone's wife. Was she? No. "Fine then," said Baba. "Do not go about saying that I, Baba, am an adulterer." The amazed and startled crowd then dispersed.

This is a very rare occurrence. No Kanuri publicizes his sex life. However, Baba was so concerned over his reputation that he decided to have us witness his extra-marital affairs in order to demonstrate that he had nothing to hide from anyone. The example does, however, point up the very sharp distinction between the relations of a married man and an unmarried, versus a married, woman. And a moment's reflection shows that Baba was right in his use of metaphor. Adultery with a married woman *is* akin to thievery in Kanuri eyes, because the husband "owns" his wife's sexual services and has in effect paid for them. To take these services is to deprive him of this sole right, making his bridewealth payment meaningless as well as decreasing his ability to control resources, i.e., his power.

It is important to realize here that the affect displayed in the above case had little to do with sex per se. It was Baba's respectability as a trustworthy community member that was being challenged. Kanuri regard emotional involvement or display of any kind as weakness. Women are the ones who manifest sexual jealousy over their treatment as co-wives or because they feel less self-esteem when their husband is behaving as though he might be going outside marriage for sexual satisfactions. All informants freely admit that women experience jealousy over the necessity of sharing a husband, but that is their lot—say the men.

In general, both sexes agree that women do not like polygyny. However, there is a paradox here that is generally resolved in favor of the institution. As we have seen, possibly the most important value attached to the husband role is that of provider—and the best providers are the more economically secure men. But these are also the men who can most easily afford more than one wife. Therefore, it is likely that the "best" husbands will also be ones who are more likely to have plural wives. The ethnographic generalization can also be made that Kanuri men claim three wife families are to be avoided. To have one, or two, or four is fine, they say, but with three wives there is trouble, fighting, and divorce. When asked why this should be so, they discuss triadic relationships in general. With two or four, there is always the possibility of equal groupings on each side of an inter-wife conflict, but with three it is always the most likely possibility that there will be two against one. There seems to be no consensus or cultural knowledge of who allies with whom in terms of wife order. That jealousy (*kanduli*) is a built-in concomitant among wives, or by a wife toward the possibility of her husband taking a second wife is universally accepted as the condition of women in Kanuri marriage.

One rather infrequent method of decreasing such jealousy is to keep wives separated in different compounds. Although only a few cases like this turn up in our sample of over 700, no informant considered them to be deviant in the moral sense. In all such cases, the husband's economic activities kept him alternating, either seasonally or more regularly, between several localities. In each, he kept a household and a wife. Thus his wives never interact within the same compound. A few report that such wives are rarely jealous since they have sole access to the husband when he is "home." This has been corroborated by a woman who has agreed to such an arrangement.

The pattern is interesting structurally as well, since it can amount to a matrilocal marriage or at least an uxorilocal deviation within a normally virilocal and patrilocal culture. I would speculate that such a pattern has been useful in the past, especially to desert travelers in the long distance Saharan trade. Travelers could then marry women in various oases and have a safe place to stay when they stopped en route. The girl could stay with her people and the man thus had a link to those who controlled the local resources. In a sense he was establishing his own entrepôt by marriage.[6]

Continuing with the topic of affect, it is clear that marital partners of many years standing do come to have a strong bond of affection and feeling of companionship for one another. However, the idea of being passionately involved with any woman, wife, or lover is repugnant to Kanuri men informants to whom I have spoken on the topic. As one informant put it:

Love of the heart [emotions] is dangerous and can lead to much trouble. If I love someone, then what happens to them happens to me. Then I feel I want to kill her because I am not my own master since what happens to her happens to me.

Other informants tell stories of men demeaning themselves because of their emotional involvement with a particular woman. These stories usually involve a wife who has run away to her *luwali* or is threatening to do so. The man then spends all his money on gifts for her, hoping to make her stay—but she still leaves. In one such story, the man finally went to the Emir and said he was going to commit suicide (an almost unheard of thing in Bornu) unless he could get his wife to return. (The traditionally legal way to do this is for the Shehu [Emir] to declare the woman to be his own slave, thereby depriving her of any legal rights—then the Shehu gives the wife as a gift to her former husband.)

The important point here is that, although emotional involvement is considered a possibility in marriage or any heterosexual relations, men believe such feelings must be kept under strict control. Women are fundamentally viewed as values to be utilized. Some are better than others across a series of judgmental scales: cooking, trustworthiness, beauty, sexual ability, and so on. But men must never become emotionally dependent upon any particular woman or "She makes a slave of you," said a young city dweller.

Legitimate fertility is a highly valued attribute in a Kanuri woman. For reasons that are not completely clear, as we have seen, fertility is low in the Bornu population. No known effective contraceptives are used. Venereal disease is widespread, especially gonorrhea, but several medical workers in the area believed that the problem was complex and as yet poorly understood. In human terms, many woman are encountered who have never given birth to live young although virtually all women are married at some time in their lives. This scarcity in fertility is one of the major reasons why men wish to marry and leads to a high estimation of wives who do in fact produce live children, at least while they are producing and caring for them. This does not mean that fertile women are never divorced; it does lead to the hypothesis of an inverse correlation between fertility and divorce.

Another cultural indication of the value of fertility is the concept of the *bənji* This is a child in the womb that will not come out. Kanuri medical beliefs include the possibility that a woman may conceive but for some unknown reason the embryo remains and the pregnancy is in a continual state of arrest. I have had women report such arrested pregnancies as being anywhere from two to twelve years old. Sometimes they document the "fact" by referring to the non-occurrence of a menstrual period at the beginning of the *bənji* period. Obviously, in a society of high infertility and high value placed upon this scarce activity, the bǝnji concept alleviates some of the anxiety and frustration of wanting children by providing a rationale for non-achievement which says in effect that failure is only partial.[7]

Another means of avoiding infertility is uncommon today and restricted primarily to a few wealthy and powerful households where concubines (female slaves) are still kept. Because the female slave is the subordinate of a wife, the latter, if she is infertile, takes over the child of a concubine and calls it her own. Everyone "knows" that the child is not a product of the wife's womb, but they speak as if it was. The child ultimately knows of his or her true maternity, but the fictive maternal relationship is sociologically complete, including inheritance rights, and no one makes much of the biological link of the child to a slave girl. This is as close to true adoption as Kanuri institutions come and I would speculate that it was much more common in the past when slavery was a widely used form of expanding household size.

Although fertility is valued, illegitimacy is abhorrent. Because so much status is dependent upon agnatic descent, a fatherless child is seen as someone who is less than half a person. Possibly the most common way to open up a conversation about identity in Bornu is to ask "Who is your father?" To have none, or no other agnates, means that a man does not have a group that will be responsible for him in court. For a woman, it means that her potential husbands have no agnatic group to deal with, although she might get a mother's brother to act as her luwali. The result is that almost all extra-marital pregnancies produce quick marriages with low bridewealth inducements. Often a poor or low status man who could not easily obtain a wife, or another one, is induced by the girl's family to marry her. Whether he knows of her pregnancy or not seems to be a moot point, with size of the community being the determining factor. It is hard to hide such news in small isolated villages. Older informants say the system works quite well, although they add accounts of World War II when an American air force base was built at Maiduguri. Because of the expected skin color differences of children resulting from interracial extra-marital matings, the system began breaking down and infanticide is said to have been initiated. The practice is traditionally unknown and not carried on at present.

One final point with respect to children is the effect on family life of high divorce coupled with the idea that the children remain with the father, unless they are not yet weaned. This does not mean that all children must stay when their mothers leave. In some cases, especially of young girls, the child might be sent to live or visit her mother for varying periods. Or the child might be sent to the household of another kinsman altogether. One of the most frequent factors affecting such decisions is the nature of the relationships in the household which the mother is now leaving. Does the remaining co-wife (or wives) have children of her own? Does she feel threatened by this child? Will she look after it properly? Informants tell of hard times they have had when they were left to the mercies of a cruel or unsympathetic co-wife of their mother after she was divorced. More infrequently, stories are also told of co-wives who turned out to be kinder and more nurturant than their own mother. In general, however, the relationship is a difficult one and can produce tension between the husband and wife when the husband discovers she is mistreating his children by other marriages.

A male child poses a threat to mother's ex-co-wives because ultimately he will inherit, or is likely to inherit, his father's household. When he does so, his mother (her divorced previous co-wife) will return as mother of the household head and she will have to leave, or at least have no legal right to remain. Thus the co-wife can see the child as a threat to one source of security in her old age.

There is also tension between husbands and wives over the limits of proper expectation. Phillips (1953) comments on this point, in what has come to be the characteristic way of describing it. Thus he points out that, in Zaria, different degrees of purdah are agreed upon before marriage is entered into, and the determinant variables are wealth and ruralism. In Bornu, and I suspect elsewhere in the northern emirates of Nigeria as well, these agreements on what each spouse may expect of one another are really rather vague. The wife knows roughly how much purdah any particular man expects and he knows roughly what freedom she considers essential, but there is much room for argument since these guidelines do not ever fit every case.

Possibly the best examples of such tension points are situations involving cooking for extra people or the visiting of kin by the wife. The wife may know something of her cooking responsibilities before she enters the marriage, but the husband may be using this new marriage to expand his social network. Thus he may invite people to eat on sudden notice and demand that food be brought for him and his friends. When it is not forthcoming, or comes and is poorly done or skimpy, the man may feel he is being shamed before people he is trying to impress with his largesse and hospitality. The wife feels she has been shamed and dealt with unfairly, since no warning was given of the need for such extra work, and the result is an undeserved demonstration of incompetence. Such occasions produce tensions and arguments. The wife may tell the husband to warn her in the future so they may both be better prepared—that way lies reconciliation and cooperation if the husband agrees. He may instead tell her she must be ready at all times because he never knows when extra people will be offered his hospitality. She may agree and cook more from then on or she may disagree and say that she did not realize this marriage involved so much extra work—implying that had she known she would not have entered into such an agreement and possibly it might be better to end the relationship.

No matter how strict the seclusion of a Kanuri wife, she has a jural right and obligation to return to her own kinsfolk for important occasions such as *rites de passage* or when someone is sick. Again, although these rules are quite clear, husbands and wives may disagree on the exact way in which such obligations are to be carried out. He may feel that she should wait a few days before going, or stay for a shorter period, and she may not agree. The structural rules governing her rights of return run counter to the ideology of dominance, since this is one area of the wife's life over which the husband does not have control, and this conflict can create tensions, especially if other factors are already contributing to mistrust and conflict. Thus one man in a rural village was extremely agitated over his wife returning to her village several miles away. He already had reason to suspect her fidelity and knew that she would be traveling through the village of a former husband. His suspicions were almost intolerable and yet he could not prevent her from going. This marriage ended in divorce a few months later. What this means as well is that marital unions that are village endogamous suffer fewer tensions over the woman's kin obligations since she can visit them regularly and return at night.

The above tensions over kinship obligations are well known in the literature (Fallers 1957), but the problem of descent and the husband-wife relationship is more complex. First, there are the wife's kin who, as noted above, maintain their connection and demand her participation in their ceremonial activities (to say the least). However, there are other factors. The woman's family, especially the *luwali*, may have a special relationship to the husband or his kin which existed prior to the marriage and from which the union resulted. Thus the husband may be a client-follower of the girl's father-cum-*luwali*. To cement the relationship and reward the client, the father gives his daughter, or one of the girls of the household over whom he has some power of marital dispensation. The break-up of this union does not destroy the patron-client relationship, but its continuity helps to strengthen and maintain it. Therefore, when the wife runs off to complain to her *luwali*, he tries to persuade her to return to her husband. Indeed, unless physical injury is involved, *luwalis* generally try to act as reconcilers of marital disputes. In this sense, the wife's kin are operating to perpetuate and maintain the union.

I have on rarer occasions observed the reverse situation in which a wife's kin helped to break up a marriage. The wife is generally very young and her descent group, especially her *luwali*, have decided that the marriage is unsatisfactory. This judgment can result from the husband's desire to move to a distant place, or to his fall in fortune or both. The *luwali* then instructs his young relative to induce a divorce by misbehaving. The husband finally becomes fed up and divorces the girl.

In both of the above kinds of cases, the assumption must be made that the wife will be influenced by her relatives. This is much more applicable to younger girls and women. The woman goes through successive marriage and/or grows older as she becomes progressively more independent in her decisions about marriage and divorce. Thus the effect of descent upon the wife's behavior in marriage is partly a function of the age of the wife.

An influence not discussed in the literature on Africa but mentioned quite regularly by informants is that of the husband's descent group members. Women sometimes say, "His mother talked against me," in explaining the reason for a divorce. It should be remembered that the wife enters her husband's family in a more encompassing way than he ever enters hers. This is especially true of patrilocal unions in which she must suddenly cope with the husband, his agnates, and the wives of these agnates, as well as his mother and possibly her co-wives. This receiving group can make such an entry harder or easier by being more or less helpful, more or less friendly and hospitable, more and less proud and formal. If they, or at least the most powerful among them (especially the husband's mother), decide that she is less attractive or acceptable than they might wish, then the marriage can suffer through their influence on the husband and their treatment of the wife.

By the same token, acceptance by the husband's group, fully granted only after years of faithful wifehood and demonstrated loyalty to his interests and those of his kin can provide a deep security to the wife. In such cases she does, in actual social terms, become an accepted member of her husband's family. In such situations (which are quite rare), the man's entire kindred will help to maintain the marriage because this particular wife is now such a fully active and accepted member. And even though she can be lost through divorce, unlike those who are born into the group, she still has a similar place because she has earned it through the years.

Above and beyond all of the sociological factors that enter into marriage are qualities of personality. Although wealthy people can afford to be more uncompromising and therefore are more rigid in enforcing standards, while poor husbands cannot generally afford such privileges because they are more dependent on their wives, this is not the whole story. Indeed, the very idea of being uncompromising suggests that certain psychological qualities are related to marital relations in Bornu, no matter what other factors may be determining the stability of the union. This deduction is corroborated by field work. Certainly men and women known for their short tempers and sharp tongues were also seen as high divorcers. Contrarily, men and women who were gentle and kind were thought to be more flexible and tolerant and therefore were believed by informants to be low divorcers. Field work does not corroborate this latter folk view. I knew and observed many mild mannered, gentle, tolerant men who were high divorcers. On the basis of intimate interpersonal knowledge with only a few of these at higher status levels, I interpret this to mean that these men are tolerant and kind and judicious more out of fear than from a deep-seated openness of flexibility of personality. They are self-controlled because emotional displays bother them very much. Therefore, when the possibility of conflict and emotional outburst enters their own family life, they cut it off through low thresholds for divorce.

This theory explains the case of Mallam, above, who divorced his wife for merely going out the front door to buy perfume. Mallam is a highly respected member of the community. People bring their troubles to him—for his calm gentle ways are widely known. Yet he manifested classic "color shock" on a Rorschach test.[8] When asked several days afterward why he had rejected all color cards in the test, Mallam said "I saw such terrible things on those particular cards that I could not speak of it to anyone." As an informant, Mallam was excellent, speaking without hesitation on any topic. However, his account of any event always censored extreme behavior. A husband-wife quarrel that ended in physical violence was described as "a disagreement." He constantly used circumlocutions to refer to events where outbursts of any kind had occurred. Thus his gentleness was basically a kind of fearful repression of affect. People reacted to this as an asset on his part. Yet his calmness was only surface deep. He literally could not cope with real conflict in his interpersonal life, and therefore kept divorcing wives rather than come to grips with the tensions that produced the conflict.

On the other hand, I have observed flexibile, tolerant men who were also low divorcers. The basic difference that I as a participant observer have seen in these men, as opposed to the type exemplified by Mallam, is their sense of personal security—their lack of fearfulness. They were more accepting of the vicissitudes of life in general and tend to be persons who "roll with the punches." Such men are tolerant of deviancy in general and therefore tend to use the divorce option only after continual breakage of rules finally makes them realize that something must be done.

For women, I am less sure of my ground because of my lack of intimate interpersonal contacts with very many of them. However, even with scanty contacts, I think there are some grounds for saying that uncompromising, rigid women as well as men tend to divorce more often than flexible cooperative ones. However, with women there is also, I believe, a deep psychological rejection of male dominance which when it cannot be repressed causes either conflict or in very rare cases (for Kanuri) culturally determined trance states (*bori*) in which men are screamingly rejected. Sometimes this rejection can take the form of rejecting sexual activity. One woman described how she had a small animal in her vagina that bit her when she had intercourse. She was twenty or twenty-one years old and had been married four times, but never for more than six months! When I asked her why, she told the story of her problem with sexual intercourse. For some reason, which I do not pretend to understand, she has a reaction to intercourse which produces sharp physical pain during the act. If the origin of this symptom is not physiological, then I would hypothesize that this is another manifestation of this same rejection.

Summary

When two people are in a hierarchical superior-subordinate relationship, the structure or "rules of the game" define the authority relations between them. As we have pointed out, Kanuri husbands are dominant. This is a social and cultural premise of the society. However, as in all hierarchical relations, there is a tension between legitimacy (accepting his dominance) and trying to make the relationship less unequal in authority (a competitive struggle for power). That is to say, just under the surface of legitimacy of dominance lies the constant potential of defiance by the subordinate. The strict segregation of men's and women's work and activities serves to exaggerate the force of this defiance, since it turns men and women, husbands and wives, into semi-separate "classes" in which the subordinate class has various legitimate and illegitimate means to obtain greater amounts of power than is theirs by cultural definition. This interpretation in terms of power and authority leads to the question of stability. If instability in marital unions is the "surface" manifestation of the authority distinctions between husbands and wives, then what brings more and less stability? Is there more stability if the husband possesses all of the necessary ingredients of power so that his will cannot be successfully challenged, thereby enhancing legitimacy and decreasing defiance? Of, is it "better" to reduce the authority distinctions thereby easing the desire for revolt? This is the basic question that we have asked of the quantitative data, which will be illuminated in later chapters.

Chapter 10
The Dissolution of Kanuri Marriage

Bohannan (1963) has pointed out that marriages can be dissolved in a number of ways—by separation, desertion, annulment, death, and divorce. All of these *can* occur in Bornu, but in a strictly record-keeping or statistical sense only separation, death, and divorce can be counted for purposes of analysis, and separations are almost always temporary. Therefore, actual data on dissolutions can be converted into death or divorce because that is what ultimately occurs anyway. In some societies, especially those undergoing very rapid change, the definitions of these concepts in operational terms is extremely difficult. Thus, when common-law unions break up, should the act be dubbed divorce, desertion, separation, or what? Is it different from the breakup of legally recognized unions in which the locally recognized traditional formalities of initiating a marriage have been honored. The Kanuri are a relatively stable society, and four of the five forms of dissolution—death, separation, desertion, and divorce—are clearly demarcated from one another culturally so that operational distinctions can be made in locally derived and easily understandable terms. Let us look at these in turn.

Death

The Kanuri distinguish between something that is dead or has no life in it (*nuna* = dead) and the event which marks off the change from being alive to being dead (*kərmu* = death). Death as an event (*kərmu*) triggers into action a series of rituals and clear-cut obligatory behavior for the surviving spouse in a marriage. A funeral (*shitəra*) must be performed within twenty-four hours and the body buried in a local burying ground (*kəbbar*); generally, this occurs in the early morning. Afterward, a mourning period is carried out for some time before ordinary activities can be carried on.

When a wife dies, messages are sent to the husband's kin and most especially to the kin of the dead wife. People of the neighborhood and kin gather at the compound where she died and begin to prepare the funeral. There is very strong compulsion to attend funerals, so that close friends, neighbors, and fellow villagers always go. Relatives will often travel several days, missing the funeral itself, but still they feel they must be there to declare and enact their relationship to the deceased. Traditionally, husbands wore their robe inside out and their caps either at the very back of the head or not at all. At present these customs are not practiced widely, especially in the cities and among the younger Western educated groups. Koranic *mallams* or priests gather outside the gate of the compound along with the other men. Women go into the compound and help prepare the corpse which must be washed. During the washing, an *nzaye* or giving of small amounts of money to the husband is held, after which the *mallams* say prayers and read from the Koran. Traditionally, *nzaye* are held at all *rites de passage* except funerals, but in the past few years city people have begun to practice it at funerals as well. This reflects the growing expense of having funerals as well as the Kanuri idea that parts of ceremonies are modular and can be attached to many different kinds of rituals.

The washing of the body is accompanied by wailing and keening. At several of these, I observed the wail of the women turn into a song in which the words "A woman's life is hard" were repeated over and over again. After the washing, the body is wrapped in three separate new white cloths—one for the loins, one for the head, and one which covers the entire body. The wrapped corpse is then put on a bier and carried by men to the area outside the gate of the compound where a special death prayer is led by the *mallams*.

The body is then taken, by the men, to the burial grounds outside the village or city where it is put into a previously prepared grave. The grave has a narrower long ditch at the bottom of a shallow pit. Sticks and leaves are placed over the inner grave to protect the body from the earth, prayers are said, and the upper grave is filled with earth.

The husband now enters the mourning period (*taji*) of one year. He remains at him home receiving friends and relatives at his gate sitting on a mat silently praying or accepting the condolences of his visitors. The man may do this for three days or seven—it is a matter of how far the kin must travel, and how pressing are his worldly concerns. During the first three to seven days of mourning, the husband must refrain from all sexual intercourse. Coming out of mourning is called "turning the calabashes" (*kəmo frəmta*). This derives from the custom of turning the calabashes that held the water for the body washing of the deceased right side up at this time. Calabashes used for this purpose are turned upside down after their use on the day of the funeral. At the time of the "turning of the calabashes," prayers (*sadaka*) are said by a small assemblage of men and the initial restrictive mourning period is officially over. However, if the mourning period was held for only three days, then another assemblage of men led by *mallams* is held to commemorate the death. Forty days after the death another *sadaka* is held, and one year later it is held again.

The husband is a possible heir to his dead wife, although her woman's goods go in practice to her female kin. However, jurally speaking, the husband may lay claim to being an heir even if he has divorced her within seventy days.

A man should wait a decent length of time (one to two months) after the death of a wife before remarrying if he already has another wife in his family. However, if a man has no other wives, especially when there are children or other cooking and womanly duties left unstaffed, it is quite legitimate to marry soon after the wife's death.

Ritually, the death of a husband is treated in similar fashion. However, a wife must wait out the *tabari* of approximately four months and ten days (more precisely, 100 days) waiting period before she can become a *zower* or single marriageable women who has been married before. This is the widespread Muslim waiting period after a marriage to ascertain whether she is carrying the previous husband's child.[1] During this period, the Kanuri woman is *kamba*—a widow—or, as one informant put it, "She does work in the house, but she is not allowed to see marriageable men or arrange for her remarriage in any way." Informants seem universally confident that, during widowhood, this strict confinement and chaste behavior is always carried out in practice. A few very pious and socially "correct" women, more so in the upper classes, will not marry until the last prayers for the dead are said one year after the husband's death.

Distinctive female practices do exist. Kanuri hairstyles for women all include hair plaiting, but a widow lets her hair go unplaited and parted in the middle. A plain black or white gown is worn, and prayer beads given by the dead husband's kin are carried and used while the widow sits in front of the compound or in it during the mourning period. A shawl is used to cover the head at all times, especially if there are men about—even close kin. During the 100 day waiting period, a water pot is placed near the husband's sleeping room in the compound and the widow pours water from this vessel over herself seven times early on each Friday after his death. This, plus the undoing of the hair and the plain clothes, make the widow unattractive, both to other men as well as the "shade" of her husband so that he will forget her. If he does not, lore has it he will return constantly to her in her sleep, or even while she is awake, and ultimately drive her mad.[2] On the first Thursday after the 100 day period in the husband's compound, the widow, or widows if the man had more than one wife, cook a ram and give the meat to *mallams* and old unmarried women as charity. In the evening, players come and are paid to sing and drum; the women sing as well and beat pestles so that the dead husband will not come to claim his widow as his own. The drumming and singing keep the wife awake and the ghost away. It is in dreams during sleep that the ghost may come, and thus the wife must try to stay awake all night to prevent herself from dreaming of her late husband. On Friday morning, she splashes water over herself seven times from the water pot near her dead husband's sleeping room for the last time. That evening she is free to return to

TABLE 10:1. AGE SPECIFIC DISTRIBUTION OF MARRIAGES ENDING IN DEATH FOR 741 KANURI UNIONS

Age	Age at Time of Marriage					% of all unions contracted at this age	Age at Time of Spouse's Death				
	Men Reporting	Women Reporting	Total	%	Acc. %		Men Reporting	Women Reporting	Total	%	Acc. %
10-14	0	7	7	18.4	18.4	6	0	1	1	2.6	2.6
15-19	8	1	9	23.7	42.1	9	0	0	0	0	2.6
20-24	8	0	8	21.1	63.2	6	6	2	8	21.1	23.7
25-29	3	2	5	13.2	76.4	5	4	3	7	18.4	42.1
30-34	2	1	3	7.9	84.3	1	3	2	5	13.2	55.3
35-39	0	0	0	0	84.3	-	4	0	4	10.5	65.8
40-44	2	0	2	5.3	89.6	4	4	2	6	15.8	81.6
45-49	0	2	2	5.3	94.9	9	2	1	3	7.9	89.5
50-54	1	0	1	2.6	97.5	5	0	1	1	2.6	92.1
55-59	1	0	1	2.6	100.1	11	2	0	2	5.3	97.4
60+	0	0	0	0	100.1		0	1	1	2.6	100.0
Totals	25	13	38	100.0			25	13	38	100.0	

the household of her own kin. A few never do, especially older women who know they cannot marry again and have nowhere to go. Others remain because their sons inherit the compound and they then become the respected mother of the compound head. Still others—the vast majority—do return to their own kin, or rent rooms (in the city) and seek new husbands.

The interesting points to notice in all of this are the greater elaborateness of widowhood and the Kanuri view of marriage, such that marriage and widowhood last one hundred days after the death of the husband. Not until then are *both* over with. The greater elaboration of the female mourning rites are all connected to the wife's subordination to her husband—*even after his death*. Special precautions must be taken to ritually break his desire to hold onto her. She washes ritually at his sleeping hut—as she did after intercourse—indicating symbolically that his sexual connection to her is now broken forever. However, men, who also wash after intercourse, do not do so as part of mourning rituals for wives. The pointed desire to keep the husband's ghost away, to prevent the wife from dreaming of him, is a constant reiteration of his desire as a ghost to maintain his control over her—especially during the *tabari*, waiting period, when she is still officially or jurally married to him. In other words, even though he is dead the husband-wife relationship continues for the 100 day period. This is the essential difference between losing a husband as opposed to a wife. When a man loses his wife by death, the marriage is dissolved forthwith. But this is not the case when a wife loses her husband. Thus the rituals of mourning are more elaborate for a wife because she is in effect still under the jural control of her dead husband, and disengaging from such a supernatural relationship requires more elaborate operations.

It is this special status of the wife during the waiting period that creates a totally different conception of widowhood among the Kanuri. For them a widow *(kamba)* is the status given to a woman during the 100 day waiting period after her husband's death. As we have noted, a few women elect to maintain the status throughout an entire year. But when the period is over, *so is widowhood.* The wife then becomes either a *zower* (an unmarried previously married and marriageable woman) or a *kamurso* (an old woman, and therefore an unmarriageable one).

Besides these cultural norms and symbols, the most striking thing about marital dissolutions brought on by death in Bornu is their scarcity. Only 5% of the 741 unions in our sample ended through the death of a spouse. If we restrict this calculation to completed marriages, leaving aside those that are still extant, the rate of dissolution rises to 8% (8 per 100 marriages)—still strikingly lower than the American figure of 65%.[3] In other words, for very high divorce societies there is a tendency for widows and widowers to be relatively uncommon occurrences.

Furthermore, the distribution of deaths (given in Table 10:1) is quite distinctive. In low divorce societies like the U.S.A., where death is the major source of marital dissolution, the rate of spouse deaths increases steadily with age and duration of marital unions. In Bornu, deaths are spread over all durations, although 54% of them occur before the tenth year of marriage, while only a small fraction (8%) of U.S. spouses die in the same period. Conversely, if we look at completed marriages—those already ended by death or divorce—and focus on older people who are 50 or over when they lose a spouse, then 12% of such Bornu unions are dissolved by death in this later life period, in contrast to 91% for the U.S.A.[4] Even among the elderly, Bornu marriages are dissolved by other means besides death. Indeed, looking at Table 10:1 it is possible to conclude that it is those who marry young, especially the girls who are most prone to experience the loss of a spouse by death (even if the overall probability is not very great). Thus over half of those women reporting dissolutions by death said they were widowed during their first marriages. This reflects the very large age disparity in some of these first marriages for girls whose parents give them to old men. The fact that men report over half of their loss of wives by death before she was thirty-five is due almost entirely to death in childbirth. In general, then, very few Kanuri marriages end in death—and over half of these occur when the marriages are still of short duration (under ten years) and when the widowed partner is still quite young. The common occurrence in low divorce societies like the U.S.A. of elderly couples living out their days together is rare in Bornu.

Desertion

To the Kanuri, as in Western society, desertion is an illegitimate act in that the deserting partner has not obtained the formal legal right to renounce marital obligations. The word *kaso* or run away is used to refer to such a dissolution, as is the phrase *kararo gawo*, to have gone to bush or to have hidden in the bush. The fact that no special term is used reflects the extreme rarity of this practice. All informants have heard of one or two cases, I have observed one myself, but none turned up, or was admitted to, in our sample of over 700 unions. The reasons for this will become clear as we describe its practice and the sanctions applied to it by the society.

When informants relate stories of actual desertion cases, it invariably turns out that it is the husband who has deserted. When desertion by the husband becomes suspect, the woman generally returns to her kin so that she can find support and food. After an indefinite period of waiting to hear from her husband, she then complains, through her *luwali* or through the head of the compound she is staying in. The complaint goes up the political hierarchy and at each step she re-tells her story. The courts (at each level) question her about the wayward spouse. Has she not heard anything from her husband at all? Has he sent her anything? Does she know where he is at present? What does he look like? Is he tall or short? Does he have any scars? What kind of tribal marks does he have? What is his name? Who was his father?

The court is generally the district Alkali's court for such cases because the matter involves using the politico-judicial system of the entire state. The judge or Alkali then initiates a search by sending a letter to the central office of the Bornu Native Authority, i.e., the central administration of the emirate. Letters describing the details of the case then go out to all district heads and all Alkali courts of the emirate. If the man is living in Bornu, he will be found—and informants say that in most cases they know of, the man has been discovered. I have recorded several instances where the husband fled beyond Bornu and therefore beyond the jurisdiction of its courts and political authority.

When the man is found within Bornu, he is brought to court and questioned. Does he wish to send something in the way of support to his wife, or does he want a divorce? Does he wish to return to her? If he would like to return and cannot afford the transport the court will provide it so that a reconciliation can be effected. The man is either given cash for a lorry, or put on a Native Administration vehicle going that way. If the man refuses to return, the court writes a letter to the official to whom the woman complained, declaring the marriage over and a divorce to be in effect one hundred days from the time she receives the news. If the woman has a child within this *tabari* waiting period, it is still considered to be fathered by the husband-deserter even though he may have been absent for many months. Informants explain this anomaly by saying that people's spirits travel at night and the husband could have impregnated her in this way. Soldiers and traders away at war or on trading expeditions use a similar argument to claim paternity of children born to their wives during long absences. Such beliefs emphasize a legal as opposed to genitorial or biological rights—a characteristic of Kanuri society as a whole.

· In those very few cases of desertion by a wife, informants agree that a man should not go to court until he has searched everywhere he possibly can by himself. When the husband has found out a few of the relevant facts concerning his wife's actions—where she might be found, with whom she is living, etc., he can send word asking her to return. If she does not, then the case goes to court. If she still refuses to return, she must repay all bridewealth and even more in some cases where the husband has spent a great deal on her. If she refuses to pay or return, she is sent to prison.

On some occasions, she might be found married to someone else. This is always a situation in which the court must act—for now a rather complex set of infractions has occurred, including adultery. The most culpable and most severely questioned person is the *luwali* of the woman. As the man responsible for dispensing her marriage rights, how and why did he allow the second marriage to take place? If the *luwali* replies that he did not know she was already married, the Alkali (judge) will say that he should have questioned her more closely and received witnesses or a letter from the first husband ensuring that she was divorced and available for remarriage. If such was not available, then the *luwali* should have contacted the first husband. If the court decides that the woman rather cleverly duped the *luwali*, then he may get off with a severe warning—generally, however, informants felt that the *luwali* would be fined for such an offense.

The woman is severely lectured by the court and may even receive a short prison sentence. The second husband is not fined, however, as he normally would be in an adultery case. His adultery has been innocently carried out because he has been duped. However, he is still infringing on another man's marital rights; he therefore loses all bridewealth that went into this unfortunate marriage and the entire affair must be written off as a loss. The first husband has the wife returned, or she must buy her way out of the marriage.

A different situation occurs if the wife runs away to live with another man to whom she is not married. When the husband discovers the pair, he takes them to court. The man and woman are both fined and the court orders the woman to return to her husband. The husband may be so angry at this point that he simply divorces her. It is possible but illegal for such cases to be settled out of court by the lover paying something to the first husband. If the two men are caught doing this, both are fined, since the first husband is illegitimately taking on the role of judge.

The interesting points here for our purposes are first of all the very clear and legal conception of marital dissolution held by the Kanuri. The woman who runs away without a divorce and remarries has in effect broken the law. Only after a legal divorce can remarriage occur. Thus desertion by a spouse cannot sever the union until the divorce is formalized. Secondly, it should be noted that in Kanuri eyes men, not women, are dominantly responsible for marriage, including the woman's side of the union. It is her *luwali* who is questioned when she remarried—for without his sanction the marriage could not have taken place. Indeed, in cases of illegal marriage by a runaway woman the judge will say, "Who is in charge of this woman's marriage?—Who is the *luwali*?" Thus even on the woman's side men are responsible for her actions. In effect, then, she is more like a ward than a free adult citizen of the state.

Actual cases of desertion are rare and difficult to observe or discuss. Men reported no desertions in their interviews, but women respondents gave the details on four examples (out of 237 unions), all of which were desertions by the husband. Three of the four were explained as being due to the onset of extreme poverty and an increase in unpaid debts which caused the husband to flee. In one of these, the wife went to the court and told the judge that her husband was in Enugu, in Eastern Nigeria. The court then declared a divorce because the man was outside the Bornu emirate. In the second poverty case, the man was located in another Bornu district. The wife was given transport to meet him there and he divorced her at court. The third case involved another indebted and impoverished husband who disappeared. His wife remained in his household for two years and finally her husband's older brother divorced her for her husband, thus dissolving the marriage. As an agnate and head of the family, he has the right to do this in his brother's absence. The fourth case involved a husband who said he would send for his wife when he moved to the city. But he never did, and she finally went to him. He sent her back to her family and then sent a letter divorcing her. She explains the desertion by saying that he wished to marry someone else and did not want her any more.

The Kanuri word for separation is *ger'atə* to be angry, to quarrel, or to be annoyed with someone. As one informant put it, "Sometimes there is an argument between a husband and wife over responsibilities and obedience and she leaves, going back to her family or to her *luwali*." This is quite distinct from desertion because both parties are aware of the location of the other. Indeed, in some cases a husband asks the wife to return because he wishes to discuss the disagreement with her *luwali*. However, a number of informants—especially young Western educated husbands—take sharp exception to this idea and claim they would rather deal with the wife herself.

In some cases, a woman returning to her family for a ceremony complains to her *luwali* about the husband and says she does not want to return until matters are settled between him and her husband. Responses by *luwali* vary. Often, especially if this is the first time or the girl is young, the *luwali* would say that she must return because she came home for ceremonies and not for the settlement of marital problems. However, if this complaint is one among many previous ones, the *luwali* may agree to arbitrate the matter and therefore allow the wife to remain in his compound.

In other cases, the wife may send a message to the *luwali* telling him of the disagreement between herself and her husband. He may agree that she return, or he may send word telling her to remain with her husband until he arrives to arbitrate with the husband. If the wife runs away in anger or fear to her *luwali*, the latter sends a message to the husband to arrange a meeting so the two men may discuss the matter. In cases where the wife has been very badly treated, the *luwali* can threaten him with court action or request that the husband pronounce a divorce.

Often the husband may appoint a friend to go to the *luwali* and speak for him, especially if there have been serious difficulties involving harsh words. Again, if the *luwali* is the wife's father or older brother (senior male in-law), the husband has to be on strict terms of in-law respect and even partial avoidance. Thus an intermediary can speak more freely. When I performed this task, the husband, whom I represented, did not tell the story as it seemed to the wife and the *luwali*. The husband claimed there had been a quarrel because she was jealous when he mentioned that he might soon marry a second wife. The *luwali*, however, told me that his daughter had been badly beaten by the husband; she was brought, and in front of witnesses I acknowledged that she did have a number of bruises on the back of her neck. Later a divorce was decreed—my efforts had proved to be to no avail.

The actual incidence of such separation is quite high, especially for marriages with very young girls who may run home several times after being married. Informants feel that many—at least half—of such separations end in a reconciliation and the return of the wife. However, our quantitative data do not bear this out. Among 741 unions, there were 365 in which 591 separations were reported. Of these 591, only 34% resulted in the return of the wife. Generally speaking, if the wife does not return after two or three weeks, then divorce ensues. Separation, then, is often a prelude to divorce.

Annulment

There is no specific term for annulment in the Kanuri language. Instead, the people see annulments in terms of specific grounds for divorce. I lump these together as a separate category of rules governing marital dissolution in which expectations considered to be necessary to marriage are unfulfilled and the marriage is therefore considered legally ended because in effect it was never satisfactorily contracted in the first place. These grounds are so widely agreed upon that no attempt is made to keep the marriage going or reconcile the partners; everyone accepts the fact that these conditions unalterably produce dissolution. It is not divorce because such conditions occur at the very beginning of a marriage and operate to prevent the union from being fully created. In this sense, the union is being set aside before it is fully recognized.

The first of these conditions is male impotence. A man must consummate a marriage within ninety days or else the marriage is considered null and void. The woman returns to her *luwali*, who applies to the local politico-judicial system to set aside the marriage. The man and woman are questioned, and if the judgment goes against the man, he then loses all bridewealth and the marriage is dissolved. Men often divorce the girl or woman first rather than face the public shame of their own impotence. Later he will report such a union to have ended in divorce—but the girl or woman reports it as a case of impotence.

It is extremely difficult to assess the actual frequency of such annulments since men never report them. I have observed two cases in rural Bornu in which marriages were abrogated for non-consummation. Neither case went to the courts and one of them utilized the ninety-day rule, while the other was over in two weeks. Women respondents reported four cases (out of 237 unions). Three of these were first marriages for the women; i.e., they were young girls aged ten to fourteen. The fourth was between a twenty-one year old divorcee and a man of thirty. In this latter case, the woman reported the impotency to her *luwali* after the wedding night, and the husband was given three days by the *luwali* to prove himself. When he still proved impotent three days running, he was forced to divorce her and the matter did not go to court. In the other three cases, the period before a divorce was declared (by the husband on the insistence of the *luwali*) varied from nine months to one year. In most of these cases, there is an attempt to avoid the exact legal rules so that, to all intents and purposes, the dissolution can be interpreted locally as a normal divorce, thereby saving some face for the husband—especially when he has proved potent in other marriages.

Second, there is a rule that if a young bride who has never been married before runs away from her husband's house to return home (separation) and does so three times within a short space of time at the beginning of her marriage, then she should not be forced to return to her husband. Although everyone knows of this technique for ending a marriage to a young girl, I have recorded no specific cases of it.

Third, there is the problem of physical disability. It is possible for a bride and groom who are married through the efforts of their kin to be total strangers to one another, meeting for the first time on their wedding night. In such cases, if the husband has had no previous knowledge of this woman's physical defect, then the marriage can be legally ended without any contest, in agreement with general Muslim practice.[5] The man feels he has expended effort and finance to obtain a proper wife. If something obviously less than this turns up, he can simply refuse to have her enter or stay in his household. Whether such rights also apply to women is debatable. Informants say that in theory the rule applies to both sexes. However, they point out that the woman or girl contracting such a marriage is under someone's authority and she should obey if that person knowingly contracted the marriage with a husband having a physical defect. Again, therefore, it is the *men* controlling the marriage and not the woman being married who constitute the legal parties involved.[6]

One young man recounts how he was farming in a rural area on land owned by his older brother. The rest of his kin lived in the city. When he sent word asking for a wife, the family sent back a message assenting to his request and they arranged the marriage. When the wife arrived in the rural area, the husband saw that she had a withered arm. He sent her back without a word, saying that no one had ever informed him of this defect in his bride-to-be. His family lost the bridewealth in this case because they had created the deception. If he had agreed to marry the girl knowing of her arm, then there would be no grounds for annulment.

In all of these instances, dissolution is supposed to occur automatically at the very beginning of a marriage because some well-accepted property of marriage is unacceptably missing or unfulfilled. In Islamic law this is referred to as "judicial divorce" pronounced by a court. Here we have called it annulment.

Divorce

As we have seen, all of the other forms of dissolution except death and annulment are convertible into reconciliations (i.e., continuations of the marriage) or divorce. Thus all Kanuri marriages end ultimately as deaths or divorces. In the Kanuri language, to divorce or *dəpta* also means to cut or break, although most commonly it refers to a divorce action. However, these additional meanings provide some understanding of the Kanuri way of looking at the subject. To them, relationships are very real, tangible parts of their lives, and thus divorce is quite rightly seen as a cutting or breaking of marriage. Indeed, the word is often accompanied by a gesture in which the person makes a downward cutting motion with the outstretched palm.

Relationships of any kind are valued. Indeed, I have gone as far as to suggest that, in their cultural view of social reality, Kanuri view social relations as a form of currency which they consciously use to obtain other values (Cohen 1965). But this is not the whole picture. Divorce, when it occurs, is described as a "bad thing," and long marriages are valued and considered blessed. However, when I discuss divorce procedures in other societies with Kanuri friends, they express horror and disbelief. If people wish a marriage to be over, they say, then putting barriers in the way is unpleasant in the extreme. Thus, although the Kanuri think divorce is unfortunate—as are all breakups of social relations—the continuation of an unsuccessful relationship is much more to be avoided. Therefore, they wholly subscribe to the widespread Islamic rule of divorce which ordains "that an adult, sane husband may irrevocably divorce his wife" and thereby sever the marriage bond, or at least start the process of disengagement which then precludes remarriage with the same man unless or until the wife has been married to another man and this marriage dissolved in its turn by death or divorce.

This brings us to the problem of definition. I would define divorce as the break-up of a marital union between two living spouses in which both partners are free to remarry. To the Kanuri, separation and desertion are only temporary dissolutions because the partners are still legally married. This means (a) that the woman in question is not free to remarry (nor the man if has three other wives) and (b) the matter can and must be only temporary, leading toward either a return of the spouses to a common residence, or to a divorce.

A simple case will illustrate how stringent are such rules. In recounting his marital history, one informant said of a wife "She was going to Mecca—so I divorced her." When questioned further, he explained the situation. She was a good wife and they always got along well together. However, her family (mother, father, and older full brother) were going to Mecca—on foot—and she wished to accompany them. Such a trip often takes two to five years. The husband says that he and his wife discussed the matter. Both agreed that she should go. However, the husband told her father (who was also *luwali*) if her family did not return but settled somewhere else, then it would be better for the woman if she were free to remarry. If she did return to Bornu, he said, then he would marry her again—for she was a good wife. He therefore divorced her. That was eight to ten years ago. He has heard recently that she and her family settled in Khartoum on the way back from Mecca. She has married again. In other words, the husband felt it was in the best interests of his wife that she be a divorced woman so that if necessary she could remarry.

Divorce action is simple and direct. The husband says "*Nyia dəmgəna*" (I have divorced you) in front of witnesses, and the divorce is in operation. He says it only once, in order that the other two pronouncements allowed under law may be saved for use at later times. It is Kanuri belief that the third time such a pronouncement is made, reconciliation of any kind is impossible, as is remarriage. By law, women may divorce, but it is complicated and very much the exception, often involving adjudication in court. On the other hand, very few divorces actually reach the courts in Bornu. When they do, it is for special reasons involving grievances and a desire for retribution which must be enforced by the state. In our sample of approximately 450 divorces, only 15 (3%) are reported to have involved recourse to the courts. This may be on the low side because informants do not like discussing court cases involving themselves. However, participant observation supports this low figure. Rarely, among many cases of divorce, have I ever observed a case that has gone to court. This means that normal Kanuri divorce cannot be studied by consulting court records.[7]

Following from the premise of corporate legal responsibility of agnates that exists in Kanuri concepts of kinship, it is possible for a man's agnates to pronounce divorce upon his wife if he is absent for any length of time. They are often responsible for her upkeep if she elects to remain in her husband's compound, and so it is considered permissible for them to divorce her. In practice, however, this only occurs when a woman has been deserted by her husband, which as we have seen is quite rare.

Divorce leads immediately to a three month and ten day (100 days) *tabari* or waiting period which can be extended to include the wife's pregnancy period if she is with child. During the *tabari*, as with death, the woman is still considered to be legally bound to her ex-husband. She should remain chaste; any discovery that she has a lover can lead to court action and adultery fines. During this "waiting" period, the husband can revoke the divorce decree, and reconciliation is then affected with no special ceremony unless it is the third time, which is theoretically irrevocable.

With both separation and divorce, reconciliation before there is a complete dissolution is marked by the giving of a few gifts to the returning wife. This occurs less often in separations, more so after a divorce pronouncement. It is also customary for the *luwali* to send a small gift, usually grain, to the husband when the reconciliation has been successfully accomplished. Such exchanges tend to solidify and symbolize the fact that the partially severed relations have now been restored.

In practice, however, things are somewhat different. Divorce pronouncements that result in reconciliation during *tabari* do not seem to count. Many informants also claim that remarriage with the same man occurs after the *tabari*, but the woman must marry another husband first before remarriage to the original husband after the latter's third divorce pronouncement. Despite such variation, almost all of our cases of remarriage involve marriage to someone else before a remarriage. And we have no instances in which people remarry each other more than once. In other words, if a formal divorce and waiting period are carried out twice, people do not seem willing to chance it a third time.

Unlike widowhood, the wife returns to her family for the *tabari* period or, in the city, she may leave and rent a room.

Among the Kanuri, the husband is not necessarily responsible for her maintenance during the waiting period, although this is a widespread practice in other Islamic areas.

Jurally, it is possible for a husband to have his wife remain in his compound during the *tabari* period, even though it is not practiced. The husband may say "I have divorced you," silently addressing himself to Allah. He then takes note of the day; for 100 days he does not eat the woman's food, giving it to his friends and to charity. He also refrains from sexual intercourse with her for the entire period. He can then call her into his presence and say to her "I have carried out *tabari*; you may now leave my household and remarry if you wish." The object of such a secret divorce would be to ensure his wife's chastity and to see for himself if she is with child. The custom is almost impossible to practice because the woman would in fact discover the ruse and demand a publicly stated divorce statement or run away from the man's household.

The possibility of reconciliation after the divorce pronouncement leads to discussions with the *luwali*, the use of intermediary peacemakers and the like, as in the case of separations. However, only a minority (16%) of divorce pronouncements lead to reconciliation rather than a completed divorce. In only a few cases (8) was there more than one per marriage. In other words, divorce pronouncements are serious events and when they occur, the marriage is generally severed.

In legal terms, a woman can initiate divorce proceedings against the husband's wishes by demanding a divorce and saying she is willing to pay for it. In Islmaic jurisprudence, this is known as *khul'*; the Kanuri word is *fida*, which informants say represents the worth of the marriage bond. The exact amount varies from, "Everything the husband ever spent on her including the bride-wealth, and other marriage expenses," to an agreed upon fee. In general, it is felt that a woman does contribute to her husband's welfare and this should also be taken into account. In theory, the matter may or may not go to court, depending upon whether the spouses can agree on the terms of the settlement.

The actual incidence of such cases seems extremely low, although this is difficult to measure since male informants are universally reluctant to admit that they have ever been through such a divorce. Women do discuss such matters and we recorded three cases in which women informants claimed to have paid *fida* (out of 171 divorces). In the first case, she was 20 and he was 60 years old. He was very jealous and constantly watched her and had her followed. Eventually he threatened her life. She asked for a divorce, he disagreed, and they went to court where the *fida* was settled. In the second case, there was also much jealousy even though the ages of the spouses were closer—she was 17 and he was 30 years old. However, he beat her rather badly and she then refused to sleep with him and asked for a divorce. He would not divorce her and they went to court. In the third case, the woman reports that she used to take cooked food twice a day to her very old parents who lived in the same village. Her husband said she was committing adultery during these visits and he finally beat her and then started doing it quite regularly. She asked for a divorce and he refused unless she paid *fida*, which she did, and then left his home. This case did not therefore go to court. All of these marriages were with young women, and two of them lasted one year or less (the other was three years).

An extreme custom associated with *fida* is called 'closing the hut' (*njim zəktə*). Here, the man demands that the wife give him all of her possessions, i.e., he takes everything in her hut or sleeping room as *fida* and then allows her to leave. In recounting a well-known story of such an event, informants tell of a wife who was enraged at her husband's demands for *fida* and sent a message to her sister to come and bring an extra woman's shift dress. She then went to her husband and in the presence of his friends she took off all her clothes and jewelry until she was naked. She then said "Take everything. I am leaving!" and put on the clothes brought for her by the sister. Her intent was to shame the husband, and informants agree that she succeeded.

In summary, however, *fida* is still a rare phenomenon. Most men will in fact make a divorce pronouncement if the wife insists, or the wife enrages him so much that she succeeds in making him divorce. Therefore, there is in fact little need for *fida* at present—although it could become important in the future.

In a very few cases, again only reported by women, the wife complains to the court that her husband or possibly his family have mistreated her in a serious way. If this mistreatment is judged to be valid and important, then the court may declare a divorce without the consent of the husband and without *fida*. In other words, in extreme cases, a man's right to compensation for divorce against his own will can be abrogated. In one such case, a husband borrowed and then stole more property from his wife, and subsequently lost it all gambling. The wife took him to court where the judge ruled that the husband must pay back his debt to the wife; the marriage was declared to be over and she was now in *tabari* (waiting period). Thus the court felt that the husband's conduct against his wife was sufficiently illegal that he should be punished and divorced whether he liked it or not.

The Divorce Rates

The actual frequency of divorce is a well-trodden path in terms of conceptualization so that there are now a number of well known ways of computing such rates. Ever since the work of Barnes several decades ago, there have been three standard rates in anthropology applied to non-Western data (Barnes 1944). These rates are:

(1) The A rate = The number of divorces as a proportion of the total number of marriages.

(2) The B rate = The number of divorces as a proportion of all completed marriages.

(3) The C rate = The number of divorces as a proportion of all marriages except those ending in death.

Basically, these rates are useful in giving an overall depiction of a marriage cohort and in showing the differences among rates when extant marriages are controlled for as in (B), and when death is controlled for as in (C), as opposed to a gross measure where none of these controls are exerted as in (A).

The Kanuri rates are extremely high when taken from our overall sample. Of these 741 marriages, (A) 64% of those ever contracted have ended in divorce; (B) 91% of all completed marriages ended in divorce; and (C) 68% of all marriages, excluding those ending in death, are terminated by divorces. For purposes of further analysis, the sample itself will be used. However, in order to obtain corrected figures which can be used to characterize the Kanuri as a whole, I have done two things: (a) separated rural from urban data which is 1:1 in the sample and 8.81:1 in the population, and (b) I have used only data from males which cuts the sample of marriages down to 504. This latter control was introduced because I believe that the urban women's sample is biased toward unmarried women, resulting from the high incidence of secluded married women in the city. This bias shows up in a higher overall rate of divorce for women than men in the sample itself. Using these controls, the best estimates of divorce rates for the population as a whole can be obtained by keeping male divorce data from rural and urban areas separate as in Table 10:2. The table also gives rates from elsewhere in Africa and the U.S.A. for comparative purposes.[9] Kanuri rates in general are among the highest ever recorded. It should also be noted that the corrected figures for Kanuri society are 10% lower than those indicated above for the sample as a whole, in which rural and urban respondents are equally represented. It is also quite obvious from this table that the U.S.A. is in fact a comparatively low divorce society.

Another way of depicting this high divorce rate is to look at marriage and divorce per person, using the individual rather than the marriage itself as the unit of analysis. When the sample data were gathered, no criteria or quotas were set for marital or divorce experience except for the limiting condition that everyone in the sample should have been married at least once. Thus this spread of marriage and divorce experience is due to other factors. The most striking thing about these data (in Table 10:3) is the low number of people who have been married only once (24%), and the high number of people (71%) who have been divorced at least once. In other words, divorce is an experience that ultimately touches almost everyone in the society in some way.

Finally, the most detailed way of looking at the divorce rates is accomplished by creating age-specific and duration-specific divorce tables. Such tables locate where the greatest and the least degree of stability is occurring in the marital experience. Several problems have been encountered in creating such tables for the Kanuri. First of all, the tables cannot with any ease or confidence be corrected to represent the population as a whole. To do so, I would have to be confident that my overall transformation techniques also apply to sub-sections of the rural and urban population by age and marital duration. Therefore, the tables describing detailed breakdowns of marital stability by age and duration are for the sample only. In general, these rates are slightly higher in the sample

TABLE 10:2. KANURI DIVORCE RATES WITH COMPARABLE DATA
FROM OTHER SOCIETIES

Society	Divorce Rates in Percent		
	A	B	C
Urban Kanuri (men)	74	98	75
Rural Kanuri (men)	52	79	56
Kanuri (corrected)	54	81	58
Bakweri (women)	42	66	54
Yao (women)	35	68	41
Ngoni (both sexes)	29	56	37
U.S.A. (1950, both sexes)	3	22	3

TABLE 10:3. FREQUENCY OF MARRIAGES AND DIVORCES IN THE SAMPLE

Frequency Per Person	Married	%	Acc. %	Divorced	%	Acc. %
0	0	-	-	62	28.8	100.0
1	51	23.7	23.7	49	22.8	71.2
2	64	29.8	53.5	37	17.2	48.4
3	41	19.9	72.6	23	10.7	31.2
4	21	9.8	82.4	10	4.7	20.5
5	9	4.2	86.6	10	4.7	15.8
6-8	12	5.6	92.2	13	6.0	11.1
9-11	7	3.3	95.5	2	.9	5.1
12-14	3	1.4	96.1	3	1.4	4.2
15+	7	3.3	100.2	6	2.8	2.8
	215	100.2		215	100.0	

than in the population as a whole because of the over-representation of urban marriages which are more unstable.

Secondly, there is a problem with missing data. Not all respondents could remember the full details of each marriage, especially unions that took place many years ago. In other cases, people simply said they did not know the answer and it was difficult to push too hard for fear of angering the respondent or creating a response ourselves where none was in fact remembered. Missing data is, however, spread fairly evenly over all of the material with a slight tendency to locate more frequently in the divorce records of older persons with very high marriage and divorce rates. In other words, missing data tend, if anything, to bias the results in the direction of more stable unions, i.e., opposite to the sampling biases.

Thirdly, there is the problem of extant unions. Recently, Barnes has suggested a technique for transforming extant unions into completed ones, thus enlarging the sample and making all unions comparable (Barnes 1967). If his technique is not utilized, then extant unions lower the rate unless they are subtracted as in the "B" rate calculation. I have decided not to convert extant unions to completed ones because (a) it would make all divorce rates look alike, since almost all unions end in divorce, and (b) such transformations assume no serious social or legal change in divorce proceedings in the immediate future—an assumption that is probably untrue for Bornu.

Given these difficulties, the tables (10:4 and 10:5) still tell a great deal about Kanuri marriage and divorce. Divorce rates are derived from the data in the tables so that the reader can if he wishes replicate these calculations. The rates should be read with their definitions in mind. Thus "A" rates in the age-specific table indicate that 67% of all unions contracted between the age of

TABLE 10:4. AGE-SPECIFIC MARRIAGE AND DIVORCE DATA FOR 688 KANURI UNIONS*

Age at Time of Marriage	No. of Unions Occurring (N=688)	% of Total (N=688)	Acc. %	No. of Unions Ending in Death	% of Total (N=43)	Acc. %	No. of Extant Unions	% of Total (N=225)	Acc. %	No. of Divorces	% of Total (N=422)	Acc. %	Divorce Rate per 100 unions "A"	"B"	"C"
10-14	118	17.2	17.2	8	18.6	18.6	31	13.8	13.8	79	18.7	18.7	67	91	72
15-19	105	15.3	32.5	10	23.3	41.9	20	8.9	22.7	75	17.8	36.5	71	88	79
20-24	127	18.5	51.0	9	20.9	62.8	38	16.9	39.6	80	19.0	55.5	63	90	68
25-29	95	13.8	64.8	7	16.3	79.1	29	12.9	52.5	59	14.0	69.5	62	89	67
30-34	84	12.2	77.0	3	7.0	86.1	34	15.1	67.6	47	11.1	80.6	56	94	58
35-39	53	7.7	84.7	-	-	86.1	26	11.6	79.2	27	6.4	87.0	51	100	51
40-44	47	6.8	91.5	2	4.7	90.8	19	8.4	87.6	26	6.2	93.2	55	93	58
45-49	21	3.1	94.6	2	4.7	95.5	10	4.4	92.0	11	2.6	95.8	52	85	58
50-54	21	3.1	97.7	1	2.3	97.8	9	4.0	96.4	11	2.6	98.4	52	92	55
55-59	9	1.3	9.9	1	2.3	100.1	2	8	96.8	6	1.4	99.8	67	86	75
60+	8	1.2	100.2	-	-	-	7	3.1	99.9	1	.2	100.0	13	100	13
	688	100.2		43	100.1		225	99.9		442	100.0		64	91	69

Means for Sample

*53 cases of missing or imperfect data (=7%), making a total of 741 cases.

TABLE 10:5. DURATION-SPECIFIC MARRIAGE AND DIVORCE DATA FOR 708 KANURI UNIONS*

Duration of Unions in Years	Extant Unions	% of Total (N=226)	Acc. %	Deaths	% of Total (N=35)	Acc. %	Divorces	% of Total (N=447)	Acc. %	Size of Sample per Duration	% of Total Sample (N=708)	Divorce Rates Per 100 Unions "A"	"B"	"C"
0-.9	19	8.4	8.4	2	5.7	5.7	111	24.8	24.8	708	100	16	98	16
1.0-1.9	16	7.1	15.5	1	2.9	8.6	76	17.0	41.8	576	81.4	13	99	13
2.0-2.9	14	6.2	21.7	3	8.6	17.2	56	12.5	54.3	483	68.2	12	95	12
3.0-3.9	18	8.0	29.7	1	2.9	20.1	43	9.6	63.9	410	57.9	11	98	11
4.0-4.9	10	4.4	34.1	4	11.4	31.5	33	7.4	71.3	348	49.2	10	89	10
5.0-7.4	27	11.9	46.0	4	11.4	42.9	63	14.1	85.4	301	42.5	21	94	21
7.5-9.9	22	9.7	55.7	4	11.4	54.3	32	7.2	92.6	207	29.2	16	89	16
10-14	33	14.6	70.3	3	8.6	62.9	14	3.1	95.7	149	21.0	9	82	10
15-19	28	12.4	82.7	9	25.7	88.6	14	3.1	98.8	99	14.0	14	61	16
20-24	16	7.1	89.8	0	0	88.6	3	.7	99.5	48	6.8	6	100	6
25-29	12	5.3	95.1	1	2.9	91.5	1	.2	99.7	29	4.1	4	50	4
30+	11	4.9	100.0	3	8.6	100.1	1	.2	99.9	15	2.1	7	25	8
	226	100.0		35	100.0		447	99.9						

*33 cases of missing or imperfect data (=4%), making a total of 741 cases.

10-14 ended in divorce and, for the duration-specific table, 16% of all unions end in divorce during the first years of marriage. "B" rates show that, for those unions contracted between ages 10-14 that have already ended, 91% of them were terminated by divorce. Similarly, in the duration table, of those unions that ended during the first year of marriage, 98% did so by divorce. "C" rates are quite similar to the "A" ones in this study because so few marriages end in death, which is what this rate controls for.

The main conclusion to be drawn from these tables (10:4 and 10:5) is the consistently high rate of divorce. This is most clearly so in the age-specific tables where the "B" rate is 91 per 100 and varies only from a low of 85 to a high of 100. In other words, no matter what the ages of the persons involved at the time of marriage, the great majority of Kanuri unions end ultimately in divorce. This consistency does, however, hide an interesting variation that turns up in the duration specific tables. Divorces are quite high, as a percentage of all marriages during the first year of marriage (16%), and they decrease steadily to 10% in the fourth year.

Put into other terms, most divorces (93%) occur during the first two years of marriage. Indeed, 71% take place before the fifth year. Marriages therefore vary in length but are characteristically short in duration. In other words, most divorces occur in the early periods of marriage, even though one-third of them are stretched out over the rest of marital careers. The statistical reason why divorce probabilities remain fairly high as time goes on is that there are so few marriages actually achieving longevity that the few numbers of divorces in these later periods still account for a healthy proportion of marital completions.

The final point to be made about the divorce rates cannot be seen in Tables 10:4 and 10:5 unless they are broken down by sex. This is not presented here because the numbers in each cell become too small, creating artificial instabilities in the data. However, one point is quite clear. Men continue to marry and divorce throughout life—women do not. Since divorce takes its toll of most unions, there is therefore an age-class of old women who are single and unmarriageable. The divorce system creates them; the society must take care of them by accommodating itself to this concomitant of high divorce.

Institutionalized Results of High Divorce

Old women are taken care of by junior relatives, usually a son, sometimes a younger brother; in one case, even by an ex-husband who was referred to as "brother." In general, they sell cooked or uncooked food and act as friendly "grandmothers" to the children of the compound. Unless they have independent means from trade or inheritance, they are often rather poorly dressed, and even unkempt. Life has passed them by, their ideal womanly role is over, and they are in some sense a surplus of human material which the system must because of its humane values organize to take care of.

A very different position is accorded to the younger marriageable women between unions—the *zower*. When very young, she returns to her agnatic kin who look after her and soon arrange a second marriage. However, her freedom increases enormously with subsequent divorces, especially the city women who rent rooms and may have several paramours who support them. As one woman put it, "This is our time to have more than one husband, just as men have more than one wife." In general, however, such women are in fact searching for a husband and a more permanent home. Living in a rented room in the city means that she must earn money for food, rent, and other necessities. This comes mostly from sexual liaisons with men. In rural areas, *zowers* generally do not pay rent and their liaisons resemble trial marriages in which the woman cooks food for her "lover" and he gives her market money once a week, as he would to a wife. By contrast, the city *zower* may try for such an arrangement, but economic necessity makes her role more difficult and therefore more accessible to simply monetary return in exchange for sexual services. However, a *zower* is not thought of as a prostitute. The Kanuri have a word for prostitute (*alangnoma*) which means a woman who entertains as many men as possible per night in return for a set fee. *Zowers* are women between marriages; the society has adjusted to high divorce by creating a clear role for the divorced woman.

An important and ubiquitous feature of high divorce is the fact that most children "lose" a mother. She is still their mother and they visit her, bring her and send her gifts and so on, but life in a common household is usually not continuous between children and their mother. Boys seem more affected by this than girls. At least many more of them than girls claim that the worst thing to ever happen was when their mother moved away at the time of their parents' divorce. In such cases, there is strong suspicion that a co-wife is not, or will not be, a proper mother. Instead, the father's sister becomes a special relative to the children of the divorced union taking on in many families the role of a mother surrogate.

Although these data tell us how divorces are distributed in terms of age at the time of marriage and duration of the union, they do not provide any insight into who divorces more or less, and why this should be so. It is to such questions that we now turn our attention.

PART IV
THE ANALYSIS OF DIVORCE

Chapter 11
Sociological Correlates of Marital Stability

Up until this point, we have been essentially asking descriptive questions. The answers have provided a picture of what Kanuri marriage and divorce is like as a way of life. In a qualitative sense, we have also asked other kinds of questions, as in Chapter 9 on married life when we posed a few hypotheses about why things are as they are. Now, however, we must turn to a more systematic posing of these questions. From now on, we shall ask why. Why does the divorce rate vary and what is associated with such variance? Can theory help us? And why do the correlates of divorce operate as they do? This is the thrust of Part IV and the ultimate goal of this study.

Grievances: Dominance as an Irritant

The reasons that people are willing to give for their own divorces are tempered by the conditions under which such information is gathered, plus the feelings and memories of the respondent. In other words, as an insight into why a particular divorce occurred, such information is misleading—indeed, purposely so, since most people recounting such reasons try to put themselves in a good light and shift the blame to the other person. Thus most of our respondents felt that each of their divorces was due to bad behavior on the part of the spouses. Furthermore, because these data were gathered in a formal interview situation, it is doubtful that the full details as seen by the respondent were ever completely recorded. Divorce is a personal matter, even in Bornu where it is common, and some people are simply not used to the idea of discussing such events with anyone but their most intimate friends. As a result, discussions concerning the reasons for a particular divorce pronouncement varied a great deal from person to person. In general, the responses were of three types. First, there were very curt one sentence answers, signaling a desire to avoid going into any detail. In such cases, the most laconic and uninformative response was to blame the divorce on "fate." In this way the respondent was being polite, proffering an answer, but avoiding the necessity of revealing anything about his divorce. Secondly, there were brief answers in which the respondent tried to summarize the events leading to the divorce; thirdly, a number of respondents went into great detail describing each divorce as if it were a complex dramatic plot. Examples of each of these types of answers are given below for each sex.

Man Speaking
(1) It was fate: she went out without permission. (Curt)
(2) She (wife) said, "I am not going to farm for you." I said, "But we need the farm for our food and for money to clothe ourselves. Why can't you farm? If you will not do it then you are divorced." This was the first time such a thing had ever happened. (Brief)
(3) She ran away once and I divorced her once. When she ran away her *luwali* sent her back and sent some millet and when I gave the *luwali*'s millet[1] to the returned senior one, the junior wife became angry and asked for her share; when she got none *she* ran away to the city. One of my daughters died in the household and I sent this runaway wife a message ordering her to return immediately in order to help with the cooking for those coming to the funeral. When she received the message she moved instead into the Shehu's palace from the city ward where she had been visiting her *luwali*. I went to the city to the house of the *luwali*. The *luwali* said, "Why didn't you come to get your wife and escort her back to your village?" I answered that there had been a death in my family. The *luwali* then sent for one of his wives (who was originally from the palace). (She asked the same question as the *luwali* and received the same answer.) This woman then sent a message to the palace and the

wayward wife appeared. She and I then went back to the village by lorry. When we returned she brought water for my prayers. After prayers I called her to me and said, "I brought you back here because it was very shameful for me to divorce you in the city in front of your relatives. Pack your property and leave my house. I divorce you." (Detailed)

Woman Speaking

(1) He drank and went with other women. (Curt)

(2) The father's sister of this husband wanted the husband to marry her daughter. The girl came to live with us when she was very young. I would have to bring up this child so that she could marry my husband. I refused and asked that he divorce me if he wished to do this. (Brief)

(3) There were two divorces. The first time he told me to give water to his horse, but the horse ran away and I ran after it to bring it back to the compound. When I returned my husband slapped me for going out without permission. I cried and ran home to the *luwali*. Later I returned to this husband and he divorced me. However, at the *luwali*'s household the matter was discussed and the *luwali* persuaded me to return two weeks later. [The divorce was, therefore, not completed.] The second time this husband sold all his possessions and went to Fort Lamy. He was going to stay there for a while and then work his way over to Mecca to perform the pilgrimage. He sent a message to me to join him. My father (who was the *luwali*) objected strongly and said I couldn't go. The husband then sent a letter divorcing me after receiving news that I would not join him. He was a good husband and I am sorry about it, but I did not want to leave my own family to go so far away. (Detailed)

Most commonly, the reasons for divorce are brief as in the second examples given above for men and women. However, there are a sufficient number of the longer ones that are rich in detail and general ethnographic information. In addition, we also collected a number of reasons for separations and other disagreements. These are no different than those given for divorce. Thus the reasons given for divorce are present in some cases of divorce, but also present when there is no divorce. In other words, grievances between husbands and wives are necessary but not sufficient grounds for divorce. Furthermore, other reasons not stated may also have been important to explain any particular break-up. Therefore, the reasons for divorce that are given by respondents form a catalogue of issues that create difficulties between spouses.[2]

The reasons given for a divorce vary widely. For analytic purposes we have lumped these reasons into fifteen categories given in Table 11:1 to show sex and location differences that are statistically significant. Except for the wife as a productive asset which is mentioned more often in rural areas, and sexual problems which are mentioned more in the urban areas, the location of the marriage makes much less difference than the sex of the speaker. Indeed, reasons given for divorce in urban areas are highly correlated with those given in the villages (r = .83). The sexes differ significantly on four basic reasons for divorce: (a) wife as a productive unit (men high; women low); (b) husband as a provider (women high; men low); (c) sexual problems (women high; men low); and (d) co-wife problems (women high; men low). Furthermore, the sexes are not correlated significantly in their explanation for divorce.

Looking at Table 11:1 as a whole, it is important to note that approximately 85% of all reasons are accounted for by the first seven categories in the table. In other words, these are the most common explanations used by the people themselves in describing a divorce. When secondary school students were asked to write essays explaining Kanuri divorce, these same issues emerged, although the differences between the sexes disappeared (Cohen 1970b). Thus the differences between men and women are due primarily to personal involvement in the divorce rather than to a biased view of divorce held by each sex.

Male dominance is accepted universally in Bornu as a major reason for divorce. However, the way we have coded this item, it should more properly be called wifely insubordination. Thus very few respondents, male or female, mention excessive tyranny by the husband, or brutality, or even concern over male dominance. As with our analysis of spouse roles, the chief concern here is that the wife did not properly comply with the obligations of subordination. She went out without permission, she visited her kin without permission, she was disobedient, she refused to do his bidding across a wide range of culturally acceptable requests. No matter whether they were men, women, rural or urban, respondents agree that marital conflict does not result from the norm of male dominance itself, but the reaction to it by women who will not fully accept its implications.

TABLE 11:1. REASONS GIVEN FOR DIVORCE PRONOUNCEMENTS
BY SEX AND LOCATION

| Reasons for Divorce | % Sex Reporting | | % by Location | | |
	Men's (N=446)	Women's (N=317)	Urban (N=580)	Rural (N=183)	Total (N=767)
1. Specific issues of male dominance	17.5	12.6	15.1	16.4	15.5
2. Wife as a productive asset	22.6	2.5*	12.1	21.3*	14.3
3. Husband as a provider	4.0	22.7*	12.8	8.7	11.8
4. Sexual problems	8.3	16.1*	12.8	7.7*	11.5
5. Bad behavior & bad character of spouse	11.0	11.4	12.2	7.6	11.1
6. Co-wife problems	8.3	14.2*	10.5	11.5	10.8
7. In-law problems	9.4	11.9	11.2	8.2	10.5
8. Fate	4.0	0	1.9	3.8	2.4
9. Husband dislikes the wife	3.6	0	1.9	2.7	2.1
10. Sickness of spouse	2.7	.6	1.7	2.2	1.8
11. Wife refuses to move to or remain in a distant place	1.3	1.6	1.4	1.6	1.4
12. Supernatural causes	.4	3.2	1.7	1.1	1.1
13. Political party membership of spouse	.2	.3	.3	0	.3
14. Husband's age	0	.6	.3	0	.3
15. No information given	6.5	2.2	4.3	7.1	4.7
Totals	99.9	99.9	99.9	99.9	99.9

*X^2 is significant at the .05 level or better; sample size is determined by numbers of reasons given per group.

The wife as a productive asset is referred to almost as much as male dominance, and to some extent this set of reasons is merely a special type of male dominance issue. Thus men complain that "she refused to cook," or "she would not work on the farm" or "she would not feed my guests." All of these reasons imply that the husband's authority is being rejected. On the other hand, the category also includes items that reflect on the skill of the wife as a productive asset, such as "she cooked poorly." Women rarely mention such reasons, and among men it is more often the rural man who is concerned about such matters.

The next item—husband as provider—is almost the mirror image of wife as productive asset. Now it is women instead of men who rely on this explanation, and urbanites do so more often. Here is the area *par excellence* of wifely expectation. These are her areas of legitimate demand. If the husband is a bad provider, he failed in his contract and therefore he must accept the blame for the divorce. No wonder then that this is the largest single category of women's response, taking up 23% of all reasons given by women respondents. As already noted, urban women are often on their own and are concerned over material goods and security. It is not surprising, therefore, that urban people, especially women, see this as being more important than rural since the latter are closer to subsistence economy, while city dwellers must rely on the markets and cash to obtain a living. Living is less secure and more expensive in the city, and urban women are responding to this insecurity.

All respondents tend equally to complain that the reason for a divorce lay with the bad behavior or bad character of the spouse. Women complained of men who beat and insulted them for no reason, or who carried out immoral and illegal acts. Men complained of vulgar, crude, immodest women or wives who cheated, lied, and stole household property.

Co-wife problems are reported significantly more often among the reasons given by women, and there are no rural or urban differences in this category. When men report such problems they refer almost invariably to co-wife jealousy as the reason why the divorce occurred. Women also mention this more often than other co-wife problems, but they also report physical fighting among co-wives, arguments about fertility, and failing to inform a present wife that a new one is coming. Women are more concerned with co-wife problems and go into more detail in describing such conflicts.

In-law problems are referred to about as often as co-wife difficulties. Men and women both mention conflict between a wife and her husband's kin, usually his mother, as a reason for divorce. However, women rarely mention trouble between their kin and the husband, while men report this more often than any other reason. Other reasons mentioned are that the wife's or husband's kin broke up the marriage or the husband's and wife's kin quarreled. All of these reasons indicate the consciousness that each spouse has of the ability of his or her affines to interfere and cause trouble in their marriages.

The last seven reasons in Table 11:1 account for about 10-15% of those given by respondents to account for their own divorces. They are also minor reasons in the essays of the secondary school students, and one, "political party membership of spouse," does not occur at all.

How realistic are these reasons for divorce? From the stories told by respondents and from many other interviews on this topic, I conclude that they are real irritants and in all probability did accompany the divorces they are said to have caused. The difficulty with this folk explanation is the fact that many instances can easily be found and recorded in which events or issues said to have caused divorce in one marriage are present in other unions as well, but are not claimed by either partner to be the cause of a particular divorce. Again, as already noted above, we must conclude that reasons given for divorce are necessary but not sufficient grounds for its occurrence. When a break in relations occurs between persons, groups, or nations, there must be an excuse or specific grievance which defines the break-up.

But to say that such specific grievances actually explain or predict the break in relations is naive. The shooting of a crown prince didn't really *cause* World War I, just as the Gulf of Tonkin did not really *cause* the bombing of North Vietnam, and the murder of Martin Luther King did not really *cause* riots in American ghettos in any full sense of the word. Instead, a more sophisticated view of causality would hold that a set of conditions obtain in one situation such that the grievance sets off the break-up in relations while in another where these conditions are not present the grievance leads to conciliation, compromise, or increased tension, but not a break such as a war, a riot, or a divorce. It is to these conditions that we now turn.

Conditions for Divorce

Demographic Variables. The conditions for divorce refer to those empirical correlates found, or posited by theory, to vary significantly with marital stability. In order to study these conditions I constructed simple ordinal scales for those variables not dichotomized into present-absent categories. At first it might seem inaccurate to take an interval scale such as number of divorces per person and transform it into high, medium, and low amounts of divorce. Yet a moment's reflection indicates that in a society where divorces vary anywhere from zero to over twenty, the sociological conditions which predict and possibly explain the differences between three and four divorces are not significant features of social life. On the other hand, when all cases of high marital stability are lumped together and compared with medium and low groups, then the conditions accompanying such differences in stability can be isolated and compared.

In strictly demographic terms, Kanuri marital stability varies with age, sex, fertility of the union, and whether the marriage in question occurs in an urban or rural setting.

Men marry more often and divorce more often than women in the sample with a mean of 2.9 divorces per man and 2.4 for women; variance is also much greater for men, as would be expected in a polygynous society. Nearly all of our measures of divorce are related to the informant's age. The simplest relationship is between age of the informant and numbers of divorce. Nearly 60% of all low divorcers (0-1 per person) are under 35, while 90% of all high divorcers (6+ per person) are over this age. There is also a positive relationship between durations of marriages and age per person such that longer marriages are associated significantly with more advanced age for both sexes.[3] However, when this relationship is examined per marriage instead of per person, the picture changes somewhat. Among those marriages ending in divorce, the least stable unions as measured by duration of marriage contain a heavy concentration of women over 40. Among extant marriages only, the longest durations are between men of all ages and women between the ages of 15-34. These data reflect the fact that most people divorce in Bornu, and the older they become the greater is the likelihood they will have divorced more often. On the other hand, many women remain unmarried after a divorce which occurs in their forties or later because men prefer younger women of childbearing age as wives. This explains why our most unstable age group is women over forty. These women have less to offer their husbands than younger women and are also in many cases systematically dismissed by their husbands who explain such actions by saying straightforwardly, "She was too old," or as several women put it, "He married a younger wife and divorced me." The fact that the longest extant marriages are with women in their middle years indicates that young girls tend not to stay with first husbands whom they are forced to marry by parents.

This should also be seen in the light of another finding. Marriages are significantly more stable (as measured by both duration and whether the marriage ends in divorce or not) when a spouse judges his or her partner to be in a young age group (15-25) than when the partner is reported to be older than this. In other words, the ethnographic generalization that there is a value placed on young marital partners is supported. These overall tendencies, however, mask the phenomena of a very few, very long, and very stable marriages with women who have, as we have previously noted, overcome the system by being close, intimate helpmates to wealthy and/or powerful husbands. Finally, it is interesting to note that there is no relationship between men's ages and the duration of marriages ending in divorce. From the man's point of view, other factors besides his own age determine how long a marriage will last before it is terminated by divorce. Thus, in general, age is related to divorce; however, it seems to be important for women's marital careers, and only peripherally if at all for men's. This reflects the ethnographic generalization that women have a definite period of life (14-45) devoted to marriage and remarriage while men go on being married throughout their adult lives. This point is shown in Table 11:2 where 96% of all women's divorces occur before she is 35, and all female divorces are over by the time the woman is 45. Men, on the other hand, are only half through their divorces (53%) before they are 35, and still have 12% of their divorces after they are 45. On the other hand, woman have 10% of their divorces before they are 15, when most men have not yet been married.

Fertility was recorded per marriage, as well as the wife's record of pregnancy and giving birth in previous marriages. It was thought that because fertility in marriage is so highly prized, especially by men, that even a record of previous pregnancy and/or childbirth might be related to marital stability. This hypothesis was not confirmed. There is no discernible relationship between a woman's previous record of fertility and the stability or durability of a subsequent marriage; in other words, a reputation in this field doesn't count—only results.[4]

Whether men or women are reporting, it is clear that pregnancies and the birth of live children are significantly associated with marriages that do not end in divorce and with longer durations. This does not mean, however, that fertility stops divorce; it simply slows it down. The association

TABLE 11:2. AGE AT TIME OF DIVORCE (N=250 FOR MEN; 155 FOR WOMEN)

Age	Percent of Men's Divorces	Accumulated Percent	Percent of Women's Divorces	Accumulated Percent
10-14	0	0	9.7	9.7
15-19	2.8	2.8	29.7	39.4
20-24	16.0	18.8	27.7	67.1
25-29	17.2	36.0	21.3	88.4
30-34	17.2	53.2	7.1	95.5
35-39	12.8	66.0	2.6	98.1
40-44	12.8	78.8	1.9	100.0
45-49	9.2	88.0	0	-
50-54	6.4	94.4	0	-
55+	5.6	100.0	0	-
Totals	100.0	100.0	100.0	100.0

of fertility with marriages not ending in divorce is in most cases one where very young children are involved. In this sense, the duration measure of marital stability is more precise. This measure does not ask whether there is a divorce or not. Indeed, we already know from the last chapter that most Kanuri marriages end in divorce. However, the association of longer durations with fertility (either pregnancies or live births) indicates that men tend to hold on to such wives for longer periods of time before divorcing them. Thus fertility inhibits divorce by increasing the duration of such marriages while the children are still young. This is shown quite distinctly in Table 11:3. Similar tables can also be constructed for other measures of marital stability, but these would simply belabor the same point—that not all long marriages are fertile but almost all fertile marriages tend to be longer.

TABLE 11:3. DURATIONS OF MARRIAGE AND THE BIRTH OF LIVE
CHILDREN (MEN REPORTING)

Live Children Born to this marriage	Duration of Marriage		
	Low 1-7 years	Medium 8-13 years	High 14+ years
0	178	88	52
1	18	21	15
2	3	11	19
3 and over	0	6	29

As a gross demographic distinction, divorce is very strongly related both in frequency and duration to whether or not it takes place in a rural or an urban area, with significantly higher frequencies and lower durations in urban areas. This relationship holds whether we use the person as a unit of analysis or the marriage and it holds for whatever measure of marital stability we use. Indeed, the relationship is so strong that by itself it tells us very little since it is basically dependent upon other social factors having to do with dominance and dependency which are in turn correlates of the rural-urban distinction. As noted in Chapter 10, 74% of all urban marriages had ended in divorce at the time of the study, compared to only 52% of all rural unions. In terms of numbers of divorces per person, the results given in Table 11:4 show that very high and even medium divorce rates are predominantly urban phenomena, while lower frequency of divorce per

TABLE 11:4. PERCENTAGE OF PERSONS HAVING DIFFERENT AMOUNTS
OF DIVORCE IN RURAL AND URBAN AREAS*

| Site | *Percentage of Persons by divorce per person* | | | |
	Low (0-1)	*Medium (2-5)*	*High (6+)*	*Totals*
Urban	25	55	20	100% (N=100)
Rural	75	22	3	100% (N=115)

*X^2 = 54.50; p < .01

person is present in the rural areas. The same is true of durations, which are shorter in urban areas and longer in rural areas. Thus 72% of all urban marriages recorded are low durations (1-7 years), while only 44% of rural marriages are in this category. On the other hand, only 11% of those urban marriages recorded are long duration (14 years and over), while 31% of all rural marriages can be characterized as long. Thus living in the urban center tends to increase the number of divorces per person and decrease the length of each marriage.

Socio-Economic Contribution of each Spouse to the Marriage. Theory as described in Chapter 1 suggests that, in general, things which tend to divide spouses from one another create instability (disjunctiveness), while activities which contribute to their operation as a working unit create stability (conjunctiveness). In this sense, children may be seen as a conjunctive bond that stabilizes a union. However, there are many areas of life which are ambiguous in terms of this theory and only a detailed understanding of any particular culture allows us to judge a practice as conjunctive or disjunctive. Thus wealth may be seen as a contribution in one sense and a disruption in another.

On the conjunctive side, it seems fairly obvious that the more each spouse contributes to the welfare and socio-economic status of the other partner, then the more valuable such a union becomes to the receiving party; consequently these unions should be more stable. And our data tend to support such a notion when it is primarily the woman making the contribution. Thus unions in which the wife helps on the farm, goes to the well to get water, and generally assists her husband, have significantly lower divorce than marriages where wives do not make such contributions. There are no differences between men and women reporting on such experience. Marriages involving such help are striking as well in their greater durability. Table 11:5 indicates that where women are reported to help their husbands with farm work then 41% of such marriages

TABLE 11:5. FARM HELP AND MARITAL DURATIONS*

| *Wife's Contribution to Farming* | *Duration in Years* | | | |
	% Low (1-7 yr)	*% Medium (8-13 yr)*	*% Long (14+ yr)*	*Total %*
Wife does not help	60	23	17	100 (N=154)
Wife helps husband	28	31	41	100 (N=161)

*X^2 = 35.04; p < .01

have long durations; conversely, where no such help is reported, only 18% are said to be fourteen years or more in duration. Another way of emphasizing the same point is to count all marriages ending in divorce as opposed to all others. Of these, 66% of those not ending in divorce involve a marriage where the wife helps her husband on the farm.[5]

In a society where male dominance is such a strong value and where purdah or wife seclusion is considered a primary indicator of such a value, there is a culturally accepted relationship between a man's social rank and the degree of purdah. In other words, one way of looking at purdah is to see it as a status-enhancing practice for the husband. To carry such logic further, we can argue that a wife, by being in purdah, contributes to her husband's status; she is also less likely to create jealousy on his party by wandering freely outside the household, and therefore purdah should contribute to marital stability. Indeed, many informants actually say that purdah (*kulle*) maintains marriages. On the other hand, by increasing the restrictions surrounding female subordination and enhancing male dominance, purdah could also be said to create conflict, since women must still go out of the household on ceremonial occasions. Furthermore, men whose wives are in purdah expect higher standards of submissiveness and therefore have lowered threshholds of dissatis-faction. In other words, on the face of it, conjunctive theory could predict both more and less marital stability in more secluded marriages depending upon what the researcher chooses to have the practice represent.

The results come down quite clearly on the side of the second interpretation. Both sexes reported significantly more marriages ending in divorce where the union was described as one involving female seclusion. Thus where men try to keep women in greater seclusion, and therefore under greater domination, there is more divorce, not less.

In terms of the husband's contribution to his wife, conjunctive theory would predict that the more a husband gives his wife, the greater the bond between them. This idea is strengthened by the importance placed on the husband's provider role in both the image of a good husband and in the reasons given for divorce. This hypothesis, however, turned out to be difficult to test. Answers to direct questions about gifts to a wife were overly general and difficult to pin down. In the area of market money given by the husband, the results are somewhat better but still unclear because the significant relationship was between the amount of market money and whether or not the marriage ended in divorce. This can be interpreted to mean that adequate market money given by a husband is related to more stable unions. On the other hand, since most marriages not ending in divorce are still extant, the relationship could represent the general rise of prices in the area during the last several decades. We will return to this discussion later when reporting on the results of the multivariate analyses.

Another more abstract way of looking at this same point, and including another set of ideas, is to examine the socio-economic status of the husband. Theoretically, the higher the status of the husband, the better able he is to provide for the welfare of his wife. Furthermore, in the society at large, the wife's status is derived in part from that of her husband (Cohen 1970i). Since Kanuri value higher status position and since social mobility is obtained primarily from establishing profitable social relations, it is profitable for the wife to prolong such a relationship. Therefore, we can predict that higher status is related to lower divorce rates.

To measure socio-economic status, the occupation of the husband was placed on a scale of occupations first arranged as to higher and lower status in the 1950's and replicated more recently in the 1960's by another investigator (Cohen 1970i; Spain 1969). The scale was arranged into five ascending categories at first, but the lack of very low and very high status people forced us to adopt a simple three point scale of low, medium, and high status for purposes of analysis. Low status is defined as traditional farmer, craft worker, or small petty trader; medium as more successful traditional farmer, small wholesale or market trader, successful craft worker in a well-paid craft such as dyeing, and low paid salary workers in the political or economic system. High status was reserved for well-to-do traders with their own canteens, and high paid salaried officials in the political and economic system.

In general, there is a relationship between low status and low divorce. But there are no significant differences between the divorce records of middle and high status husbands. Thus 76% of medium and 71% of high status husbands have marriages ending in divorce. On the other hand, when the husband is ranked as low status, only 56% of the marriages have ended by divorce. The same thing occurs when we use durations per marriage; these latter results are given below in Table 11:6, in which medium and high statuses are lumped and compared to low status men. Over half of those husbands not ranked as low in status have short durations, or 13% more than among low status men. Conversely, more lower status husbands have long durations than non-lower status ones.

TABLE 11:6. PERCENT OF LOW STATUS AND NON-LOW STATUS HUSBANDS
HAVING DIFFERING MARRIAGE DURATIONS*

Status-Rank	Marriage Duration			
	% Low (1-7 yr)	% Medium (8-13 yr)	% High (14+ yr)	Total %
Low (N=212)	38	40	32	100
Not Low (N=198) (medium and high)	51	28	21	100

*X^2 = 8.41; p $<$.02

The results are the reverse of what might be expected from conjunctive theory, since those men best able to provide for their wives divorce more than the lower status men and have fewer stable unions of long duration. The results also tend to contradict an interpretation I made ten years before (Cohen 1961a). On the basis of more adequate data, I now feel that (a) my previous results were not wrong but myopic and (b) that higher status men are stricter and more dominant with their wives and therefore have a lower threshhold of divorce than their poorer low status neighbors who are more dependent upon wives and must therefore think twice before divorcing them. In the previous work, I noticed that the longest marriages and the most stable ones were between women and upper class men. I find that this is still true but for very few cases of *women*. These same men are usually high divorcers who have a stable relationship with a particular wife who has become a confidante and helper. In other words, in large scaled terms, my previous observations are wrong; in more fine-grained terms, they are correct for a small "sub-class" of upper class unions.[6]

Bridewealth may be viewed as a contribution made by the husband to the marriage, since he and/or his relatives and friends are providing these funds and gifts in order to create the marriage itself. In conjunctive terms, this means that the husband and his group are contributing, and therefore the greater this contribution the greater the stability of marriage. This view is echoed in the anthropological literature (Gluckman 1951; Fallers 1957). If we add the amounts for the two major bridewealth payments (*luwaliram* and *sadaga*) and scale these in Nigerian pounds, we can compare bridewealth to divorce. The results of this comparison are somewhat ambiguous for men reporting, although the most stable unions are associated significantly with the lowest bridewealth. However, there is a general loading of bridewealth payments into the middle ranges (especially for completed marriages) that indicates a desire not to admit to payments that are judged low or high. Women, on the other hand, seem less secretive about such information and tend to show more variance than men in their reporting of the bridewealth. This is due partly to their greater openness in general concerning marital matters, and also to the fact that several of them reported bridewealth received rather than bridewealth agreed upon originally, some of which often takes the form of a long term debt on the part of the groom, although customarily this debt should be retired in order that a divorce be pronounced. In other words, women's reporting on bridewealth seems by all accounts to be more accurate than men's.

The results of women's reporting on bridewealth and divorce are given in Figure 11:1. The graphs indicate quite clearly the direct relationship between low bridewealth and divorce.[7] This is especially true of low bridewealth and its relationship to higher stability as measured by no divorce. Bridewealth in Bornu, therefore, does not stabilize marriage; in fact, it would be more correct from strictly correlational data to suggest the opposite.

Why bridewealth should be related inversely to marital stability can be understood in terms of the correlates of bridewealth itself. Bridewealth is high for first marriages of young girls, most of which end in divorce. Bridewealth also increases with rank and wealth of the groom and, as we have seen, there is a direct relationship between status and divorce in terms of low status equals more stability and non-low status equals less stability per marital union. Therefore, like many correlations, the one indicated by Figure 11:1 is really an aspect of other factors; in this case, bridewealth reflects ability to pay, which in turn is positively related to divorce.

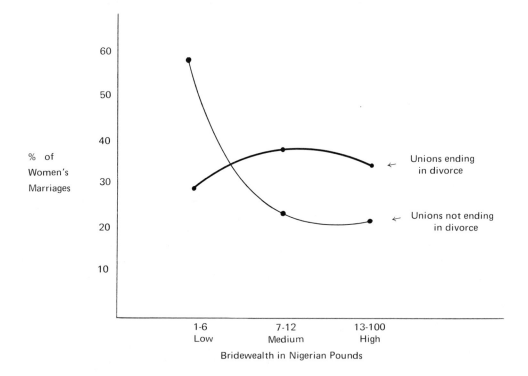

Figure 11:1. Bridewealth and Divorce in Women's Marriages.

In summary, the socio-economic contributions that husbands and wives make to marriage seem to operate in opposite directions. When the wife actively helps the husband with her labor on his farm or her productivity as a childbearer, then marriages are more stable. However, in situations where the husband is capable of making greater contributions, such as having higher status or giving greater bridewealth, then marriages seem more brittle. The only data that do not quite fit these generalizations are market money whose results are ambiguous, for the moment, and the seclusion of women. In the latter, the women contribute to the status of their husbands by remaining in the household more often and are therefore more submissive in a formal sense than wives who are not in seclusion. However, this greater dominance is, as we have seen, associated with higher divorce. Before attempting to synthesize all of this into one overall theory, let us move on to consider other correlates of Kanuri divorce.

Kinship and Divorce

Theoretically, kinship has been noted widely to contribute to marital instability in Africa in situations in which the wife must continue to carry out obligations to her own descent group members after she has married (Fallers 1957). In conjunctive-disjunctive terms, this means that the wife is pulled away from her marriage on a regular basis and, again theoretically, this weakens the relationship, thereby raising the divorce rate in comparison to situations where this is not the case.

In terms of male dominance, the wife's kinship obligations are rules of behavior requiring serious obligations to people other than her husband and therefore such obligations tend to weaken male dominance and thereby to anger and frustrate him in achieving ideal goals of wifely subordination. From several points of view, therefore, it is possible to predict that the greater the wife's maintenance of kinship ties with her own descent group after her marriage, the greater will be the marital instability. However, the theory can be carried further and stated more generally. Given the potentiality of husband-wife solidarity (conjunctiveness), compulsory obligations by either spouse away from the marital tie should weaken the union. In other words, the greater the involvement by either spouse with his or her own descent group, the greater the instability of the union.

A number of questions on ego's degree of involvement in his or her own descent group were asked on the questionnaire. These included visits to near and far kin, numbers of agnates and other descent group members in the compound, how much ego depended on the descent group for help in social and economic affairs, and so on. These have been studied independently, especially frequency of visits to near kin and far kin, and also combined into an overall index of kinship involvement by simply adding up each person's affirmative answers to questions concerning his or her interaction and dependence upon their own kin groups.

For men, most of the relationships between divorce and either their own kin involvement or that reported for their wives are unrelated to marital break-ups. The two exceptions to this are number of mother's divorces and number of patri-kin in the household, both of which are positively related to a man's divorce record. Since there is a strong chance that a man's mother will be living with him more often if she divorces more often, these two results imply the same conclusion. That is, a man's kin connections, when they involve relationships between himself and his own descent group members *within* one household, will tend to interfere with and therefore break up his marriages. Put another way, this tends to substantiate complaints by Kanuri women that their husband's kin, especially his mother, often help to cause divorces because of antagonisms that develop between them and a wife.

Results of women's interviews tend to both contradict *and* substantiate the usual hypothesis that a woman's own descent group obligations tend to interfere with her marriage. If we look at the divorces per person in relation to the frequency of a woman's visits to her own kin group members, 79% of those who visit more than once a week are medium and high divorcers (2 or more per person), whereas only 59% of those that visit less than once a week divorce this much.

Thus the hypothesis is supported when we look at the divorce records of individuals. That is to say, women who claim to visit their descent group more often divorce more often. When marriages are used as units and we take the total kinship involvement score and relate it to whether or not the marriage ended in divorce, then 67% of those unions ending in divorce have low as opposed to high kinship involvement for women. This is the reverse of what theory would predict.

These contradictory results point up an important quality of Kanuri marital experience for women. In the city, many high divorce women have become quite independent of their kinsfolk and live in rented rooms between marriages. When compared to others as persons, they show up as high divorcers with low kinship involvement. However, the weight of Kanuri individual experience is against them. When marriages are used as units of analysis, this group tends to bias the sample by overweighting the low involvement category with high divorce simply becasue this group has many more marriages per person than the rest of the sample. Thus the theory does predict for Kanuri society in general, but a small significant group of city women act in an exactly opposite way; they are more independent of their kin and they are high divorcers as well.

The Kanuri themselves say that cousin marriages tend to create more stable unions. Indeed, this is why informants claim to dislike such unions for they are more difficult to break up than ordinary ones. Kin members on both sides more often tend to pressure the couple to stay together, compared to non-cousin unions.

Men report that a significant majority of their cousin marriages (56%), but a minority (30%) of non-cousin marriages, do *not* end in divorce. In other words, there is evidence to suggest that divorce varies inversely with cousin marriage, but this does not seem to be consistently so for all divorce measures.

Another possible indicator of the relationship between descent and divorce is suggested by ethnography. Wives' families often dislike having a husband move away from the place where he married their daughter, thus taking her away from her kin. This is especially the case when the girl is quite young, and I have recorded several such instances where the family instructed the girl to misbehave and thereby cause a divorce. Quantitative checking of this point was done by asking questions about whether the marriage involved moving to a new place or remaining in the same locale for both partners and the kinds of places (hamlets, villages, or cities) that were involved.

Analysis shows that there is a positive relationship between marital durations in the rural areas and local endogamy. Thus 68% of all unions lasting nine years and over for men and women combined are between spouses from the same village or hamlet. On the other hand, there are no differences between marriages of shorter duration. In other words, whether or not a woman must leave her own home village or hamlet—making it more difficult to visit her kinfolk—does not seem to measurably affect marriages at first. However, this separation of the wife from her natal group does produce difficulties, and these tend to become more powerful over time. Almost all urban marriages are between urban residents, and therefore it was impossible to test this relationship on the urban sample.

In summary, kinship involvements by both husband and wife tend to weaken the marriage bond between them. This is especially so for a woman's obligations to her own kin, which are exacerbated as an irritant when she is not living in the same locality as her own kin. The husband's relationship to his own kin, especially to a high divorce mother who more often lives with him, also tends to interfere and create instability in his own union. On the other hand, Kanuri are right when they say cousin marriages are more stable. Thus when affines are in fact own descent group members rather than simply spouse's kin, marriages are strengthened.

Polygyny

Ethnographic evidence, plus simple logic, indicates that polygyny is a more disruptive form of marriage than monogamy. Informants readily admit this if they are men and counter it with cultural rules and values designed to smooth out the problems involved. Women often say they don't like it, but then suggest that if it is necessary then they wish to be the senior wife in the group. Logically, a husband-wife relationship is much more complex if there are co-wives who must relate to each other as well as to the shared husband. The further possibility of children's relationship to mother's co-wives and half-siblings make the structure more complex and therefore creates more grounds for conflict than in situations where this is not so.

If we look at polygyny per person, 50% of all persons in the sample with two or more divorces were married polygynously at the time of the interview. Conversely, only 33% of those with this many divorces say they married monogamously. This measure indicates that polygynous persons tend to be higher divorcers, but it leaves out persons unmarried at the time of the interview and lumps together the sexes who each have a different experience, of polygyny. In order to include all marital experience it is necessary to look at all unions in the sample and ask whether they were monogamous or polygynous at the time of dissolution or at the time of the interview if they were still extant. Table 11:7 gives these results in terms of the percent of monogamous and polygynous unions that end in divorce.

Although men and women both show a relationship between polygyny and divorce, the increase in divorce is greater for polygynous men than women, reflecting the greater numbers of marriages and divorces for men. However, despite this discrepancy, it can be fairly confidently concluded that marriages having multiple wives tend to end in divorce more often than monogamous ones. The chief reason for this is the fact that men are much reduced in status if they have no wife at all to cook for them, work on their farms, provide cooked foods for their guests, and so on. To divorce one among several wives does not change a man's marital status, but to divorce a single wife makes him an unmarried male. The greater possiblity for conflicts within polygynous unions also contributes to the higher divorce rate among such families. Thus there are more forces pushing against the stability of polygynous unions, and other forces pushing to hold monogamous ones together.

TABLE 11:7. POLYGYNY AND DIVORCE*

| Type of Union | Men (N=458) | | Women (N=236) | |
	Divorce	No Divorce	Divorce	No Divorce
Monogamy	54	46	67	33
Polygyny	69	31	75	25

Percent of Unions Ending in Divorce:

*for men, $X^2 = 9.169$, p $<$ .01; for women, $X^2 = 1.474$, p $<$ .20

An interesting structural question can be raised about polygyny by looking at the stability of its component relationships. Granted that polygyny is associated with higer divorce rates, should it be assumed that such higher probabilities attach to all of the marital relations equally, or is there some variance involved˄ To get at this point, we asked, for each polygynous union, whether each wife was junior, senior, or both, in relation to her co-wives in the marital union being discussed. This allows for an analysis of divorce by numbers of wives junior and senior to the one under discussion.

The data as given in Table 11:8 indicate two significant and important patterns of tension. When a wife has co-wives of any kind then, in general there is a higher probability of divorce than when this is not the case, i.e., in monogamy. A difficult situation arises when there is one senior wife. Then the junior has an increased probability of divorce which takes the percentage up to 74%, where it is 66-67% in the case of two or three wives senior to ego. Thus polygyny most adversely affects the fate of the second wife in a two-wife family. When we look the other way, from senior to junior, it is a senior wife with two junior wives who has a strong increase in her divorce frequency.

TABLE 11:8. DIVORCE AND THE STRUCTURE OF POLYGYNOUS MARRIAGE*

| Numbers of Co-Wives | Percent of Unions in which Co-wife is Senior to Ego (N=693) | | Percent of Unions in which Co-wife is Junior to Ego (N=688) | |
	Divorce	No-Divorce	Divorce	Non-Divorce
0	59	41	60	40
1	74	26	68	32
2	67	33	82	18
3	66	34	70	30

*$X^2 = 13.950$; p $<$ .01; df=3 $X^2 = 9.906$; p $<$ .02; df=3

The ethnographic data tend to support these findings, but only in part. Kanuri informants are agreed that of all polygynous unions a three-wife family is the most difficult. However, they disagree or have no opinion upon whom the tension sits most heavily. The quantitative material goes further by suggesting that a two-wife family is difficult for the junior wife, and a three-wife family is most difficult for the senior wife in terms of who is divorced most often. Both of these findings are consistent with the interpretation that a senior wife is the authoritative figure among the wives and faced with one junior wife, the superior position of the senior tends to make her the winner more often than the loser in any competitive struggles that ensue. However, when the husband marries a second junior wife, the tables are turned; now the single junior has an ally and, in this triadic situation, the most common recourse is for the two junior wives to form a coalition against the senior.

An alternate explanation can be used which includes husband-wife relations. It may be that in the three-wife family the husband is simply getting tired of the oldest wife, who has been around longest. But there is no correlation between age and duration of senior wife and her divorce record. Furthermore, the senior wife in a four-wife family has the same divorce record as the senior wife in a two-wife family, and the husband-getting-tired-of-senior-wife hypothesis would predict that senior wife's divorce should increase with numbers of other wives. This is not the case. Rather it is most particularly the three-wife—i.e., triadic—relationship that is most unstable for the senior wife. Thus the most likely theory for explaining the variance of divorce among co-wives is relations among the co-wives themselves, leaving aside their relations to the common husband.

In summary, polygyny is valued in Kanuri society and it also tends to be associated with higher rates of divorce. Within the polygynous family itself, the two-wife family increases the probability of divorce for the younger wife. The three-wife family increases the probability of divorce for the senior wife. This is explained by suggesting that junior wife is in a subordinate disadvantageous position, but when she finds another junior co-wife they form an alliance against the senior wife. This is less likely in four-wife families where the senior wife may equal the balance by obtaining an alliance with one of the junior co-wives.

Premarital Relations

It is often suggested in Western literature on marital stability that the types of backgrounds of each spouse and their length of acquaintance, as well as the type of relationship they have had with each other, affect their future relations within marriage. In general, the more similar these relations, then the more "conjunctive" they are—i.e., they form a basis for solidifying the union. Conversely, the less alike they are, the greater the gap that must be closed by the marriage relationship. It has also been suggested (Bohannan, personal communication) that, for Western society, experience by either partner with divorce within their own kindred lowers the threshold of ego's own decision to divorce. Finally, within this same context, it is useful to ask if there is any relationship between premarital sexual relations and divorce. Since this is presumably one of the rights being gained by marriage, then it is arguable that the more this right is restricted to marriage, the greater will be the stability of unions, whereas when access to the privilege occurs outside marriage, then the utility of marriage as access to sexual relations decreases.

For Kanuri society, none of these generalizations is supported. There is no relationship between differences in socio-economic background and divorce among spouses, nor does length of acquaintance have any affect on divorce, or the distance between husband and wife's domicile relate to marital stability. We could obtain information on premarital intercourse from women only, and again these data show no relationship to divorce. Similarly, estimated or reported divorce experience of a person's own mother and father have no systematic association with the person's own divorce record for the sample as a whole or for women.[8] Even in the realm of a woman's fertility, past fertility in previous marriages has no bearing on marital relations in future unions. The one exception to these generally negative results is that of cousin marriage, where a premarital relationship does exist and where, as already noted, there is an association with lower rates of divorce.

These results suggest that, unlike Westerners, the Kanuri see their marriages in very ahistorical terms. What has occurred beforehand is unimportant—what matters is the kind of behavior and relationship set up and carried out within each individual marriage itself. In this sense, marriage is a very practical affair and is not idealized as stemming out of a previous "romance." If it works well as an arrangement and benefits accrue to the participants, all well and good; if not, then it should be ended.[9]

The Quality of the Relationship

The relationship of husbands and wives is essentially formal. In general, each sex has its most frequent social relations with members of the same sex. The degree of intimacy, however, varies.

Furthermore, sexual intercourse provides a deeply emotional experience between spouses, at least for the wife who must remain faithful to her husband. Under such circumstances it is not surprising that some women complain of their husband's fidelity, and those that openly complain tend to divorce more often (not significant statistically) and have significantly shorter durations to their unions. These women seem to be saying both with their complaints and their behavior that they resent the greater sexual freedom of their husbands. Sexual attractiveness and intercourse is by right the prerogative of a wife and is a tribute to her acceptability and sense of self-worth. By going outside marriage for sexual experience, men deflate these rewards. Many women accept such action grudgingly; others refuse and the union becomes unstable because of their proclivity to become jealous, which leads to conflict and divorce.

Intimacy between husbands and wives, as measured by whether or not the husband tells her his secrets, is associated with longer durations and unions not ending in divorce. This latter relationship is shown in Table 11:9. It is probably inflated by biased reporting, since men very likely have a tendency to report or believe that a divorced wife did not take any of her husband's secrets with her. However, the relationship is corroborated when we examine durations. The average duration of unions in which husbands report not telling any secrets to their wives is 3.4 years, while the average for unions where some or many secrets are shared is 10.7 years.

TABLE 11:9. SHARING SECRETS BY THE HUSBAND
AND MARITAL STABILITY*

Husband reporting on his relationship to a wife	Percent of Unions		Totals
	Unions ending in death or still extant	Unions ending in divorce	
He tells her secrets	67	33	100% (N=190)
He tells her no secrets	28	72	100% (N=274)

*$X^2 = 56.067$; p $<$ .001

Many respondents tried to explain their answer to this question, and one or both of two reasons were invariably given. First, the idea of secrecy was equated to duration just as it is in the data. Respondents commented that of course they shared secrets with this particular wife—after all, she had been in the compound for over ten years. Contrarily, secrets are not shared with new wives. Some men, however, reported never telling a secret of any kind to a wife no matter how long she remained. Secondly, and more interestingly, men explained their answers by referring to whether the wife was fertile or not. If fertile, then she deserved intimacy; if not, then she was to be kept at a distance. Fertility then completes, for these men, the woman's role and makes her more of a member of his family so that he may share his intimacies with her. In this sense, fertility becomes a watershed in the quality of husband-wife relations, decreasing the social and psychological distance between them and stabilizing the marriage, not only because of the mere fact of productivity, but because of an actual change in the quality of the relationship toward greater intimacy and therefore greater stability in the social and psychological domain.

Multivariate Analysis

In order to establish some degree of priority among the sociological variables considered in the study, a stepwise discriminant function analysis was carried out on a selected set of them. This technique enables a researcher to divide his data by groups and discover which variables

TABLE 11:10. MULTIVARIATE ANALYSES OF KANURI MARITAL INSTABILITY

Percent of Differences Among Stability Measures Accounted for*

Variables Accounting for Differences and direction of relation to Instability	Whole Sample			Rurals			Urbans			Males		
	a	b	c	a	b	c	a	b	c	a	b	c
Fertility in present union (negative)	17	20	13	24	15	21	23	24	--	21	26	--
Rural (negative) Urban (positive)	18	18	18	not applicable			not applicable			15	25	--
Husband tells wife his secrets (negative)	23	15	--	36	24	--	26	13	--	25	--	--
Wife is helpful to husband (negative)	--	--	--	--	--	--	--	--	--	--	--	--
Age of Respondent (positive)	14	--	--	20	--	--	15	--	--	10	--	14
Sex of Respondent (males positive)	8	12	--	--	--	--	16	16	--			
Wife helps husband on farm (negative)	--	--	17	--	--	35	--	--	--	--	--	39
Local exogamy (positive)	--	--	--	--	20	--	--	--	--	--	--	--
Wife is obedient (negative)	--	--	--	--	--	--	--	--	62	--	--	--
Wife is kulle (seclusion) (positive)	--	--	--	--	21	--	--	--	--	--	11	16
Amount of market money given to wife (negative)	--	--	15	--	--	14	--	--	--	--	--	--
Husband's occupational rank (positive)	--	--	11	--	--	10	--	12	--	--	--	--
Monogamous Unions (negative)	--	--	--	--	--	--	--	--	18	9	--	--
Senior Wife in 3 wife household (positive)	--	--	--	--	--	--	--	15	--	--	--	--
Wife runs home (positive)	--	--	--	--	--	--	--	--	--	--	--	--
Spouse previously married (positive)	--	--	--	--	--	--	--	--	--	--	18	--
Bridewealth (positive)	--	--	--	--	--	--	--	--	--	--	--	--
Husband stays out overnight (positive)	--	--	--	--	--	--	--	--	--	--	--	--
Spouse's Age (positive)	--	--	--	--	--	--	--	--	--	--	--	--
Cousin Marriage	--	--	--	--	--	--	--	--	--	--	--	--
Total percent of Difference accounted for	80	80	80	80	80	80	80	80	80	80	80	80

*The instability measures are as follows: a = marriages ending in divorce as compared with those that do not. b = short, medium and long marital durations compared as three groups of unions. c = low, medium and high per person divorce rates compared as groups of persons using the marriages of these three groups as groups of data to be explained.

Females			Rural Males			Rural Females			Urban Males			Urban Females			Rank Order
a	b	c	a	b	c	a	b	c	a	b	c	a	b	c	
12	16	15	25	41	17	13	24	21	31	30	--	--	23	42	1
--	8	26	not applicable												2
--	--	--	38	--	--	--	--	--	33	--	62	--	--	38	3
17	19	15	--	--	--	19	14	23	--	--	--	39	12	--	4
18	11	--	--	--	--	--	--	--	--	--	18	41	--	--	5
not applicable															6
24	--	--	--	--	--	15	10	--	--	--	--	--	--	--	7
--	13	14	--	39	--	7	8	23	--	--	--	--	--	--	8
9	13	--	--	--	--	11	13	--	--	--	--	--	13	--	9
--	--	--	--	--	42	--	--	--	--	17	--	--	20	--	10
--	--	--	--	--	21	--	--	13	--	--	--	--	--	--	11
--	--	--	--	--	--	--	--	--	--	12	--	--	--	--	12
--	--	--	--	--	--	--	--	--	16	--	--	--	--	--	13
--	--	--	--	--	--	--	--	--	--	21	--	--	--	--	14
--	--	--	--	--	--	15	11	--	--	--	--	--	--	--	15
--	--	--	--	--	--	--	--	--	--	--	--	--	--	--	16
--	--	--	17	--	--	--	--	--	--	--	--	--	--	--	17
--	--	--	--	--	--	--	--	--	--	--	--	--	12	--	18
--	--	--	--	--	--	--	--	--	--	--	--	--	--	--	19
--	--	10	--	--	--	--	--	--	--	--	--	--	--	--	20
80	80	80	80	80	80	80	80	80	80	80	80	80	80	80	

among an array of them are contributing most to the differences between the groups (Cooley and Lohnes 1962). The stepwise quality of the analysis involves a consideration of the total array of variables; when that variable contributing most to the differences is found, the analysis is repeated with the remaining set. In the present work, this means that we can take our dependent measures of marital stability and ask which among our independent variables contribute most to high as opposed to low degrees of stability among marriages.

Before carrying out the analysis, several technical problems had to be resolved. The computer program for discriminant functional analysis will not accept missing data. This difficulty was overcome by assigning mean values to missing data items. Thus if age of spouse at time of marriage was not available for a union, the mean score for that item was given to that particular spouse. This acts to lower the chances that this variable will discriminate and thus biases the analysis away from obtaining results with variables for which data are not complete.

Another difficulty arises in the stepwise treatment of the data. Given a large array of variables and a large sample size, the analysis will produce a discriminant function to which very many variables are contributing. However, in general only a few are doing most of the "work," while the others each contribute to one or two percent of the differences between groups. We resolved this problem by trial and error and finally decided that the 80% level of explanation was the most efficient cut-point. Beyond that level of explanation, variables multiplied rapidly even though each considered by itself was doing very little discriminating between high and low levels of marital stability.

The Variables

Three measures of marital stability were used on our sample of marriages. First, unions were simply divided into those ending in divorce versus those not ending in divorce. Since a great many Kanuri marriages do in fact end in divorce, this sampling device is biased toward recent marriages in the no-divorce group. To counteract this bias, the next measure chosen was marital duration. There, divorce itself is not in question. Rather, the durability of the union is being considered. Finally, as a third measure, we chose the number of divorces of the person being interviewed, even though the analysis was being made on marriages as units. This measure tends to counteract the bias in the sample provided by the fact that high divorcers marry more often. Therefore, in treating each of a single person's marriages as separate units, we are in fact weighting the analysis toward the behavior patterns and sociological features of the high divorcers. However, by using the person's rate, we can ask questions not about marriages but individuals, and attempt to answer such questions by referring to the details of their marriages.

The independent variables were developed from the results of the bivariate analysis discussed above plus some trial and error runs on variables which seemed promising, especially in the area of husband-wife interaction. In general, five classes of variables have been considered. First, a number of demographic features such as age, sex of respondent, fertility, and rural or urban residence at the time of interview were considered. Secondly, we considered a small number of measures dealing with physical movement at marriage (endogamy-exogamy) and movement after marriage. Thirdly, a number of variables concerning kinship involvement by both ego and spouse were considered and, fourthly, socio-economic factors such as husband's occupational rank, amount of bridewealth, whether or not wife earns her own money, amount of market money given to the wife, were also considered. Finally, we included a group of variables dealing with the nature of husband-wife interaction, such as does the husband tell the wife his secrets, is she obedient, does the husband complain about the wife as being bad, is she in purdah, does she help on the farm, go to the well, and so on. All together, 37 measures of these qualities were included and used to compete with one another to account for marital stability.

The Results

The results of 27 separate analyses (three each for each of nine sub-samples) are given in Table 11:10. Of the 37 measures utilized from the questionnaire, nineteen (in various combinations of six to nine for each sub-sample) tend to account for 80% of the differences among the three measures of marital stability. The variables are listed from top to bottom in terms of their importance to the outcome of the multivariate analysis. This was estimated by calculating the mean percent of differences accounted for by each variable where it was relevant and multiplying it by the number of times the variable showed itself to be an effective discriminator where this latter was relevant. Thus fertility is the number one variable because it has a mean discrimination effect of 23% (the mean of all numbers listed in row #1) and it is present as a discriminator 85% of the time (23/27 of all possible runs). This product (23 x 85) yielded the highest number among all variables. In other words, no matter what the situation, fertility enters in as a factor to stabilize marriage. The only measures for which this is not the case are male and urban male per person divorce rates. In other words, the urban men—whether they are high or low divorcers—tend to have similar numbers of fertile unions. The table shows, however, that fewer of their fertile unions have ended in divorce, and the durations of these are longer. By contrast, fertility seems to be "working hardest" to discriminate per person divorce among urban women (42%) and marital durations among rural men (41%). The ranking criteria are given in Table 11:11. It should be noted that this is a very rough and ready means of establishing priority among variables that discriminate between more and less marital instability. On the other hand, it is clear that items ranked high on the list have a great deal more impact on marriage than those ranked very low.

The rural-urban distinction is the next most important discriminator accounting for some differences whenever it is not controlled for. No matter how it is measured in the whole sample, rural-urban distinctions account for a steady 18% of the differences in marital stability, with stability increasing in the rural areas. After this in importance comes intimacy and trust between husband and wife. Whether or not the respondent declares that the husband shared his secrets with a wife generally differentiates whether a marriage has ended in divorce or not and whether the duration is longer or shorter. When the sample is broken down further, this quality predicts more for men than for women and, in one group, that of the urban males, 62% of the differences in per person divorce rate are associated with this variable. The table also shows that this variable has no effect among rural women. Its extremely powerful differentiating effect among the urban men's personal divorce records points to personality and status differences. Some urban men seem to trust their wives consistently no matter what the circumstances or duration of the union. Others are exactly the opposite, not trusting a wife even when she has been in the house for 35 years. Furthermore, the non-trusting high divorcers are also consistently higher in occupational ranking than their lower divorce, trusting colleagues. As one informant put it, "It is the rich and important people who always keep secrets, for they have important things to hide."

The next most important discriminator must be viewed together with one further down the list. From ethnography and our bivariate analysis, we know that wife helping on the farm is a significant factor in depressing the divorce rate. In the present analysis, it decreases the per person divorce rate in rural areas and among men in general, while it also helps predict the stability of unions reported on by rural women. To this specific question about farm help, we added a more general yet more behavioral and attitudinal question about wifely behavior. In this item, we asked if the wife was genuinely helpful and supportive to her husband. This turned out to be the fourth most important discriminator in the multivariate study, differentiating for women but not for men—the latter generally answering this in a rather random fashion. For women, this measure consistently distinguishes between low and high stability, with the more helpful wife (by her own estimation) most often being a low divorcer, having non-divorce unions, and longer duration unions. This is more true for rural females; while it does not distinguish between high and low divorce women in the city, it does discriminate among their unions.

The men reacted politely to this question. All wives are "helpful" to some extent, and therefore it had little relevance to them. The women, on the other hand, took it seriously and answered only if they felt they honestly contributed to a husband's welfare. Thus women who see themselves as being helpful are more stable partners.

The age of the respondent distinguishes marriages that have ended in divorce from those that have not in the sample as a whole, and when it is broken into rural, urban, males or females. This is most likely an artifact of the data, since there are generally more young people who have

TABLE 11:11. RANKING THE VARIABLES THAT DISCRIMINATE
BETWEEN DEGREES OF MARITAL INSTABILITY

Variables	A=Mean Percent of Difference Accounted For	B=Percent of Total Possible Times That This Variable is Discriminating	Rank Score A X B / 100
1 Fertility in present union	23	85	19.6
2 Rural-urban residence	18	78	14.0
3 Husband tells wife secrets	30	41	12.3
4 Wife is helpful to husband	20	30	6.0
5 Age of respondent	18	33	5.9
6 Sex of respondent	13	44	5.7
7 Wife helps husband on farm	23	22	5.1
8 Local exogamy	18	26	4.7
9 Wife is obedient	20	20	4.4
10 Wife in kulle (seclusion)	25	15	3.8
11 Amount of market money	15	22	3.3
12 Husband's Occupational rank	11	15	1.7
13 Monogamy	14	11	1.5
14 Senior wife in 3 wife household	18	7	1.3
15 Wife runs home	13	7	.9
16 Spouse previously married	18	4	.7
17 Bridewealth	17	4	.7
18 Husband stays out overnight	12	4	.5
19 Spouse's Age	11	4	.4
20 Cousin Marriage	10	4	.4

incompleted marriages than old people. The fact that urban men can be distinguished by age into those having less and more divorce, while this is not so for rural men, indicates urban men are more active divorcers than their country cousins. As they advance in age, they tend to build up an accumulation of marriages and divorces that contrasts with the rural men. This same point is made by the discriminating power of the sex of the respondent. Again, it is urban men who are out in front, whereas sex does not predict well to marital stability in the rural areas.

Local exogamy is clearly a rural phenomenon in its negative effects on marital stability. For rural men, 39% of the differences among shorter and longer durations are accounted for by whether or not the wife came from the same village or hamlet as her husband. For women, the percentages are not so high, but this variable discriminates no matter what type of measure is used for marital instability. In general, then, going outside of one's own village to find a wife in the rural area introduces a strain on the marriage which results in a more brittle union than if the wife were taken from the local community.

The next variable, which describes whether or not a wife was obedient within a particular union, accounts for 62% of the difference between low, medium, and high divorcers in the urban area. It also tends to predict the stability of unions reported on by women in both rural and urban areas, especially their durability. In the urban area, where a woman's economic role is less important, the value of male dominance comes to the surface as the single most important distinguishing feature between individuals who have high as opposed to low divorce records. When the man or woman sees the wife as obedient, divorce records are low, and high divorce records are seen as associated with wifely disobedience.

Wife seclusion (*kulle*) is associated with more rather than less instability in marriage. For both men and women in the city, it accounts for shorter marital durations. This is as expected. It may seem incongruous to see marital seclusion accounting for 42% of the per person divorce rate among men interviewed in the rural area. However, a little thought explains this seeming incongruity. Of those men in the rural areas who have high divorce records, a number are not peasants but political functionaries from the city now living in the rural areas. They still maintain their urban style and keep their wives in *kulle*. In every other respect, they resemble urban men. Thus they are urbans living in the rural area and are distinguished from the peasants by higher divorce and *kulle*.

The amount of market money tends to stabilize the marriage when it is greater or judged as sufficient. The analysis indicates that this is basically a rural phenomenon discriminating between high, medium, and low divorce persons of either sex in this area. Males as an entire group do tend to be differentiated by this variable into those who are more stable in marriage, and provide more market money for their wives, as opposed to those who are less stable in marriage, and provide less market money.

Among urban men, and in the per person divorce rate among urbanites in general, monogamy tends to differentiate unions that end in divorce from those that do not. If the variable also distinguished longer from shorter durations in the same direction, i.e., that of more stable marriage, it would be possible to report it with more confidence. As it stands, it is quite possible that monogamy distinguishes more stable unions from less stable ones simply because polygynists have greater chances to divorce. Thus the multivariate analysis of this variable adds little to our knowledge.

The remaining six variables show no clear-cut pattern except possibly that of the wife running home to her family. This distinguishes two of our three measures of stability for rural females. Thus, when reported by these women, this factor predicts less marital stability. It should be noted that bridewealth payments do not discriminate except between unions ending in divorce and those not ending in divorce among rural men. I interpret this to be a class phenomenon in which a few upper class, high divorcing men are residing in the rural areas and this quality of bridewealth has predicted their higher marital instability.

Finally, it is important to note which variables had very little or no power to discriminate high from low marital stability. None of the direct kinship involvement measures concerning wife visiting near or far kin, or concerning total kin involvement for either spouse, showed up in any of the analyses. Duration of acquaintance before marriage does not discriminate, nor does the distance that the wife has to come if she came from a different place. The husband's complaints, or the wife earning money, or the husband moving to a new locale during the marriage, were not sufficient to distinguish among groups with different marital stability. Fertility in previous marriages and false pregnancy were not sufficient either.

If we use Table 11:11 to give us some idea of the relative importance of sociological variables affecting Kanuri marriage, then the following table, 11:12, sums up the multivariate findings. We will return to a synthesis and theoretical interpretation of these results in the concluding chapter after looking at the rest of the quantitative materials.

In summary, the sociological variables reflect a number of underlying factors which, inductively, we can abstract as the causes of stability and instability in Kanuri marriage.

TABLE 11:12. SUMMARY OF MULTIVARIATE ANALYSIS

Impact of Variables	More Stable Kanuri Unions	Less Stable Unions
More Important	Union is fertile	Union is not fertile
	Rural residence	Urban residence
	Husband tells wife his secrets	Husband does not tell wife his secrets
	Wife is considered helpful	Wife is not considered helpful
	Person responding is young	Person responding is old
	Wife helps husband on his farm	Wife does no farming
	Community endogamy	Community exogamy
	Wife is considered obedient	Wife is not considered obedient
	Wife is not in seclusion	Wife is in seclusion
	Wife is given sufficient market money	Wife is given insufficient market money
	Husband has lower occupational rank	Husband has higher occupational rank
	Monogamy	Polygyny
Less Important	Not senior wife in a three wife family	Senior wife in a three wife family
	Wife does not run to her home often	Wife runs away to her home often
	Spouse not previously married or married only a few times	Spouse married previously many times (more than 4)
	Husband does not stay out overnight	Husband stays out overnight
	Spouse is young	Spouse is old
	Spouse is a cousin	Spouse is not a cousin

First, there is the contribution of the wife to the marriage. Most important of these is the childbearing qualities of the wife. Possibly this is in turn due to the low fertility rates of Kanuri women. Whatever the reason, fertility stablizes marriages, and this is true no matter what other conditions hold during the union. Secondly, there is a group of qualities associated primarily with rural life. These include rural residence itself, wife helping on the farm, and wife not in seclusion. In other words, and not surprisingly, the economic contribution of a wife is more salient to the husband's success in the rural areas where she is an essential factor in his productivity and success. The contribution of the wife to the family and to her husband—just how helpful she really is, as seen by women—cross-cuts rural/urban distinctions and predicts marital stability. Thus the primary determinant of marital stability among the Kanuri is the contribution to the union made by the wife—objectively, in terms of children, and in the views of the husband and the wife. In general, the greater her contribution, the more stable the union.

Second, there is a complex of qualities that all reflect in some way the ideology of male dominance. Most clearly indicative is the idea that obedience of the wife is positively related to marital stability. But again, as with the contribution of the wife, a group of factors subsumed under the rubric of urban residence actually indicates reference to male dominance. Thus purdah for women is almost exclusively an urban phenomenon, except for urbanites living as administrators in the rural areas. Furthermore, urban wives do not farm or go to wells for water. Finally, their husbands are on the average of higher social rank than their rural counterparts. Purdah means that the wife is by definition more tightly controlled, since she is in formal seclusion. Higher social status and wealth for urban husbands means they require less contribution from their wives to their economic enterprise. Instead, they want decorum and subordination. Their wives must stay home and behave properly or the marriages are severed and new, more ideally submissive women are sought out. Richer men, who are mostly in the cities, can afford to divorce more often and attempt to enforce ideals of male dominance; therefore they divorce more often.

Third, urbanism per se is also an unstabilizing force in Kanuri marriage. There are many single men in the city and thus a divorced woman can always find a liaison with some man, either married or unmarried, who will support her. Because there are many other women doing the same thing, and it is an independent and non-submissive role, there is some attraction to city life and its more independent status for divorced women. Urban men, on the other hand, feel they can usually get another wife from this corps of available unmarried women. They find it easier to divorce wives, especially if the husband is a demanding and authoritative person who insists on rigid standards of wifely decorum—standards that are not easily enforced in rural areas where women must leave the household to work in the fields and go to the wells.

Fourth, there is the quality of the interpersonal relationship itself. This is very likely dependent upon personal qualities of the actors, but is also a result of stable and unstable marital experience as well as a cause. Thus shared intimacy, lack of sexual jealousy by the wife, lack of conflict as reflected in the wife running home to her kin, all point to the fact that if the husband and wife are bound up in some intimacy with one another and there is trust about—or at least lack of concern over—the husband's extra-marital affairs, then we may predict a more stable union.

Fifth, polygyny is an institution that stimulates marital instability. By adding wives, a man diminishes the strength of his relationship to any one wife. The most fragile of such arrangements is the three-wife family where the senior wife is in an extremely unstable position, or to a lesser extent the junior wife in a two-wife family. Any polygynous union creates a greater stress on marriage than a monogamous one. The only exception to this is the senior wife as a political partner who tolerates her husband's having many junior wives for short durations while she remains to rule the roost.

Finally, there are several factors indicated by only one variable each. Women are loath to leave a good provider and quick to find fault with a bad one. Thus, all else being equal, good provider husbands have more stable unions. Women who are taken away from the local community prove to be partners to more unstable unions. Obviously, the pull of their kin living in another locality causes a strain on the marriage that local endogamy does not. The remaining factors are demographic characteristics of a high divorce society that reflect increasing divorces with increasing age, plus the probability that older women will be divorced and not remarried simply because they are getting old.

Chapter 12
Psychological Correlates of Divorce

In the very large literature dealing with marriage in the Western world, emphasis is placed upon the importance of psychological variables which predict or explain the differences between stable and unstable unions. Marriage counseling stresses individual adjustment, and marital problems are often given as reasons for initiating psychotherapy (Leslie 1964). Even when a marital problem is judged to be non-psychological, we tend to assume that there is still an important level or aspect to it which is essentially psychological. This is due to the fact that ultimately we think in individualistic terms so that even the break-up of marriages is explained as being acceptable or inadvisable because these unions were or were not "productive of healthy personalities of happiness or satisfaction" (Leslie 1964:915). In other words, our ultimate test of the success or failure of a marriage is in terms of the psychological rewards it provides for the individuals concerned.

Sociologists and anthropologists have, as we have already noted in Chapter 1, emphasized sociological variables and their relationship to measures of marital stability. Indeed, there are exceedingly few if any studies in anthropology which investigate directly the impact of psychological factors upon marital instability. A question emerges about the relation of psychological qualities of spouses to marital stability among a non-Western people such as the Kanuri. The question becomes even more intriguing in the face of a high divorce rate, since marriage break-up is in fact a normal everyday occurrence and happens ultimately to a majority of all marriages. Under such conditions, there are grounds for arguing that psychological factors are irrelevant, since divorce is so common that no matter what type of persons are involved the outcome is still an eventual break-up. On the other hand, as we have seen, there is variation; some unions are very short and others much longer, some people divorce a great deal and others much less, so that individual psychological differences may very well be systematically important. Synthesizing these ideas cross-culturally would lead us to expect psychological factors to be of greater significance in societies having lower divorce rates, while higher rates of divorce would be associated with a declining impact for psychological variables.

As a working null hypothesis, we can start with the notion that there are no psychological differences among persons who differ systematically in their marital stability. This is in fact the way in which the work for this chapter has been planned and executed. Having decided to examine psychological data, the problem of method and technique emerges as crucial. What sorts of variables should be considered and what sorts of data gathering devices should be employed? The first of these questions was answered by reference to both ethnographic material and a common sense deduction. In general, it has been my experience that people with records of very high marital instability in Bornu tend to be more intolerant of conflict and less flexible in their reactions to conflict in interpersonal relations. Case material on the reasons given for divorce tend to substantiate this view. In effect, the observation simply says that people who are less tolerant of conflict in general will be less tolerant of marital conflict in particular. It was decided therefore to use this as a guiding theme and to create a testing device adapted to the culture which would be aimed at eliciting responses to situations of conflict or potential conflict between individuals and groups.

The instrument took the form of a series of artist drawn pictures depicting easily recognizable Kanuri scenes and people interacting. After pilot testing, eighteen of these cards at three separate degrees of clarity or chiaroscuro, a set of twelve were chosen and administered to 161 men and women in the rural and urban areas who varied in age and marital history. It is my view that such picture tests are not particularistic psychological tests which get at specific aspects of personality. Instead, I see them as an efficient means of obtaining a focused set of responses from a set of informants concerning a constant type of social interaction situation.[1] Psychological data are then inferred from such responses through whatever type of analysis the researcher wishes to apply. In other words,

> A TAT is rather like a questionnaire. . . .The formulation of the question posed by an individual picture is accomplished, then, not in words but by the selection and management of pictorially represented symbols [Sherwood 1958:162].

It should therefore be made clear that the results of such a TAT investigation are partially determined, as with all questionnaire material, by the types of pictures used in the investigation. Since the total range of Kanuri behavior and experience is not represented, interpretation must be restricted to those aspects of life represented by the "question," i.e., the picture. Thus what emerges is not a well-rounded or complete profile of personality among the Kanuri, but those aspects of personality relevant to the topics chosen for investigation.[2]

The Cards

The picture cards are shown in Appendix II. They were given consecutively to each respondent, who was asked to tell what was happening here. When human figures were not perceived, these were pointed out with no sex, age, or location identification. The interviewer simply said, "Here is a person with a head, arms, body, and legs," pointing out the figure on the cards. In this way, stimulus standardization was ensured. There are no significant statistical differences or any other discernible differences in total scores per person where such directions were given, as opposed to instances when this was not the case. The following summaries provide a brief description of each card and some typical responses given by respondents.

Card 1: School room scene with pupils at their desks, teacher at the blackboard, and a man leaning in the window from the outside. Except for the man at the window, it is a perfectly ordinary, easily recognizable scene. The man could be benign (another teacher, a parent), or more threatening (someone coming to check up on the teacher or cause trouble for the teacher). Responses generally followed this pattern.[3]

Card 2: A man reclining with vague mat-like or wall-like background and a shadow-like figure in a doorway. Again, responses varied from "a man resting" to "he is rich." Some people mentioned the figure in the doorway; others did not.

Card 3: A man sitting on a chair in front of a modern (i.e., expensive) house with a kneeling figure in front of him. Some people did not notice the figure in front, but most viewed the sitting man as wealthy and/or powerful, dealing with a supplicant who was greeting him or requesting something from him.

Card 4: A group of five men, two in the foreground and others behind. This was often seen as two men greeting one another, with their followers or subordinates behind each of them. The scene appears polite and respectable and most people saw it as a non-conflict situation. It was assumed that to see conflict in such a picture required distortion of the symbolic content such that even outwardly benign situations involved possible threats or difficulties.

Card 5: A woman sitting under a tree with a filled basket in front of her and a man, arms akimbo, looking at her. The woman's hand is raised as if gesturing, reaching, or supplicating for something. Responses to this card varied more than for any other—from sexual connotations, to a request by the woman, to severe conflicts.

Card 6: A man and a woman. The man's right hand is raised as in greeting, or as if he may hit the woman, or as if he has something in the hand. There is a faint line indicating that he may be pointing behind him with his thumb. Responses varied from a simple greeting, to sexual themes, to husband-wife conflict in which the man is telling the woman to get back into the compound.

Card 7: Two men sitting outside a covered market stall or shaded area. One man holds an antelope horn (used in sorcery) and is on the mat. The other is looking at objects on the mat.

There are bone-like or elongated objects off the mat. This picture was drawn to depict a medicine-seller-cum-sorcerer and his potential customer. Although many respondents saw supernatural types of activity on this card, only a small minority mentioned sorcery, or even mentioned the antelope horn, preferring to call it a hoe, or bow and arrow, or something else. I interpret this as repression of the obvious stimulus because of its unpleasant connotations.

Card 8: A man seated on a dias with people in two groups in front of him and one man with bare arms (= poverty) kneeling in the foreground. A man over at the right is sitting on a chair. Almost all subjects saw this as an adjudication situation usually in a court room. The nature of the case itself varied. A minority saw it as a chief and his followers. This card (and Card 12) were designed to obtain stories about conflict even from people who avoided conflict responses on other cards. In general, the subjects did respond as desired, since it is extremely difficult to discuss an adjudication procedure without mentioning conflict of some kind.

Card 9: Two women seated in front of huts. The open door of one of the huts indicates that they are inside a compound. Responses varied from two women friends, to mother and daughter, to co-wives.

Card 10: A man and a woman; almost exactly like Card 6 except that the woman's hair could be grey and the man's right hand now has its fingers extended upward. This gesture could mean "I want food," or he could be explaining something, or be seen in the act of hitting her. His hatlessness, which is made much clearer here than in Card 6, reflects informality or possibly servile status. Responses varied from very benign interactions to severe conflict.

Card 11: Three men in front of a compound. First man (at left) is in a cheap robe with a parcel under his arm. Second man is in poor clothes with his arms up at chest level and his hands partially closed in a fist-like manner. Third man (with back to us) is dressed more richly and is facing the other two. Responses varied from physical fighting to an excited story-teller with an audience.

Card 12: Man on a dias with two groups in front of him. Very similar to Card 8, except that the group to the right of the card contains a middle-aged woman. Again, most people saw this as an adjudication situation and many viewed it as a dispute between a man and a woman, most often married.

The Sample

These picture-tests were given to a sample of men and women in the urban and rural areas having both high and low divorce records. We also tried to obtain variation in socio-economic status and age. Although such variance is represented, the sample would have to be much larger than the 161 tests finally accepted for analysis if we wished to control for all such variance. Instead, we simply tried to make sure that ranges of possible sociological variation along several dimensions were present in the sample preventing it from being made up of only one particular segment of the society.

In all, 167 persons were interviewed. Six have been excluded because they are judged to be full rejections of one sort or another. In one case, the person left the interview. In five others, varying degrees of overt rejection are manifestly present in the protocols. In the most overt case, the subject saw only Europeans in the pictures and claimed he could not tell what they were doing because the researcher, and not he, was a European. In the other four cases, subjects gave one or two word answers on each card and refused to interpret any action. Lesser degrees of rejection on specific cards occurred but the protocols as a whole were judged to contain sufficient projective material to be scored.

The analyzed sample contains 93 men and 68 women, ranging in age from 16 to 69. The men are about one-third below thirty, one-third between thirty and forty, and a third over forty. The women are mostly under thirty-five, and half of them are under thirty. Thus there is a bias in the sample toward young women. Testing by comparing younger and older women has produced some significant differences in their responses and these will be considered when the projective materials are related to marital stability.

In terms of socio-economic status using occupational rank as an indicator, the men are just over one-half low status with the remainder split into one third middle status and the rest (one-sixth) with high status occupations. Using the occupation of present husband or last husband (if the woman is single), the women are distributed in a quite similar pattern. Just over half the men are monogamous, and just under one-half have two or more wives at the time of the interview. The men's marriages range from one to forty-one with a mean of 5.90 (median = 4), while the women range from one to thirteen with a mean of 2.8 (median = 2). For both sexes, the ratio of rural to urban is approximately 2:1. This results from our wish to have respondents in the sample from the city, the rural village, and the rural hamlets. However, as in the sociological material, there are no systematic differences between persons from the two types of rural settlements, and these data have been lumped into a simple rural-urban dichotomy. In other words, the sample contains men and women who reflect most of the ranges of basic sociological characteristics.

On its own, it is impossible to judge the representativeness of such a sample, since it is not randomly chosen. However, because a number of similar variables are used in this sample and in the one from which the sociological data were taken, it becomes possible to assess the reliability of the relationships being established. If the relationship between independent measures and marital stability occurred in the first instance because of unknown sampling biases, then chances are they will not show up on another sample. Contrarily, if the same relations are re-established using a different sample, as this one is, then we can have much more confidence that the relationships in this study are in fact present in the society as a whole.

The Dependent Variable

For the psychological materials, the unit of analysis is the person, and therefore the measures of marital stability must be attributes of the person rather than the marriage. Accordingly, we created three separate measures of stability. The first is a simple per person score for numbers of divorces arranged into high, medium, and low on a similar basis as that used for the sociological data in the last chapter. The second measure is derived from the durability of an individual's marriages. Given the fact that most people have more than one marriage, we reasoned that the mean duration per person is a good overall approximation of stability which can correct for biases occurring in the per person rate. However, if the more stable person has only very recently married, then this short duration would decrease his mean duration score. Therefore, we created a third measure which is mean duration of only those unions ending in divorce. This last measure produces a number of persons with no score because they have not yet had any divorces, and these were assigned mean scores for purposes of analysis. In other words, no measure is perfect. Each sheds light on a particular aspect of marital stability and each tends to distort the picture in some way. Table 12:1 gives the distribution of persons in relation to these three measures.

TABLE 12:1. MARITAL STABILITY MEASURES
OF RESPONDENTS FOR PICTURE TEST

Sex of Respondent	Number of Divorces*			Mean Duration of Respondent's Marriages**			Mean Duration of Respondent's Marriages that end in divorce**		
	Low	Med.	High	Short	Med.	Long	Short	Med.	Long
Men (N=93)	49	22	32	38	44	21	26	52	15
Women (N=68)	37	22	9	33	19	16	28	24	16

*Low = 0-2 (Men); 0-1 (Women): Medium = 3-5 (Men); 2-4 (Women): High = 6+ (Men); 5+ (Women)
**Short = 0-2 years: Medium = 3-5 years: Long = 6+ years

Analysis of the Protocols

Qualitative. The picture-tests have been analyzed qualitatively by a clinical psychologist. The entire set was given to Dr. Sydney Levy who has done much work on TAT tests in the U.S. and who has also interpreted similar tests for the Bena of East Africa as a consultant to another anthropologist. Dr. Levy's report (Levy n.d.) notes that he knew nothing of Kanuri culture before seeing these materials but did have data on the sex, age, occupation, and marital history of each person whose test results he was examining. The result is corroboration of many of the interpretations I have made about Kanuri culture and society plus some tentative hypotheses concerning psychological differences between high and low divorcers.

Dr. Levy sees the Kanuri world as an hierarchical one in which status differences are very sensitively responded to and where wealth is important and highly prized. He sees the people as being very concerned over respect, over the prerogatives attached to roles (getting one's due), and over seeking outside mediation to conflicts that arise between persons or groups. He is impressed that although they recognize the existence of the supernatural, i.e., of magic and sorcery, they are much more concerned with the intricacies of human social life and the practical possibilities and problems which emerge from such interaction.

Looking for common psychological themes that run through the tests, Dr. Levy interprets the tests to mean that the Kanuri are well aware of human emotions as experienced by others but they have little empathy for their fellows and speak of such emotions "with pride and detachment." Again, in personality terms, there is great stress on giving and getting what seems to be appropriate. "Giving and receiving are intensely cathected, being the monotonous focal point of story after story. They are the springboard of interpersonal relations and a variety of social, economic, and legal actions." He feels that this is probably the most dominant psychological trait in the sample as a whole (Levy n.d.).

In marriage, the tests indicate to Dr. Levy that Kanuri husbands wish to be sexually potent and attractive, to obtain obedience from women, and to be good providers. Men also consider women to be easily, indeed almost immediately, available for sexual or marital purposes. This he feels puts women into the position of being commodities in the eyes of men because they can be obtained as easily as other kinds of goods and services. In marriage, he sees the role bargain that we have already seen in the chapter on the role images of each spouse. The woman must be well behaved, i.e., submissive and obedient. The husband in turn provides the wife with her due—attention and material goods.

To a Western psychologist like Dr. Levy, the Kanuri seem to be "a divorce-obsessed people." He sees them as subscribing to stereotyped explanations of marital breakdown. In conflict situations, the role bargain is rejected and reversed. Wives are disobedient, uncooperative, dishonest, and too demanding; husbands do not provide for their families, marry extra wives without discussing it, and are impotent. The suspicion is widespread that husbands will not treat co-wives equally, favoring instead the younger one.

Finally, Dr. Levy suggests that the following qualities are associated with high divorce among the men.

(1) Anxiety concerning the desire for and intensity of feelings by men about their dominance vis-a-vis women. This can be seen as well in strictness over purdah and the suspicious feelings that are attached to it, if and when the wife does go out of the compound.

(2) High divorcers see women as fickle and easily led astray by their impulses to be unfaithful, to cheat, and to steal.

(3) High divorcers are also strong status-seekers and their interest in wealth seems especially strong and envious.

(4) High divorcers give more attention to the details, complications, and subtle nuances of behavior. In other words, they tend either to be more perspective socially or to read more into the behavior of others than low divorcers.

(5) Among the younger men and those of higher status, the higher divorcers seem also to be more cynical about people (not trusting good intentions in others). Lower status high divorcers appear to be put upon, victimized, betrayed, and conscious of women's unreasonable demands.

Among high divorce women, he suggests the following regularities.

(a) High divorce women show less warmth of feeling and willingness to ameliorate situations. They are quick to take offense ("The tone of petulance, of, 'If I don't get what I want, I quit.' is notable" [Levy n.d.].

(b) These women are strong, independent, forceful, willing to be contentious, and to demand their rights.

In general, then, Dr. Levy sees low divorcers as more cooperative, more flexible, with greater gentleness, and having a greater degree of self-criticism. Some of the men seem also to be more fearful than their more self-confident high divorce neighbors.

Quantitative Analysis. In order to test some of these qualitative interpretations, a quantitative analysis of the test results was planned and carried out. As with Dr. Levy, we read over the protocols and began isolating particular qualities judged to be present in the stories. Operational definitions were created for these categories, and coders counted how many times each of these was present per individual. A preliminary coding of the data resulted in unacceptable levels of reliability among three coders. A number of the definitions of variables were changed, and I and a research assistant continued to discuss each lack of agreement, creating rules for ambiguous cases until we found ourselves agreeing on 85% or better of the coding per person. This ultimately led to an instruction booklet in which definitions plus the fullest possible range of examples were given so that each coding could be compared with previous ones.

Another problem arises over single versus multiple coding. Ideally, each statement should be coded only once and thus all coding is independent. However, using phrases as our units of analysis, it becomes impossible to judge which among several of our categories a particular phrase most aptly represents. In such cases, we assume that human utterances are connotative involving multiple meanings. Consequently, we decided to score the same statement several times if this is considered an accurate rendition of the meaning. Thus the phrase ". . .she is asking for her money" was entered as (a) *getting one's due*, since a wife should receive money as a matter of right, and (b) *communication*, since she is getting her point of view across successfully. In several instances, double coding is built into our definitions because one of the categories is an aspect of the other which we wished to look at more closely. Thus both debtor-creditor relations and adamance are particular types of relations or responses to relations in which getting one's due is a central theme. Similarly, illness is an attribute of physical condition and insubordination is an aspect of illegitimacy. Thus, the more general the category and the more related sub-categories there are to be coded, then the more likely it is for the general category to receive a higher score. In other words, if there are many sub-categories which also reflect some general level we are in effect measuring these sub-qualities and the more general level at the same time by double coding. In this sense, and also because human utterances are complex in meaning, I believe multiple codings per phrase is justified. Table 12.2 gives the definitions and results of the coding for the entire sample of men and women; men and women have a rank order correlation of .91 for the way in which they responded to the pictures.

From the distributional evidence, it is clear that Dr. Levy's generalization about concern over getting one's due and about hierarchy, i.e., status and subordination as dominant features in the protocol, is in fact correct. The high incidence of successful communication, occupational setting, and recognition of form, simply attest to the successful manner in which respondents were able to see their ordinary everyday world in the cards. The high amount of affect, especially negative affect, along with other conflict categories such as hostility, third party mediation, illegitimacy, insubordination, divorce, and others, indicate again a recognition of the cues that were purposely built into the pictures. However, from previous ethnographic work, both Dr. Levy's conclusion and the test results were somewhat surprising to me, since I expected the quantity of affect statements to be relatively low.

Instead of negating either my ethnographic conclusion of these test data, I would rather look for an explanation that covers all of the findings. In all likelihood, the Kanuri are inhibited in the use of affect in their interpersonal lives—I have observed this too often not to be confident of it. These results show, however, that they recognize affect, perceive it, but (a) as Dr. Levy concludes, they do not empathize with it, and (b) they do not respond in kind, but instead restrict, control, or inhibit their own affective responses to a marked degree.

TABLE 12:2. CODING OF PICTURE TEST MATERIAL
FOR 161 KANURI MEN AND WOMEN

	Number of Times Coded
1. *Getting one's due*: a concern over culturally-recognized reciprocation for services rendered.	2986
2. *Status*: a recognized difference in ranking between persons where ordinal distinctions are made with reference to age, sex, wealth, religion, socio-economic position, education, etc.	2647
3. *Communication*: getting a point of view across successfully to another person or to a group.	2322
4. *Occupational situation*: descriptions which tie the scene to an ordinary work-a-day world.	1592
5. *Recognition of form*: an unmodified recognition of person, place, or thing. (No multiple coding allowed here. If respondent recognized a form but we could not code it under any other category, then we gave him a score for "form.")	1454
6. *Affect (total score)*: any description or statement revealing an actor's emotions or mood. (A=negative 730) (B=positive 467).	1197
7. *Physical attributes*: mention of or description of body parts or postures.	1084
8. *Form in action*: same as (5) but with the added idea of an activity of some kind going on. (Only scored when other scoring impossible and no multiple coding allowed.)	1082
9. *Subordination*: Recognition of status distinctions which involve an authority relationship between actors.	844
10. *Hostility*: A scene depicting quarrelling, fighting, menacing, hitting, types of activity between actors.	795
11. *Rejection*: a refusal by the respondent to make a further statement about a scene or activity he has identified on the card.	743
12. *Third party mediation*: conflicts which involve resolution by person(s) other than those directly involved.	735
13. *Role*: activity culturally associated with a particular occupation or status.	675
14. *Flexibility*: (A) a significant change in the way the respondent perceives the pictures or the plot (=512); (B) willingness on the part of people in the stories or the story-teller to acknowledge more than one point of view (=104).	616
15. *Marital Situation*: any situation of husband-wife interaction (A=involving conflict 325) (B=involving no conflict 197).	522
16. *Illegitimacy*: any act which is improperly deviant from the accepted rules of the society.	512
17. *Ambition*: striving for the achievement goals (A=unrealistic or unattainable, 100, B=attainable, 405).	505
18. *Insubordination*: an actor's disregard of his or her subordinate role when such subordination is a legitimate part of his relationship to others.	458
19. *Illness*: statements alluding to physical abnormality caused by sickness.	428
20. *Kinship*: mention of persons as members of a consanguinal or affinal kin group.	417
21. *Friendly situation*: a scene or statements depicting amiability and agreement between actors.	414

TABLE 12:2. CODING OF PICTURE TEST MATERIAL
FOR 161 KANURI MEN AND WOMEN (CONT)

	Number of Times Coded
22. *Westernization*: descriptions of people, places, and things which are derived from Western life ways.	379
23. *Sex*: number of times sexual intercourse is referred to.	267
24. *Respect*: use of the word respect and/or general recognition of the legitimacy and propriety of superiors to demand attention and subordination.	259
25. *Adamance*: desire or inability to compromise.	256
26. *Generosity*: willingness to give of one's resources within one's means.	244
27. *Animal Metaphor*: the use of animal-like activity or substitution of animals for human form or shadings in the pictures.	225
28. *Cooperation*: interpersonal relations characterized by agreement and helpfulness.	224
29. *Debtor/creditor relations*: an interpersonal relationship in which debt is being contracted, discussed, paid off, or requested.	211
30. *Curiosity*: action or activity by one or more actors provoked by a desire to see what is going on.	211
31. *Marriage*: the number of times mention is made of marriage, or getting married.	209
32. *Lack of Communication*: a breakdown of interpersonal understanding.	200
33. *Divorce*: the number of times divorce is directly referred to.	186
34. *Piety*: activity, in the pictures or other utterances that indicate a positive attitude towards religious injunction; or the use of common Islamic speech patterns such as "only Allah knows how this will turn out."	181
35. *Supernaturalism*: statements about religion either Islam or the occult which involve the invocation or results of non-empirical forces; or the recognition of a figure as a supernatural being.	146
36. *Situational change*: the conversion of a friendly scene to one of conflict or vice versa i.e., the resolution of a conflict (harmony to conflict = 96) (conflict to harmony = 34).	130
37. *Victimization*: the outcome of interaction such that a person has, or feels he has, been duped, cheated, or injured.	128
38. *Extra-marital relationships*: any personal man-woman interaction marriage in which there is a connotation of sexual relations as well as a possible part of the relationship now or in the future between: (two unmarried persons = 97) (a zower and an unmarried man = 21) (a married woman and a man = 4).	122
39. *Dependency*: the reliance of one person on another person or object.	100
40. *Male-female interaction*: extra-marital and non-sexual; involving conflict 21, involving no conflict 56.	77
41. *Foreign*: African people and/or places outside Bornu.	75
42. *Co-wife situation*: co-wives interacting.	65
43. *Uncodeable statements*	17

To construct measurements from raw scores, we decided to divide all non-dichotomous variables into trichotomous ones (low, medium, and high). For the sociological measures we used similar criteria to those in the questionnaire data. For the psychological data we assumed the more times a person mentioned a content category the greater was the salience of this quality to him as a person. In other words, if individual A sees dependency in many of the interpersonal relations depicted, while individual B does not, then we assume that A is more prone to perceive dependency, more sensitive to it, and it has more meaning and saliency for him than for individual B. These data were then aggregated into high, medium, and low scores, separately for each sex. This latter point follows from the fact that the sexes differed significantly in productivity, i.e., number of codable responses, depending upon the interviewing procedures. I carried out the men's interviews with an assistant and often used my own knowledge of the language to stop and ask questions. Women's protocols were gathered by a Kanuri woman and a non-Kanuri-speaking American woman. Since it is known that longer protocols produce higher frequencies of content categories (Child, Storm, and Veroff 1958:491) it was proper to correct for this by using separate criteria for dividing each sex into high, medium, and low scores per content category.

Men and women are, as already mentioned, very similar in overall response distribution. Significant differences occur in expected ways. Thus men see more debtor/creditor relations, more competitiveness, and men mention marriage more often. Women, on the other hand, see significantly more co-wife situations, dependency, and respect relationships. However, given all the possible distinctions that could have occurred, these seem slight indeed.

Age differences by sex provided very few significant differences among the responses to the cards. Younger men had more form in action responses which indicated only that they had more responses that were difficult to code, since this coding was used only when we could not use some other category but the respondent had in fact made a recognition of the form and viewed it as carrying out an unspecified activity. In other words, older men were more relaxed informants and tended to project in more detail. Younger men, on the other hand, produced less detail and were more careful in their judgments. More interestingly, older men mentioned kinship situations significantly more often than their younger counterparts. I would interpret this as a greater interest in this subject that goes along with age among the men.

Among women, age differences are present but, as in the case of the men, they are quite negligible. Older women produce rejection responses significantly more often than younger ones, and older women are more flexible in the way they tell the stories and they mention flexible people significantly more often. I would interpret such results as indicating contradictory tendencies. Some older women are angry about the test situation and produce many responses such as "I don't know," which keep them in the interview but convey the idea of non-cooperation. Thus they do not have to actively reject the test but indicate displeasure by not telling a story. Younger women as a group are more cooperative.

Compared to age and sex differences, which seem slight, rural-urban distinctions in response to the test are more significant, especially for women who differ in the two locations across a greater number of variables. In general, rural men are less eager to project stories and plots, and this is reflected in their high form in action score (given only when there is no plot development), as well as rejection scores. Rural men also see more flexibility and situational change indicating an ability to be less adamant about their own interpretations of social interaction. Rural men also see co-wife situations, kinship interaction, and competitiveness less often. I would interpret this as simply reflecting the real life experiences of these men. Our urban men in this sample do have more kin in their households, more co-wife situations in their own marriages, and certainly competition (many of them are traders) in their everyday lives, and the fact that they notice these qualities more often in the pictures expresses these sociological conditions.

Like their menfolk, rural women see much more flexibility in the pictures and fewer co-wife situations. However, the rural women are also signficantly lower than their urban counterparts in seeing hostile situations, debtor-creditor situations, victimization, foreignness, physical attributes, affect, and the action of supernatural forces. On the other hand the rural women see significantly more extra-marital interaction between men and women, and they mention sex as a subject more often. I would interpret these results partly at least in a similar fashion to the men's data. Urban women are more often in purdah and interact less with men openly in extra-marital situations, whereas this is not uncommon in rural areas. Similarly, they see non-Kanuri Africans more often.

However, all of the remaining differences point to a generally more relaxed, less pressured, or oppressive way of life for rural women. The association of more hostile situations, victimization, debtor/creditor situations, affect, and the activity of the supernatural with urban women's perceptions of interaction, indicates a much greater sense of tension. These women see interactions as potentially stressful and fraught with danger much more easily than their rural counterparts. Conversely, I would interpret the rural women's greater mention of sexual relations as even more proof of their sense of relaxation and ease. Men and women are interacting in these pictures; a major aspect of such interaction is the possibility of sexual intercourse, and the rural women are able to express this. This does not mean urban women do not see such activity as easily or as often. However, what they seem more eager to express are the *negative* effects and aspects of human interaction.

Psychological Variables and Marital Stability Measures

Looking at all variables measured in the picture-test interviews, the most striking results occur if we simply use the measures of marital stability referred to above as dependent variables, allowing them to be related to all other data collected in the interview. Overwhelmingly, it is the residence, occupational status, fertility of union, etc., that produce significant relationships to marital stability measures. As already noted, these results serve to replicate and therefore strengthen those of the last chapter. They indicate very forcefully the greater significance of sociological as compared to psychological variables in predicting Kanuri marital stability. Put more precisely, when the multivariate analyses were carried out it was impossible to study the psychological variables without omitting the sociological ones. If left to compete with sociological data, psychological materials hardly ever entered into the results. The discriminant function analyses were carried out, as in Chapter 11, using the criterion that 80% of the differences between high, medium, and low divorcers and durations would be explained. This means that sociological variables can be estimated to account for 80% of these differences. In other words, marital stability in Bornu is first and foremost a function of the social and economic conditions within which marriage is practiced.

In order to study the "non-sociological" qualities more closely, let us look first at a bivariate analysis of all the picture-test variables that are significantly related to the measures of marital stability. These are given in Table 12:3. Originally, all variables, including the dependent variable, were trichotomized into high, medium, and low. However, this produced 3x3 tables, many of which had cells with numbers under five. When this occurred, the tables were collapsed by lumping the medium and high categories of picture test variables, and if further lumping was still necessary, the medium and high categories of the marital stability measures were also lumped, making either a 3x2 or a 2x2 comparison.

Table 12:3 is a summary of significant relationships between our psychological variables and our measures of marital stability. Although the TAT results may provide insights into Kanuri personality at least in terms of these stimuli, only these factors listed in the table can with much confidence be related to our central problem of marriage relations. Before interpreting these results, let us turn to the multivariate analysis.

As in the case of the sociological variables, we decided to run a multivariate analysis to rank the variables in some order in terms of their impact on marital stability. Accordingly, we ran discriminant function analyses on the sample and sub-samples of the data just as we did in Chapter 11. However, as already noted, a serious problem not present in the previous analysis loomed large in this one. In order to obtain any results whatsoever, we eliminated the sociological variables, restricting our analysis only to the relationship between TAT results and marital stability. This means that a set of variables associated with only a small amount of the difference between high, medium, and low marital stability is being examined, and re-examined on partial samples, in order to obtain an insight into the relative importance of these variables in predicting such differences. For this reason, the percent of difference explained is inaccurate and has been omitted.

The results are as one would expect; some of the previous bivariate findings are corroborated and a number of other variables having no statistically significant relation to marital stability turn

TABLE 12:3. TAT VARIABLES RELATED TO MARITAL STABILITY*

Variables	No. of Divorces		Mean Duration		Mean Duration of Unions Ending in Divorce	
	Men	Women	Men	Women	Men	Women
Flexibility (B)	-.75	--	--	--	--	+.36
Co-wife situation	+.44	--	-.47	--	--	--
Dependency	--	-.41	--	+.41	-.31	--
Creditor-debtor	+.37	--	--	--	-.28	--
Marriage	--	--	--	+.54	--	--
Insubordination	+.37	--	--	--	--	--
Subordination	--	--	-.36	--	--	--
Affect (total)	--	--	--	--	--	+.40
Flexibility (total)	-.37	--	--	--	--	--

*All tabulated relationships are at the .05 level of significance or better; the statistic used is the (corrected) contingency coefficient which is derived from X^2; $c = (\sqrt{X^2/N + X^2})$. Positive and negative signs have been added to indicate the direction of association. N = 93 for men; 68 for women. See, McCormick, T. C. Elementary Social Statistics. New York, McGraw Hill 1941, p. 207, for this correction table which raises the value of c because it varies from zero to less than 1.00 depending upon the degrees of freedom.

up due to random factors. These random factors distribute some variables unevenly among the groups. This unevenness is picked up and dealt with by the computer whether or not such variables are significant according to other qualitative and quantitative criteria. Thus we have rejected all findings that are not corroborated statistically by some technique other than the discriminant analysis itself.

Using the above criterion and a number of separate computer runs on the sample and sub-samples of the data in which we controlled for rural urban distinctions and sex differences, six of the nine variables listed in Table 12:3 consistently appeared as discriminators of differential degrees of marital stability. The results were then ranked in the same way as in Chapter 11 and this ordering and its interpretation appear in Table 12:4.

Among all of the TAT variables, dependency is consistently important in differentiating among persons of varying degrees of marital stability. However, it operates quite differently for each sex. For women, it suggests that those who feel dependent upon others, or more correctly who more often see dependency situations when interpreting social interaction, are more stable marriage partners. Their dependency makes them better wives, as it were, less likely to conflict with their husbands and more likely to be compliant because of the saliency of dependency to their own perceptions. Conversely, independent women, or women with low perception of dependency, are less likely to make the compromises necessary to maintain a marriage.

For men, however, the reverse is true. High dependency scores are related to low durability and many divorces. This could be due to age differences among men, but when this is checked we find no relationship between age and dependency scores. I interpret these results in a similar way to Levy's (n.d.) ideas on male dominance. Kanuri men who are concerned about dependency are in my view expressing a concern over dominance per se; that is to say, they are very prone to recognize status distinctions and dependency relations which are significant aspects of status differences. These results then tie in with the high interest by such men in insubordination, subordination, and reacting to the social situation in terms of who owes what to whom.

There is, then, one common underlying thread running through a number of these variables as they apply to men who are prone to marital instability. This is a very strong sensitivity to status distinctions and all the concomitant behaviors implied by such differences. In relation to this same syndrome, divorce prone women are the opposite. For them, lack of dependence, i.e., sensitivity

TABLE 12:4. SUMMARY AND RANKING OF PSYCHOLOGICAL VARIABLES
RELATED TO MARITAL STABILITY AND THEIR INTERPRETATION

Impact of Variables	*People in More Stable Unions*	*People in Less Stable Unions*
More important causes of marital stability and instability	*Dependency*: Women feel dependent / Men feel independent	Women feel independent / Men feel dependent
	Insubordination: There is attention paid to insubordination, less anxiety and anger about it. It is accepted as normal.	There is much stress on insubordination. It is easily noticed, easily reacted to by men, it is more easily practiced by women.
	Flexibility (B): There is a willingness to see more than one side in an argument.	An unwillingness or less willingness to see both sides of an argument.
Less important causes of marital stability and instability	*Creditor-debtor*: There is less likelihood that these people will react to social situations in terms of who owes what to whom.	There is more likelihood that these people will react to social situations in terms of who owes what to whom.
	Affect: These people will be more open, aware, and expressive of the emotional component of human relationships.	These people will be less open, aware and expressive of the emotional component of human relationships.
Importance of these variables is unknown in relation to the above, although they are significantly associated with differences in marital stability	*Marriage*: These people speak more freely about marriage.	They tend to mention the topic of marriage less often.
	Subordination: Related to insubordination above; these people tend to notice the hierarchial nature of relations less often; they are less status conscious.	These people notice hierarchical relations more often. They are concerned with status-distinctions and mention them a great deal.
	Flexibility (Total): These people are generally more flexible. They change their minds more easily and are not rigid in their approach.	These people are less flexible, more rigid, adamant in their way of handling and viewing interpersonal relations.

to status distinctions, and independence or lack of compliance are the key tendencies in relation to this all important quality.

Dependency, insubordination, subordination, and creditor-debtor relations are all aspects of the same quality, namely, status distinctions and their meaning in interpersonal relations. Men who are extremely sensitive to such norms are maritally unstable; women who tend to reject such norms are also maritally unstable.

The second feature of these variables is what we might call the flexibility-rigidity continuum. Flexibility itself comes out twice in the analysis, showing it to be an important quality. I would interpret both affect and mention of marriage to be part of this same quality. The divorce prone person, man or woman, seems on the basis of these results to be a more rigid and unbending person, less willing to see two sides to a question, and less willing to change their minds about an interpretation. It seems logical to suggest that this rigidity would make it more difficult for them to recognize and cope with emotional experience and to discuss personal topics such as marriage. Ethnographic experience bears out such generalizations.

In summary, psychological correlates of marital stability are not nearly so important as sociological ones. However, they do have some impact and are closely related to the sociological level. Thus our null hypothesis that there are no psychological differences in marital stability can be said to have been disproved. Instead, we have found that two distinct psychological reactions tend to be systematically related to marital stability: (1) concern over status distinctions and their associated behavior by men, and rejection of such distinctions or independence of them by women; and (2) rigidity or lack of flexibility with its concomitant inability to cope with affect.

Reduced to such simple terms, the psychological qualities associated with marital stability do not seem very surprising, in light of Kanuri society and culture. But we should remember our technique. These data derive from a test in which the respondent makes up a story about an interaction. The kinds of perceptions he makes are those he is most prone to have when he is in any social situation whose details are unclear and whose meaning he must guess at. This extends as well to the so-called unconscious or repressed responses. Because of the obviousness of sorcery in Card 8 and almost total lack of sorcery response, yet use of the supernatural to describe this card, I would judge it to have produced a repression of the obvious and a production of utterances more socially acceptable in the interview situation. This, however, reflects what the Kanuri person does in fact do in normal social life, since such conversation is not usually carried on in public. In other words, the so-called psychological correlates are highly conditioned by their social context and the sociological attributes of the speaker. These, rather than "pure" psychological features, are what we have measured and related to marital stability.

Chapter 13
The Prospects and Nature of Change

All societies change, and today the non-Western peoples of the world are actively engaged in widely ramifying programs of development that will ultimately affect every facet of their lives. In other contemporary Muslim societies that have undergone significant change, there has been a steady pressure on the ease of divorce and an attempt to raise the status of women from its traditional position of inferiority and subordination. It is almost a certainty that ultimately such policies and pressures will come to Bornu just as they have already come to Turkey, Egypt, Morocco, and Tunisia, to name only a few examples.

From the point of view of Bornu itself, it is also important to ask what kinds of forces are operating within the society to produce change and what effect these will have on marital life and stability in the coming years. The forces of modernization sweeping across the world are exerting pressure for less easily acquired divorces in Muslim areas and rising status for women. However, such forces do not act in a vacuum; instead, they are brought to bear on a society already facing its own internal pressures, many of which are already acting upon marital stability. The difficulty of such an exercise is the assessment of any ultimate outcome, since a number of forces which can be assumed to be present in the modernization process can, according to our analysis, affect marital stability in opposite directions. Let us look at some of these in turn.

Forces Stimulating More and Less Marital Instability

From our previous analyses, we have seen that urban residence is associated with more marital instability. It is quite clear from census material and from my own experience in Bornu over the past decade that urban centers are steadily expanding and that the proportion of urban to rural people is also growing (urbanization). All other things being equal, this is a force for increasing marital instability.

Although it will occur much more slowly and affect far fewer people, it is also safe to predict that standards of living, personal incomes, and the numbers of economically successful people will also rise in the future. This can be seen in the increased numbers of shops and trucks owned by local people, as well as in the growing numbers of automobiles, and individual trips to Mecca by airplane. This, too, is a force for increased marital instability since we have established a positive relationship between socio-economic status and divorce. However, it is not that simple. Increased income means an increased ability to provide market money, and this acts in the opposite direction to stabilize unions. This means that if increases in wealth affect only a minority, placing them among the higher classes of society, then for them marital instability can be predicted to increase, while if the money is spread more widely and is used to increase market money given to wives, then it will help to stabilize marriages.

Our analysis has also established that men's reliance upon women's labor in the rural areas helps to make marriages more stable. This means, according to our analysis, that the mechanization of rural labor, or an increased reliance on male wage labor, will make rural families more like their urban counterparts and raise the divorce rate in the villages.

It also seems clear from what has gone before that if ideas of male dominance, wifely obedience, and contemporary male sensitivity to rank and status distinctions remain important, then marital instability will remain at a high level. I shall have more to say about this in the concluding chapter, for ultimately these are the key factors in both understanding and predicting the future of the Kanuri marriage system.

Given the accuracy of our analysis, we can also predict that increases in fertility per union, monogamy, husband-wife intimacy through the sharing of secrets, less kinship involvement by each partner, more equal status for women, and more flexibility in interpersonal relations will produce more durable unions and less divorces per person. If women also see a greater amount of interpersonal dependency in human relationships, this too will contribute to more marital stability.

The difficulty with this kind of theorizing is its "vacuum-like" quality. In order to pose questions of our generalizations and turn them into projections for the future, we must make that most ridiculous of all scientific assumptions by saying, first and magically, "all other things being equal." But they are not, and therefore the multiplicity of factors and events affecting the future of marital stability cannot be assessed by simply projecting our present findings into a theoretically constant and unknown future. Indeed, it is by reversing this argument that we can gain insight. Thus we must assess what we know of the future and thereby assume that in fact all other things will not be equal, if we wish to gain a foothold on the diviner's path.

Whether we are in Bornu or Tierra del Fuego, the basic nature of change going on the world today revolves around Westernization and its concomitants of increased living standards, health facilities, communications, rising status for women, and so on. But since Westernization is producing an increase in forces that both increase and decrease marital stability, it becomes necessary to try and sort out some of its particular effects. This is a large task, and we have been able within the confines of this present study to get at only a few of the specific effects of this complex process.

In order to accomplish the task of isolating some of the influences of Westernization, we have gone to the institution most openly committed to the propagation of Western values and institutions—that is to say, the schools of Bornu.

The School Study: Marital Values
Among Post Primary School Students in Bornu

We asked young men and women in both the secondary schools and the teacher training colleges of Bornu to write an essay on "My Future Marriage." All of the girls wrote their essays in 1965 and the boys in 1966. Arrangements were made with the cooperation of school authorities to have all of the students write their essays at the same time. Instructions were given out to the teachers; a graduate student and I moved from room to room during the essay writing to ensure standardization. A prize for the best essay per school year was offered in terms of English composition. Later these were given out at a public gathering of the school.

The instructions asked each student to consider the type of life they would like to lead when they were married, the type of relationship to spouse, the kind of spouse, the type of housing and material possessions they would have, and the position they would hold in the community. In addition, each student was asked to answer a few questions about his or her family background, religion, ethnic group, father's occupation, whether their family was polygynous or monogamous, and as far as they knew it, the marital and divorce history of their parents.

Unlike the other types of data collected for this study which used Kanuri ethnic membership as a universe for analysis, the essays come from approximately 650 young men and women (ages 13-30) who claimed membership in over fifty ethnic groups which were either Christian or Muslim in religion. Some of them, for example the Bura, have representatives of both religions. Thus the sample was ethnically heterogeneous.

The coding of this material was done by reading over the material carefully and arriving finally at a satisfactory set of components which represented a generalized semantic structure of the essays from which we derived our coding categories. We decided that the most obvious first division was into sets of interpersonal relationships being described: (a) husband-wife, (b) co-wife, (c) ego with other kin and (d) ego with non-kin. We then listed all qualities that described such interactions and set up coding definitions for these and finally each of these qualities had to be judged to be traditional or modern or applicable to both the traditional and the modern setting. Unrelated to these interaction components were a set of materials we called "style of life," which referred to house type, material possessions, use of servants in the home, etc. These were also broken down into attributes and each of these then judged to be modern, traditional or both.

The ten interaction attributes are defined as follows:

1. *Independence*. Action without deference, without deferring to the wishes or considerations of alter.

2. *Dependence*. Action showing a definite deference to an alter.

3. *Equality*. Action involving a definite reference to ego and alter having similar rights and prerogatives. Simple reciprocity is not equality. If ego does A and alter must therefore do B, it is not enough. Both ego and alter must each have the right to do both A and B.

4. *Superiority*. Action or wishes showing a desire to have alter submit to ego without any reference to standards of improvement.

5. *Inferiority*. Recognition of the need or desirability of ego's submitting to alter.

6. *Competitiveness*. Indications by ego that he should or will exceed alter with reference to some standard or goal.

7. *Cooperation*. Action or desire to help an alter achieve his or her goal.

8. *Positive Affect*. Ego expresses a desire for positive emotional response from alter; e.g., kindness, love, liking (but not generosity, which means ego needs alter in order to achieve ego's own goals).

9. *Improvement*. Action or desire to make alter achieve ego's goals or vice versa in terms of some standard of getting better.

10. *Uncodeable*. None of the above.

The style of life attributes were defined as follows:

1. *Education.* An expressed interest in education for self, alter, or others such as one's children.

2. *Religiosity*. An expressed interest in religion as an important part of life.

3. *Female role model*. A general desire to be or have a "good wife" and/or "good mother"; i.e., to live up to or have one's wife live up to an ideal image or standard for the female role.

4. *Male role model*. A recognition that there is an ideal and desirable role for men without any specific reference to the husband-wife dyad which would be scored in the relationship dyad above.

5. *Occupation other than housewife desired for a woman/or wife*. (a) female type jobs, (b) jobs now defined as male jobs.

6. *Desirable occupation for the husband.*

7. *Status-striving*. Action or expressed desire by ego indicating an attempt to make others recognize that ego (or ego and spouse as a couple) have high status, or action directed towards achieving such recognition.

8. *Uncodeable*. None of the above.

Results

After a number of training sessions, a research assistant and I achieved an acceptable level (78%) of reliability. This was improved upon by having her put aside all difficult codings and these were done together. Often, a coding rule would develop out of such ambiguous cases. For scaling purposes, we have assumed as we did in the TAT analysis that the more often a subject is mentioned in an essay (i.e., stressed) the more salient it is for the writer. Similar scaling has been used for both sexes and other comparisons, since there are no significant differences in the lengths of the essays (except by grade level in school) which could produce differences in frequency simply on the basis of length.

In general, the results show that women are more oriented to change in their conception of married life than are the men. The girls aspire to modern types of activities, relationships, and material possessions more often than boys. But the difference in their traditional types of responses are striking, 64% of the boys use traditional means of describing things or aspire to traditional life style in their marriages, as opposed to 11% for the girls.[1] Yet both sexes overwhelmingly (91% of the boys; 99% of the girls) mention some modern changes they want to include in their own marriages. In overall terms, it is as if the boys want the best of both worlds, past and future, while the girls rarely see much to want from the past but unanimously wish to see changes occur in married life. If we break this down into relationships on the one hand and life styles on the other, it becomes apparent where the differences in viewpoint are. Again, the girls are very high on modern and low on traditional responses in general for both relationships and life style. However, only 49% of the boys mention modern types of relationship qualities (compared with 89% of the girls). On the other hand, 92% of the boys mention some traditional qualities of relationships that they wish to have in their marital careers with wives and others, compared to 10% for the girls. Both boys and girls, but the latter significantly more so, wish to have modern life styles in the future. In other words, the biggest differences are over the type of relationships that will obtain after marriage, although even in terms of life styles, girls desire a more modern setting for their marriages.

What types of differences do they manifest in the descriptions of their future marriages? The boys mention relationships between themselves and their kin significantly more often than do the girls. As shown in Table 13:1, the majority of the girls (73%) do not even mention this relationship, while only 46% of the boys omit it. In other words, the boys tend to see their marriages as a part of and related to their wider kin networks as is the case in more traditional society. The girls, on the other hand, see their future marital relationships more in terms of the husband-wife dyad alone, cutting this relationship off from the kin ties of each partner. Thus, although both sexes mention the husband-wife relationship more often than all others (because of the subject of the essay), girls mention this dyad significantly more often than boys.

TABLE 13:1. PERCENT OF BOYS AND GIRLS MENTIONING RELATIONS
TO KIN DURING THEIR FUTURE MARRIAGES*

No. of Times Mentioned	Boys (N=393)	Girls (N=255)
0	46%	73%
1	29%	21%
2 or more	25%	6%
Total	100%	100%

*$X^2 = 55.593$; $p < .01$

Girls, especially when they are young, are very involved with their kin. Even though they move away at marriage, most unions are locally endogamous, and the wife returns for ceremonies, visiting and between marriages. Another explanation would be that girls are more concerned over their marriages, especially these school girls who have passed beyond the age of first marriage and are not yet married. In other words, this is a sensitive and vary salient topic for them, and their intense attention to the husband-wife relationship reflects its importance. Boys, on the other hand, although approaching the age of marriage, have not gone beyond it and marriage, albeit an interesting topic, is only one of their concerns. Indeed, it seems from speaking to them that their chief concern by far is that of the career choices they must soon make.

Another interesting difference between the girls and the boys occurs in the realm of independence. As shown in Table 13:2, more of the girls make independence statements concerning relationships, and they make them more often per person than the boys. In other words, the girls see themselves acting as independent agents, not deferring to others, whether the other is a husband, boss, kin member, or neighbor. The boys, on the other hand, see much less of this; indeed, half of them have no codeable independence ideas in their essays. Related to this is the

TABLE 13:2. PERCENT OF BOYS AND GIRLS USING INDEPENDENCE STATEMENTS
TO DESCRIBE RELATIONSHIPS IN THEIR FUTURE MARRIAGE*

No. of Times Mentioned	Boys (N=393)	Girls (N=255)
0	49%	33%
1-2	44%	33%
3-4	7%	23%
5+	1%	11%
Total	100%	100%

*X^2 = 78.104; p $<$.01

relative number of persons and frequency per person of statements of equality for each sex. Thus 37% of the boys make no codeable statements about equality in interpersonal relations, and this rises to just over 60% if we limit the analysis to the husband-wife dyad. On the other hand, 81% of the girls do make such statements in general, and a similar proportion use such qualities to describe the type of husband dyad they expect to carry on in the future. The girls, therefore, are expressing a desire for independence and equality in their interpersonal relations especially their marriages and the men are expressing just the opposite point of view. It should be remembered from the last chapter, that independence by women is associated with divorce prone marriages.

The opposing view can be seen in the statements concerning superiority by ego (the essay writer) over other people. As shown in Table 13:3, 52% of the girls do not make such statements, while only 6% of them make three or more of them per essay. On the other hand, 58% of the boys do make superiority statements, and 28% of them make three or more per essay—mostly of course with regard to the husband-wife dyad. Again, it should be remembered that status consciousness by men is also related positively to divorce.

TABLE 13:3. PERCENT OF BOYS AND GIRLS USING SUPERIORITY STATEMENTS
TO DESCRIBE RELATIONSHIPS IN THEIR FUTURE MARRIAGE*

No. of Times Mentioned	Boys (N=393)	Girls (N=255)
0	42%	52%
1-2	30%	42%
3-4	28%	6%
Total	100%	100%

*X^2 = 49.007; c = .39; p $<$.01

Other statistically significant differences between the sexes are not surprising. Thus the girls discuss an ideal model for husbands more often than the boys; they also discuss children more often and they mention their own salaried job more often. However, a significant proportion (74%) of the boys do mention the possibility that their wives will have employment outside of the house, if she has some education. Boys also mention ideal role models for wives significantly more often than the girls do.

Above and beyond these quantitative measures, there is a strong quality of resentment and desire for change in marital relations that is easily seen in reading the girls' essays. They see themselves as the vanguard of a new era for women and marriage; one in which there will be much more equality between the sexes, in which marriages will occur solely because there is mutual attraction which is "spiritual," not physical alone. They want their husbands to be good-looking and often say so, but more often, and even when they mention physical appearance, they stress this desire for affection, kindness, and a sharing of life's problems *and* decisions. In the few cases where girls actually mention polygyny, they all say that they must be the senior wife or they will leave. Their idea of the ideal marriage is a monogamous neolocal home with servants to take care of the housework while both the husband and wife have salaried jobs in the civil service. Essentially, it is a Western model adapted to new elite status in a new nation setting. Some quotes from the essays illustrate these points quite dramatically:

> The main thing marriage should have is love, and as [here in Bornu] they lack true love, marriage always breaks.

> The kind of treatment given to wives in the families is very bad indeed. Women are regarded very low in Nigeria, i.e., in my tribe when a man dies only the boys that he had are mentioned but the number of the daughters is not given. This all makes the women feel they are not human beings.

> When a man beats his wife no case is taken on it. I wonder what the Government thinks about this. You cannot go into the street and beat a man, you will [be] put into the jail if you do so. But when a wife is beaten nothing happens to the husband.

> I am against men because I am a woman.

> They only marry for beauty and high possessions. Such people find it difficult to live when they begin to understand each other.

> We must be equal but there is nothing that hurts men's feelings [more] than a wife to tell him that they are the same and that she will follow her own decision and not his own.

> We will [have] servants because my husband will not allow me to work in the house.

> Of course yes! I would like to have a job also.

> We will eat on the same table [a taboo in traditional society].

> During the breakfast hours, I would carry my husband on the honda (motor bike) [refers to coming home at 9-10 a.m. for breakfast; she sees herself owning the honda and giving her husband a lift!].

> I will not like my husband to go to the cinema or any public place or to picnic with other women. I am really against this and I will never have it.

In a small majority of cases however traditional views came out strongly as in the following:

> I must obey my husband whatever he tells me to do I must do, I must do it even I don't want it. Because if a woman married she is under her husband's CONTROLE [sic].

> What men need from their wives is respect. What wives need from their husbands are to love them and buy them whatever they liked.

The boys, on the other hand, seem to stress traditional values of male dominance, wifely obedience, and polygyny, albeit they would like modern conveniences with the possibility even of an educated or semi-educated wife who knows something about modern hygiene. However, the equality, the emotional sharing and loving, the husband-wife intimacy found in the girls' essays are simply not there. School life is preparing these young men for a career in the modernizing local and, possibly, national elite. Despite this, they still see their own marriage and family life in a traditional framework in terms of the types of relationships they expect and want their conjugal units and their kinsfolk. As one of the girls put it, women want love, men want respect. The following typical and strikingly traditional quotes from the boys illustrate this synthesis of their views.

> If she [future wife] is proud. . .I will simply dismiss her and look for another.

> The kind of girl I think will be best wife for me is a discipline girl, hygienic girl, and good in manner of respect and also she may be literate.

> The life I would like to have [is] as my fathers, he lives with so many people in his house and so many people also are his friends, therefore I wish to be as him.

> I like to be a husband of a Kanuri girl. . .because we have same tribe and I know all the way of their living, so I could do what is necessary to be good husband.

> She [my wife] must be less education than me because if a person married a girl more educated than he, she will soon disagree.

> To marry a highly educated lady is dangerous.

After three or more years when she is born a child I will take no notice on her because no body will love her because she will be old at that time. . .and. . .I will soon divorce her and have another one.

We will be teaching in the same school because womens are not to be trusted.

And after I married one girl then again I will try and marry another one.

When I married two wives I will warn them to be social to each other.

. . .if you haven't many wives you will be in shame.

As for me I should rather marry a very ugly girl who can obey my rules. . .I wouldn't want my wife to be wandering from compound to compound talking with other men. . .talking and laughing with a girl causes temptation.

My father will stay with me.

I will arrange everything with her parents.

We must all be very obedient to our parents [after he is married].

When I get married I will try to live peacefully among my wives and children as well as the community.

We will not go to bars and places of high life.

On the other hand, in a few cases some vision or desire for a marriage more like that seen or desired by the girls is evident, if not in the entire essay, then here and there in a phrase or two, as in the following quotes:

There are many differences that will exist between the kind of life I will lead with my wife and that carried on by the ordinary people of Bornu province. . .they don't keep their wives as parders [partners] and [instead they] treat them as slaves.

So I feel that by being a nurse my wife will render a great help to the community as I do as a teacher [this idea of husband and wife as a nurse-teacher team turned up in many of the girls' essays].

To my personal point of view. . .my parents are not supposed to arrange the girl [first wife] for me—no! I am to have the agreement with her.

To sum up my life should not be totally westernized neither should it be too local.

The contrast taken from these typical statements from boys and girls generally in their middle to late teen-age period is striking. Both the girls and boys see themselves as entering into the educated elite but there the similarities stop. It is as if the boys realize that even though they may drive to work from a modern household to a modern office, they can maintain the quality of traditional family life just as in many of the very modern offices the quality of traditional bureaucratic and political relationships have persisted.

The girls, however, are ultimately, at least for the present, being quite unrealistic. No man, except possibly a few university graduates, of which there are still only a handful from Bornu, would accept this vision of egalitarian marriage in more traditional terms. Indeed, many young men find these post-primary school girls too educated and refuse to marry them. A number of them are used as "outside" wives to very wealthy and/or powerful politicians. These men need a wife who can get along in the wider world outside Bornu, who knows English, and can thus serve for public occasions if and when such social life is necessary.

The other attraction these girls offer is that of health. Most wealthy, powerful, or semi-educated Kanuri men accept the Western connection between hygiene and health. They feel that these girls are well trained in such procedures and will therefore make better housewives.

For a very tiny minority, the dream of an egalitarian Western type of marriage comes true, at least for a time. I have observed several of these, generally between a teacher wife and a husband who either teaches as well as has some other civil service post. Such women are happy and fulfilled, but I suspect their husbands are somewhat mortified to have given up so much of their traditional authority. Interestingly, all of the cases I have recorded of such unions have terminated in divorce.

An important methodological point helps to partially explain why these stark contrasts exist between the boys and the girls. The boys and the girls each live in separate school compounds at some distance from the city of Maiduguri. Thus each sex lives a segregated existence which sets them apart from their various social backgrounds and in constant touch with the Westernized school atmosphere, and Western or Westernized teachers. On this basis, we hypothesized that each sex would in fact belong to a "school culture" that obliterated differences among them of religion, ethnic membership, age and socio-economic background.

When tested statistically, this hypothesis is confirmed such that we are unable to find differences within the girls' or boys' essays based on sociological differences among them. However, that is only part of the picture, since the sociological differences between the girls and the boys are significant. There are more Muslims, more members of large centrally organized ethnic groups, among the boys, and they are older as a group when compared to the girls. The girls' sample then contained more Christians, more from smaller acephalous ethnic groups, and they were more often from larger towns and cities than are the boys. If we lump the boys and girls together and then compare Muslims versus Christians, larger ethnic groups versus smaller ones, then some of the differences we have attributed to sex reappear, especially equality (a Christian idea), and superiority (a Muslim idea as well as an idea held by members of larger ethnic groups). Members of larger ethnic groups also mentioned dependency significantly more often than those from smaller groups. Can we not say, then, that all our so-called sex differences are really a reflection of these other sociological distinctions rather than attributing such differences to sex. The answer is yes and no. Yes, because many of the sex differences are also distinctions associated with more and less urbanism, Muslim versus Christian views of marriage and sex roles, and size of ethnic group. No, *because we have found no significant differences within each sex by religion or ethnic group size, etc.* In other words, the social and cultural differences in each sample can be used to explain the overall sex differences which differ between the sexes but are homogeneous within themselves. Thus the major influence on the boys' views of their future marriages are traditional Islamic religious ideas, the nature of husband-wife roles among the larger ethnic groups of Bornu (the more hierarchically organized ones), and more representation of the views of rural people, i.e., more traditional ones. By contrast, the girls are influenced by greater numbers from small ethnic units who are Christian and ideologically committed to its modern teachings on marriage, the family, and an egalitarian role for women. Thus Christian and Western ideas about women and marriage are entering Bornu through the institutions of the girls' schools, although this is not happening among the boys.

The Prospects for Change

What all of this means for the future can only be estimated rather than measured and predicted with any assurance. At present, there are sociological forces operating which tend, on the basis of our analysis, to both increase and decrease marital stability. If, on the other hand, we look at the young people who are most changed by the new forces of Westernization in the more advanced schools (a very small group), the boys still hold to traditional views while the girls have taken on a vision of radical change. The conditions for more widespread education for girls are growing very slowly, while the conditions for accepting an egalitarian view of women are not present at all in contemporary society. Thus this view of marriage will remain in the school—as only one among many parts of its dissonance in values from that of the society as a whole. When such societal conditions change, then the school and their views will begin to expand as other facets of the culture, the government, the mass media, and the courts, begin to accept and propagate such views as well.

For the immediate future, the prospects indicated by this analysis are for a continuation of high rates of marital instability. The educated girls are being socialized into a post primary school sub-culture that accentuates egalitarianism and independence—qualities that can be predicted to produce tension and conflict in marriage if the men are not trained or attracted to change their traditional views of the spouse roles. However, post-primary school sub-culture for men is perpetuating the traditional view of marriage relations. The boys manifest the same qualities, e.g., status consciousness associated traditionally with brittle marriages. Therefore, it seems clear that unless legal steps are taken to deter the high rate of divorce—it will continue even among modernizing elements of the population.

Chapter 14
Dominance and Defiance:
The Inevitability of Entropy in Human Affairs

We have come a long way. Now let us return to the beginning and ask a few simple questions for which, hopefully, the preceding chapters will have provided answers. Why do the Kanuri have so much marital instability, and what makes this vary within the society? How does this explanation compare with contemporary theories about marital instability? And, finally, what does all this tell us about the human condition? Without some attempt to find answers to these questions, especially the latter ones, the study of Kanuri marital relations remains just that: one more case study added to scores of completed ones whose synthesis must await aggregation by a researcher seeking generalizations. However, I take a more Liebnizian view of the socio-cultural substance. Humanity's life is not so various that any particular piece of it does not contain many of the elements common to all. It is with this basic epistemological position in mind that this study has been carried out; now it is time to face the challenge of these assumptions and see in fact how far we have come with such an approach.

A Theory of Kanuri Divorce

Although it has served as a backdrop for this entire study, it is of central importance to recall that the Kanuri are a Muslim people. Islam has been in this area for nearly a millennium and has had a profound affect on the daily lives of the people of Bornu for five hundred years. Divorce in Islam is easy, and almost everywhere Islamic communities have experienced high rates of marital instability. In Islamic social and legal philosophy, marriage is an extremely important institution, but it is a contract and can be broken when the arrangement has proven unsatisfactory. Marriage in Islam is not sanctified or made holy by religion. Instead, the religion divides and sub-divides the legal duties and obligations of the spouses to one another so that adjudication of the contract can take place with reference to a body of law. Unlike Western traditions, then, there is little or no religious force that holds Islamic marriage together. In the Western traditions, the Church ties the couple together and only the Church can or should be able to untie the knot. The couple not only have duties and obligations to one another but to supernatural forces that control the universe (including their marriage). To dissolve a marriage by other than death in the West is, traditionally, to deal with supernatural forces that have solidified the union and the socio-legal institutions in society that reflect widespread belief in these supernatural forces. This is not so with Islam, and therefore divorce has never been a serious problem in Islamic society—as long as the basic assumptions of the law have been accepted, particularly its definition of the nature of marriage and the role of women.

This, then, is the most obvious and probably the most potent reason why marriage is so brittle among the Kanuri. However, it is not the whole story. Given what I have said of Christian marriage, it is obvious that even if divorces could be had for the asking, Western marital instability would never approximate that of the Kanuri without severe and drastic changes in the nature of the society and its values. Until recently, it was easier to obtain a divorce on legal grounds in North Dakota than in most of the states of the U.S.A. Yet this state has, if anything, more stable unions than some others in the country. Thus ease of divorce cannot fully explain the frequency of marital break-ups. Beyond a certain point of marital instability, the potential dislocation of each break-up must be countered by social arrangements which soften the ramifying effects of such an action so that its effects are minimized in the society as a whole. Without such socio-cultural support, a very high rate of marital instability reflects and helps to aggravate social disorganization; with such support comes a *system* of social life adapted to brittle marriage, or conversely, a social system in which high rates of divorce are possible.

The basic support for marital instability in Kanuri social structure is the nature of household organization. Divorce breaks up continguous and continuous contacts among family members but it does not break up households. Indeed, households are the basic corporate units in the society (Cohen 1967a). They can be broken by the death of a senior male and/or conflicts which send constituent members off either to set up their own units or to join other households. Such disintegrative forces are counteracted by others, such as the wealth and power of the household head, client relationships, and other factors which can override the fissiparous tendencies of the domestic cycle. In such a situation, household organization, persistence, growth, or dissolution is basically a function of forces other than marriage and divorce. Marital dissolution, then, simply severs an active husband-wife relationship. Children are taken care of, the household of the husband can easily survive, and the woman either returns to a household of her own descent group or sets herself up as an independent divorced woman.

In a system of brittle unions there is a tendency, as we have seen, for older women to become an unmarried age-class in the society. There is no rule against marrying older women, but with short marital durations and younger women being more desirable as mates, as well as children being a universally desired goal of marriage, then older post-menopause women find it exceedingly difficult if not impossible to remarry once they are divorced. The tendency can be seen among wealthy, high-divorce Western men who continue to marry young women throughout their lifetimes. However, when an entire system uses such a practice, some means of dealing with, or caring for, old women must be available. For example, a law or rule forbidding any man over fifty to marry a woman younger than forty would solve the problem because brittle unions would result in remarriages among roughly similar age mates in the society. The Kanuri have solved this problem by having younger men take care of their mothers or older women in general. Thus the household as a corporate group simply expands to take care of members of this older group, distributing them throughout the population as generally venerable and respected members of their own kin groups.

If households are stable and men stay put when there is a divorce, then women must move, and even move about, between marriages. Thus to maintain a high divorce rate there must be a clearly recognizable and legitimate role for a divorced woman, no matter whether she is living alone or with kin. When this role is illegitimate or scorned, such negative status will inhibit women from taking on the position of divorcee. The status of *zower* is an extremely well established role for a divorced woman among the Kanuri, a concept which they seem to have had for a very long time. Indeed, in the pre-colonial period there even seems to have been some organization among the divorced women. There is no shame attached to the role, so that no negative evaluation is made of either spouse after a divorce has occurred. In other words, the changes in social roles accompanying a divorce do not necessarily create a hardship for either party.

One more support structure is necessary if the effects of high divorce are to be handled without major social disruption. Some techniques are necessary to assure the parties concerned that the fatherhood of unborn children be allocated in a manner agreeable to all parties concerned. Given the fact that knowledge of the exact nature of biological reproduction is fairly new to mankind, then fatherhood, especially sociologically ascribed fatherhood, can and does vary independently of the biological contributions of a particular man or woman. The Kanuri make such distinctions even more difficult with their concept of *bənji*—a child in the womb that will not come out in the normal nine month period. As Muslims, the Kanuri solve this problem (although not completely) by demanding a waiting period of 100 days for the woman after a divorce in order to determine if she is pregnant. The solution is only partial because the *bənji* concept can allow for a paternity claim after the three month period, and such cases, although rare, do occur.

These six qualities, listed in Table 14:1, are therefore the basic enabling causes for the brittleness of Kanuri unions. In this sense they are necessary, but not sufficient causes for a high divorce rate. Without them, it would be difficult for an unstable marital system to operate as part of a stable social system. With them, unstable marriage can be a non-dislocating, i.e., a normal part of social life. It follows that unstable marriages can in fact be part of a stable system of social relations.

TABLE 14:1. THE STRUCTURAL PREREQUISITES OF A HIGH DIVORCE SOCIETY

The Structural Prerequisite	*Kanuri Means of Expressing this Feature*
1. Ease of divorce: little or no procedures necessary.	Islamic legal code and marriage ideology.
2. No supernatural sanctions or sanctity attached to marriage.	
3. Some means of keeping social dislocations, especially care of children, at a minimum.	Separation of household and family as organized units in society.
4. Maintaining an age-class of single old women.	Absorb old women into the households of their kin.
5. Legitimacy of the divorced person, especially the woman's role.	Women as zowers return to kin or go out on their own.
6. Legal means of establishing fatherhood of children after divorce.	Waiting period after divorce for women before they can remarry to see if she is pregnant.

These features are the basic conditions which allow a society to absorb a high divorce rate without that rate itself producing further change, or being changed by the social structure. But these qualities cannot explain why divorce within such societies takes place or why some people within such societies divorce a great deal while others do much less of it.

The first point of significance to cope with in a general way is our basic finding that sociological variables accounted for the vast majority of differences among persons with varying degrees of marital stability. It has been suggested that this results from the fact that almost everyone in Bornu divorces at some time or other, and therefore personality distinctions are not as relevant to such variance as they are elsewhere. This leads, then, to another generalization: namely, that psychological causes of marital instability vary inversely with the divorce rate as to their predictive and causal power in restraining or facilitating marital break-ups. Put another and more recognizable way, we can say that among societies with comparatively low rates of divorce and few support systems for its maintenance (like the U.S.A.) divorce is more likely to be associated with psychological determinants or "incompatibilities," whereas in high divorce societies, break-ups are more likely to be associated with the sociological qualities of the marriage and have less to do with psychological qualities of the actors.

This means that, once the enabling prerequisites are available, certain sociological qualities take over to determine which marriages will be more and which shall be less stable. For Kanuri marriage, the specific nature of these variables, as well as the way in which they operate, is given in Chapter 11. This does not mean that there are no psychological factors associated with marital instability. Certain kinds of personal reactions to social interaction have been shown to be significant correlates of stability, and we discussed these in Chapter 12. Now I would like to put these separate analyses together into an explanation of Kanuri marital experience, attempting at the same time to look for the general qualities of which our case material is only one example.

The Stabilizing Syndrome

A number of features all tend to produce greater degrees of stability in Kanuri unions. However, for the most part, they can be subsumed under a general category concerning the positive contributions that each spouse makes to the marriage. Over and over again, in the ideal image of the husband, in the reasons for divorce, and finally in the questionnaire items associated with more stable unions, the husband as a good provider for his wife and family turns up as an important factor in stabilizing marriage.

Similarly, but in a more complex fashion, the various contributions made by women are positively associated with marital stability. This is strikingly true for fertility, but holds as well for her work on the farm. From more limited but richer ethnographic data we have seen her usefulness as a cook who creates independence for her husband and thereby raises his status. And for a very few marriages, especially of some powerful political leaders, a wife may ultimately become a trusted partner whose loyalty to her husband and his responsibilities add to his ability to do a good job.

In effect, this syndrome is simply another way of looking at the division of labor in human society. Instead of merely describing it, we are saying men and women in any society vary with respect to the division of labor. Some are better at supplying, or fulfilling, or achieving their side of the role bargain, and the more successful they are at it, the greater is the stability of their marriages. Again, however, this is not the whole picture. It would be if all marriages involved a similar division of labor, as they do in very simple hunting and gathering societies. But Kanuri unions vary in this regard such that the more rural and lower status unions require more services from women than marriages with urban and higher status men. Thus, the more the services of women are required, then the more stable are the unions. This sounds like a dependency argument, since it really says that the more women actually do in the way of economically productive work, then the more men wish to hold on to them. Presumably, such men are dependent upon them. However, it should be remembered that in our psychological data the more dependent *women* were high on marital stability, while the more dependent men were low, which is the reverse of what one would expect from the above generalization. This is an important loose end whose contradictory nature will be tucked in later.

Finally, at the psychological level, flexible, open reactions to interaction and a lack of concern with status distinctions also contribute to stability. What this means is that men and women who are able to be less rigid, less concerned with their rights, less concerned with the jural rules governing their relationship, will tend to last longer as mates. The flexibility characteristic is probably a universally adaptive quality that explains greater stability of social relationships in general across all cultures, and applies within each to marriage as well. However, the notion of concern over status distinctions is more limited. It implies that if there are social system features which make relationships less unequal, then some people will be less bothered, while others will react strongly. Those who react less, or who are less concerned, tend to have more stable unions.

The Instability Syndrome

A complex of qualities tends to create less stable unions in Bornu. In my view, all of these variables are to a significant degree the outcome of the ideology and practice of male dominance in Kanuri society, aggravated by the hierarchical nature of the society and its stress on inequality. As we have seen, the ideology of male dominance pervades the marital relationship, it is embodied in the image of the ideal husband-wife relationship, and it is dramatized in the wedding ceremonies. Unions reported on as having had less wifely obedience are less stable.

The fact that urbanism emerges as positively related to instability reflects this same idea. As already noted, the city woman does not contribute as much, economically, to the marriage as her rural counterpart. Thus she is also dominated more. She is kept in seclusion, and she is more often married to a high status man who is used to, or who wishes to, obtain respect and discipline from his family and supporters. Such men are more concerned with status; our tests have shown that this is what they strive for and often achieve. The results also show that such men share fewer secrets with their wives. Concerned as they are with their superior status and the fact that as husbands they do not need a wife's productive work so much, they feel compelled to keep their distance socially from their wives and maintain the superior authority which the culture grants them as a right. Along with this goes lack of emotional involvement or concern for the psychological side of interpersonal relations, as well as inflexibility or an inability to change positions once a disagreement has been initiated.

Such men, being more successful, more interested in prestige and respect to those higher up in the social order, are also more likely to be polygynists. This mode of marriage itself defines man as superior, since he can take several wives into subordination (wifehood), whereas the reverse would, in Kanuri terms, be unthinkable. Polygyny, which is also associated with marital instability, rests upon the assumption of male dominance and superiority.

In other words, all of the major qualities that are associated with marital instability are also aspects of male dominance. Conversely, many of the qualities associated with marital stability are aspects of more egalitarian relations between husband and wife. Monogamy, sharing of secrets, non-purdah, and less concern over status distinctions are the best examples of these. It is almost as if women as an entire class are saying "You may try to dominate us and use us for your own benefits, but we will do our best to subvert your authority and when we can make things more equal then we will stay married to you."

The ideal of male dominance is just that—an ideal. Lower class men in rural areas and in the city, more flexible men, those who for myriad reasons can never expect ideal conditions in their own lives, do not insist so strongly on their own dominance, and their marriages are more stable. But those in a position to demand the best for themselves, or who try to live up to the ideal values, can be rigid and demand high standards of wifely subordination. Their thresholds of tolerance for wives is therefore much lower and their marriages are always unstable.

The fact that men who are high on marital instability measures also have some tendency to be more sensitive to dependency reflects this same point. Unlike their more maritally stable colleagues, they are less egalitarian. They also see dependency more often because such a recognition involves status distinctions. In other words, men who are divorce prone are also sensitive to rank hierarchy and other aspects of Kanuri culture that emphasize inequality. Conversely, women who accept hierarchy and inequality as well as its marital expression—male dominance—have more stable marital careers. The system of high divorce is thus based ultimately upon status distinctions and hierarchical relations which put husbands and wives into the more general position of superiors and subordinates. All of this occurs in a society in which such dyads are considered to be the most important kind of social relation in the system as a whole.

Entropy, Dominance, and Divorce

All superior-subordinate relations are governed by two opposing forces: legitimacy and entropy (Cohen 1970). Legitimacy describes those forces, values, customs, and supports which maintain the authority of the superior over the subordinate and bind the subordinate to his inferior position with respect to the power his superior wields over him. Contrarily, entropy is the resentment, and striving for equal or more power, on the part of subordinates. Thus all situations of social inequality have inherent in them the potentiality for change in a direction of more equality or even a reversal of the inequalities.

The husband-wife relationship in Bornu is an example of a legitimated superior-subordinate relationship. However, except for a very few rare women who achieve a form of partnership with their husbands, almost all Kanuri women are ascribed their lower status by birth and can never reverse their subordination within marriage. The result is a constant tension in the man-woman relationship, a constant seeking by the woman for means to increase her power and thereby equalize the relationship. When this occurs, i.e., when entropy begins to operate, then marriages are more stable. Each partner is contributing his and her share and there is less tension over the inequities.

In the extreme case, the woman who craves freedom and despises or seriously cannot cope with wifely subordination, there is the role of free *zower* or divorced woman. In this role, she has no need to be subordinate, but if she wishes to remain free she must fend and provide for herself, while her married sister, although less free, is at least fed.

However, divorce lies at the end of the road for most marriages, whether they are more or less stable. When the more egalitarian relationship occurs, it is more satisfying to the woman. Her husband is not so authoritarian and demanding. His range of tolerance is greater, and he sees her more as a human being with feelings and emotions like himself. But now it is the husband who is in trouble. He lives in a culture whose ideals he is constantly transgressing in his everyday behavior with his wife. In Kanuri terms, she has subverted his legitimate authority, thereby making him a less adequate and successful man. This can only go on so long. Ultimately, a situation arises, she takes one too many liberties, and he can take it no longer.

What this means is that inequalities in social interaction are always fraught with tension. When such inequalities include an intimate relationship such as that of husband and wife, then the tensions are even greater. If this takes place in a social system with our six enabling features, a very high divorce rate will result, varying per person with the amount of tension created in the marriage by the social and psychological characteristics of the partners.

The Theoretical Relevance of the Study

In many respects, the ideas and facts presented here have had little relevance to divorce theory as that theory is described in the first chapter of this book. In overall terms, our approach to divorce as a discontinuity in interaction which therefore permits us to more adequately understand continuity or stability, has been vindicated. If we wish to know something about social order, about its repetitive, systemic qualities that carry society through time, changing but continuous, then we must know about those factors that disrupt the continuity. By looking at divorce, we have been able to measure a number of qualities that contribute to continuity and discontinuity, and to posit the general theoretical idea that underlying all social order is a drive toward social equality which, when not satisfied, produces tension and conflict that must be adapted to.

Ideas from elsewhere in social theory have helped us to formulate hypotheses and derive variables, as well as descriptive modes, that are relevant for the study of marital stability. But I believe that a full understanding of high divorce frequencies would have eluded us if we had elected to remain within one theoretical or methodological approach devoted to this topic. In this sense, the study has not been so much a test of various theories of divorce as an attempt to measure and understand the nature of divorce in one particularly high divorce society. In some cases, attempts were made to carry out direct tests, as in the case of kinship; at other times, direct tests were impossible. For example, within the context of this study it has not been possible to make a clear-cut operationalization of the key variables in the Gibbs (1963) theory of tight and loose social structure, in which tight structure is correlated to low divorce.

In retrospect, however, some comments are in order. Central to Kanuri marriage is the ideal of male dominance. Yet, as we have seen, the more this ideal is adhered to, i.e., the more "tightly" structured is the marriage, then the greater should be the instability of the union—which is contrary to what the Gibbs theory would predict. The theory fails to question the focus of legitimacy and accepts such forces as givens in the situation being studied. But legitimacy as here theorized is constantly under pressure to change and never is fully accepted. Indeed, I would suggest that the greater the demands for conformity in a social system, the greater the tension, i.e., those forces that challenge or subvert legitimate patterns of authority. When such tensions become intense, they must be expressed in some way; in marriage, this most commonly means a high divorce rate, is such is allowed in the legal structure of the society. Despite this qualitative assessment of the plausibility of Gibbs' (1963) theory to the Kanuri data, it should be noted that it is not easy to reliably characterize Kanuri social structure as a whole as "loose" or "tight," and nothing in the present literature allows us to make such generalizations. Some features of Kanuri life are "loose," some are "tight." For this reason, the theory of divorce created by Gibbs cannot be said to have been adequately tested.

By contrast, descent group theory has been used as an important part of the present research. Ever since Gluckman's (1950) work, descent has been an important element in the explanation of variance in divorce between one society and another. However, the results have been somewhat complex and not fully predicted by theory. As Fallers' (1957) work suggests, women who return to visit their own kin more often are also higher divorcers, in general. However, in the city the highest divorcers are among women who visit their kin infrequently, which is the opposite of the theory. We have shown that these are extremely independent women and that the theory works for the divorce records of individuals; but when marriages are used as units, the greater numbers of divorces per woman reverse these results. For men, on the other hand, the theory says very little, referring instead to the interference of descent in the woman's absorption into her husband's group. However, our data show that a *man's* descent group members tend to detract from and interfere with *his* relations to his wife. Thus the theory should be reformulated and extended to include the idea that descent group involvement of either spouse after marriage is negatively related to marital stability. This is exacerbated by the practice of unilocal residence in which an in-marrying spouse is a stranger entering into a well organized extended kin group.

A corollary of the original descent theory concerned bridewealth, which was posited as a correlate of a system of more stable unions. This may be so when societies are being compared, although it is difficult to characterize a society as one of high or low bridewealth when there is enormous variation of bridewealth among marriages. However, among stratified, high-divorce societies like Bornu, bridewealth is inversely related to marital stability—the opposite of that predicted by theory. In such situations, those men who can pay the most are the most rigid about marital behavior and they are the least bothered by bridewealth payments. They are therefore willing to lose money, or pay it out repeatedly, in order to obtain "proper" (i.e., respectful) subordination.

Marriages and bridewealth can be seen not as an aspect of descent but rather as part of an alliance pattern among groups (Leach 1957). However, there is no indication in our data that special alliances between groups or persons (e.g., a chief and his client) through marriage produce any significant change in divorce probability. For the parties concerned with such alliances, the most important quality of the alliance is the idea that the marriage was in fact initiated and carried out. Person A gave a girl, whose marriage he either controls or has influence over, to person B. Whether or not the union lasts, the noteworthy point for all concerned is the fact that the event has taken place. The durability of the union is a matter outside the control, more or less, of the alliance that created it. Obviously it is useful for a man to have socially prominent in-laws or to be related by marriage to someone with whom he already has many links. Indeed, in particular cases, such prior or would-be relations may help stabilize a union. But this is not enough. It is impossible on the basis of this study to predict marital stability on the basis of the alliances being created by the union. Alliances can help to initiate marriage; indeed, they tend to express such relationships. But the fate of the marriage is unrelated to such consideration.

When the present study is compared to demographic research, such as that by Ardener (1962) for Africa or Jacobsen (1958) for the U.S.A., several difficulties arise. The most obvious is comparability. Because each of these studies has been conducted in separate contexts using different techniques, clear-cut comparison is sometimes difficult. Thus Jacobsen (1958) has very large population sizes plus good per annum rates of divorce. Such data are extremely difficult to collect for Kanuri, and thus my so-called "rates" are in fact proportions or probabilities per cohort of persons or marriages. Thus I had to use portions of the Jacobsen data to calculate divorce frequencies that were comparable to those used up to now. On the other hand, in our multivariate analysis we have developed our own measures of marital stability. This includes duration measures, per person and per marriage. Each has shortcomings, and these are counteracted by the other, thus producing a kind of triangulation of measures. Divorce rates or probabilities are, in my view, only indicators of the more general concept of stability but do not portray stability in all its facets. Hopefully, future work in other parts of the world will produce data which can be compared to these Kanuri results using these more comprehensive measures.

In terms of results, this study has corroborated previous work in some respects and, in others, it has gone beyond to newer generalizations. Thus, like Ardener (1962), I too have found age and sex differences associated with marital stability. I have also found junior wife status to be more unstable, but have gone beyond this to show that such is the case in a two-wife family, while in a three-wife situation, the senior wife has the unstable role. We have interpreted such instabilities to be the result of co-wife interaction rather than husband-wife relationships. Such findings must now be checked in other polygynous societies in order to assess the level of generality of this finding.

Using theory from sociology has proven to be interesting and useful. Jessie Bernard's (1964) imaginative adaptation of escalation theory is an accurate way of describing the process of marital conflict. And in a number of places throughout the qualitative analysis, I have used it as the conceptual framework for depicting the movement of events. However, to have framed the entire analysis in these terms would have created gross limitations for the study. Escalation assumes a conflict and then describes the course of events during the interchange. It does not explain why the conflict is there in the first place, nor which person or groups are more or less prone to engage in such conflict. Thus two parties, each with the same set of "grievances," may react differently. Possibly the theory should assign ways of analyzing differential reactions, and also differential kinds and amounts of power, to the participants. Then the way in which such forces have developed and how they are used to maintain peaceful or non-peaceful relations could be analyzed. Only then could escalation theory provide a full framework for the analysis of divorce, and possibly other conflicts as well. Without such detail, escalation theory provides a convenient set of terms for describing a conflict but not an alternative form of explanation.

The same can be said for conjunctive theory. As I see it, conjunctive theory states that those factors of social and personal background, as well as of marital conditions, which tend to unite spouses into a more solidary unit, are predicted to lead to greater marital stability. In general this is true, but the present study, interestingly, disconfirms what seems to be a very simplistic, almost tautological, theory. Thus degree of previous acquaintanceship and similarity of social background (two important variables in the U.S.A.) have no effect on Kanuri marriage stability. Purdah, which separates the wife from the community and links her closely to her husband (and his authority), thereby creating conjunctiveness, is associated with higher amounts of instability. Thus conjunctive theory may have limited application cross-culturally, at least in situations in which the conjunction (or coming together) and similarity of spouses' backgrounds also produced inequities and tensions.

Possibly the least important theorizing for present purposes has been the social psychological realm. Psychological variables simply do not account for much variance in high divorce societies. However, if we consider these variables alone, then flexibility among men and dependency among women stand out as qualities of personality that probably have cross-cultural significance as being positively related to marital stability. Central to the present analysis is the finding that insubordination by women is negatively associated with the stability of their unions. However, I would think that the greater emphasis on hierarchy and subordination in the society as a whole, the greater the effect of this variable upon marriage. As with the work of Clignet (1970), work in social psychology must go beyond the search for successful or unsuccessful unions and seek instead for the psychological features that are correlated with different types of marriages in different systems.

At the end of Chapter 1, I said that ultimately to study another society and its culture is to try to understand ourselves. By some, this study could be interpreted to be a vindication of our own way of life, of monogamy, of more emotionalism in marriages, and more eqalitarianism between spouses. Nothing could be further from my intentions. If there is such a thing as an ideal marriage system, I am convinced that neither the Kanuri nor the Westerner approximates to it. What is much more likely is the possibility that both we and the Kanuri will change in terms of what we have been in the past and what each of us wants in the future.

Our own divorce rate is probably too low and we need more marital break-up, more easily accomplished, to free people and allow them to lead the kind of lives they want. Our society does not possess the enabling structures for a high divorce society that I have distilled from the Kanuri case study. Therefore, even if we could divorce as freely as the Kanuri, I believe we would opt not to because other factors would inhibit us from doing so. We have no institutions for taking care of divorced unmarriageable older women; we have great difficulty with "broken" homes because the household and the conjugal family are congruent; and we still call divorce a "failure" in a success oriented society. Our view of the mature healthy personality is one in which we see spouses especially as "working through their problems" or coping with them. We believe with Oscar Wilde in *De Profundis* that to live with difficulties in the husband-wife relationship and work them out, if possible, can produce "better," more profound, or more mature partners to a marriage. So far, I do not see that commune life as practiced by a few of the younger generation, or any other suggested reform, can wipe out our own past and its effects on our future.

On their side, the Kanuri will as they modernize produce more rights for women and tend to make divorce somewhat more difficult legally. However, enabling conditions for divorce are still present, and although the rate will ultimately decline it will be fairly high for the foreseeable future because male dominance as an ideology is so deeply imbedded into the culture and history of the society. Thus the tensions arising out of more rights for women, and the pull of the past will keep marriages brittle even though Kanuri society itself must ultimately accept more egalitarian marriages.

In saying all of this, I am in fact reflecting what is possibly the major finding of this study. For almost his entire history *Homo sapiens* has seen the man-woman relationship in unequal terms. Women's physical properties, her somewhat weaker physique and her childbearing capacities have worked together with incest prohibitions to turn her into a value manipulated by men for the continuity and productivity of the species. Throughout, her humanity has constantly ameliorated this semi-commodity status, but ultimately her common membership in humanity must determine that she be given a place of equality in society. Not to do so, as we have seen, produces tension and conflict. Ultimately, then, equality among men, between men and women, indeed between individuals and groups, is the basis of stable relations in a changing world.

APPENDICES

APPENDIX I

Questionnaire - General Information

1. Informant number

2. Site number

3. Present age

4. Sex

5. Are you presently married?

6. (Male) How many wives do you have at present?
   (Female) How many co-wives do you have now?

7. (Male) How many concubines do you have at present?
   (Female) How many concubines does your husband have?

8. (Male) How many concubines have you had in the past?
   (Female) How many concubines has he had in the past?

9. How many times have you been married?

10. How many times have you been divorced?

11. (Male) How many wives have died while they were married to you?
    (Female) How many of your marriages ended by the death of your spouse?

12. (Male) Have any of your wives ever run away and never returned (no divorce)?
    (Female) Has your husband ever run away from you and never returned (desertion), i.e., there
       was no divorce?

13. (Male) How many wives that you divorced have you remarried?
    (Female) How many husbands who have divorced you have you remarried?

14. (Male) Were any of your marriages annulled after the wedding?
    (Female) How many of your marriages were annulled?

15. (Male) How many compounds did you live in during the first 5 years of your life?
    (Female) How many compounds did you live in before your first marriage?

16. What is the total number of compounds that you have ever lived in?

17. Tell me the length of time you stayed in each of these compounds and your relationship to the
       household head.

18. (Male) Tell me the age, sex, and relationship to you of all in your compound.
    (Female) Tell me the age, sex, and relationship to you of everyone in your compound.

19. (Male) Total in compound (calculated).
    (Female) How many people altogether are living in your household?

20. Total number of kin in compound (calculated).

21. Total number of clients in compound (calculated).

22. How many of your kin live in adjoining compounds?

23. (Male) How many of your kin live in this ward?
    (Female) How many of your kin live in the same ward as you?

24. How many of your kin live in this same town?

25. How often do you visit kin who live nearby?

26. How often do you visit kin who live far away?

27. How many times was your father divorced?

28. How many times was your mother divorced?

29. What was your father's occupation?

30. (Male) What is your present occupation?
    (Female) What occupation do you have for earning money?

31. (Male) Tell me the sex and relationship to you of everyone who helps you with your occupation.
    (Female) Who helps you with this occupation?

32. (Male) What occupation would you like to have in the future?
    (Female) What sort of man would you like most to marry?

33. (Male) Do you think you will ever get it?
    (Female) Do you think you will ever marry such a man?

34. (Male) Do you farm?
    (Female) Do you help your husband farm?

35. Were there periods when you did not farm?

36. Why?

37. (Male only) Tell me the sex and relationship to you of everyone who helps you farm.

38. (Male only) Tell me all of the occupations you have had in your life from earliest to most recent, and for each one tell how long you had it and your relationship to the man who taught it to you.

39. (Male) Tell me all the things that make a good husband.
    (Female) Tell me what a good husband is.

40. (Male) Which of these is most often not done?
    (Female) Which of these things are most often broken?

41. Tell me all the things that make a good wife.

42. Which of these things is most often not done?

43. (Male) What are the important customs that are most often broken by men in Bornu?
    (Female) What are the important customs that are no longer practiced?

44. How many years of Western-type schooling have you had?

45. How many years have passed since you last attended such a school?

46. (Male) How many times during your life have you been to court?
    (Female) How many times have you been to court as a principal?

47. (Male) If you have a horse, who gave it to you?
    (Female) Do you have little gold, not much—not little, much gold?

48. (Female only) How did you get your gold?

Questionnaire - Marriage Specifics

1. Informant number.

2. (Male) Wife number.
   (Female) Husband number.

3. How old were you when you married this wife (husband)?

4. (Male) How old was this wife when she married you?
   (Female) How old was this husband when you married him?

5. (Male) Had she been married before or was she a previously unmarried woman?
   (Female) Had he been married before or was he a previously unmarried man?

6. How many times was she (he) married before she (you) married you (him)?

7. Were you both living in the same village (town) when you were married?

8. Was your town a hamlet, a town, or a city?

9. (Male) If wife's town different—see number 7—ask 8.
   (Female) If husband's town different—see number 7—ask 8.

10. (If different towns) How far away was your town from your wife's (husband's) town?

11. How long did you know this wife (husband) before you married her (him)?

12. Tell me the story of how you came to marry her (him)?

13. How many relatives were with you (him) in the same house or close by when she (he) married you?

14. How many of these were in your (his) father's family?

15. How many of these were in your (his) mother's family?

16. How many relatives did she (you) have near by your (his) house at the time of the marriage?

17. How often did she (you) visit relatives that lived close by?

18. How often did she (you) visit relatives that lived far away?

19. Did you (your husband) think your wife (you) visited her relatives too often?

20. Did you (your husband) suggest that she (you) go less often?

21. What was your (your husband's) occupation when she (he) married you?

22. What occupation did you (he) change to during this marriage?

23. How was your (your husband's) income (wealth)?

24. How many times did you (your husband) move to new houses in the same town during this marriage?

25. Did your wife (you) have relatives near by these new houses?

26. Did you (your husband) have relatives near by these new houses?

27. Did your wife (you) disagree with these moves?

28. Did you (your husband) move to new towns during this marriage? How many?

29. Did she (you) disagree to these moves?

30. Did your wife (you) have relatives in these new towns?

31. Did you (your husband) have relatives in these new towns?

32. How many years of Western-type schooling did she (your husband) have?

33. How many years and months did she (you) stay with you (him)?

34. Is this woman (man) still living?

35. If this woman (man) is not living with you, is she (he) living in a hamlet, a town, or a city?

36. Did she (he) die while she (you) was (were) married to you (him)?

37. Was this marriage annulled?

38. How many times did she (you) run away?

39. How many times did she (you) return?

40. How many times did you (she) divorce her (you)?

41. How many times did she (you) return after you (he) divorced her (you)?

42. Did this marriage finally end in divorce?

43. What were the reasons for the divorce?

44. How many wives (co-wives) were in the compound when this divorce occurred?

45. How many were senior to her (you)?

46. How many were junior to her (you)?

47. Were you and she (he) relatives to one another?

48. What kind of relative was she (he)?

49. If she (he) was a relative, when was she (were you) promised to you (him)?

50. What was her (his) father's occupation?

51. How was her (his) father's wealth?

52. Was he (his father) a common person or an aristocrat? Important.

53. How much was the *luwaliram*?

54. How much was the *sada*'s?

55. How many saris and shirts?

56. Was this wife (were you) in seclusion?

57. How was the beauty (handsomeness) of your wife (husband)?

58. (Male) What occupation did she have for earning money when she married you?
    (Female) What occupation for earning money did you have when he married you?

59. How often did she (you) work on your (his) farm?

60. How often did she (you) go to the well?

61. When you were married to this wife (husband), did your (his) occupation take you (him) away from home very often?

62. How many relatives (of his) helped you (him) on the farm during this marriage?

63. How many non-relatives helped you (him) on the farm during this marriage?

64. (Male) Did this wife always "follow" you (was she obedient)?
    (Female) Did you always follow your husband?

65. Do you (did you) sometimes tell secrets to one another?

66. (Male) Does your wife (this one) assist you with a lot of things?
    (Female) Do you (did you) assist this husband with lots of things?

67. (Male) Did you (do you) give this wife many things?
    (Female) Did your husband give you many things?

68. (Male) What kind of gifts do (did) you give her?
    (Female) What kind of gifts did he give you?

69. (Male) How much money do you (did you) give her for market?
    (Female) How much money did he give you for market?

70. How many times was she (were you) pregnant before you (he) married her (you)?

71. How many children did she (you) have before she (he) married you?

72. How many times was she (were you) pregnant before she married you (while married to this husband)?

73. How many children did she (you) have while married to you (this man)?

74. Give all of their present ages, or ages at death, and their sex.

75. How many false pregnancies did she (you) have?

76. Tell me the stories of these false pregnancies?

77. Was she (he) from the same or different tribe? What was the name of the tribe?

APPENDIX II

TAT Cards and a Sample Protocol

The pictures which follow show the TAT pictures, and accompanying each one is the protocol from an urban man—respondent number 16. He was 34 years old at the time of the interview. He is a small contractor who builds local houses in the city. His father, he says, was a mud builder in the city. He has one wife at home at present who has been in the house only five months; she is the latest of six marriages, all others of which ended in divorce and none of which lasted longer than seven years. He has two young children by his second wife who is the one who stayed the longest. I chose this protocol because it seems to be of medium length and in no way extraordinary when compared to others. Numbers in the protocols refer to figures, counting from left to right in the picture.

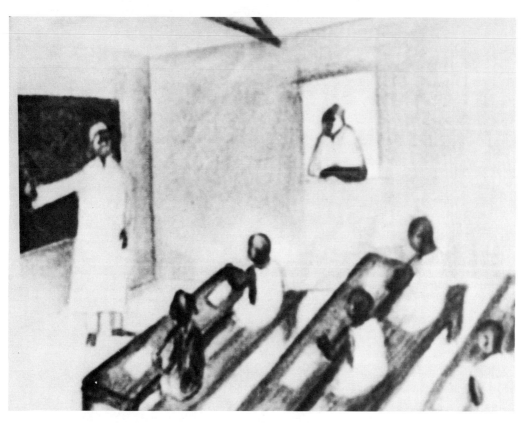

Card No. 1. Kids, want learning and knowledge—all Africans. He has come to see what they are doing (in window). Someone from somewhere else seeing whether these young men are progressing. He may be an adult educator—probably looking to benefit from the lessons. He is here on his own accord and stands to benefit.

Card No. 2. A sick man—an old man rather poor and sick. This man lacks a lot of things, health, he is aging and not well looked after. He looks (as if) he is not hungry. A man standing in a door—no, a woman, not his wife: he is too old for her—probably his daughter, or a visitor. He doesn't look like he is *not* dying. He is not well clothed. *Just old*, not much wrong.

Card No. 3.
The sitting man is someone with some position of some kind. He has not much power, but some. The man in front is paying his respects. He is not mistreating the young man— everything is well. The man in front is not unafraid, just respectful. The big man does not look angry or sad. Chair man appreciates and respects the man in front of him (kneeling) (reciprocal). Nobody is afraid here.

ANTHROPOLOGICAL STUDIES

Card No. 4.
(3) is the father
o f e v e r y o n e
there. They are in
their ward. They
have been waiting
(for him) to tell
them something.
He is telling them
how to follow his
example of being
good and respect-
ed by everyone.
Everybody is pa-
tiently listening
to him attentive-
ly. They look (as
though) they will
follow what he
says. They re-
spect him a lot.

Card No. 5. A woman under a tree. She looks tired and has sat down. She needs help probably from the man. The man looks reluctant. She wants him to lead to a place where there is water or people. She has been on a long journey. They don't seem to have seen each other before—just met in the bush. The man does not look sympathetic. The man has not decided what to do yet. Probably he does not think very much of the woman, but it might be that the man is only interested in what is here (basket or pail). Probably the woman is trying to give him this, but NO he is not taking it.

Card No. 6. A
man and a
woman, married,
in front of a
house. They are
not happy with
each other. He is
telling the woman
to go in. The
woman has just
come out of the
house, and she is
being ordered
back. She is going
to go in. She is
going in, and he
will follow, and
be nice to her
when she goes in.
Everything will
be all right. She
looks (as though)
she obeys her
husband nor-
mally. Whatever
is between them
will be (straight-
ened) out. They
will reach an
agreement.

Card No. 7. In a village. (2) has come to (1). (1) is the host. (2) is a diviner. He has come to tell something to (1). The diviner has come to deceive (1) and get things from him. He (2) is in the middle of it. (1) is listening; (2) is in the middle of divination. (1) wants to know how much his own people like him. He is in doubt about how much people like him. He cannot get the truth from a diviner (who can!). A diviner (was) not invited; the man (is) using the opportunity but it will not do any good. The object of (2) is to cheat (1) and go.

Card No. 8. Court scene. All (are) court members here, and the court disputants have not come yet. (3) is a small girl come to greet the big man. (She greets and departs?) (1) and (2) are from the *family* of the Big Man (4) (Alkali). (5) to (8)—court members. The family has come to see if there are any messages for the house. Not there permanently.

Card No. 9. Mother and daughter. (2) = *fero.* (1) = mother in front of their house. The daughter has not yet married, and the mother is telling the daughter the things to do to lead a good married life when she (daughter) gets married. "Obey your husband," the mother says. "When the husband calls you—go!" the mother says. "If he asks you to take care of something, do it," the mother says. "Try and be patient," the mother says. "Stay clean," "Cook food on time," "Don't push him too hard to get you things," "Appreciate what he does for you," "Don't look down on your husband," "Always ask for permission," "If the husband says, 'You can't go,' *then don't.*" (She says this and many other things.)

Card No. 10.
A young man is
in front of his
mother. He is us-
ing his hands to
express some-
thing. He (has)
just come from
an errand for the
mother. The man
is just standing
and receiving in-
formation. He is
looking straight
at the mother.
The mother is sat-
isfied with the er-
rand. He is still
not finished talk-
ing about the er-
rand. Probably
the mother has
come to him for
the story. They
just met in front
of his house.
That's it; he will
deliver the whole
story to the
mother, and she
will return. (It is)
not an unpleasant
story. He will es-
cort the mother
home part way.

Card No. 11. Three men in front of a house. (1) is H H. H H (1) has just been called out. (2) and (3) have called (1) out. There is a dispute between (2) and (3), and they have called (1). (2) has done some work for (3), and (2) has not been paid by (3). [They called (1) to witness that (2) has not been paid.] They are all neighbors. (2) says he has finished. (3) says the work is not finished satisfactorily. (2) has his hands up indicating how hard he has worked on the job. (1) = mediator. (1) will settle, it looks as if he can. (3) will pay on intervention of (1). (3) is still unhappy about (2's) work. There will be an understanding about work already done. It will be resolved out of court (Alkali's).

Card No. 12. (4) is a *Mai* = a King. (1, 2, 8, 5) are his people. (3) has come to pay his respects and go. (7 and 6) are husband and wife. They have come to the *Mai* with a problem. The complainant = woman (plaintiff). The *Mai* is listening to what happened. The woman has finished speaking, and the man is speaking. (They are) complaining about each (other). The man complains of disobedience. The woman complains of neglectfulness of the husband. They are now in front of the king for advice before it gets worse. It has not gotten worse yet. The king is telling them to come to an understanding. The *Mai* is going to say, "You must return home and pay more attention to one another."

APPENDIX III

Two Sample Essays

#23. A Kanuri girl of 14 from a rural town. She was in the second year of the Teacher's Training College at the time of writing. She wishes a non-traditional relationship with her husband in a typical schoolgirl fashion.

I should like to be a teacher when I finish my schooling. My husband's occupation will be teaching too. If my husband and myself were teaching in the same town, we should like to bring an electricity to our home and also we should like to build our house with a cement and we should like to cover with an linoleum. For all this the most important thing that we should like to bring to our house is record players and gramaphone to play and dance when we are free from working. Also we should like to have to buy a car when we receive our salaries monthly and in the every night we shall drive our car to go and see cinema.

My husband and I should be live together by doing what he told me to do and doing what I told him to do in the same times. I shall live with my husband without any fighting quarreling as he is my brother. I shall treat him by cooking our foods to eat at any time and he will treat me by giving me some more beautiful clothes to wear. I should eat my food together with my husband in the same room and on the same table. We should sleep in the same room and on one bed. I should tell him what I dream in the night and he will tell me what dreams in the night. Our duties will be teaching. Early in the morning when we wake, we should bath ourselves and we shall say our morning prayers. After finishing our prayers we should go to school in order to teach to our students. All these things are different from other people's ways because some women are not doing what their husband needs to do and they were always quarreling every day and every night. Therefore this must stop to live with their husbands faithfully.

People get divorced because when the wife and the husband mix their male cell and female cell, the male cell fusing the female cell, the male cell give divorced to a female cell.

Some people live together happily for many years because maybe they have some children between wife and husband that the husband does not like to leave his wife because of his children. But when the husband drives his wife the children cannot live in his father's house happily because of their mother. The people who were divorced are: When the people were divorced they will give birth to child. Some people divorced each other because they want to have a child.

There are more divorces in Nigeria than in other places because Nigerian women and men have understood everything carefully and they knew how to do everything quite clear and good easily way. I think in Nigeria there more than 450,000 children, and all these children will divorced sometime and they will become old.

#219. A Kanuri youth of 19. He is from the city and was at the time of writing in the third year of Teacher Training College. His father is one of the senior officials of the Emirate which means that he very likely has a very bright future ahead of him. In this vein it is interesting to see his publicly stated modest view of himself and his future life. His view of marriage, kinship, and community life are almost identical to older non-school men of the area.

The kind of life I wish to lead. . . .The kind of wife that I think will make the best wife for me is a girl who lives in a big house and family where she is restricted to her home and the surrounding area and not left to herself to roam about in the town. I wish to have such a wife for they usually make a very decent wife and due to the fact that they are not well acquainted with the outside in their homes, they will be likely to concentrate their minds on their own homes affairs rather than dream of going out without a definite reason.

The only difference I would have from the ordinary life is that if I were to farm I would not let my wife come out and help me farm. I would not do this because: (a) I know that most of these girls that come from big families don't usually know much about farming, (b) I don't want make her do too much work since she has household works to do, (c) I don't want her to be see around too much by other people.

My occupation would be a Primary School teacher—maybe a headmaster, and as for my wife if she is to have an occupation I would rather have her do things like sewing and embroiding things like bedsheet, or pillow-cases or cover etc just some minor jobs when she has a spare time at hand. I will of coure let her sell her works.

I would like to have a new bicycle to ride to my school, and nice house of myself which would of course be near my school and good neighbours.

The relationship between us would be of course just husband and wife like anywhere else in the province. I will let her have almost all I could if she needs it and that is if and when necessary. I shall try and keep her mind to her home and not elsewhere. I will try and have a good community around me so that we are happy. If one is alone in an area he is not likely to enjoy oneself. Attending of these parties and ceremony will lead to a happier community. And I will try and invite as many neighbours of mine as I can for my meals. Family relationship must be the base of my all plannings. Everything that I do should be under the consent of my family if necessary.

My life with my wife will be the kind of life any school teacher would lead without of course too much jumpings for the moon.

Why I think our people have divorces:

The reason why people in this part have divorces is I think, mostly due to lack of understanding of each other's reaction. There are some reasons for such things—a husband and a wife living together under one roof here will mostly head their life to divorce because if one gets too much of anything he gets tired of that particular thing. When this comes into such life they began to see out, by this I mean they start going to different directions—the husband would go to another woman and so the wife to another man. When such things happens each of them would start complain of each others whereabout at a particular to a certain time and this would to a divorce. Some of these divorces would come due to financial affairs, now this is serious as women don't go for reasons given by their husbands mostly except of course those who do understand some of the problems of men. Well, when a husband fails to satisfy his wife's demand the wife gets furious and accuses the husband of many things. This mostly lead to some bad languages and expressions and thus to divorce. Lack of food and maintaining of the house and the household would also cause divorce. Some wives who have much power over their husbands would also make claims of demand for divorce. This they do to show their power over their husbands and to the nearby community. This is not infrequent happening here but of those who do the likely cause was that when a person marries a woman while he is just an ordinary person and in their years of living he grows into a higher community and in a matter of years he is looked upon as a distinguished personality anything he does or says in the house—that is in his home is just a mere word to the wife. The wife would say she is the cause of his success and that whoever he becomes he is just that ordinary person she married years ago and will look upon him as that—this as I said is not a regular happening but I know of two or three of such events and led to a multiple divorce and reconcilation.

Some people lead a decent life of husband and wife and live long because, maybe they understand each other, they are tied a bond like children, they would have nobody to turn to, or that the girl or wife is under oppression to stay in her home—this oppression is of course from her family. Those are the reasons as far as I can remember why some life here lead to a happier and longer life while others to a shorter and uglier one.

APPENDIX IV

Kanuri Kinship Terminology

ya	Mo, Mo-Sis, Mo-Mo, Fa-Mo, any older female
yakura	Mo-Ol-Sis
yinna, yagana (rare)	Mo-Yo-Sis
rawa, raba	Mo-Bro, Fa-Sis-Hu, Mo-Hu, Mo-Hu (not own father), Mo-Divorced-Hu
aba, ba'a, baba	Fa, Fa-Bro
abakura, ba'kura, babakura	Fa-Ol-Bro
bawa, baba	Fa-Sis, Mo-Bro-Wi, Fa-Ol-Bro-Wi, Fa-other wives, Mo-co-wives, Wi of adoptive compound head
abagana, ba'gana, babagana	Fa-Yo-Bro
yangana	Fa-Yo-Bro-Wi
kaka, ka'a	Mo-Mo, Mo-Fa, Fa-Mo, Fa-Fa, any old person, Wi-grandparents, all sons and daughters of ego's own children, with less frequency—the sons and daughters of people ego calls son and daughter. For 2nd descendant generation, only as term of address
yeiya	anyone on the 3rd ascendant and descendant generation of ego's kin relations
yeiyari	anyone of ego's kin relations beyond the 3rd ascendant generation
yanyiana	Bro, Sis, Half-Bro, Half-Sis, Ol-cross and parallel cousins of either sex, ex-husband of an old woman, husband of many years
kərami	Yo-Bro, Yo-Sis, Yo-Half-Bro, Yo-Half-Sis, Yo-cross and parallel cousins of either sex
yabe	same as kərami, not used often, also any person junior to ego
shakik (rare)	full brother, sister
aba'ana (rare)	Half-Bro, Half-Sis, same father
kalala (rare)	Half-Bro, Half-Sis, same mother

tada	own son, own children's sons, own children's male grandchildren, junior male cousins and their male descendants, general term for male child of anyone
fero	same as tada, only female
diwo	grandchild (reference)
fəndi	child of a cousin marriage
kəsai	senior in-law, Wi-parents and their collaterals, Wo-Ol-Siblings (sometimes)
tiu	junior in-law, Wi-Siblings real and classificatory especially juniors, all wife's junior relatives
kamunyi	my wife (reference)
kwanyi	my husband (reference)
tiuəma	spouse of wife's collaterals
do'oma	co-wife

Kinship I

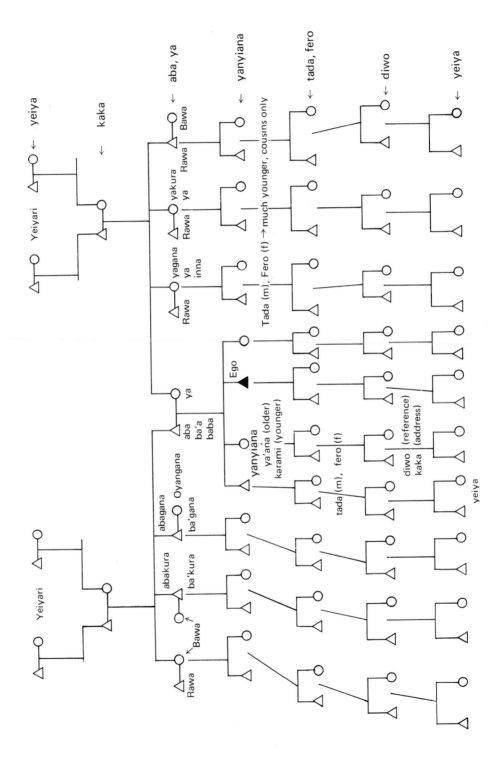

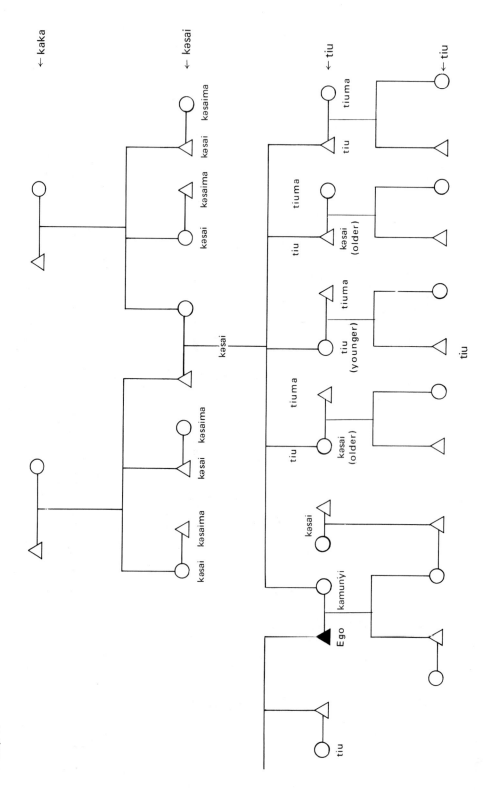

Kinship II

NOTES

Chapter 1

[1] For an example of such functionalism, see Firth 1956.

[2] See Goode 1961 for an example of such writing.

Chapter 2

[1] Dr. Spain returned the following year to carry out eighteen months of field work among the Kanuri and is now a competent speaker of the language.

Chapter 3

[1] See Cohen, R. "Conflict and change in a northern Nigerian Emirate." *In* G. Zollschan and D. Hirsch (eds.), *Explorations in Social Change*. Boston: Houghton Mifflin, 1964; Cohen, R. "The Bornu King Lists." *In* J. Butler (ed.), *Boston University Publications in African History* Vol. 2:41-83. Boston: Boston University Press, 1966; Cohen, R. "The dynamics of feudalism in Bornu," *In* J. Butler (ed.), *Boston University Publications in African History* Vol. 2:87-105, 1966; Cohen, R. "Power, authority, and personal success in Islam and Bornu." *In* M. Schwartz, V. Turner, and A. Tuden (eds.), *Political Anthropology*. Chicago: Aldine, 1966; Cohen, R. "Bornu and Nigeria: Political Kingdom in a Troubled Nation." *In* H. Volpe and R. Melson (eds.), *Communalism in Nigeria*. East Lansing: Michigan State University Press, 1970; Cohen, R. "From empire to colony: Bornu in the nineteenth and twentieth centuries." *In* V. W. Turner (ed.), *The Impact of Colonialism*. Cambridge: Cambridge University Press, 1970; Cohen, R. "Incorporation in Bornu." *In* R. Cohen and J. Middleton (eds.), *From Tribe to Nation in Africa.* San Francisco: Chandler, 1970; Cohen, R. "The Kingship in Bornu." *In* M. Crowder (ed.), *West African Chiefs*. London: Faber and Faber, 1970; Cohen, R. "Social stratification in Bornu." *In* A. Tuden and L. Plotnicov (eds.), *Social Stratification in Africa South of the Sahara*. New York: Free Press, 1970; Cohen, R. and L. Brenner. "Bornu in the nineteenth century." *In* A. Ajayi and M. Crowder, *History of West Africa*. Oxford: Clarendon, 1970.

[2] Ardener, *Divorce and Fertility: An African Study*. Page 159 shows 3.21 live births per woman and .26 infant deaths (for children under two years) for the southern Cameroons; by comparison, the Kanuri women in our sample had 1/33 live births and .35 deaths (for children under two) per woman.

[3] For a more detailed description of this period, see Cohen, R., "The Dynamics of Feudalism in Bornu" and "The Bornu King Lists," as well as the relevant chapters in A. Ajayi and M. Crowder, *History of West Africa.*

[4] In all likelihood, the Bulala were first a clan group, then later on took on the identity of a separate ethnic group. If oral traditions are to be believed, the group started as a lineage segment of the old ruling clan of Kanem—the Magumi. See Chapter 4 for a discussion of clanship among the Kanuri, also Chapelle, J. *Les Nomads Noire du Sahara*. Paris: Plon, 1956.

[5] Local traditions interpret Kanuri in two ways; *Kam nurbe*—the men of light who brought the light (i.e., Islam) to Bornu, or *kanuma*—the men of fire who conquered Bornu with sword and fire. I lean to the former because of the Arabic stem *nur* or light which is absent from the latter tradition. A strictly etymological interpretation having, as far as I know, no traditional backing, would be *kanu-ri* or place of the fire meaning possibly that where these people go there is always a settlement put to flames.

[6] Evidence of an urban tradition in the earlier state of Kanem has not been established and no actual site has as yet been identified although there have been several attempts to find one. Because Kirni Njibi in present day Niger has burnt brick walls, I would date its inception in the mid to late sixteenth century. Thus it may very well be a later Kanuri garrison built to protect the main trade route northwards.

[7] The monarch was termed *Mai* in the pre-nineteenth century or first dynastic period, and *Shehu* when the second dynasty took over. See Cohen, "Empire to Colony" and "The Kingship in Bornu."

Chapter 4

[1] See page 45 further in the chapter for the behavioral and cultural distinctions between cross and parallel cousins, involving greater shame responses for the cross cousins.

[2] The English terms brother and sister are used in the classificatory sense; in Kanuri a parent's sibling equals the parent's cousins and siblings.

[3] In the form of an hypothesis, this statement can be read as follows: the greater the authority distinctions between parents and children, the greater is the probability of grandparent-grandchildren reciprocity and licentiousness by the junior in the relationship. Although this hypothesis seems plausible, no direct test is known. Cross-cultural summary data (Textor 1967) on a very small sample (N = 25) show that societies where grandparents and grandchildren are friendly equals are also (92%) ones where grandparent authority over parents is absent. This tends to disconfirm my hypothesis and to suggest instead that where authority is weak in general there is greater probability of alternate generation reciprocity and equality. However, the opposite conditions are dramatically present among the Kanuri and a number of other African societies, suggesting a possible U-curve relationship between authority of parents and equality-reciprocity of grandparent-grandchildren.

[4] Cohen, R. *The Structure of Kanuri Society.* Ph.D. dissertation, University of Wisconsin, 1960. Page 119; Cohen, *The Kanuri of Bornu.*

[5] A smaller group was interviewed in the village of Damboa in southern Bornu. However, only five individuals from that group are considered here. The remaining twenty-five have been discarded because their primary ethnic affiliations are Marghi and many of their kin responses were quite different from those who identify themselves as Kanuri.

[6] This difference is statistically significant; $x^2 = 9.025; p < .01$.

[7] Some of these upper class men can produce agnatic descent lines that go back many generations if their families have been noble for a long period of time.

[8] Some younger informants claim never to have heard of this usage, so that I would conclude that it is dying out.

[9] If we lump the wife's older siblings of both sexes and compare this with ego's younger siblings' spouses, the differences in shame and in respect responses are significant at the $p < .01$ level.

[10] In one case, a young man has become so fond of his mother's co-wife (who is an important person in her own right) that he has become a client-son to her even after both she and his own mother were divorced by the common husband.

[11] Elsewhere (Cohen and Schlegel 1968) I have suggested that growing socio-political complexity is associated with the loss of clan exogamy.

Chapter 5

[1] Prevailing winds come from the east and northeast, bringing sand into any opening facing that direction.

[2] If we use the same correction factor (rural: urban = 8:8, 1:1) as in Chapter 3, then Bornu households have an average size of 4.6 persons (standard deviations are 6.9 for urban and 2.2 for rural households).

[3] The ranked list of occupations was collected in 1956-57 (Cohen 1970i). It was replicated by Dr. David Spain in 1966-67, ten years later, on a totally different sample with no significant differences between the two scales (Spain 1969).

[4] This figure is much lower than a previous one collected on seventy-five farmers in three rural villages in 1956-57. I now believe that the earlier figure was distorted upward by the fact that the respondents were better off then average, and were generally older members of their communities picked to participate in an agricultural experiment because of their influence. These factors would tend to make them prone to have more non-kin clients living with them than was the case with their neighbors. Thus I believe this present figure is more accurate.

Chapter 6

[1] Recent conversations with university students from Bornu brought out the idea that several wished to marry at least one Ibo girl, no matter what her religion, in order to help knit Nigeria together again after the civil war.

[2] Urban men marry previously unmarried girls in their subsequent unions significantly more often than rural men: $x^2 = 4.027; p < .05$.

[3] One case is not included because the husband and wife did not know they were cousins until after they were married.

[4] This statistic is simply a measure of admission by women of their premarital sexual relations in non-first marriages. My ethnographic data from close friends lead me to believe the figure to be significantly higher than this, but not necessarily universal. Some marriages occur so quickly and with such a minimum of contact that we may safely assume no premarital sexual relations.

Chapter 7

[1] I use the term lore here because the Kanuri consider it this way. They accept this custom as symbolism rather than for any magical results it may have.

[2] Oath-taking is called "eating the Koran." It is done by placing the right hand on the holy book; and the leprosy punishment for lying involves the withering of the hand.

[3] A *gursu* is a Maria Theresa dollar usually worth 7/- to 9/- but in marriage ceremonies it is a symbolic way of saying 5/-. In the past, and sometimes today, the *sada'ə* was always made in Maria Theresa dollars.

[4] To carry out an agreement in front of witnesses is the means by which Kanuri create legally binding contracts. Since the rules of evidence in court require witnesses, the use of witnesses means all involved are prepared in future to act in this capacity should adjudication be required.

[5] As with all personal names in this book, this particular name is a pseudonym.

Chapter 8

[1] Quoted in Levy (1957).

[2] Editorial in *The Islamic Review* (1952:40, 8:3-4).

[3] There are a few women who say a good husband is one who ". . .does not talk nonsense" but this is as close as the material comes to mentioning male modesty.

Chapter 9

[1] The example is more complicated, however, for although access to salaried jobs is open to both sexes, they are dominated by men.

[2] This practice was introduced by colonial officials who found it hard to work through the heat of the day and thus instituted the 7:00 to 9:00 a.m., 10:00 to 2:00 p.m. day. This also means that they can come back to a closed office after mid-day meals and work without outside interruptions. The practice is now well established.

[3] I am grateful to Dr. Peshkin for permission to read and use his data, part of which is now available in published form (Peshkin 1971).

[4] The original material is in conversation which I have partially changed to description, omitting nothing of relevance and adding interpretive comments. I have also changed the names of informants.

[5] If we use only completed marriages the durations are even shorter (median = 2.8; mean = 3.8) since the longer extant unions are not counted.

[6] See Richardson (1853) for an eye witness account of such marriages in the nineteenth century southern Sahara (2 vols. London: Chapman and Hall, 1853).

[7] This belief is documented for the nineteenth century as well. Barth was asked to help a woman in southern Bornu who requested medicine from him to allow her to give birth to her baby who had been in the womb for over two years. H. Barth (1968: Vol. II, 444).

[8] The only color he identified at all was on Card 2 which he labeled "blood," then "running blood."

Chapter 10

[1] Referred to as *idda* in the Koran; Levy (1957:6) gives "three courses" after a divorce and four months ten days after death of a husband. When pressed, Kanuri rely on the 100 day figure for both divorce and widowhood.

[2] This fear of a ghost or shade is also seen in the practice of giving children date necklaces to wear at the time of funerals. It is said that the shade of the deceased who may be hovering nearby along with other spirits who have been attracted to that spot by death are supposed to eat the necklaces and not the children.

[3] Calculated from P. H. Jacobsen (1959:145).

[4] Calculated from P. H. Jacobsen (1959:145).

[5] See J. N. D. Anderson (1950). Willful deception on the part of a person afflicted with some loathsome illness at the time of marriage is grounds for "judicial divorce" in Shari'a law.

[6] Anderson (1950:169) points out that in Islamic law as practiced in the traditional Near East the woman did *not* have the right of dissolution by the courts if she were married unwittingly to someone with physical disabilities.

[7] It is my suspicion that this is true for all of Muslim Nigeria and will continue to be so unless court action is made a mandatory part of divorce decrees.

[8] See Ardener (1962:38) and Jacobsen (1959:158). The calculations from Jacobsen's data were done similarly to those for the African material, except that "singles," i.e., those never married, were subtracted from the cohort to get total marriages.

Chapter 11

[1] The phrase "luwali's millet" refers to the custom of sending a gift of millet to the husband from the luwali when a reconciliation has been accomplished.

[2] The total number of reasons are taken from the respondents' explanations for a given divorce even if the divorce was later reconciled. There are no differences among reasons for reconciled divorces as opposed to unreconciled ones in quality or frequency. In calculating the divorce frequency itself, only unreconciled break-ups were counted as "real" divorce.

[3] Unless otherwise stated, all reported relationships are at the .05 level of probability or better. The statistic utilized for these bivariate analyses is the chi-square test of significance. For the demographic data almost all of the relationships are at the .01 level.

[4] The argument about whether polygyny facilitates or restrains fertility is in my view spurious. These Kanuri data show no relationship between polygyny, monogamy, and fertility from the demographic point of view—i.e., per woman. However, if we take a more common sense view of polygyny and view it from the man's perspective, then polygynous *men* have consistently more children than monogamous ones. Polygyny aids men to obtain children even if it has no effect upon the fertility of the total population seen as a breeding unit, although it could increase such figures if women are imported from other groups (Cohen and Middleton 1970).

[5] Missing data from the total of 741 cases are almost entirely in the category of wealthy men with very many marriages, divorces, and very short durations. Wives of such men do not work on farms. Thus the missing data would in fact make the relationship between women's farm work and marital stability stronger than shown here.

[6] It should also be noted that my previous generalizations were based on data taken mostly from rural genealogies intermixed with a few chiefly families and an overall small sample.

[7] These differences are significant statistically: $x^2 = 14.704$; $p < .001$; df = 2.

[8] As noted above, numbers of mother's divorces are positively related to a man's divorce record. This reflects the fact that his wives have a mother-in-law problem that is more intense than men whose mothers divorce less often. If the "experience with divorce" hypothesis were upheld, the relationship should be observed between the divorce records of each sex and numbers of divorces of both parents, which is not the case.

[9] Elsewhere (Cohen 1965) I have pointed out that this quality of using relationship in a very manipulative way is a crucial and central quality of Kanuri political and economic relations.

Chapter 12

[1] This view is shared by my psychological consultant on this project, Dr. Sidney Levy. Levy has one important criticism which should be kept in mind by others attempting to use this technique. He feels that I should have designed one very ordinary, unambiguous card and inserted it into the middle of the interview. This would produce a limited range of variance or a set of cultural norms and the researcher could then more easily estimate deviant types of responses by using this standard card as a clue to deviancy in the remainder of an individual's protocol.

[2] Spain (1969) used a set of photographs to get at possible responses to achievement situations and his content categories are different from mine.

[3] Card 1 was almost invariably responded to briefly and haltingly and we came to see it primarily as the "learning" card. Women were found to "learn" more easily when we substituted a card depicting a woman holding a child. There are no significantly measurable content differences per person or per group because of this substitution.

[4] The differences mentioned here are all at the $p < .05$ level of significance or better, using the chi-square test and frequencies of high, medium, and low per person.

Chapter 13

[1] All differences reported here are at the .05 level of significance or better using the chi-square test.

BIBLIOGRAPHY

Ackerman, C.
   1963 "Affiliations: structural determinants of differential divorce rates," *American Journal of Sociology* 69:13-20.
Ajayi, A., and M. Crowder (eds.)
   1970 *History of West Africa*. Oxford, Clarendon.
Anderson, J. N. D.
   1950 "The problem of divorce in the Shari'a law of Islam," *Royal Central Asian Journal* 37, 2, 169-85.
Antoun, R. T.
   1968 "The modesty of women in Arabic Muslim villages: a study in the accommodation of tradition," *American Anthropologist* 70:690-1.
Ardener, E.
   1962 *Divorce and Fertility: An African Study*. Published for the Nigerian Institute of Social and Economic Research. London: Oxford University Press.
Austry, J.
   1967 "Islam's key problem: economic development," *Islamic Review* Oct.-Nov.:26.
Barnes, J.
   1949 "Measures of divorce frequency in simple society," *Journal of the Royal Anthropological Institute* Vol. 79:37-62.
   1951 *Marriage in a Changing Society*. Rhodes-Livingstone Paper No. 20.
   1967 "Measuring divorce frequency." *In* A. L. Epstein (ed.), *The Craft of Social Anthropology*. London and New York: Tavistock.
Barth, H.
   1968 *Travels and Discoveries in North and Central Africa 1849-1855. Vol. II*. London: Cass.
Bernard, Jessie
   1964 "The adjustment of married mates." *In* H. I. Christensen (ed.), *Handbook of Marriage and the Family*. Chicago: Rand McNally & Co.
Block, M.
   1968 Social Change in Malagasy. Lecture given at Northwestern University, Program of African Studies, November.
Boguslaw, R.
   1965 *The New Utopians: A study of system design and social change*. Englewood Cliffs, N.J.: Prentice-Hall, Inc.

Bohannan, L.
   1949 "Dahomean marriage: a revaluation," *Africa* 19:273-287.
Bohannan, P. J.
   1963 *Social Anthropology*. Chapter 8. New York: Holt, Rinehart & Winston.
Brenner, L.
   1967 *The Shehus of Kukawa: a history of the Al-Kenemi dynasty of Bornu*. Ph.D. thesis, Columbia University.
Burgess, E. W., and L. S. Cottrell
   1939 *Predicting Success and Failure in Marriage*. New York: Prentice-Hall.
Chapelle, J.
   1956 *Les Nomads Noire du Sahara*. Paris: Plon.
Child, I. L., T. Storm, and J. Veroff
   1958 "Achievement themes in folk tales related to socialization practice." *In* J. W. Atkinson (ed.), *Motives in Fantasy, Action, and Society*. Princeton: Van Nostrand.
Clignet, R.
   1970 *Many Wives Many Powers*. Evanston: Northwestern University Press.
Cohen, R.
   1960 *The Structure of Kanuri Society*. Ph.D. dissertation, University of Wisconsin, p. 119.
   1961a "Marriage instability among the Kanuri of northern Nigeria," *American Anthropologist* 63:1231-49.
   1961b "The success that failed: an experiment in culture change in Africa," *Anthropologica* 3:1-15.
   1962 "The just-so so: a spurious tribal grouping in western Sudanic culture." *Man* Article #239:153-4.
   1964 "Conflict and change in a northern Nigerian emirate." *In* G. Zollschan and D. Hirsch (eds.), *Explorations in Social Change*. Boston: Houghton Mifflin.
   1965 "Some aspects of institutionalized exchange: a Kanuri example," *Cahiers d'Etudes Africaines* 5:353-69.
   1966a "The Bornu King lists." *In* J. Butler (ed.) *Boston University Publications in African History* Vol. 2:41-83. Boston: Boston University Press.
   1966b "The dynamics of feudalism in Bornu." *In* J. Butler (ed.), *Boston University Publications in African History* Vol.

2:87-105. Boston: Boston University Press.

1966c "Power, authority, and personal success in Islam and Bornu." *In* M. Schwartz, V. Turner, and A. Tuden (eds.), *Political Anthropology*. Chicago: Aldine.

1967a *The Kanuri of Bornu*. New York: Holt, Rinehart and Winston.

1967b "Slavery among the Kanuri." *In* R. Cohen (ed.), *Slavery in Africa*. Special Supplement to *Trans*-action Jan.-Feb.:48-50.

1970a "Bornu and Nigeria: Political Kingdom in a Troubled Nation." *In* H. Volpe and R. Melson (eds.), *Communalism in Nigeria*. East Lansing: Michigan State University Press.

1970b "Brittle marriage as a stable system." *In* P. J. Bohannan (ed.), *Divorce and After*. New York: Doubleday.

1970c "From empire to colony: Bornu in the nineteenth and twentieth centuries." *In* V. W. Turner (ed.), *The Impact of Colonialism*. Cambridge: Cambridge University Press.

1970d "Incorporation in Bornu." *In* R. Cohen and J. Middleton (eds.), *From Tribe to Nation in Africa*. San Francisco: Chandler.

1970e "The Kingship in Bornu." *In* M. Crowder (ed.), *West African Chiefs*. London: Faber and Faber.

1970f "The logic of generalization in anthropology." *In* R. Naroll and R. Cohen (eds.), *Handbook of Method in Cultural Anthropology*. New York: Natural History Press.

1970g "The political system." *In* R. Naroll and R. Cohen (eds.), *Handbook of Method in Cultural Anthropology*. New York: Natural History Press.

1970h "Preface." *In* R. Naroll and R. Cohen (eds.), *Handbook of Method in Cultural Anthropology*. New York: Natural History Press.

1970i "Social stratification in Bornu." *In* A. Tuden and L. Plotnicov (eds.), *Social Stratification in Africa South of the Sahara*. New York: Free Press.

Cohen, R., and L. Brenner
1970 "Bornu in the nineteenth century." *In* A. Ajayi and M. Crowder, *History of West Africa*. Oxford: Clarendon.

Cohen, R., and J. Middleton
1970 Introduction. *From Tribe to Nation in Africa*. San Francisco: Chandler.

Cohen, R., and A. Schlegel
1968 "The tribe as a socio-political unit: a cross-cultural examination." *In* J. Helm (ed.), *Essays on the Problem of Tribe*. Proceedings of 1967 annual meeting of American Ethnological Society.

Cooley, W. W., and P. R. Lohnes
1962 *Multivariate Procedures for the Behavioral Sciences*. New York: Wiley.

Denham, D., H. Clapperton, (and W. Oudney)
1826 *Narrative of Travels and Discoveries in Northern and Central Africa in the Years 1822, 1823 and 1824*. London: Murray.

Dole, G. E.
1969 "Generation kinship nomenclature as an adaptation to endogamy," *Southwestern Journal of Anthropology* 25, 2:105-23.

Epstein, A. L. (ed.)
1967 *The Craft of Social Anthropology*. London: Tavistock.

Fallers, L. A.
1957 "Some determinants of marriage stability in Busoga: a reformulation of Gluckman's hypothesis," *Africa* 27:106-121.

Firth, R.
1956 "Function." *In* W. L. Thomas, Jr. (ed.), *Current Anthropology: A Supplement to Anthropology Today*. Chicago: University of Chicago Press.

Fortes, M.
1958 "Introduction." *In* J. R. Goody (ed.), *The Developmental Cycle in Domestic Groups*. Cambridge Papers in Social Anthropology No. 1. Cambridge: Cambridge University Press.

1962 "Introduction." *In* M. Fortes (ed.), *Marriage in Tribal Societies*. Cambridge Papers in Social Anthropology, Number 3. Cambridge: Cambridge University Press.

Gibbs, J. A., Jr.
1963 "Marital instability among the Kpelle: toward a theory of epainogamy," *American Anthropologist* 65:552-59.

Glick, P. C.
1964 "Demographic analysis of family data." *In* H. T. Christensen (ed.), *Handbook of Marriage and the Family*. Chicago: Rand McNally.

Gluckman, M.
1951 "Kinship and marriage among the Lozi of northern Rhodesia and the Zulu of Natal." *In* A. R. Radcliffe-Brown and D. Forde (eds.), *African Systems of Kinship and Marriage*. London: Oxford University Press.

1961 Quoted by E. R. Leach in the latter's book *Rethinking Anthropology*. London: Athlone Press, p. 115.

Goode, W. J.
1961 "Family Disorganization." *In* R. K. Merton and R. A. Nisbet (eds.), *Contemporary Social Problems*. New York: Harcourt, Brace & World, Inc.

1963 *World Revolution and Family Patterns*. New York: The Free Press.

Goody, J.
1970 "Marriage policy and incorporation in northern Ghana." *In* R. Cohen and J. Middleton (eds.), *From Tribe to Nation in Africa*. San Francisco: Chandler.

Goody, J. and E.
1967 "The circulation of women and their children in northern Ghana," *Man* Vol. 2: 226-48.
Homans, G. C.
1950 *The Human Group*. New York: Harcourt, Brace & World, Inc.
Ibn Fartua
1928 "The reign of Idris Alooma." *In* R. H. Palmer, *Sudanese Memoirs*, Vol. III. Lagos: Government Printer.
The Islamic Review (editorial)
1952 "Al-Azhar, Islam, and the role of women in Islamic society: an un-Islamic statement," 40, 8, (August), 3-4.
Jacobsen, P. H.
1959 *American Marriage and Divorce*. New York: Rinehart.
Jarvie, I. C.
1964 *The Revolution in Anthropology*. London: Routledge and Kegan Paul.
Jongmens, D. G., and P. C. W. Gutkind (eds.)
1967 *Anthropologists in the Field*. Issen: Van Gorgum.
Last, M.
1967 *The Sokoto Caliphate*. London: Longmans, Green and Co. Ltd.
Leach, E. R.
1957 "Aspects of bridewealth and marriage stability among the Kachin and Lakher," *Man* 57 Article 59:50-55.
1961 *Rethinking Anthropology*. London: Athlone Press.
Leslie, G. R.
1964 "The field of marriage counselling." *In* H. T. Christensen (ed.), *Handbook of Marriage and the Family*. Chicago: Rand McNally.
Levinger, G.
1968 "Marital cohesiveness and dissolution: an integrative review." *In* R. F. Winch and L. L. Goodman (eds.), *Selected Studies in Marriage and the Family* (third edition). New York: Holt, Rinehart & Winston, Inc.
Levy, R.
1957 *The Social Structure of Islam*. Cambridge: Cambridge University Press.
Levy, S. J.
n.d. "Kanuri personality, marriage, and divorce." Mimeographed report.
Lewis, I. M.
1962 *Marriage and the Family in Northern Somaliland*. (East African Studies No. 15). Kampala: East African Institute of Social Research, p. 42.

Mitchell, J. C.
1956 *The Yao Village*. Manchester: University of Manchester Press.
1961 "Social change and the stability of African Marriage in Northern Rhodesia." *In* A. Southall (ed.), *Change in Modern Africa*. London: Oxford University Press.
Murdock, G. P.
1949 *Social Structure*. New York: Macmillan.
1950 "Family stability in non-European culture, *Annals*, 272:195-201.
Naroll, R., and R. Cohen (eds.)
1970 *Handbook of Method in Cultural Anthropology*. New York: Natural History Press.
Patai, R.
1962 *Golden River to Golden Road*. Chapter 4. Philadelphia: University of Penn. Press.
Peshkin, A.
n.d. Unpublished fieldnotes.
Phillips, A. (ed.)
1953 *Survey of African Marriage and Family Life*. London: Oxford University Press.
Rapoport, A.
1960 *Fights, Games, and Debates*. Ann Arbor: University of Michigan Press.
Richardson, J.
1853 *Mission to Central Africa* (2 vols.) London: Chapman and Hall.
Schneider, D. M.
1953 "A note on bridewealth and the stability of marriage," *Man* Article #75:55-7.
Sherwood, E. T.
1958 "On the designing of TAT pictures with reference to a set for an African people assimilating western culture," *Journal of Social Psychology* 45:161-90.
Spain, D.
1969 *Achievement Motivation and Modernization in Bornu*. Ph.D. dissertation, Northwestern University.
Stenning, D. J.
1959 *Savannah Nomads*. London: Oxford University Press.
Textor, R. B.
1967 *A Cross-Cultural Summary*. New Haven: HRAF.
Winch, R. F.
1968 "Basic societal functions." *In* R. F. Winch and Z. L. Goodman (eds.), *Selected Studies in Marriage and the Family* (third edition). New York: Holt, Rinehart & Winston, Inc.